JUJUTSU KAISEN

3

YOUNG FISH AND REVERSE PUNISHMENT

STORY AND ART BY GEGE AKUTAMI

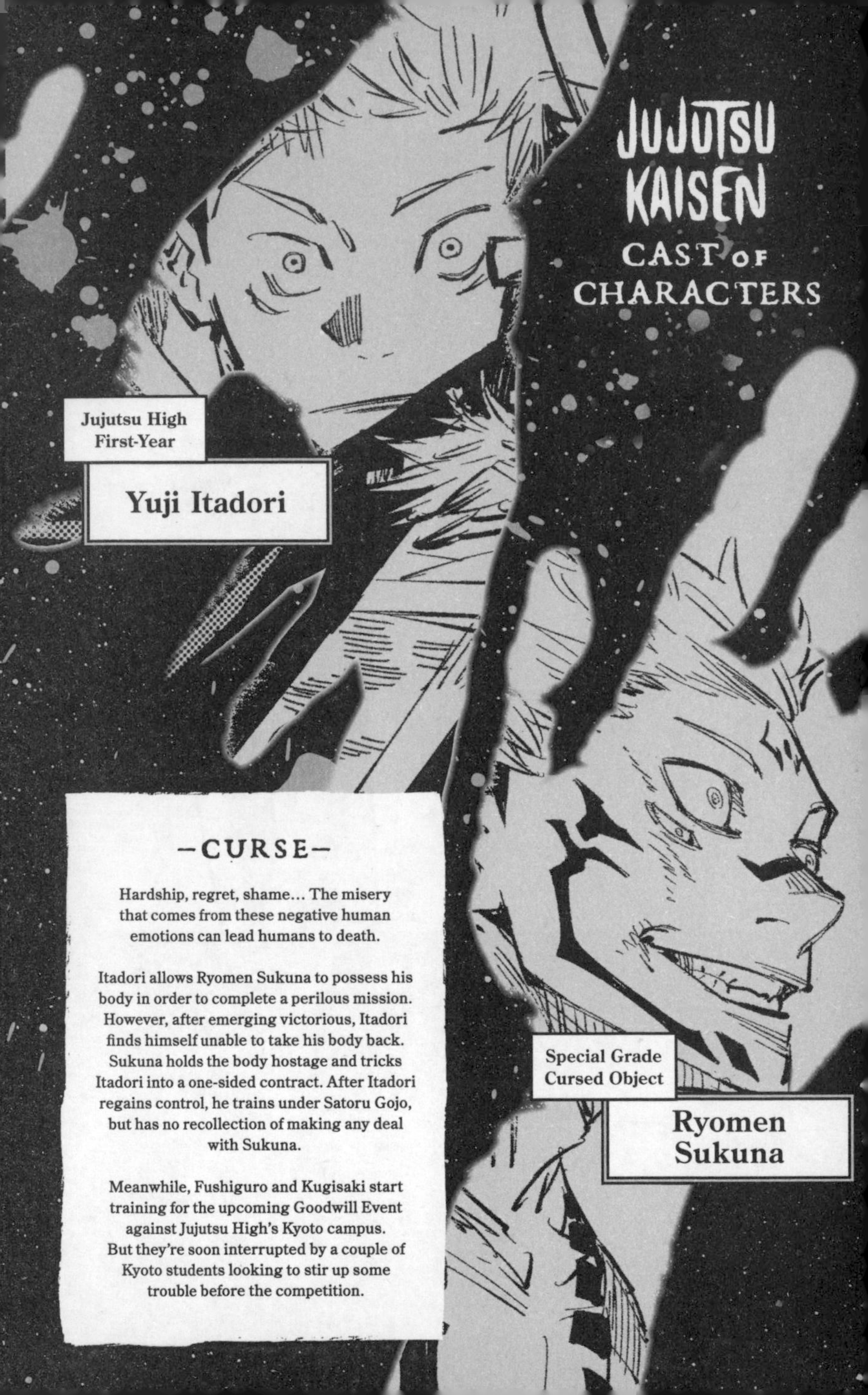
JUJUTSU KAISEN
CAST OF CHARACTERS
Jujutsu High First-Year
Yuji Itadori
Special Grade Cursed Object
Ryomen Sukuna

—CURSE—

Hardship, regret, shame… The misery that comes from these negative human emotions can lead humans to death.

Itadori allows Ryomen Sukuna to possess his body in order to complete a perilous mission. However, after emerging victorious, Itadori finds himself unable to take his body back. Sukuna holds the body hostage and tricks Itadori into a one-sided contract. After Itadori regains control, he trains under Satoru Gojo, but has no recollection of making any deal with Sukuna.

Meanwhile, Fushiguro and Kugisaki start training for the upcoming Goodwill Event against Jujutsu High's Kyoto campus. But they're soon interrupted by a couple of Kyoto students looking to stir up some trouble before the competition.

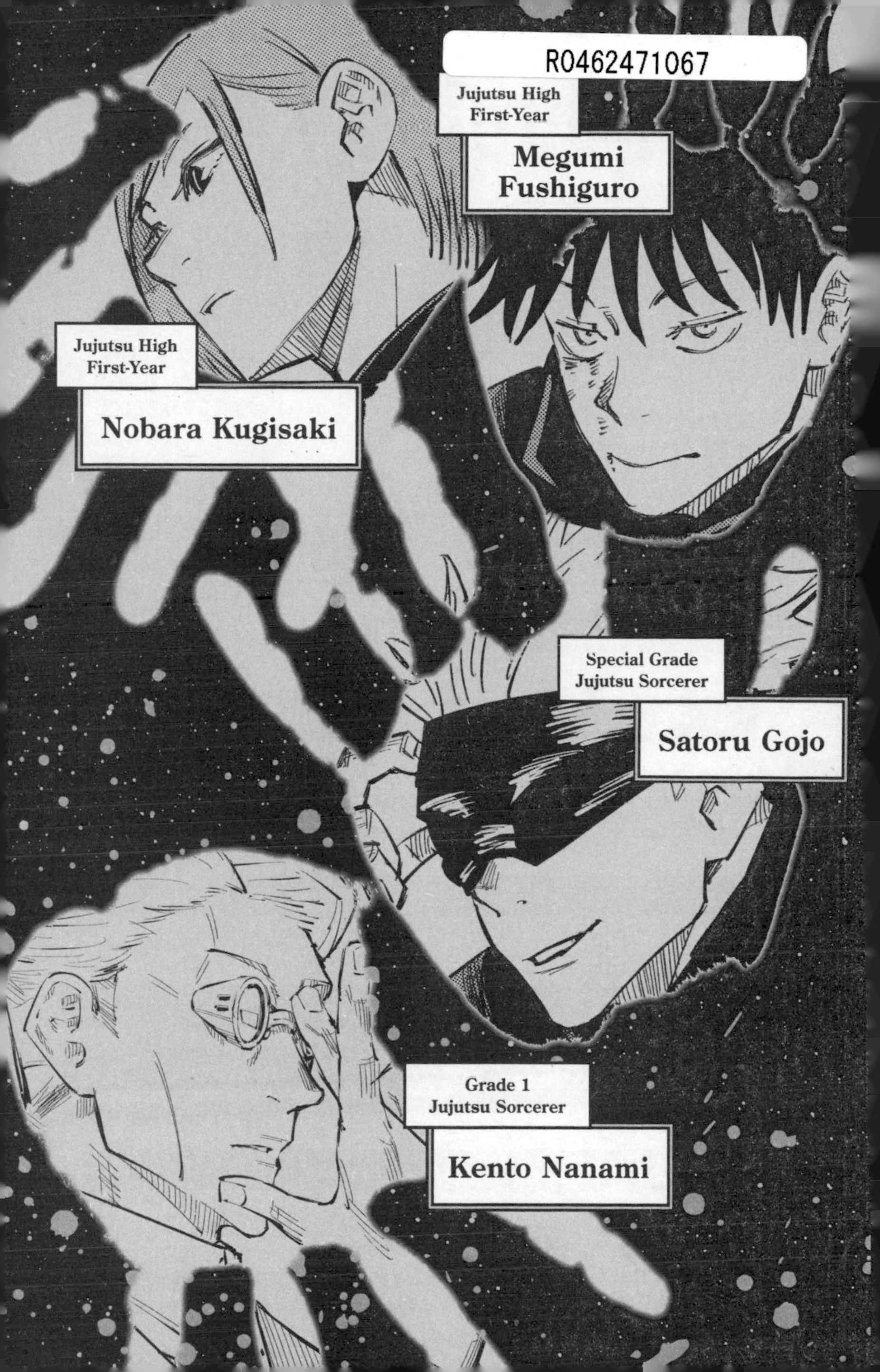
Jujutsu High
First-Year
Megumi Fushiguro
Jujutsu High
First-Year
Nobara Kugisaki
Special Grade
Jujutsu Sorcerer
Satoru Gojo
Grade 1
Jujutsu Sorcerer
Kento Nanami

JUJUTSU KAISEN

3

YOUNG FISH AND REVERSE PUNISHMENT

Chapter 17: Boring

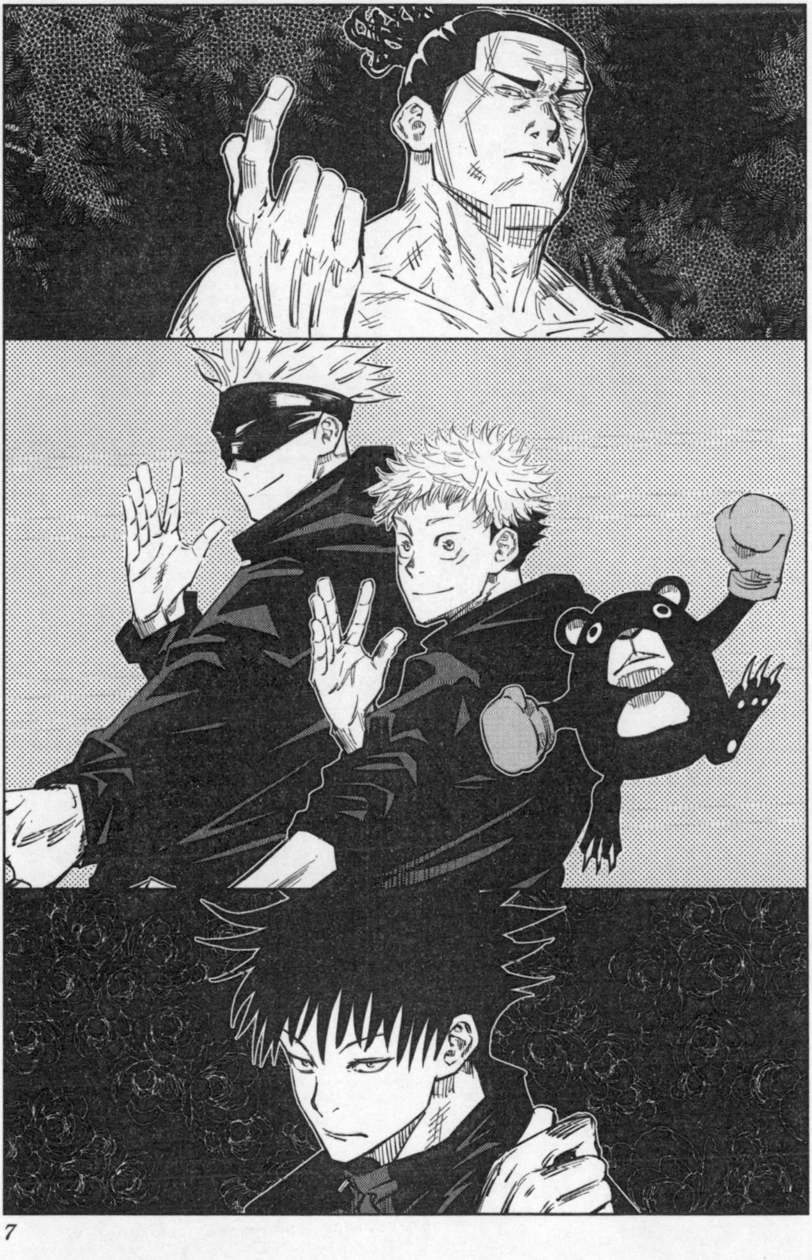

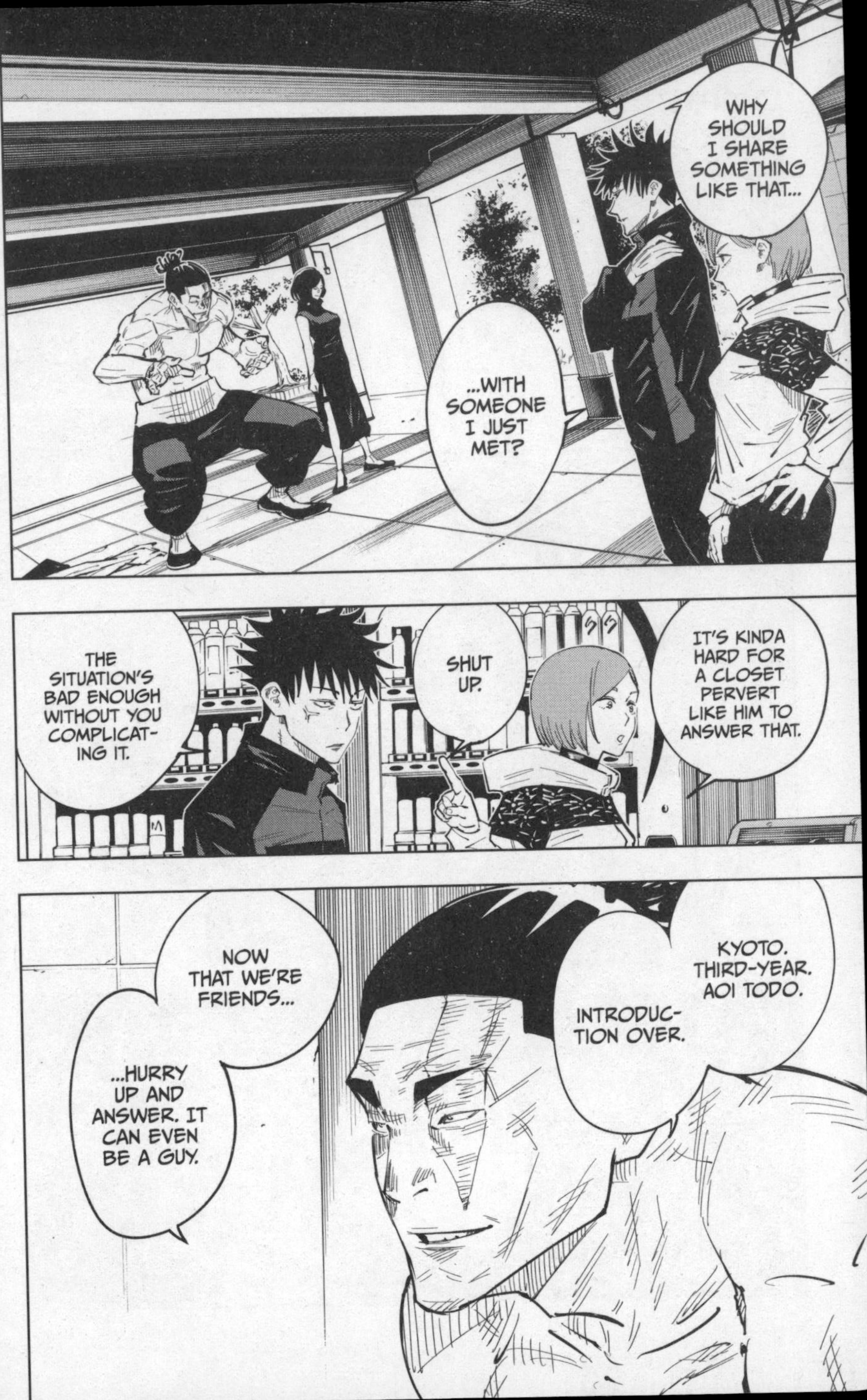
WHY SHOULD I SHARE SOMETHING LIKE THAT...
...WITH SOMEONE I JUST MET?
IT'S KINDA HARD FOR A CLOSET PERVERT LIKE HIM TO ANSWER THAT.
SHUT UP.
THE SITUATION'S BAD ENOUGH WITHOUT YOU COMPLICATING IT.
KYOTO. THIRD-YEAR. AOI TODO.
INTRODUCTION OVER.
NOW THAT WE'RE FRIENDS...
...HURRY UP AND ANSWER. IT CAN EVEN BE A GUY.

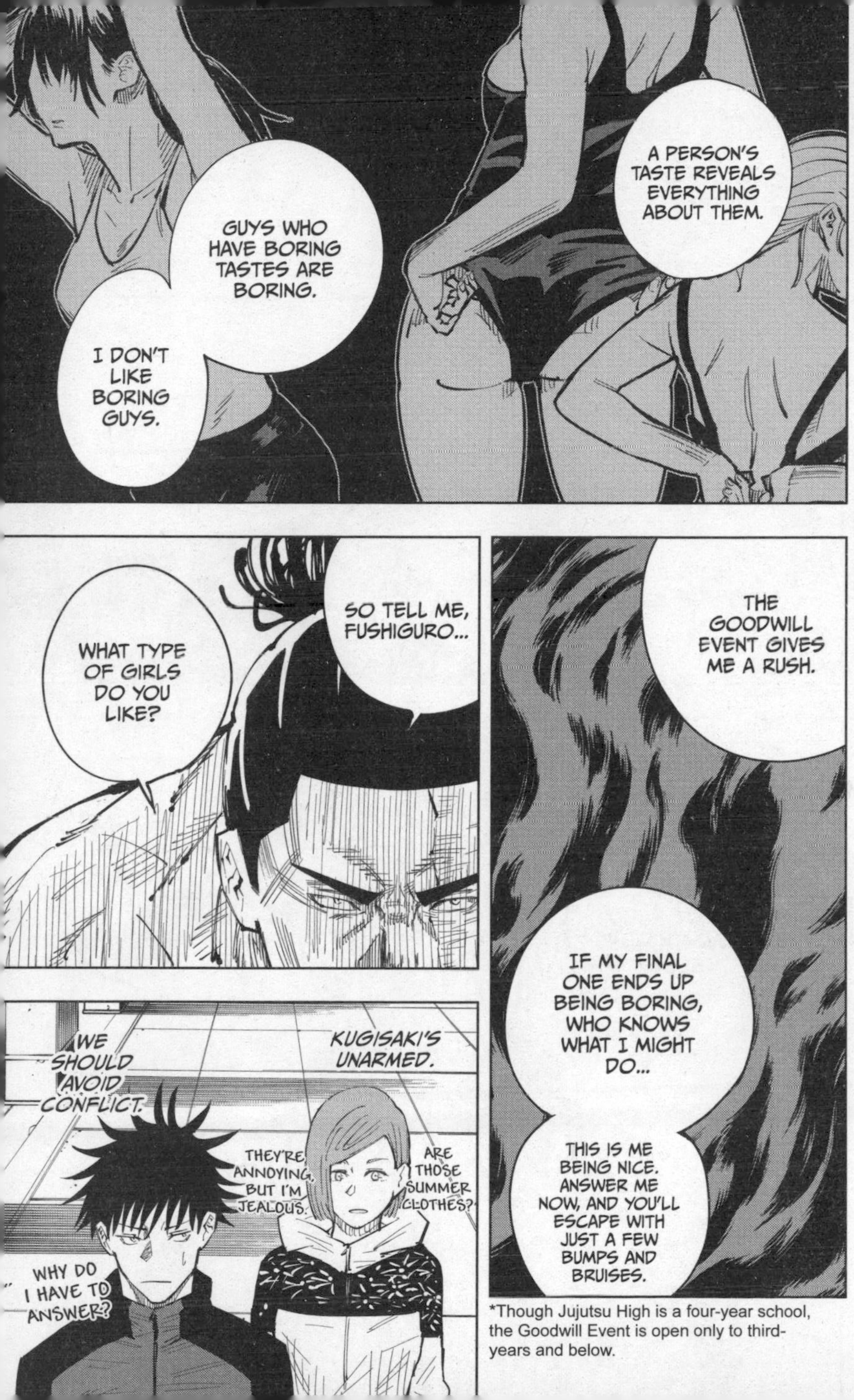
A PERSON'S TASTE REVEALS EVERYTHING ABOUT THEM.
GUYS WHO HAVE BORING TASTES ARE BORING.
I DON'T LIKE BORING GUYS.
THE GOODWILL EVENT GIVES ME A RUSH.
IF MY FINAL ONE ENDS UP BEING BORING, WHO KNOWS WHAT I MIGHT DO...
THIS IS ME BEING NICE. ANSWER ME NOW, AND YOU'LL ESCAPE WITH JUST A FEW BUMPS AND BRUISES.
SO TELL ME, FUSHIGURO...
WHAT TYPE OF GIRLS DO YOU LIKE?
KUGISAKI'S UNARMED.
WE SHOULD AVOID CONFLICT.
ARE THOSE SUMMER CLOTHES?
THEY'RE ANNOYING, BUT I'M JEALOUS.
WHY DO I HAVE TO ANSWER?

*Though Jujutsu High is a four-year school, the Goodwill Event is open only to third-years and below.

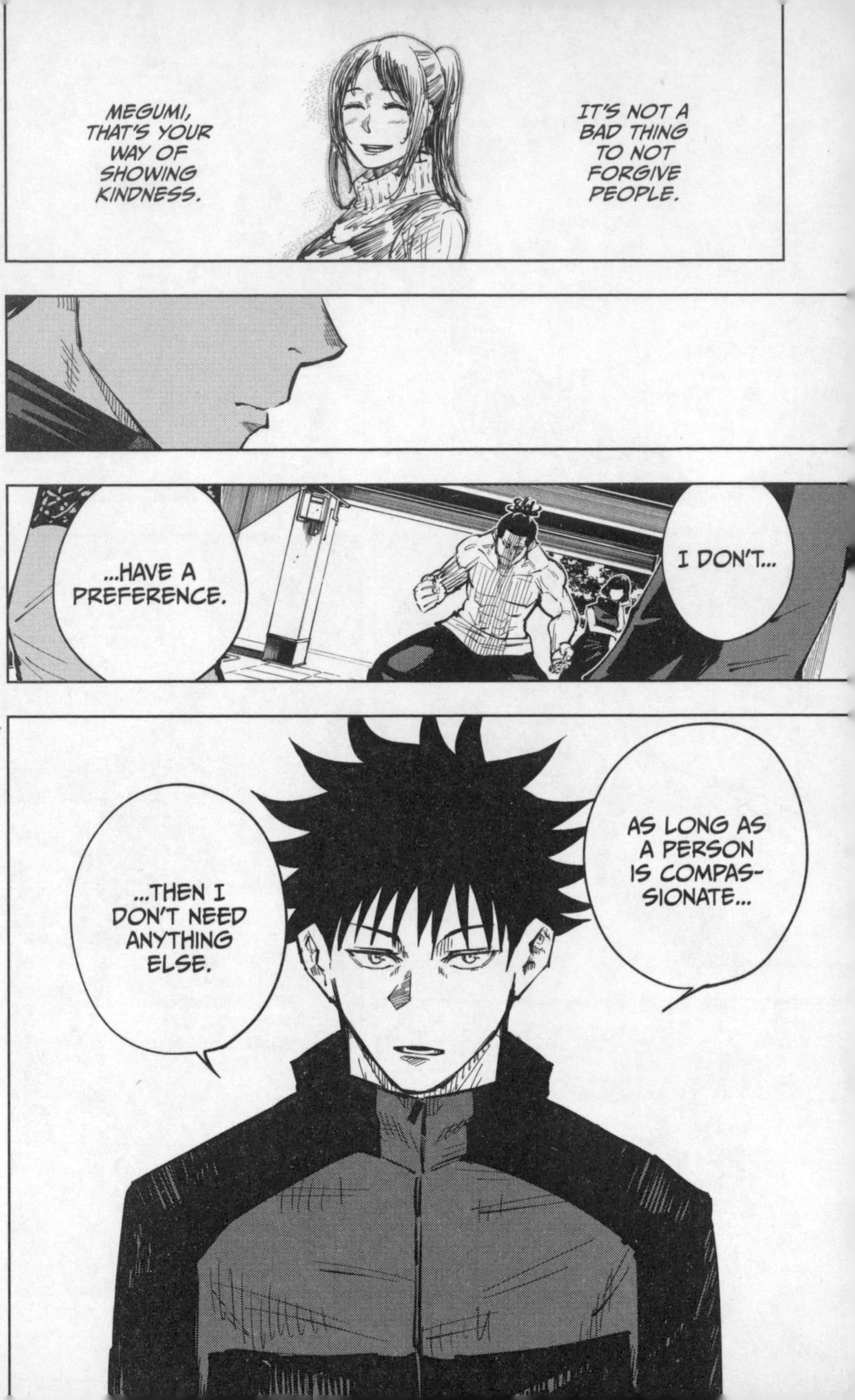
IT'S NOT A BAD THING TO NOT FORGIVE PEOPLE.
MEGUMI, THAT'S YOUR WAY OF SHOWING KINDNESS.
I DON'T...
...HAVE A PREFERENCE.
AS LONG AS A PERSON IS COMPAS-SIONATE...
...THEN I DON'T NEED ANYTHING ELSE.

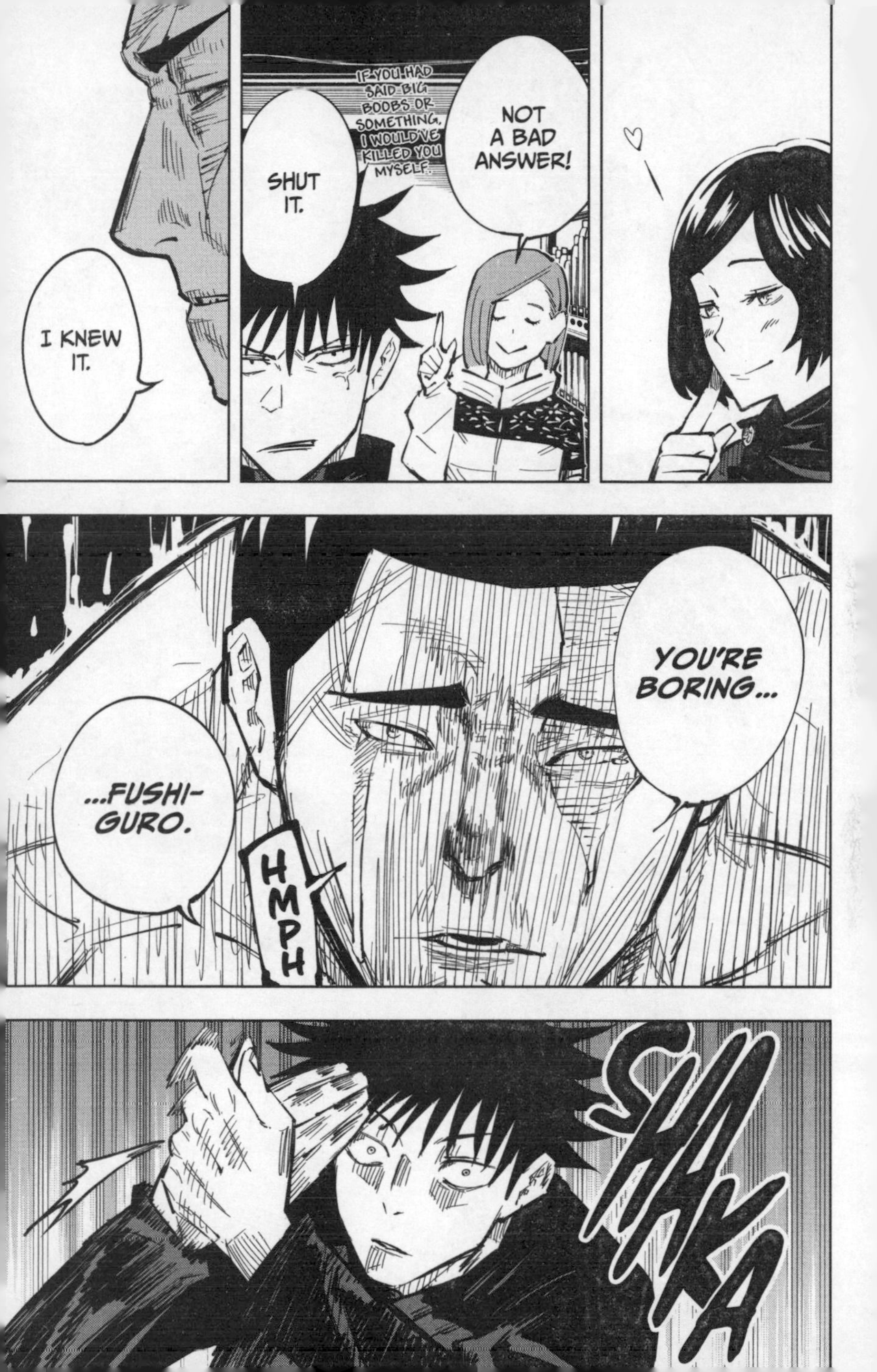
NOT A BAD ANSWER!
IF YOU HAD SAID BIG BOOBS OR SOMETHING, I WOULD'VE KILLED YOU MYSELF.
SHUT IT.
I KNEW IT.
YOU'RE BORING...
HMPH
...FUSHIGURO.

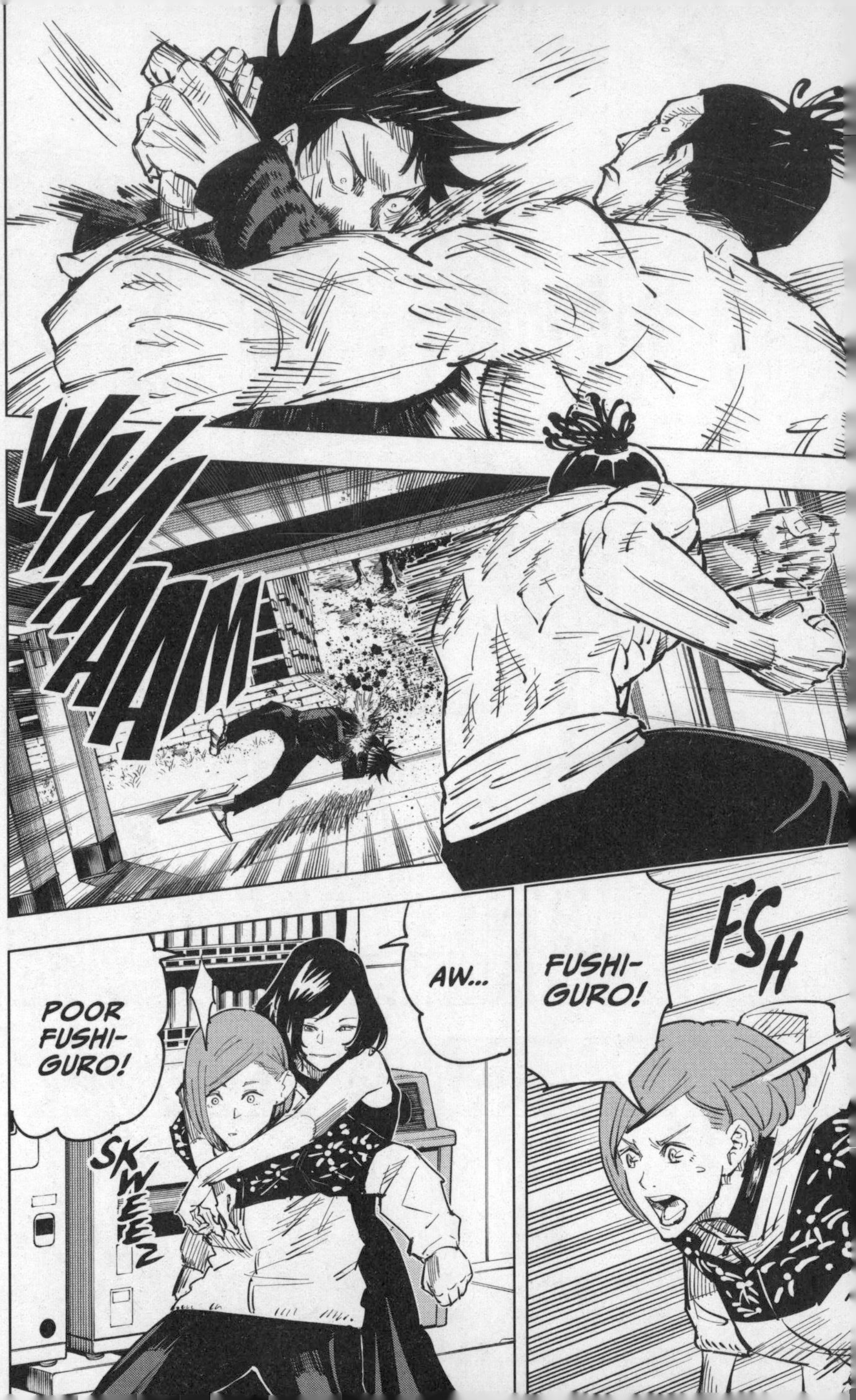
WHAAM
FSH
FUSHI-GURO!
AW...
POOR FUSHI-GURO!
SKWEEZ

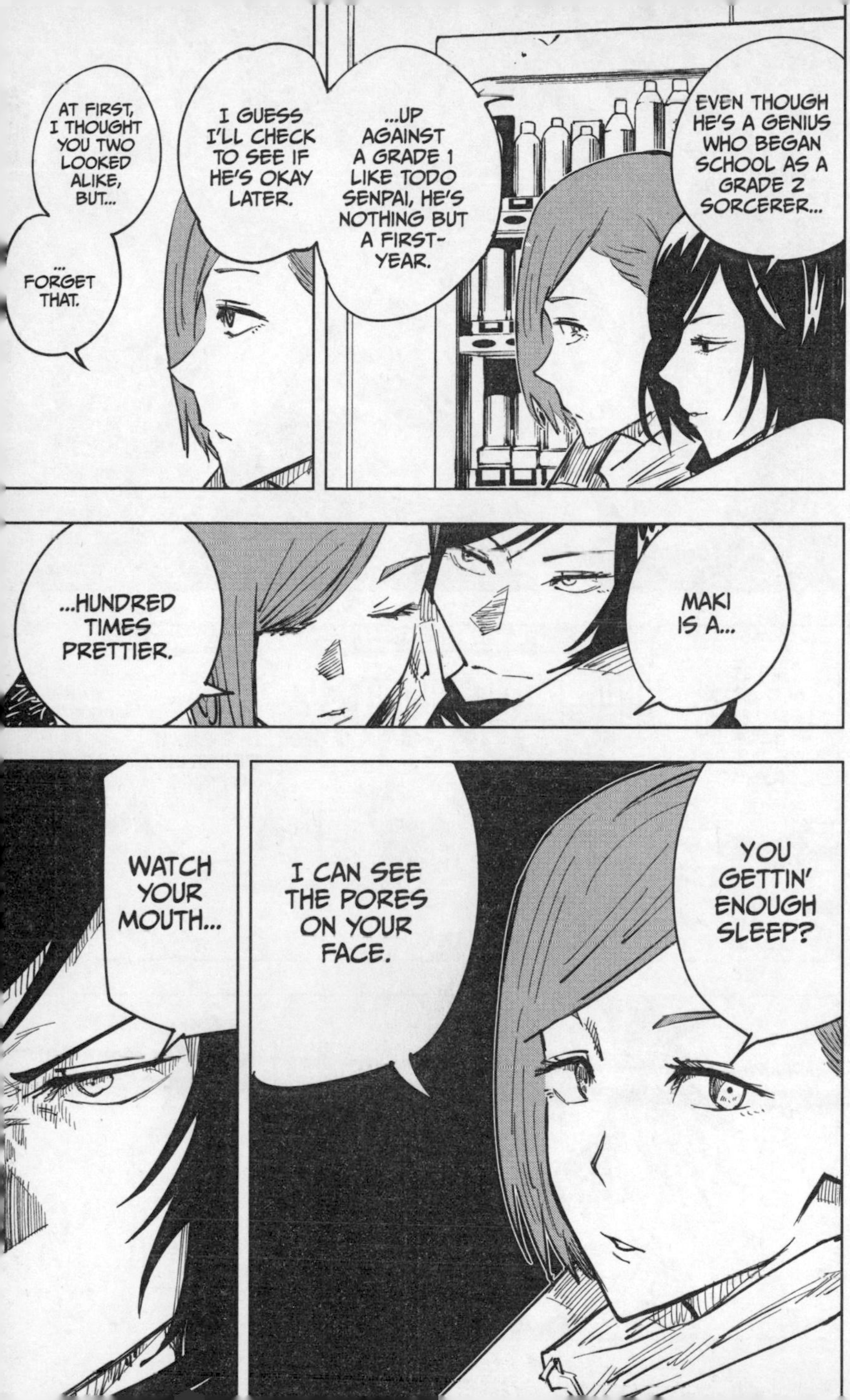
EVEN THOUGH HE'S A GENIUS WHO BEGAN SCHOOL AS A GRADE 2 SORCERER...
...UP AGAINST A GRADE 1 LIKE TODO SENPAI, HE'S NOTHING BUT A FIRST-YEAR.
I GUESS I'LL CHECK TO SEE IF HE'S OKAY LATER.
AT FIRST, I THOUGHT YOU TWO LOOKED ALIKE, BUT...
... FORGET THAT.
MAKI IS A...
...HUNDRED TIMES PRETTIER.
YOU GETTIN' ENOUGH SLEEP?
I CAN SEE THE PORES ON YOUR FACE.
WATCH YOUR MOUTH...

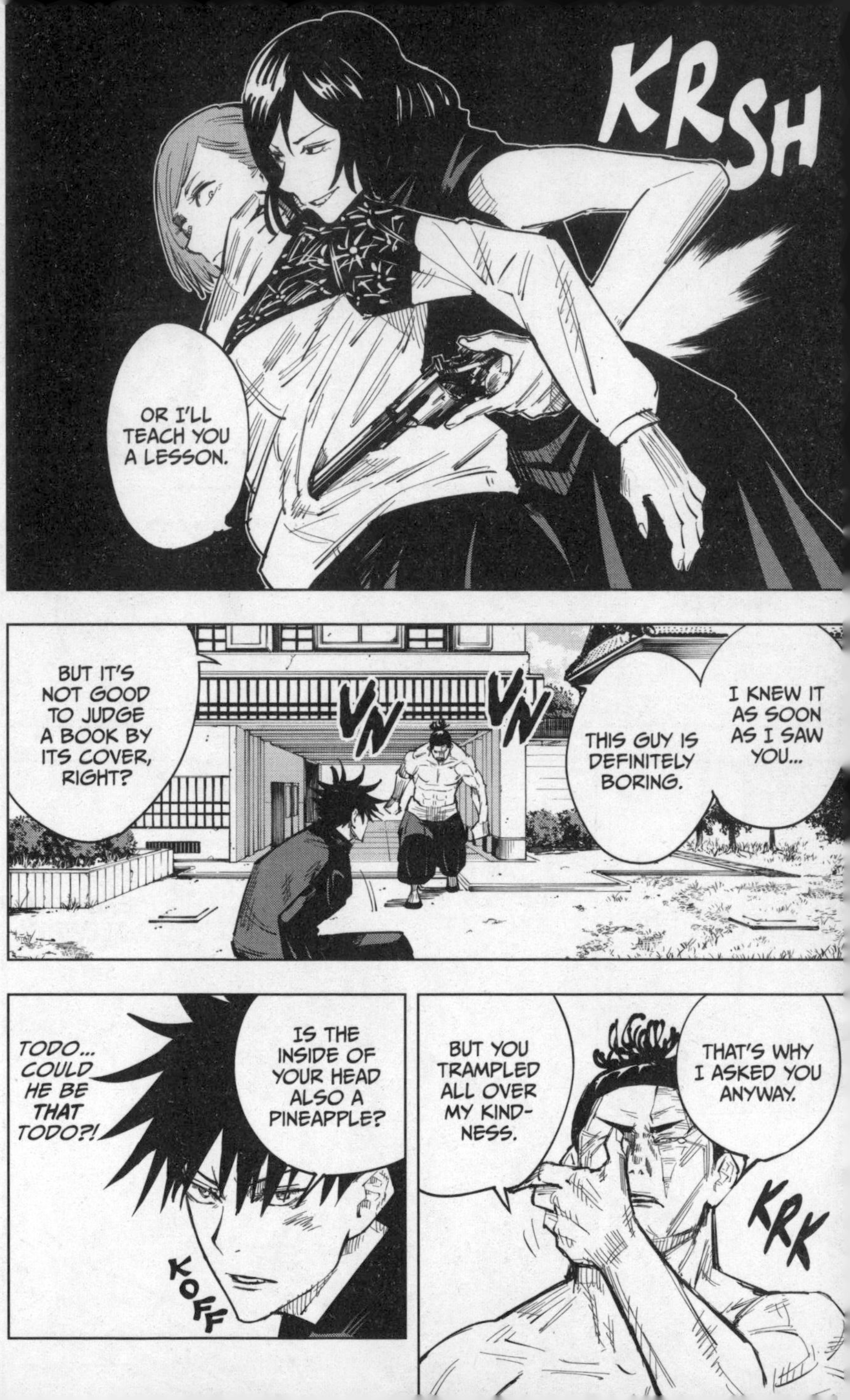
KRSH
OR I'LL TEACH YOU A LESSON.
I KNEW IT AS SOON AS I SAW YOU...
THIS GUY IS DEFINITELY BORING.
VN
VN
BUT IT'S NOT GOOD TO JUDGE A BOOK BY ITS COVER, RIGHT?
THAT'S WHY I ASKED YOU ANYWAY.
BUT YOU TRAMPLED ALL OVER MY KIND-NESS.
KRK
IS THE INSIDE OF YOUR HEAD ALSO A PINEAPPLE?
TODO... COULD HE BE THAT TODO?!
KOFF

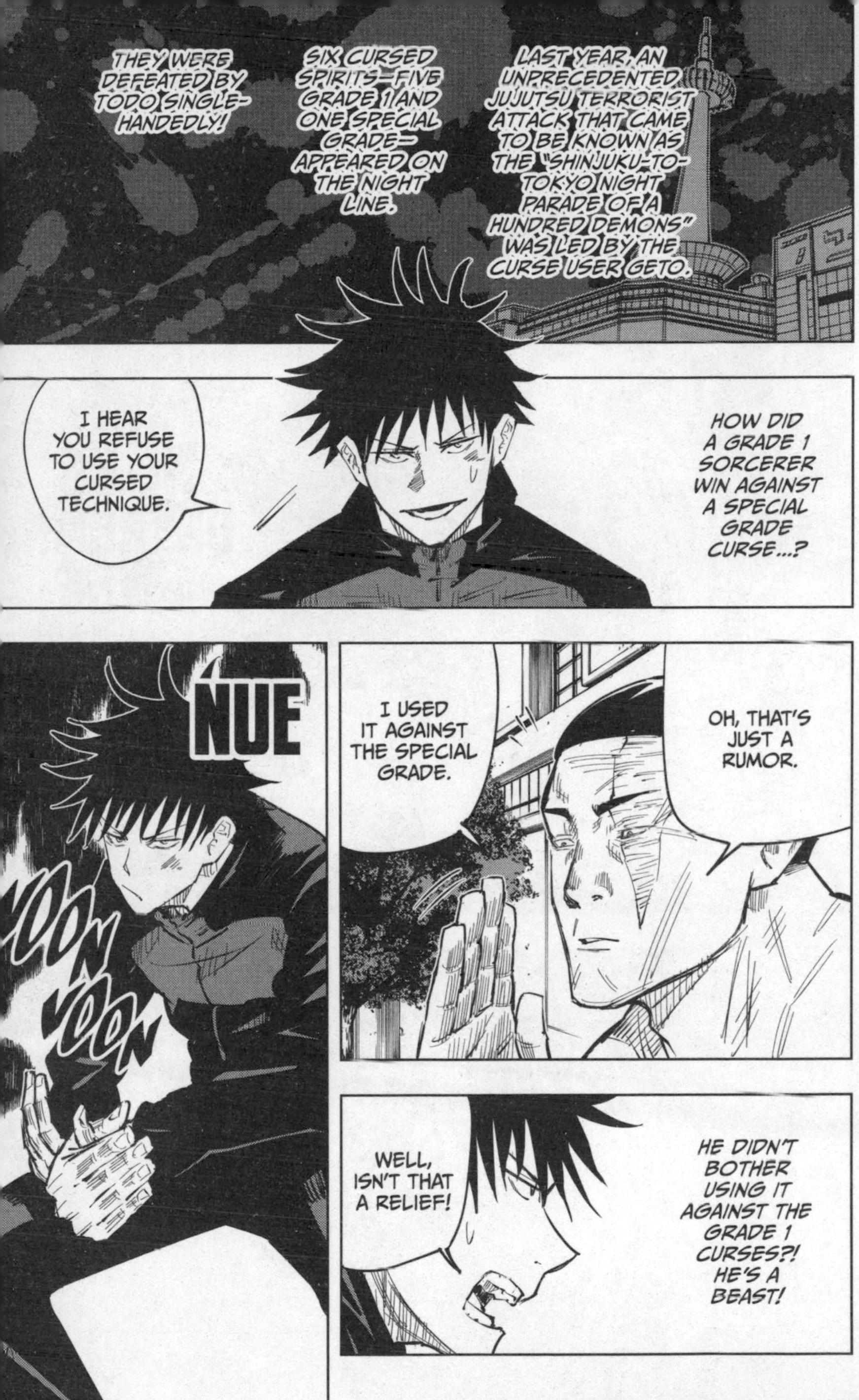
LAST YEAR, AN UNPRECEDENTED JUJUTSU TERRORIST ATTACK THAT CAME TO BE KNOWN AS THE "SHINJUKU-TO-TOKYO NIGHT PARADE OF A HUNDRED DEMONS" WAS LED BY THE CURSE USER GETO.
SIX CURSED SPIRITS—FIVE GRADE 1 AND ONE SPECIAL GRADE—APPEARED ON THE NIGHT LINE.
THEY WERE DEFEATED BY TODO SINGLE-HANDEDLY!
HOW DID A GRADE 1 SORCERER WIN AGAINST A SPECIAL GRADE CURSE...?
I HEAR YOU REFUSE TO USE YOUR CURSED TECHNIQUE.
OH, THAT'S JUST A RUMOR.
I USED IT AGAINST THE SPECIAL GRADE.
HE DIDN'T BOTHER USING IT AGAINST THE GRADE 1 CURSES?! HE'S A BEAST!
WELL, ISN'T THAT A RELIEF!
NUE
VOON
VOON

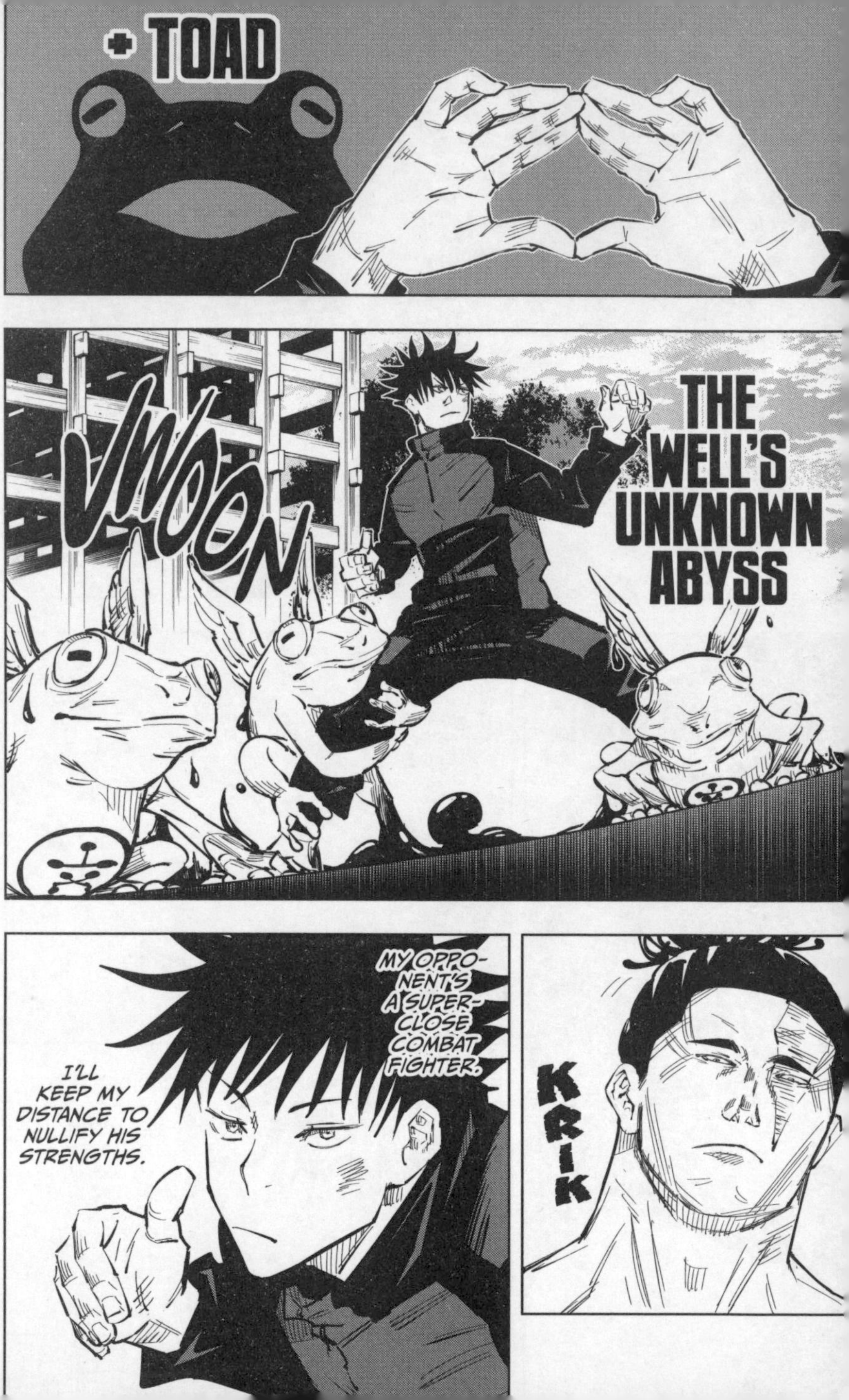
TOAD
THE WELL'S UNKNOWN ABYSS
VWOON
KRIK
MY OPPO-NENT'S A SUPER-CLOSE COMBAT FIGHTER.
I'LL KEEP MY DISTANCE TO NULLIFY HIS STRENGTHS.

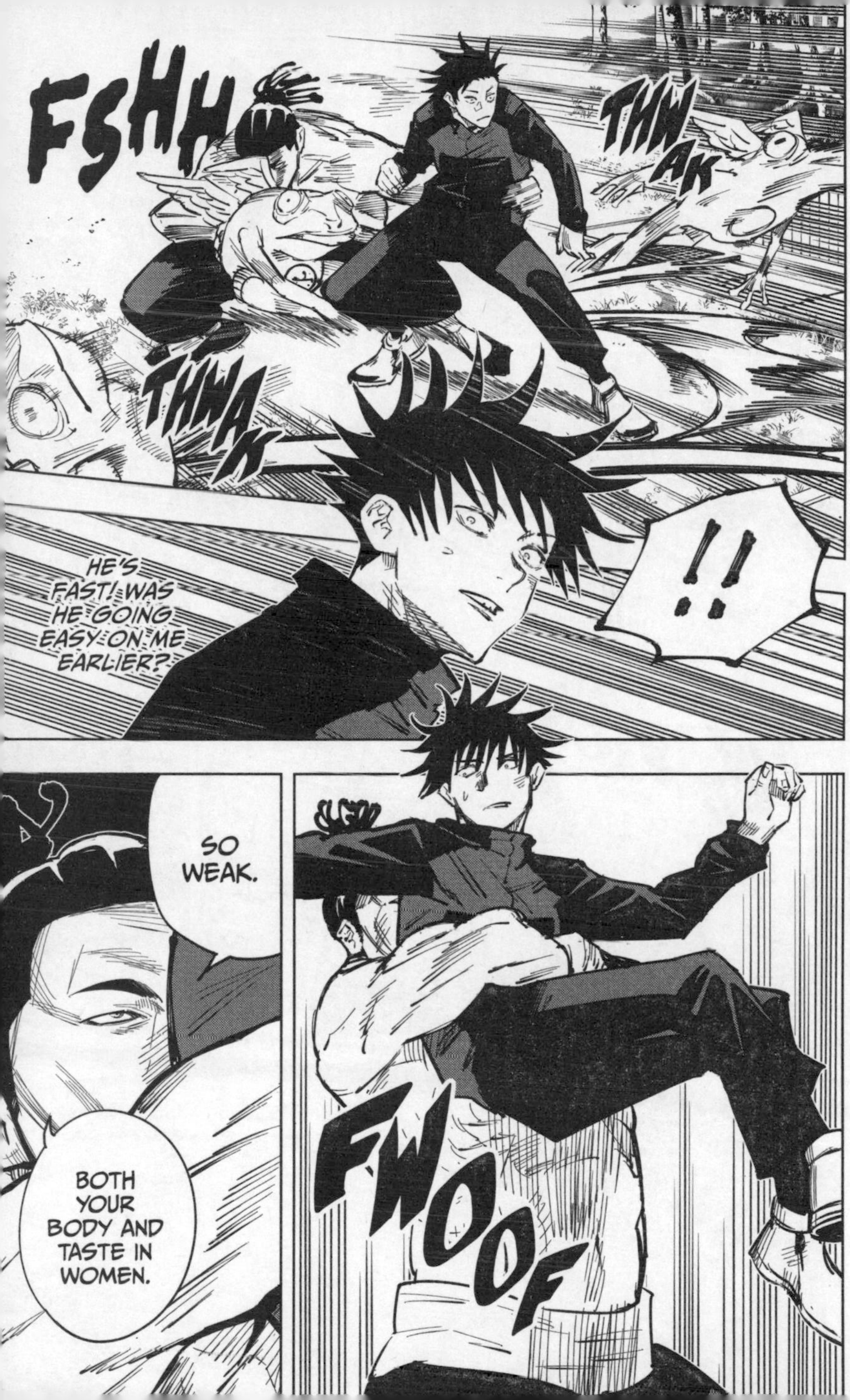
THWAK
FSHH
THWAK
!!
HE'S FAST! WAS HE GOING EASY ON ME EARLIER?
FWOOF
SO WEAK.
BOTH YOUR BODY AND TASTE IN WOMEN.

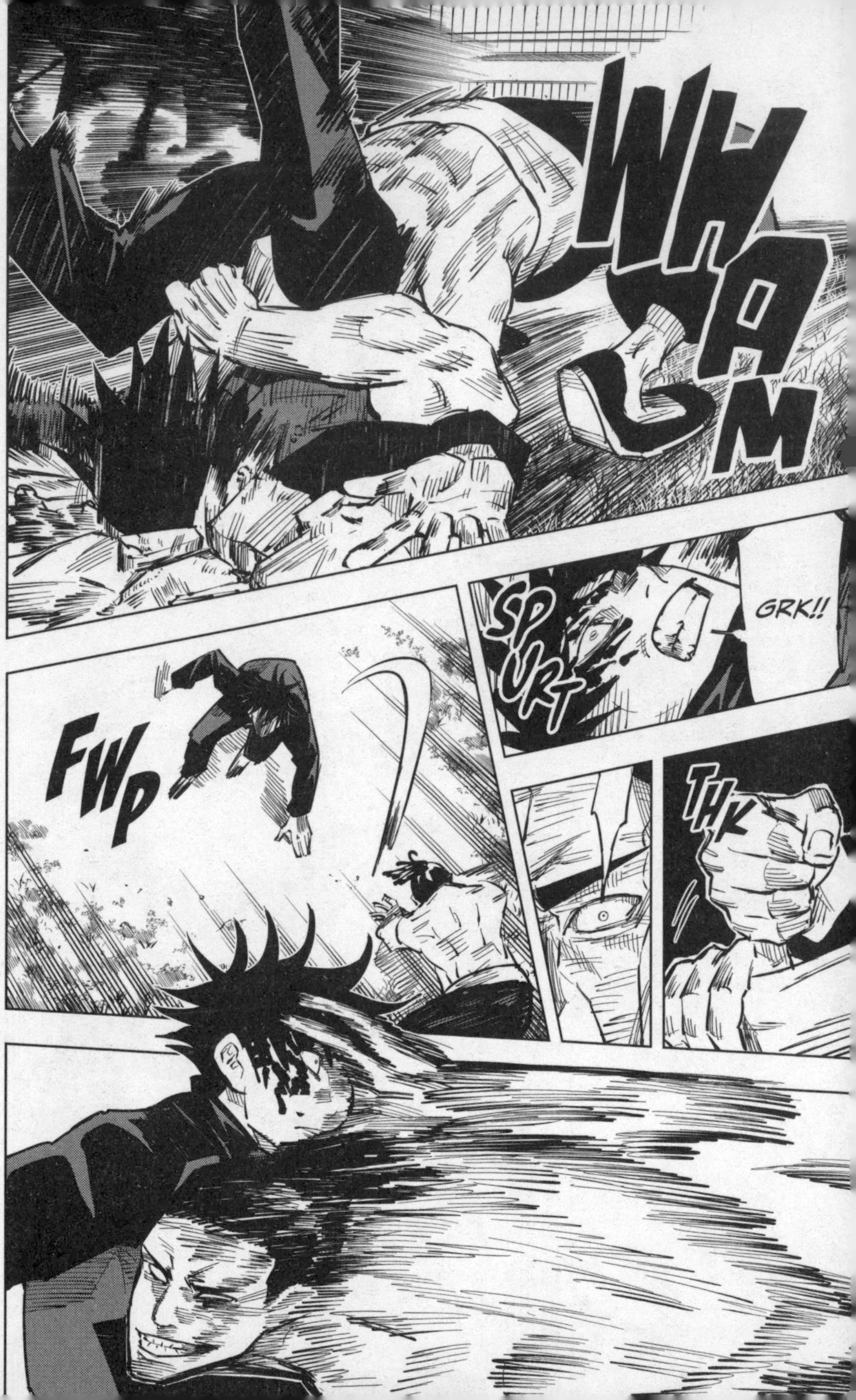
WHAM
SPURT
GRK!!
THK
FWP

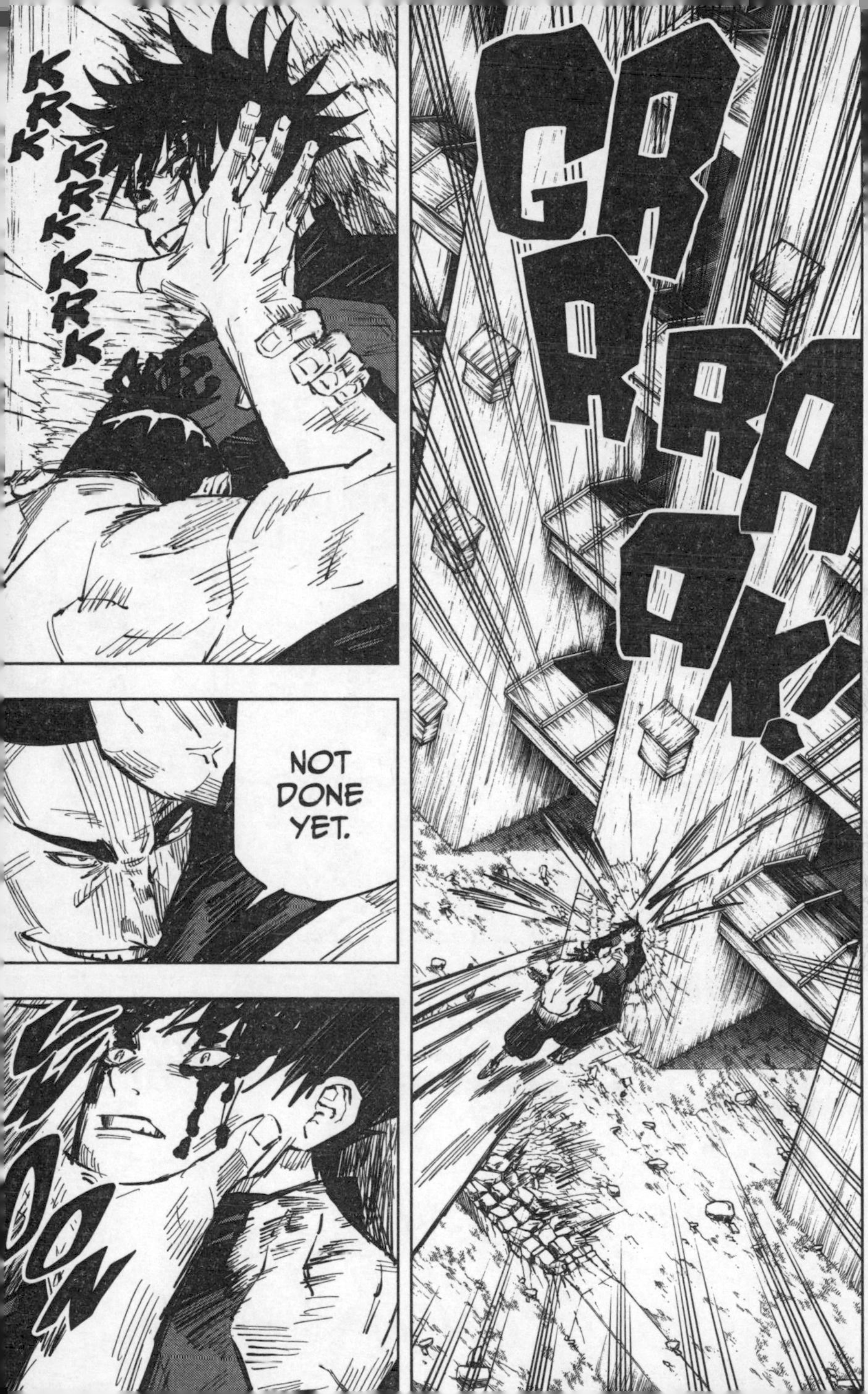
GARRAAAK!
KRK KRK KRK KRK
NOT DONE YET.

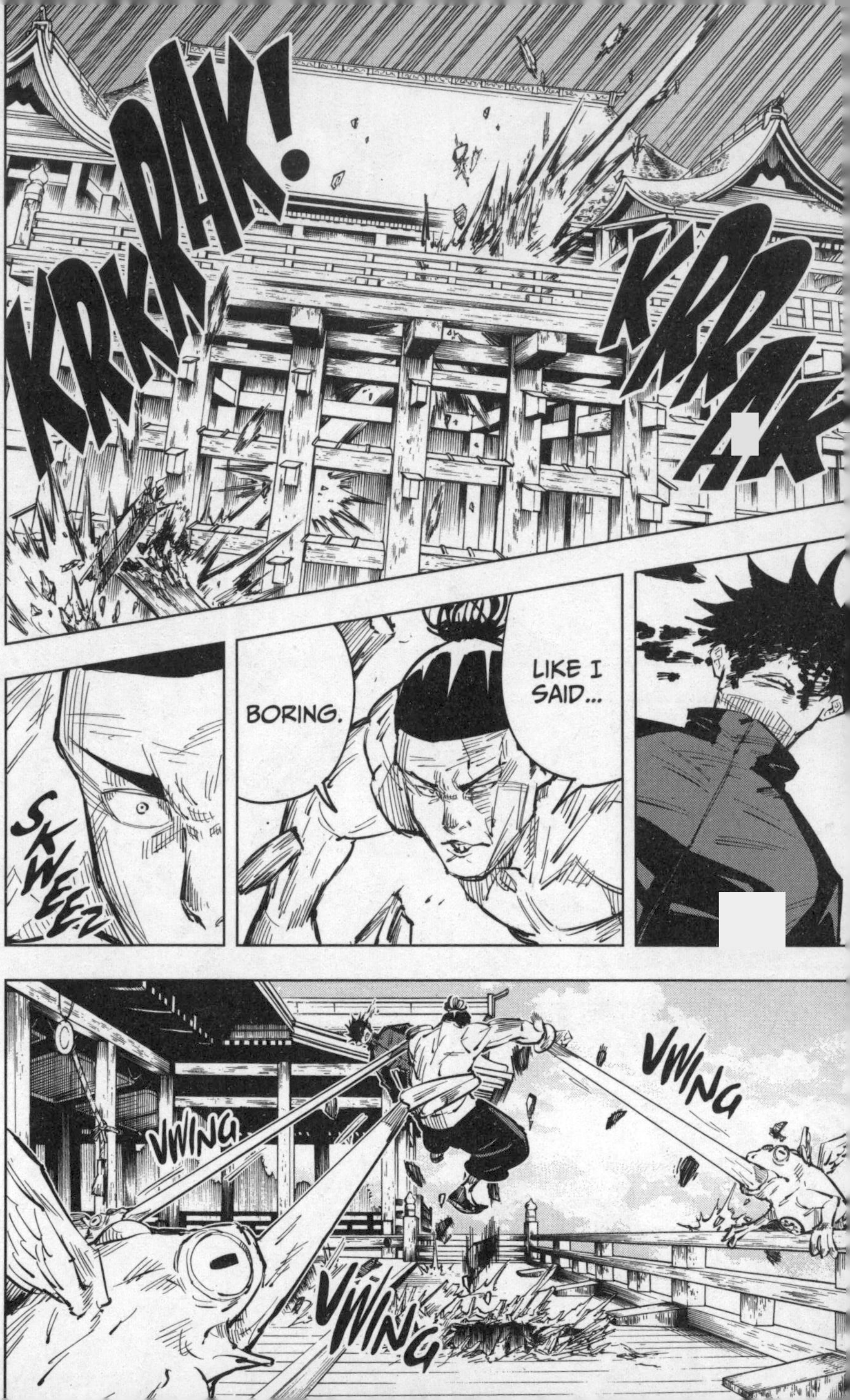
KRRAK
KRKPAK!
LIKE I SAID...
BORING.
SKWEEZ
VWING
VWING
VWING

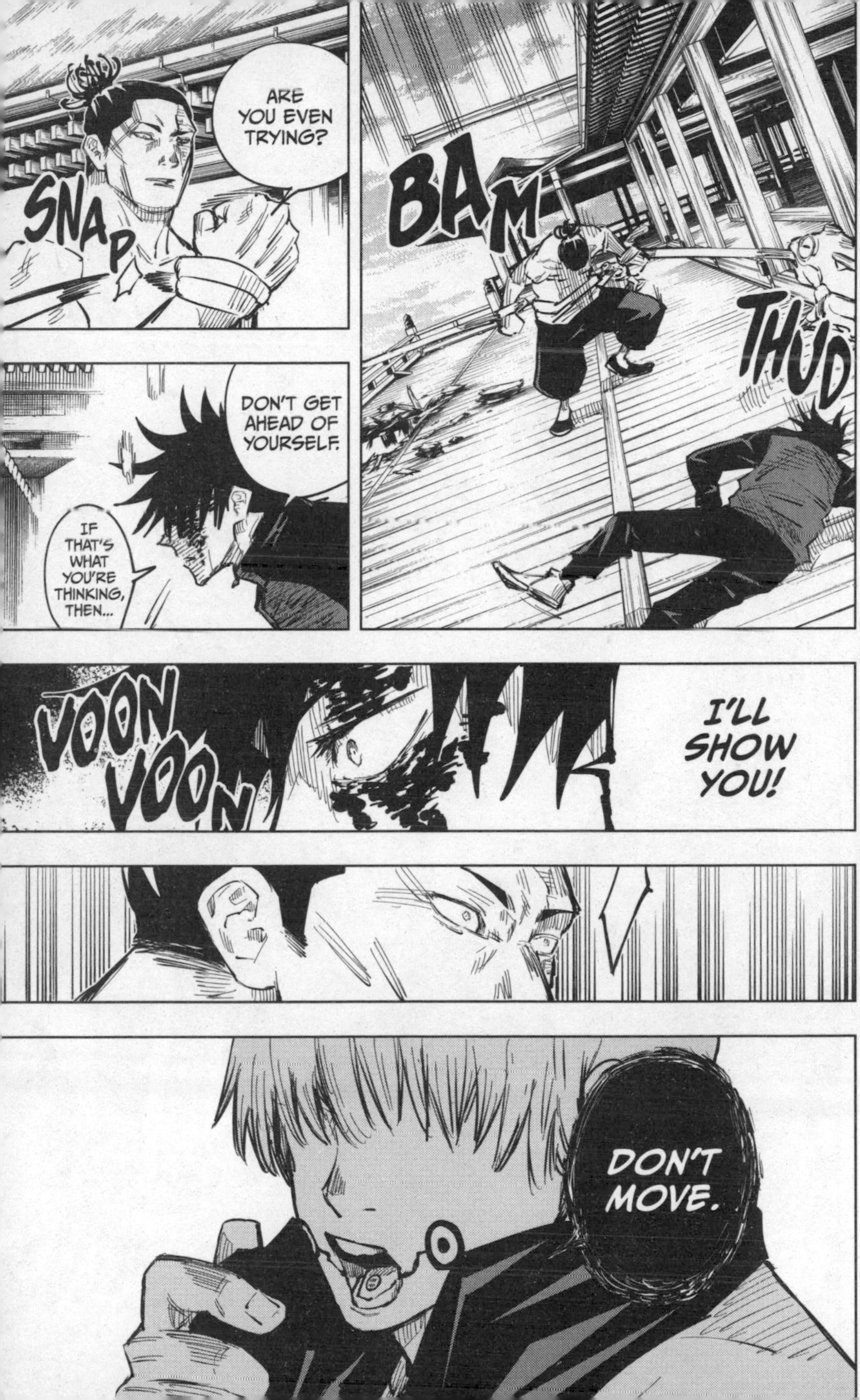
BAM
THUD
ARE YOU EVEN TRYING?
SNAP
DON'T GET AHEAD OF YOURSELF.
IF THAT'S WHAT YOU'RE THINKING, THEN...
I'LL SHOW YOU!
VOON VOON
DON'T MOVE.

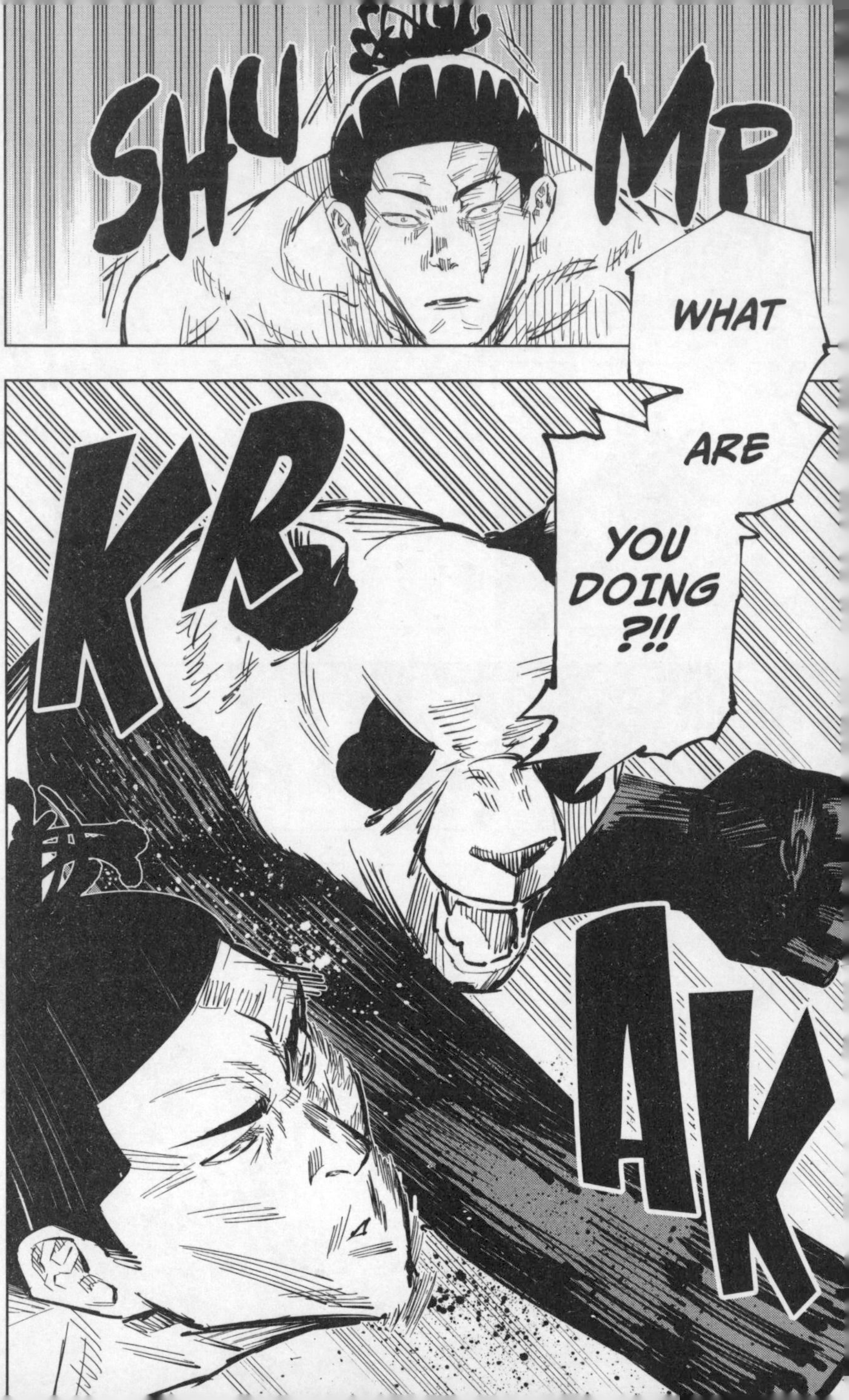
SHUMP
WHAT ARE YOU DOING ?!!
KRAK

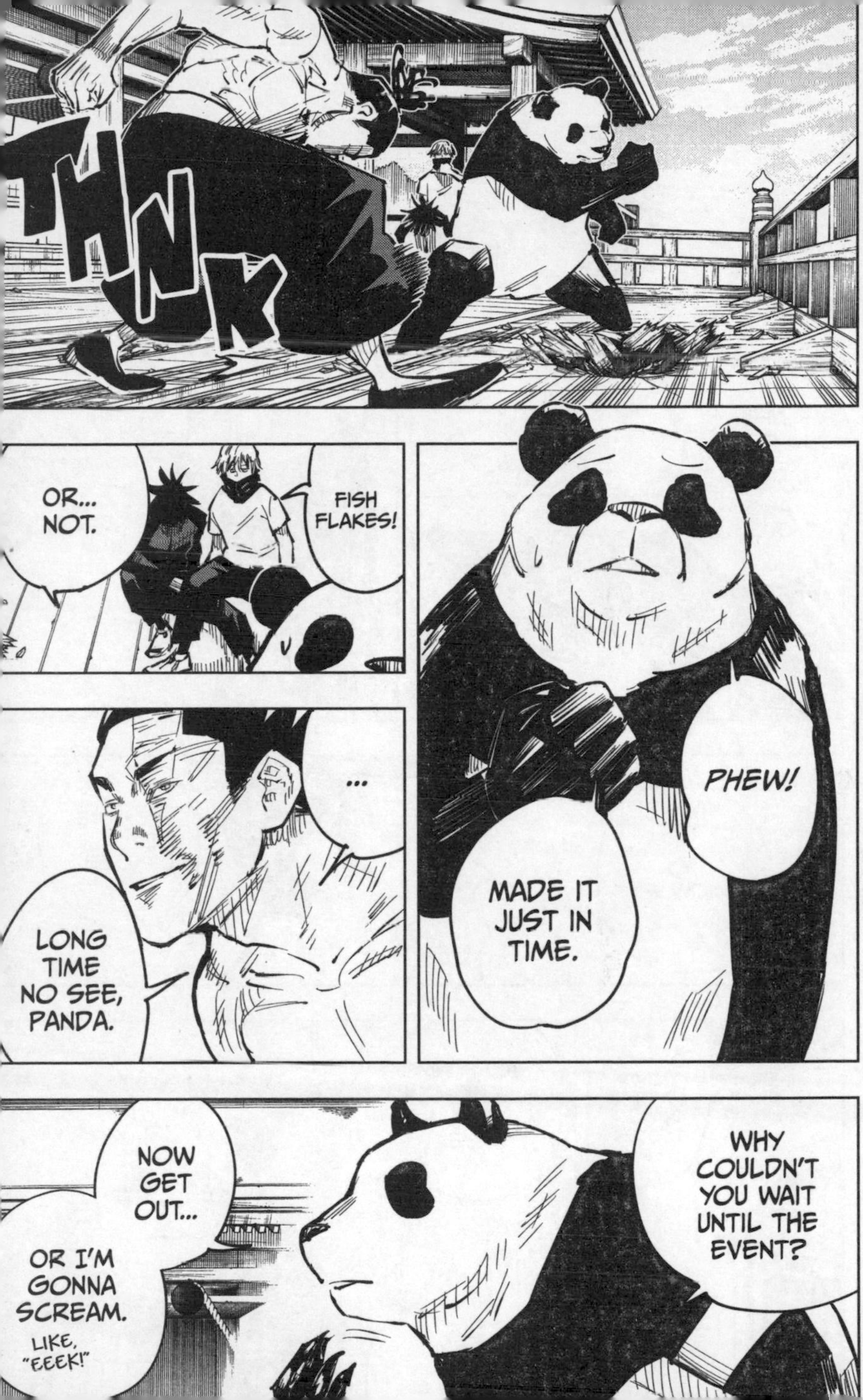
THNK
PHEW!
MADE IT JUST IN TIME.
FISH FLAKES!
OR... NOT.
...
LONG TIME NO SEE, PANDA.
WHY COULDN'T YOU WAIT UNTIL THE EVENT?
NOW GET OUT...
OR I'M GONNA SCREAM.
LIKE, "EEEK!"

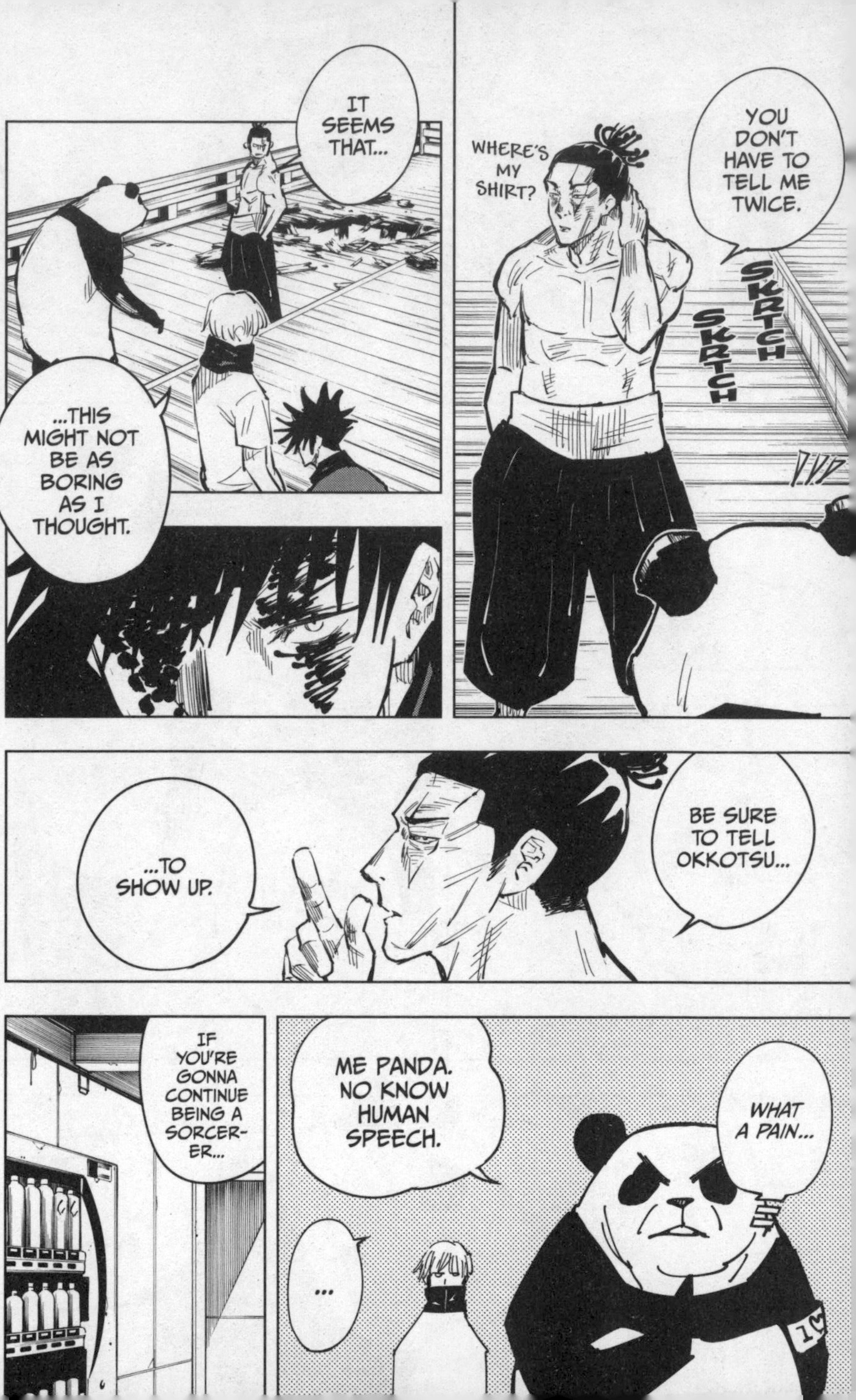
YOU DON'T HAVE TO TELL ME TWICE.
WHERE'S MY SHIRT?
SKRTCH
SKRTCH
IT SEEMS THAT...
...THIS MIGHT NOT BE AS BORING AS I THOUGHT.
BE SURE TO TELL OKKOTSU...
...TO SHOW UP.
WHAT A PAIN...
ME PANDA. NO KNOW HUMAN SPEECH.
...
IF YOU'RE GONNA CONTINUE BEING A SORCER-ER...

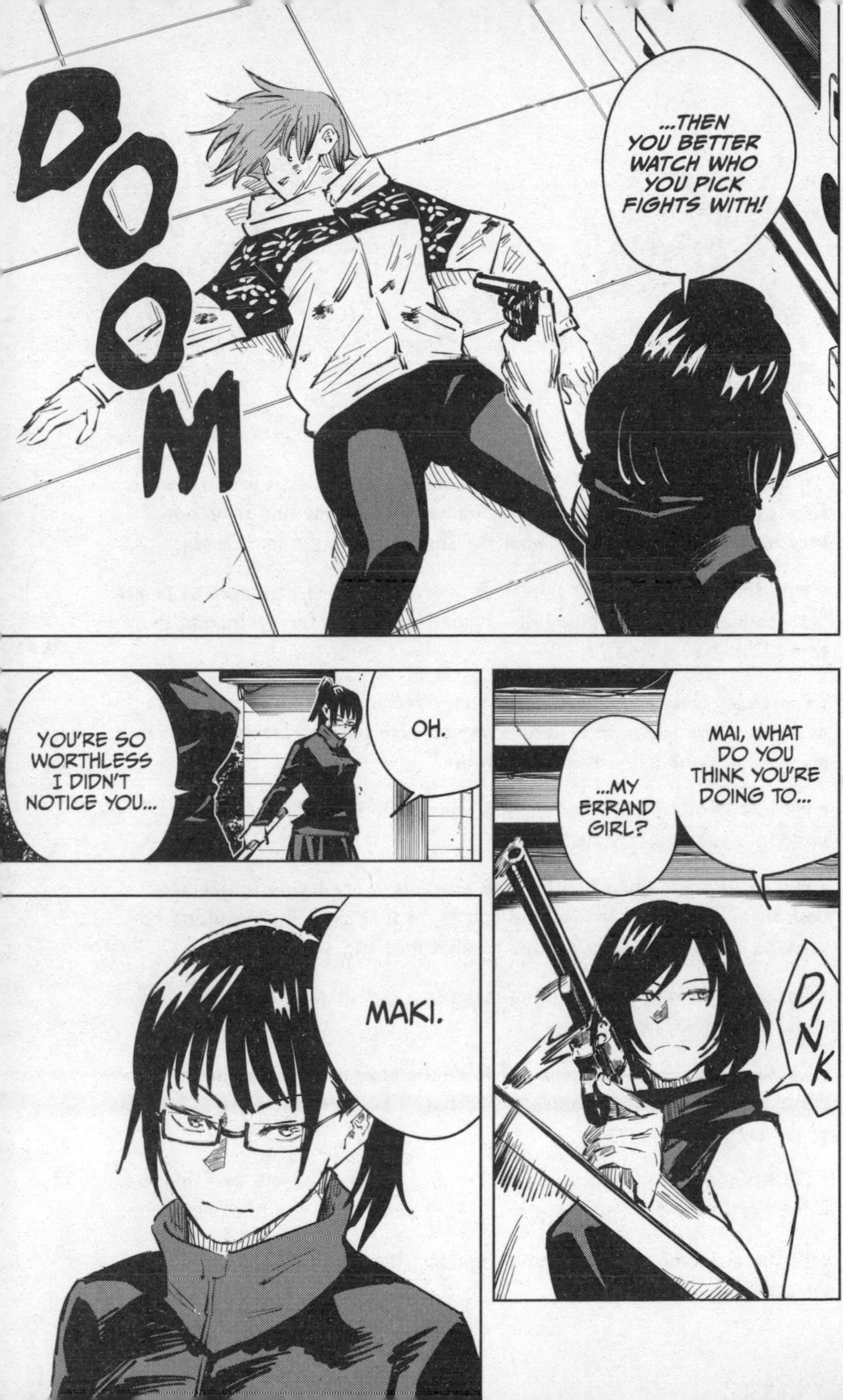
...THEN YOU BETTER WATCH WHO YOU PICK FIGHTS WITH!
DOOM
MAI, WHAT DO YOU THINK YOU'RE DOING TO...
...MY ERRAND GIRL?
DINK
OH.
YOU'RE SO WORTHLESS I DIDN'T NOTICE YOU...
MAKI.

SMACK TALK — A LITTLE CHAT

I'LL SPIT ON YOUR GRAVE!

WORDS HURT ONLY THOSE WHO SAY THEM!

• It goes without saying, but many shonen manga readers are in elementary or junior high school. I wanted to address this topic now because I don't want to limit what the characters in the manga say.

• With the appearance of Kyoto High, there'll be many instances of smack talk coming up. (I apologize to everyone from Kyoto for portraying them as sort of the bad guys.)

• I intended this to be more of a don't-do-this-stuff-at-home kinda deal. You know what I'm saying. Have you ever read something mean in a manga and done it to others in real life?

• It's possible to be scarred for life after being verbally abused while in a vulnerable state.

• But in *Jujutsu*, when fighting, the characters are trying to damage both their opponents' bodies and spirits. In that case, they wouldn't be thinking about the repercussions of what they say, would they?

• So don't you dare say anything mean to a girl in your class, especially about her pores, okay?

• I'm fine if you read *Jujutsu* and think it's boring and don't like it. But it'll make me sad if someone who hasn't even read it hates it because of the language...

• I'm sounding really virtuous, but I'm also guilty of saying bad things. I don't really have a right to preach. Just don't think too hard about it...

• To the awesome people reading *Jujutsu*... It's tough ending up like me! Be careful!!

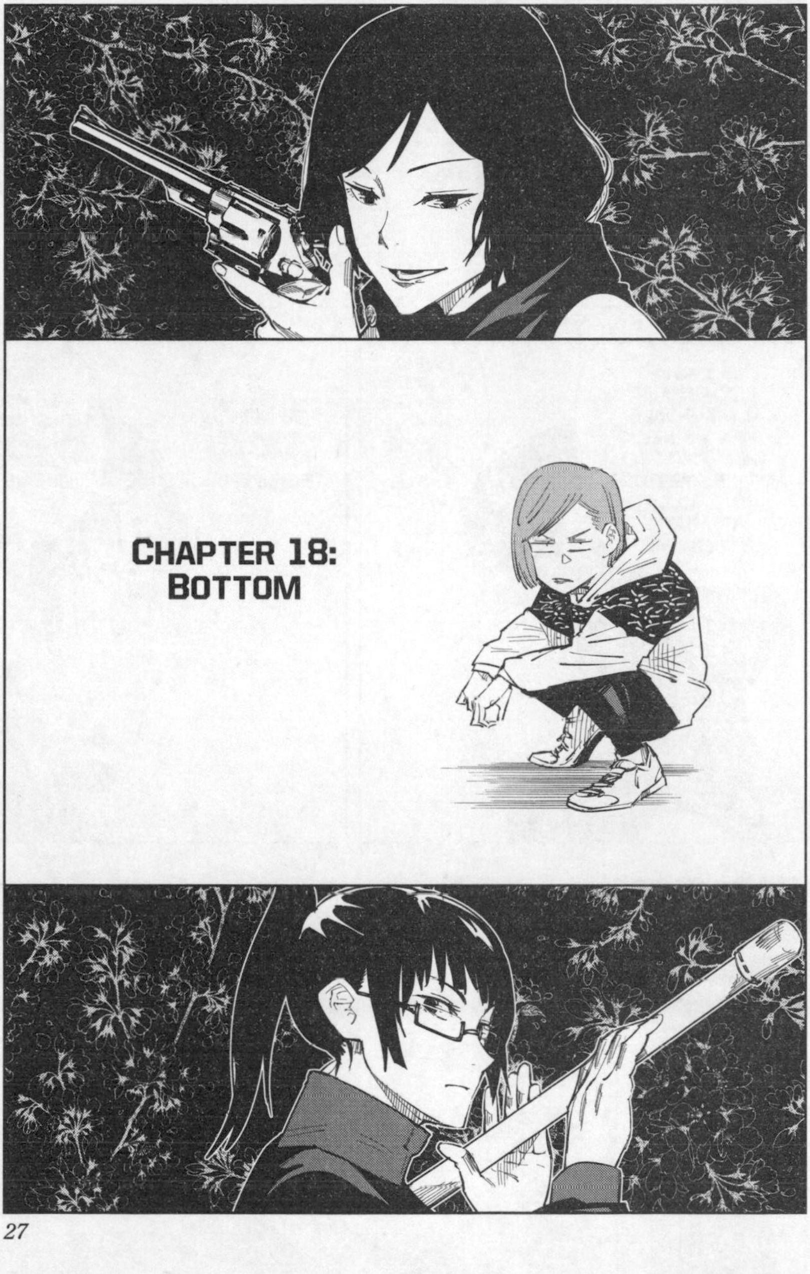
CHAPTER 18:
BOTTOM

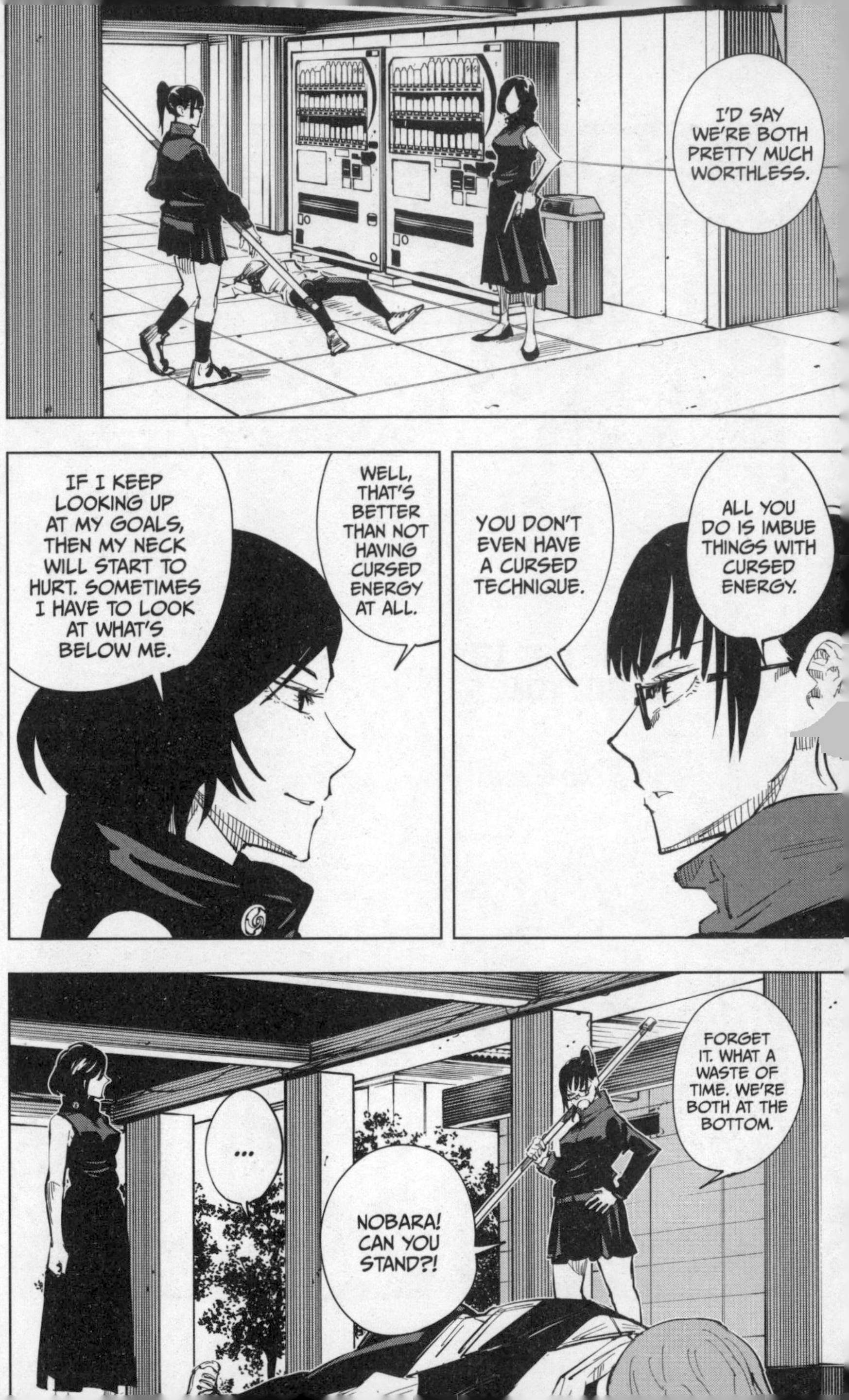
I'D SAY WE'RE BOTH PRETTY MUCH WORTHLESS.
ALL YOU DO IS IMBUE THINGS WITH CURSED ENERGY.
YOU DON'T EVEN HAVE A CURSED TECHNIQUE.
WELL, THAT'S BETTER THAN NOT HAVING CURSED ENERGY AT ALL.
IF I KEEP LOOKING UP AT MY GOALS, THEN MY NECK WILL START TO HURT. SOMETIMES I HAVE TO LOOK AT WHAT'S BELOW ME.
FORGET IT. WHAT A WASTE OF TIME. WE'RE BOTH AT THE BOTTOM.
NOBARA! CAN YOU STAND?!
...

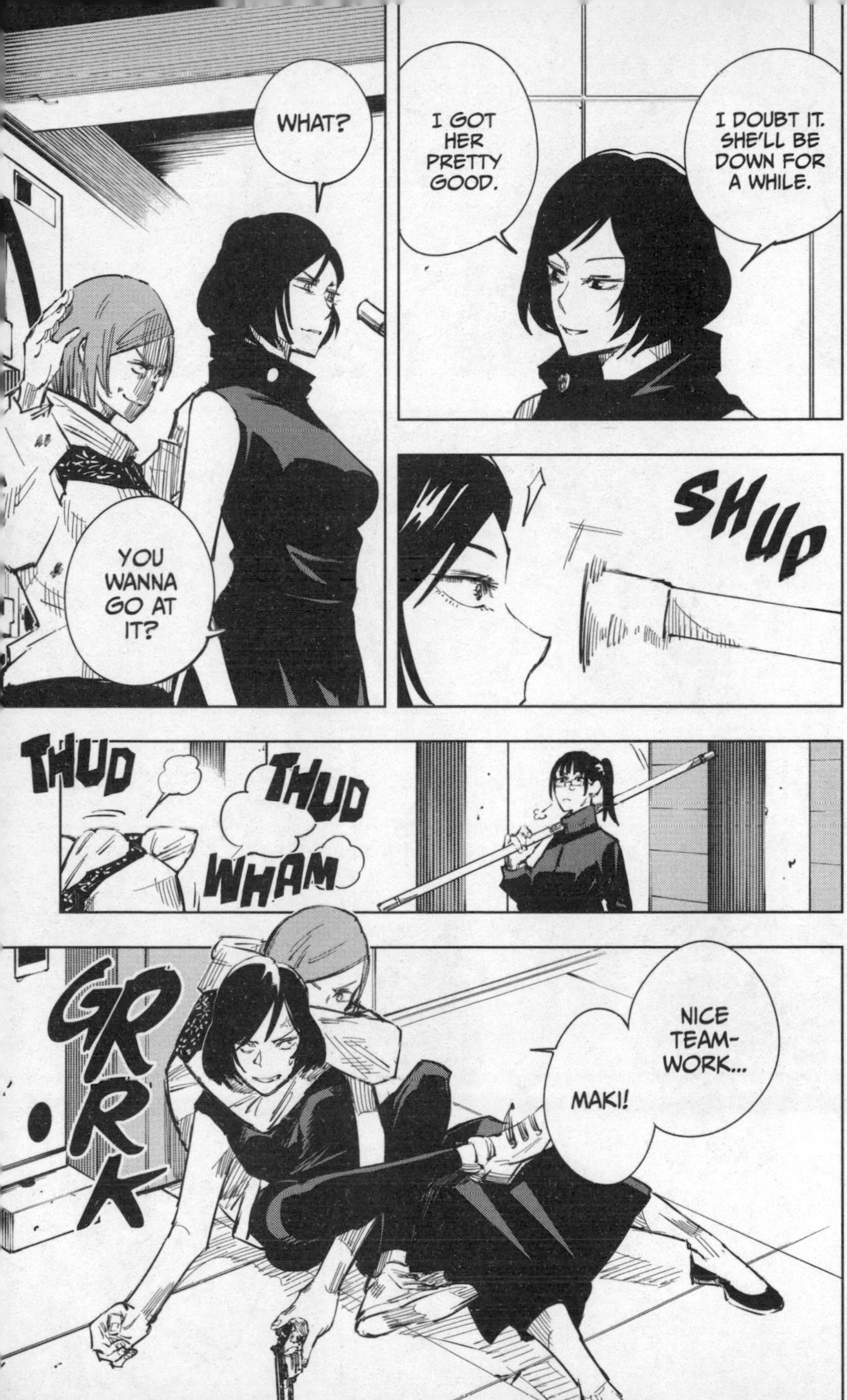
I DOUBT IT. SHE'LL BE DOWN FOR A WHILE.
I GOT HER PRETTY GOOD.
SHUP
WHAT?
YOU WANNA GO AT IT?
THUD
THUD
WHAM
NICE TEAM-WORK...
MAKI!
GRRK

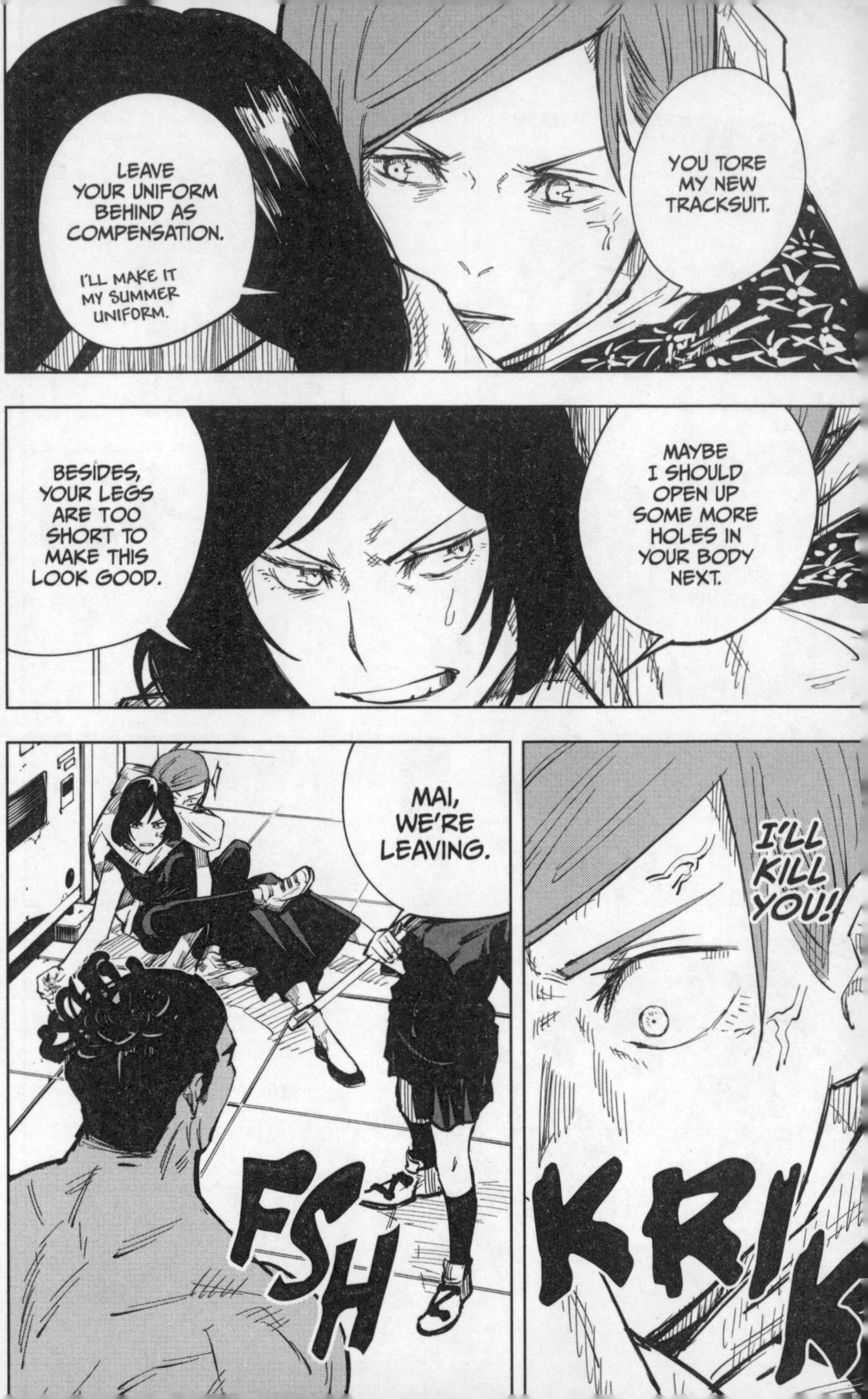
YOU TORE MY NEW TRACKSUIT.
LEAVE YOUR UNIFORM BEHIND AS COMPENSATION.
I'LL MAKE IT MY SUMMER UNIFORM.
MAYBE I SHOULD OPEN UP SOME MORE HOLES IN YOUR BODY NEXT.
BESIDES, YOUR LEGS ARE TOO SHORT TO MAKE THIS LOOK GOOD.
I'LL KILL YOU!
KRIK
MAI, WE'RE LEAVING.
FSH

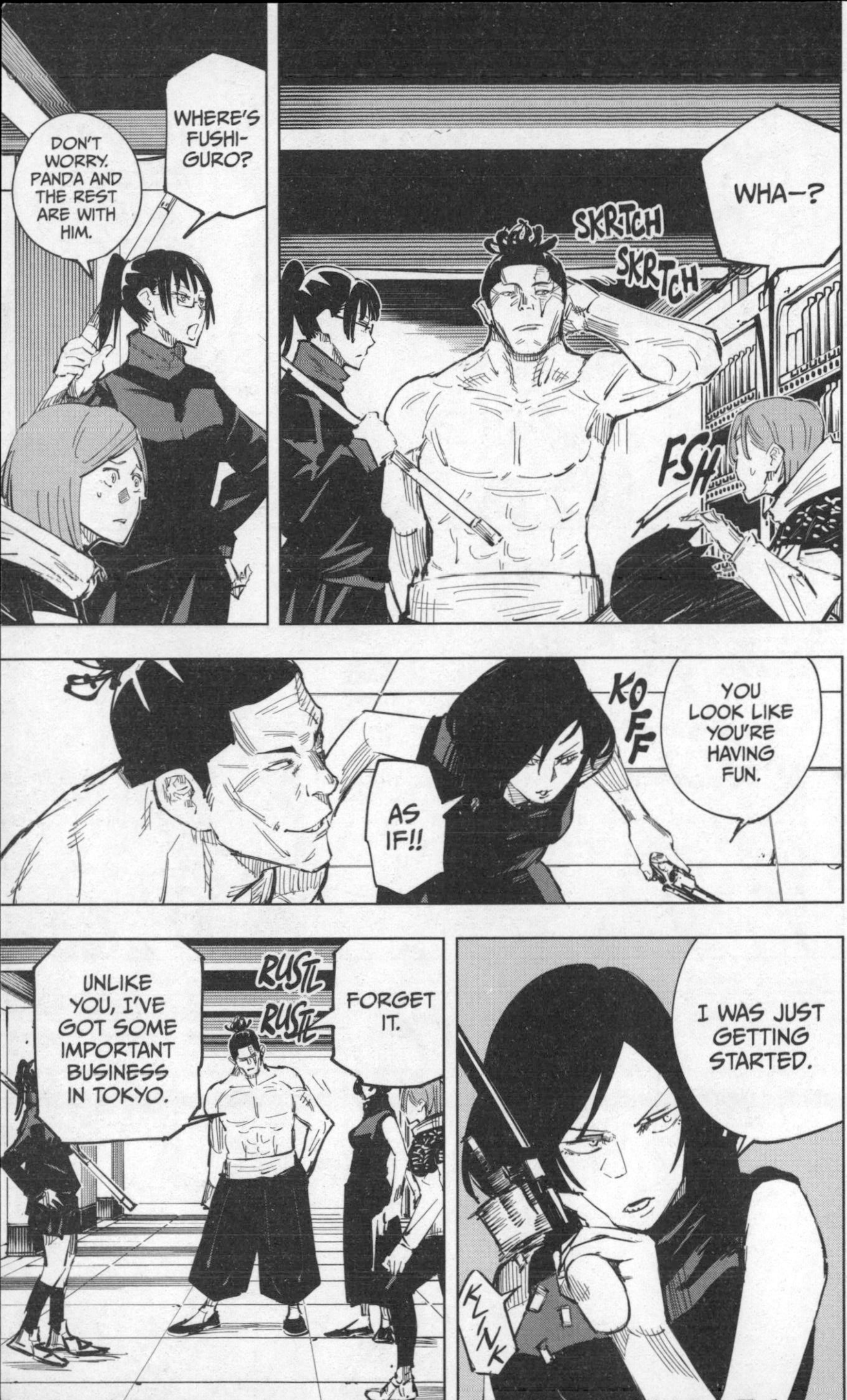
WHA–?
SKRTCH
SKRTCH
FSH
WHERE'S FUSHI-GURO?
DON'T WORRY. PANDA AND THE REST ARE WITH HIM.
YOU LOOK LIKE YOU'RE HAVING FUN.
KOFF
AS IF!!
I WAS JUST GETTING STARTED.
KLINK
FORGET IT.
RUSTL
RUSTLE
UNLIKE YOU, I'VE GOT SOME IMPORTANT BUSINESS IN TOKYO.

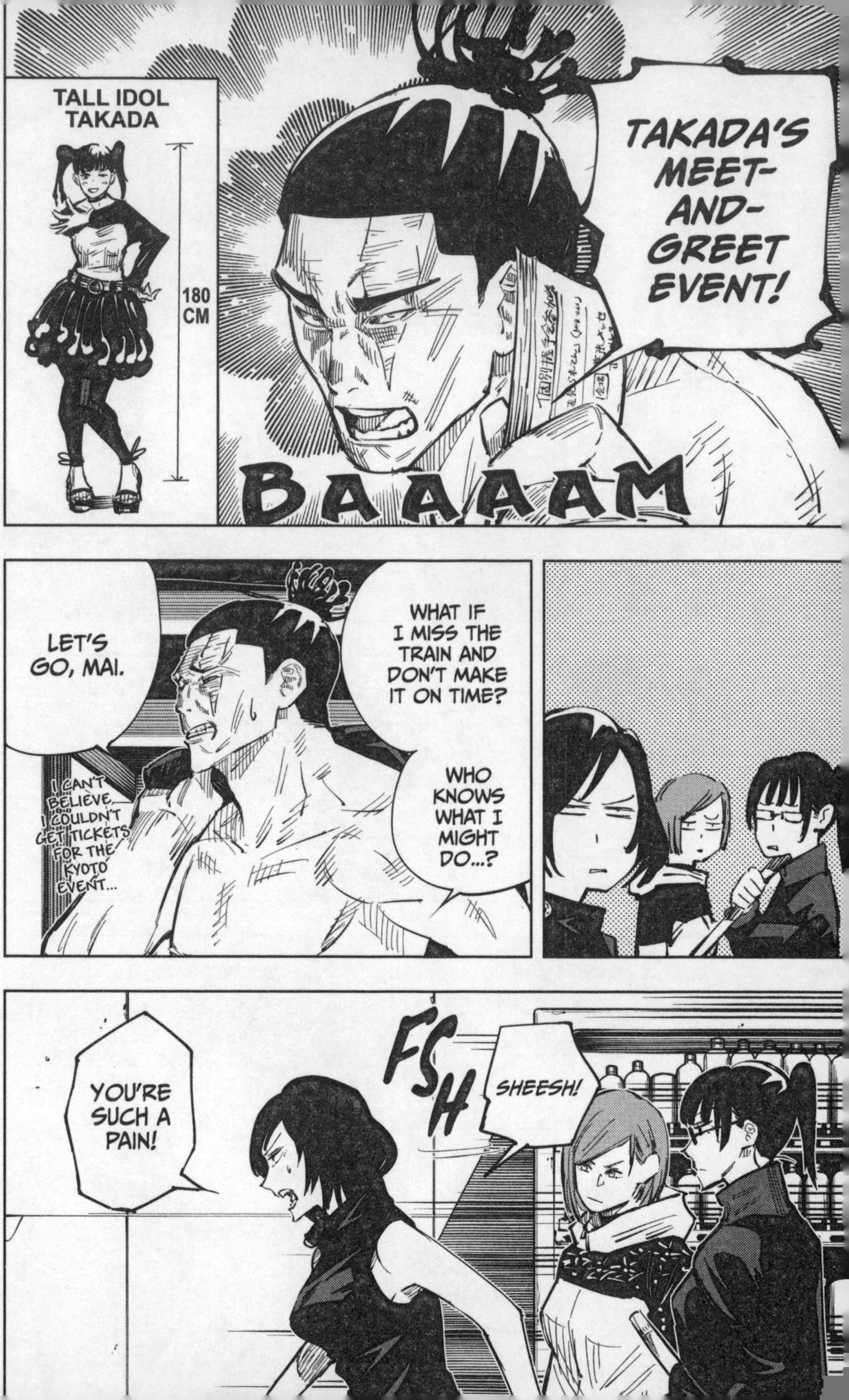
TAKADA'S MEET-AND-GREET EVENT!
BAAAAM
TALL IDOL TAKADA
180 CM
WHAT IF I MISS THE TRAIN AND DON'T MAKE IT ON TIME?
LET'S GO, MAI.
WHO KNOWS WHAT I MIGHT DO...?
I CAN'T BELIEVE I COULDN'T GET TICKETS FOR THE KYOTO EVENT...
SHEESH!
FSH
YOU'RE SUCH A PAIN!

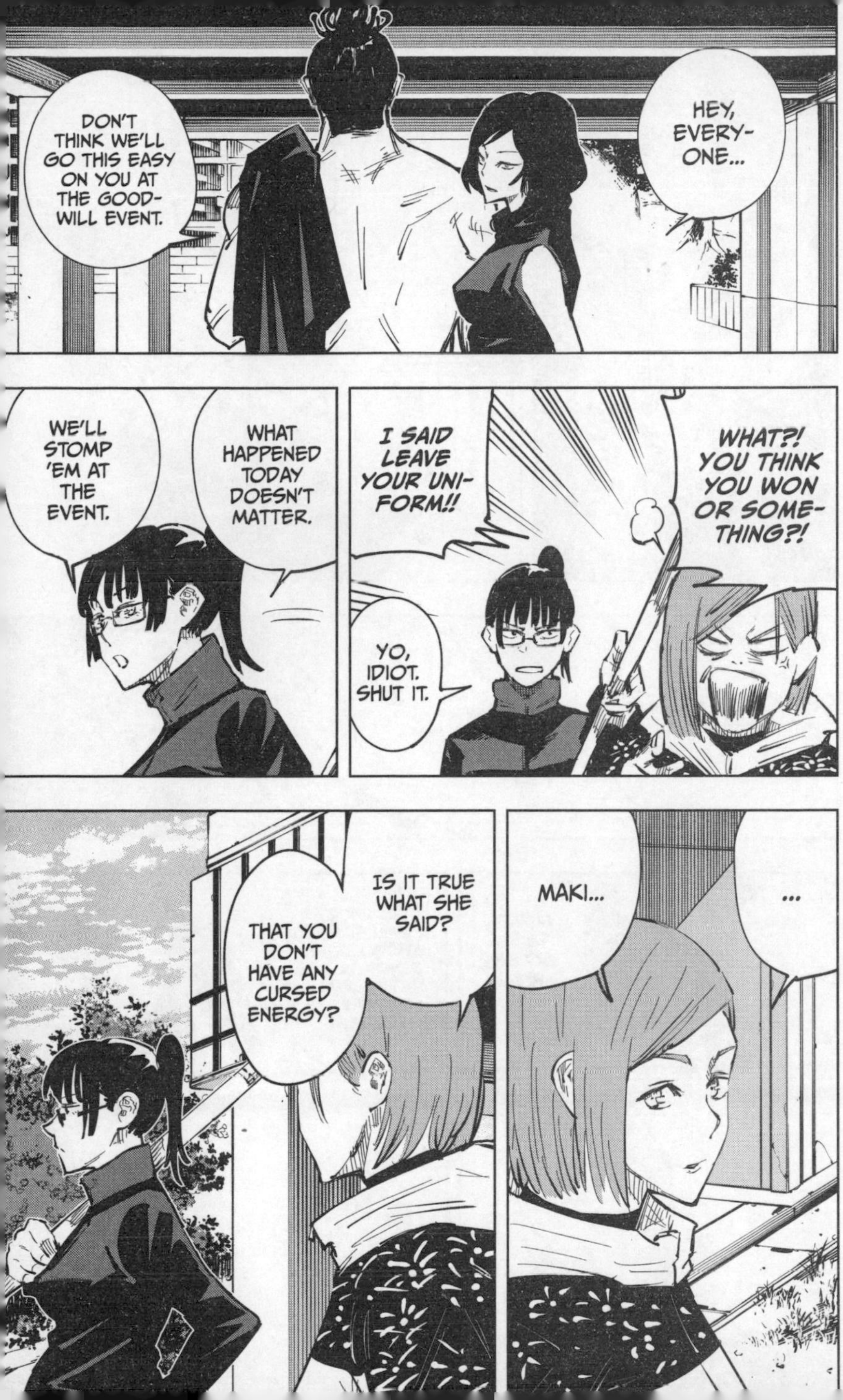
HEY, EVERY-ONE...
DON'T THINK WE'LL GO THIS EASY ON YOU AT THE GOOD-WILL EVENT.
WHAT?! YOU THINK YOU WON OR SOME-THING?!
I SAID LEAVE YOUR UNI-FORM!!
YO, IDIOT. SHUT IT.
WHAT HAPPENED TODAY DOESN'T MATTER.
WE'LL STOMP 'EM AT THE EVENT.
...
MAKI...
IS IT TRUE WHAT SHE SAID?
THAT YOU DON'T HAVE ANY CURSED ENERGY?

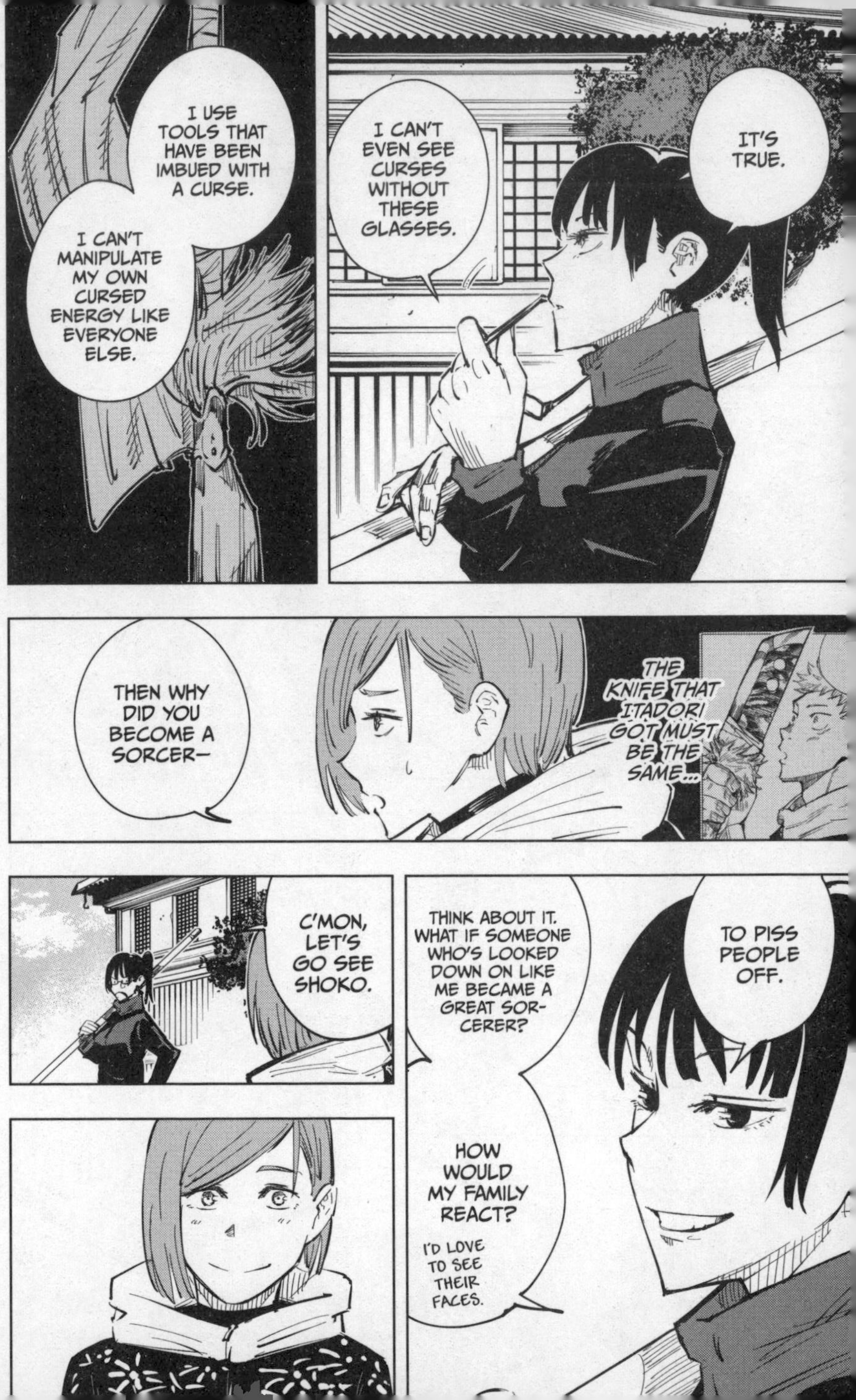
IT'S TRUE.
I CAN'T EVEN SEE CURSES WITHOUT THESE GLASSES.
I USE TOOLS THAT HAVE BEEN IMBUED WITH A CURSE.
I CAN'T MANIPULATE MY OWN CURSED ENERGY LIKE EVERYONE ELSE.
THE KNIFE THAT ITADORI GOT MUST BE THE SAME...
THEN WHY DID YOU BECOME A SORCER—
TO PISS PEOPLE OFF.
THINK ABOUT IT. WHAT IF SOMEONE WHO'S LOOKED DOWN ON LIKE ME BECAME A GREAT SOR-CERER?
HOW WOULD MY FAMILY REACT?
I'D LOVE TO SEE THEIR FACES.
C'MON, LET'S GO SEE SHOKO.

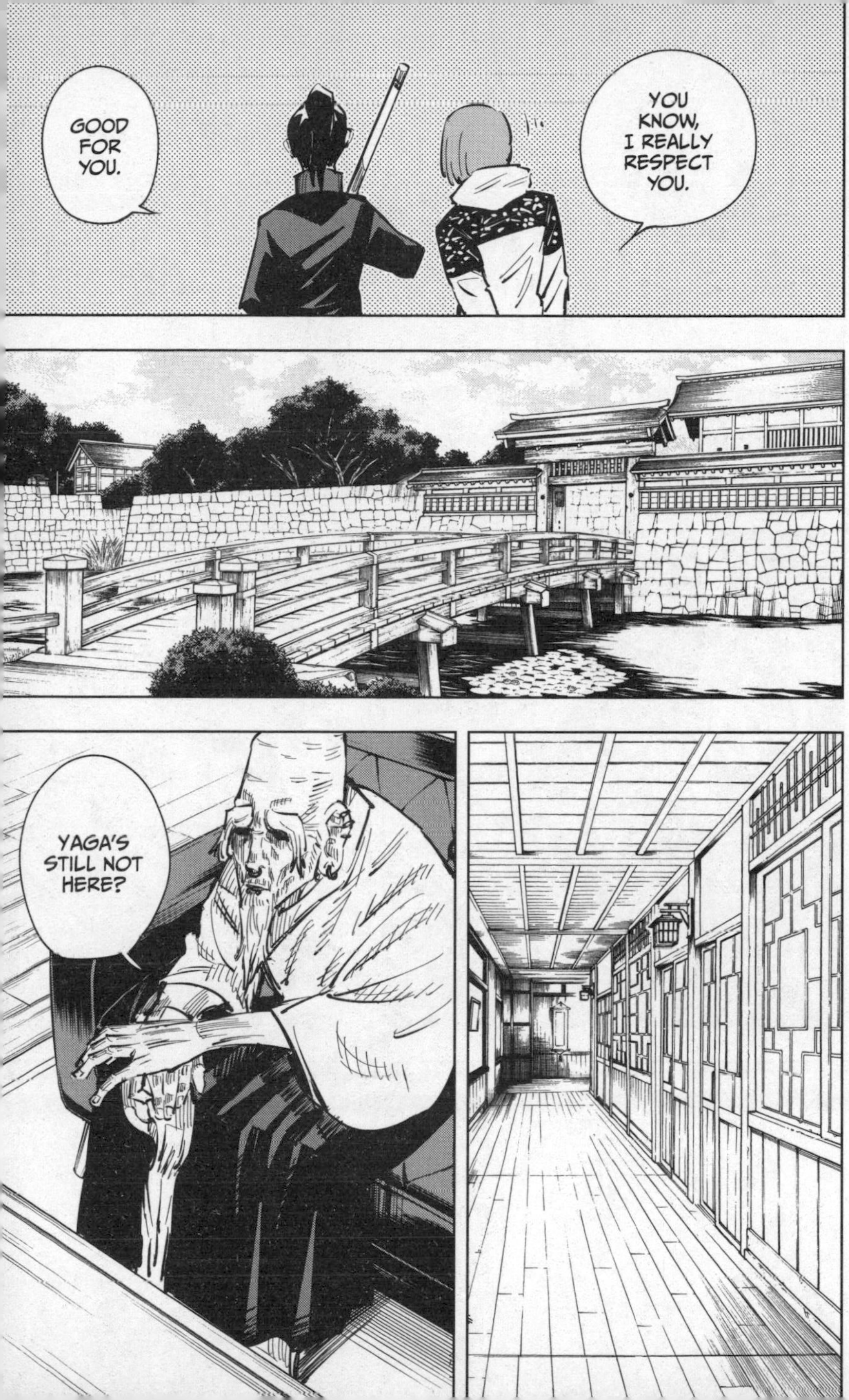
YOU KNOW, I REALLY RESPECT YOU.
GOOD FOR YOU.
YAGA'S STILL NOT HERE?

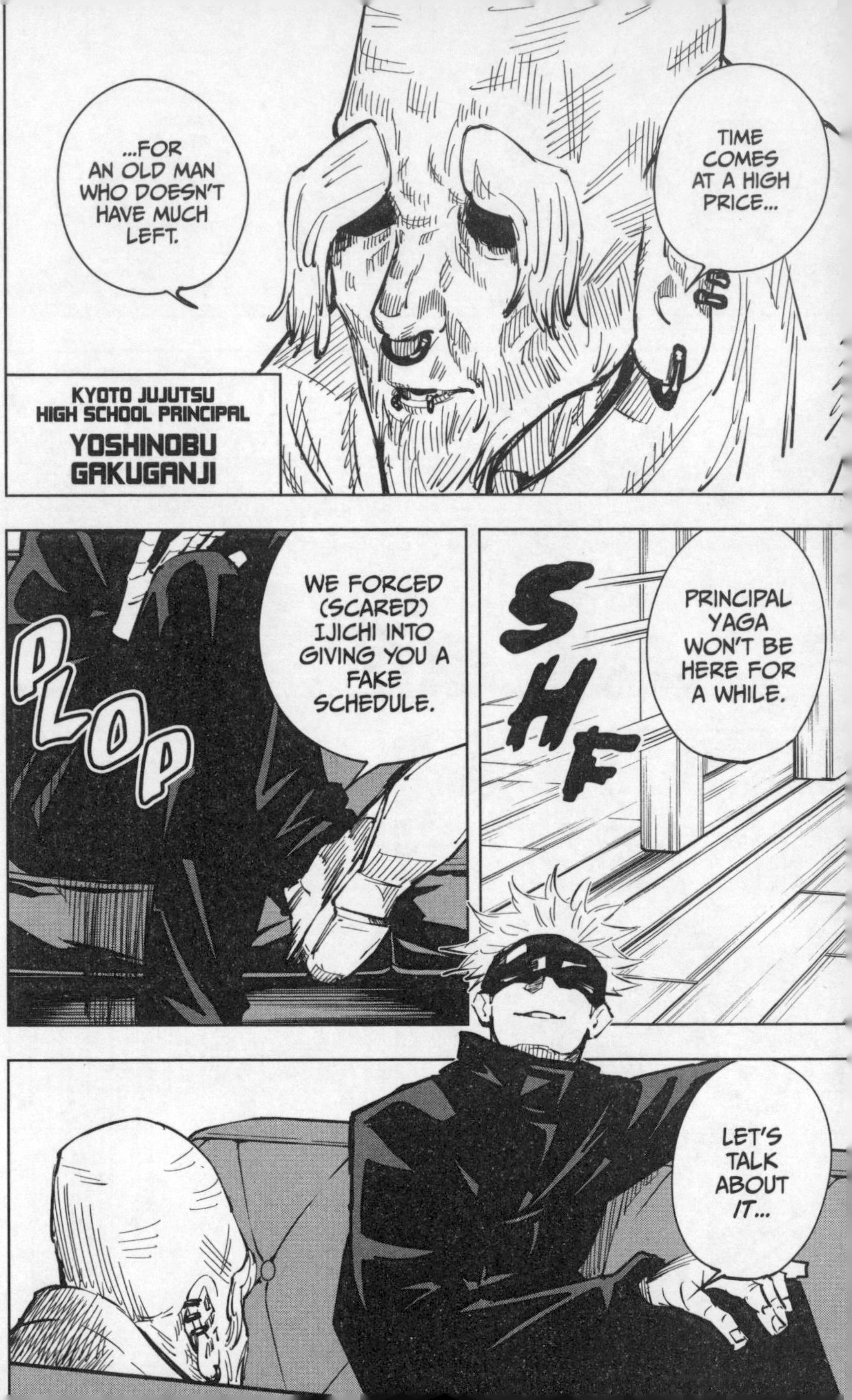
TIME COMES AT A HIGH PRICE...
...FOR AN OLD MAN WHO DOESN'T HAVE MUCH LEFT.
KYOTO JUJUTSU HIGH SCHOOL PRINCIPAL
YOSHINOBU GAKUGANJI
PRINCIPAL YAGA WON'T BE HERE FOR A WHILE.
SHF
WE FORCED (SCARED) IJICHI INTO GIVING YOU A FAKE SCHEDULE.
PLOP
LET'S TALK ABOUT IT...

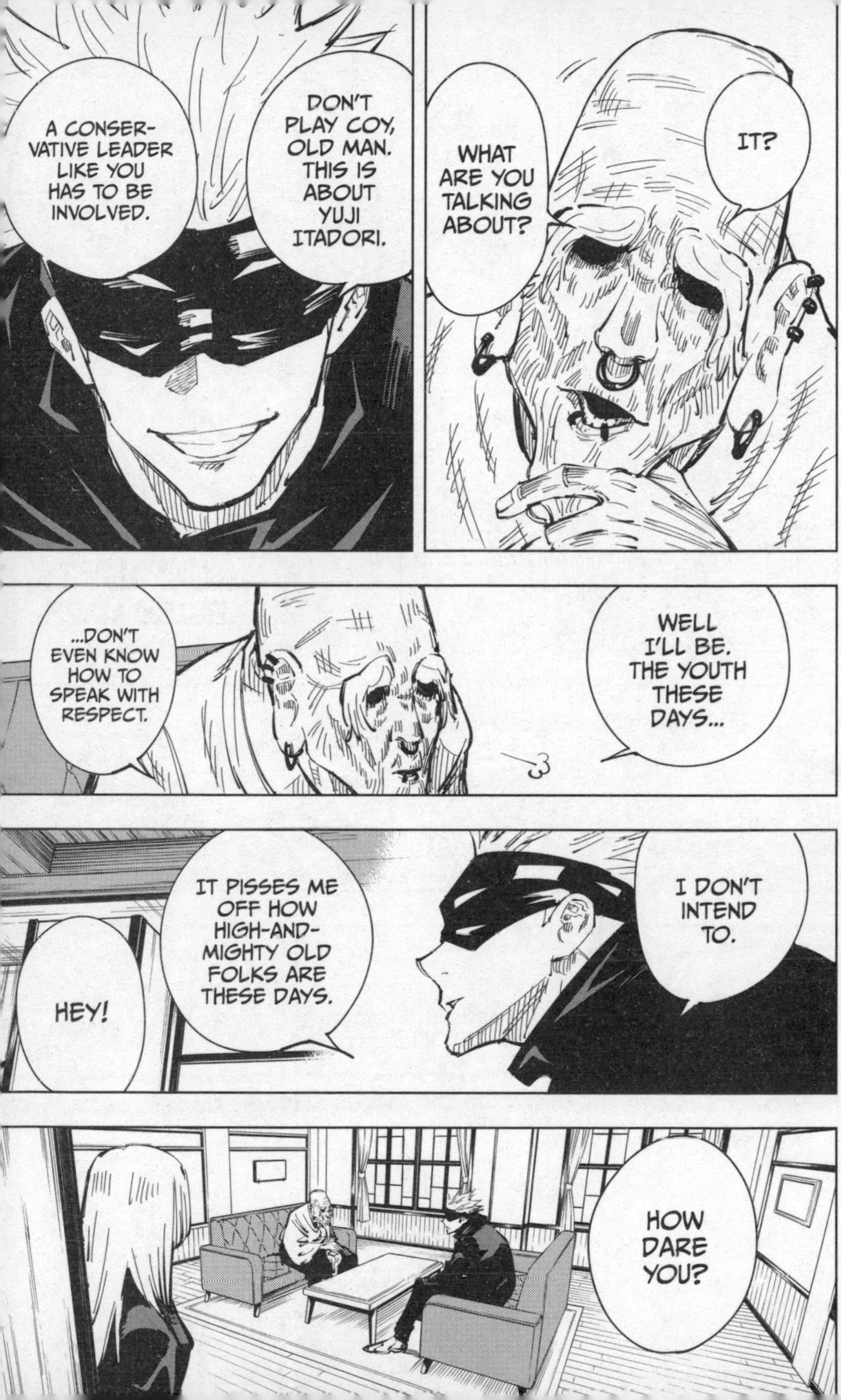
IT?
WHAT ARE YOU TALKING ABOUT?
DON'T PLAY COY, OLD MAN. THIS IS ABOUT YUJI ITADORI.
A CONSERVATIVE LEADER LIKE YOU HAS TO BE INVOLVED.
WELL I'LL BE. THE YOUTH THESE DAYS...
...DON'T EVEN KNOW HOW TO SPEAK WITH RESPECT.
I DON'T INTEND TO.
IT PISSES ME OFF HOW HIGH-AND-MIGHTY OLD FOLKS ARE THESE DAYS.
HEY!
HOW DARE YOU?

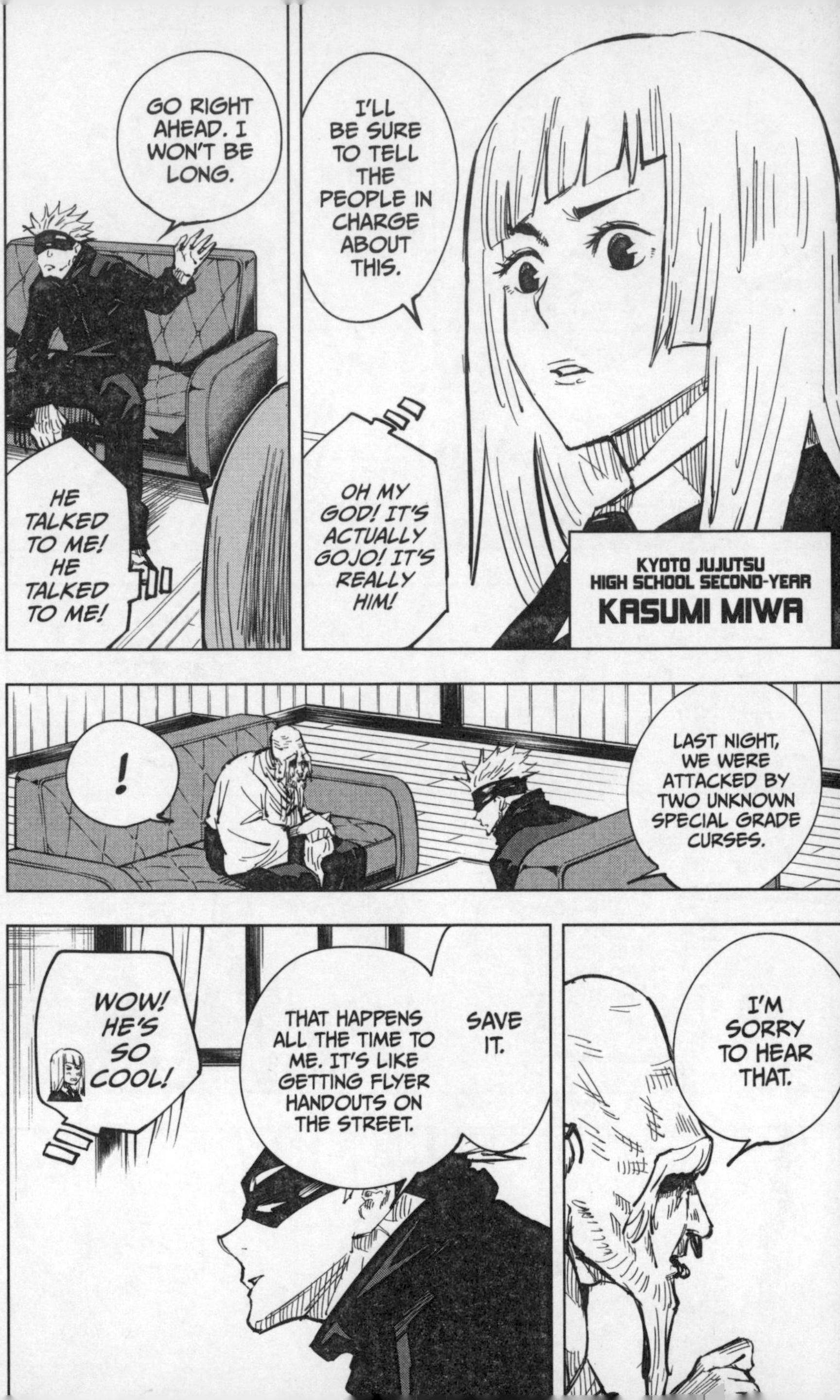
I'LL BE SURE TO TELL THE PEOPLE IN CHARGE ABOUT THIS.
KYOTO JUJUTSU HIGH SCHOOL SECOND-YEAR
KASUMI MIWA
OH MY GOD! IT'S ACTUALLY GOJO! IT'S REALLY HIM!
GO RIGHT AHEAD. I WON'T BE LONG.
HE TALKED TO ME! HE TALKED TO ME!
LAST NIGHT, WE WERE ATTACKED BY TWO UNKNOWN SPECIAL GRADE CURSES.
!
I'M SORRY TO HEAR THAT.
SAVE IT.
THAT HAPPENS ALL THE TIME TO ME. IT'S LIKE GETTING FLYER HANDOUTS ON THE STREET.
WOW! HE'S SO COOL!

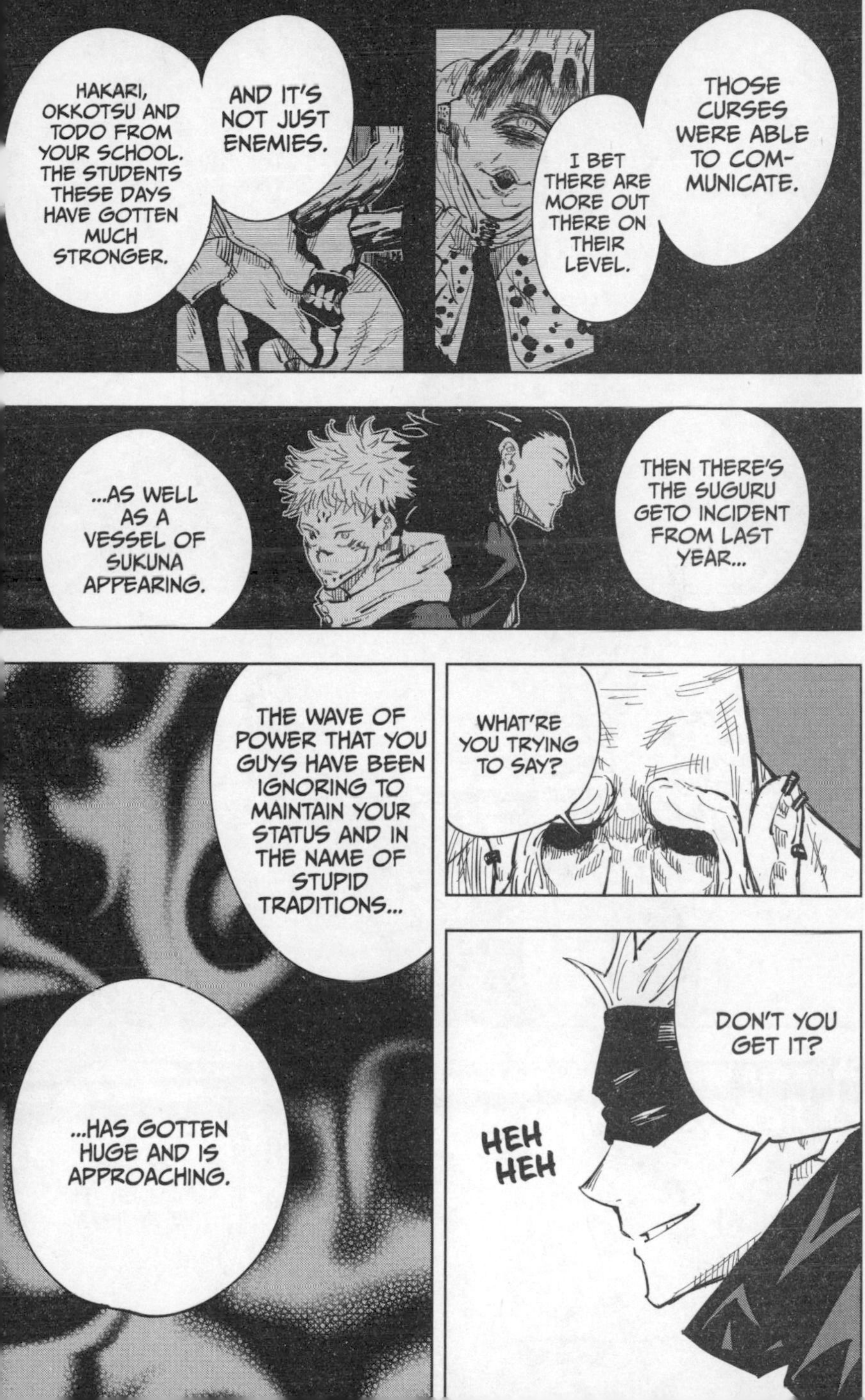
THOSE CURSES WERE ABLE TO COMMUNICATE.
I BET THERE ARE MORE OUT THERE ON THEIR LEVEL.
AND IT'S NOT JUST ENEMIES.
HAKARI, OKKOTSU AND TODO FROM YOUR SCHOOL. THE STUDENTS THESE DAYS HAVE GOTTEN MUCH STRONGER.
THEN THERE'S THE SUGURU GETO INCIDENT FROM LAST YEAR...
...AS WELL AS A VESSEL OF SUKUNA APPEARING.
WHAT'RE YOU TRYING TO SAY?
DON'T YOU GET IT?
HEH HEH
THE WAVE OF POWER THAT YOU GUYS HAVE BEEN IGNORING TO MAINTAIN YOUR STATUS AND IN THE NAME OF STUPID TRADITIONS...
...HAS GOTTEN HUGE AND IS APPROACHING.

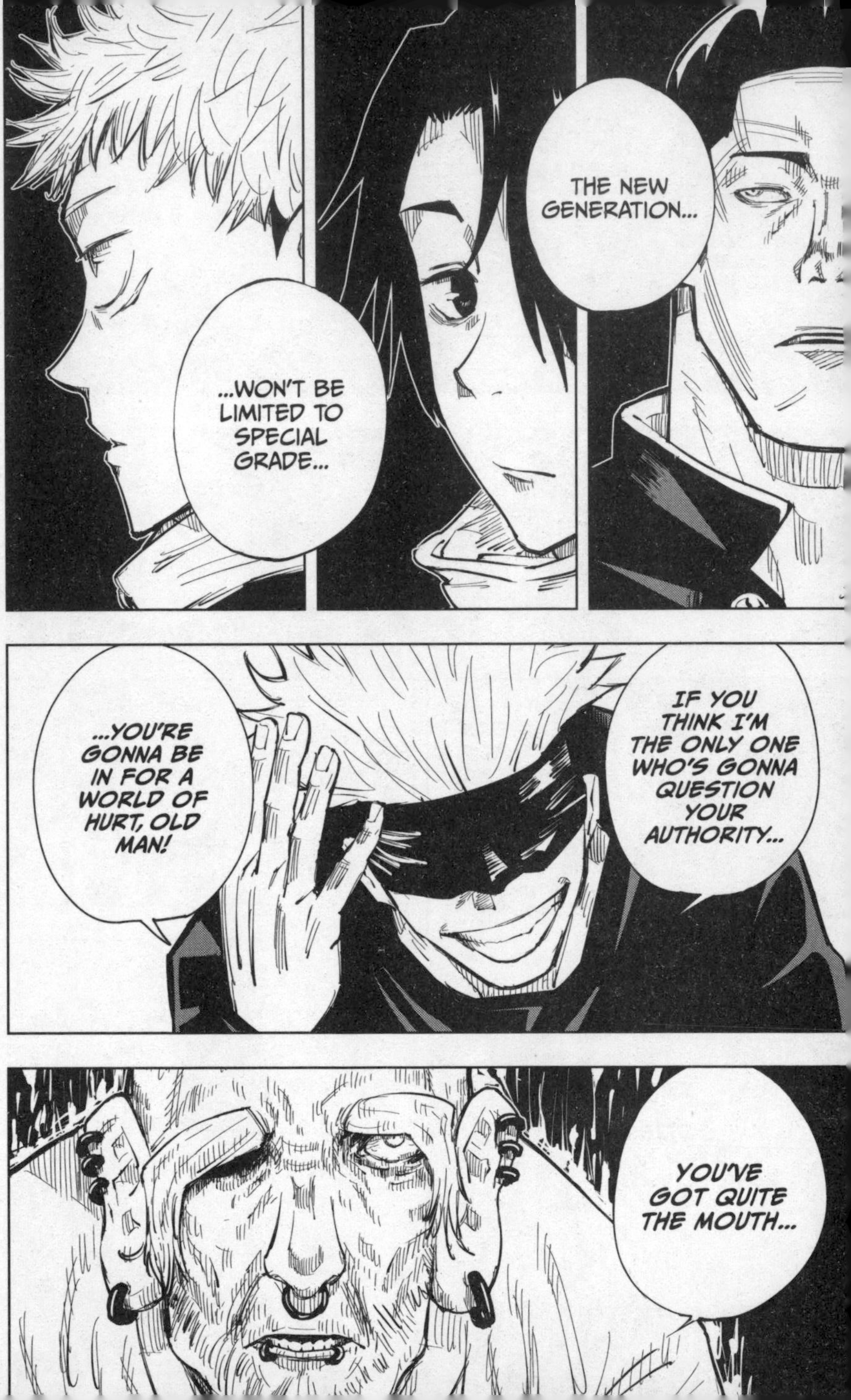
THE NEW GENERATION...
...WON'T BE LIMITED TO SPECIAL GRADE...
IF YOU THINK I'M THE ONLY ONE WHO'S GONNA QUESTION YOUR AUTHORITY...
...YOU'RE GONNA BE IN FOR A WORLD OF HURT, OLD MAN!
YOU'VE GOT QUITE THE MOUTH...

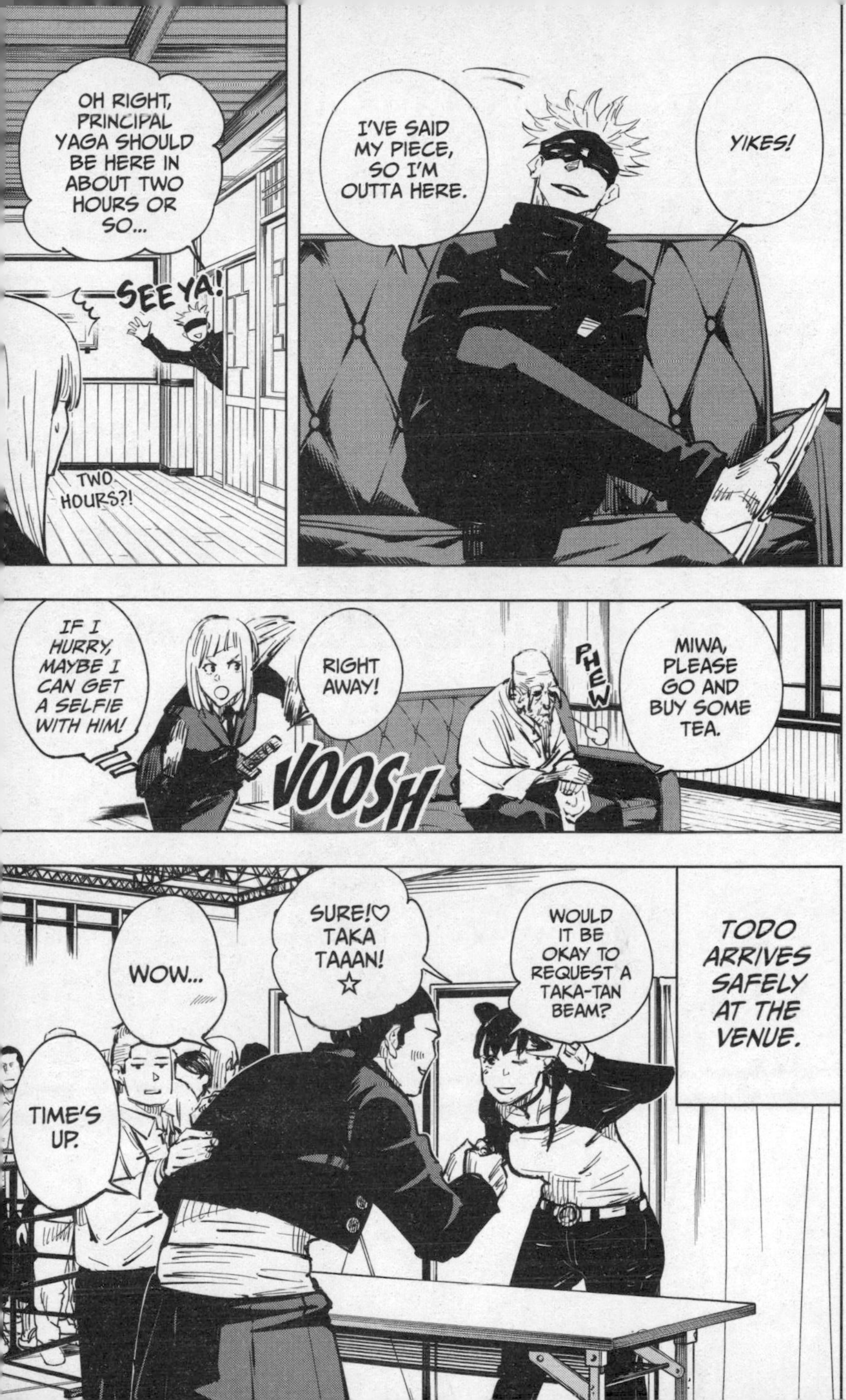
YIKES!
I'VE SAID MY PIECE, SO I'M OUTTA HERE.
OH RIGHT, PRINCIPAL YAGA SHOULD BE HERE IN ABOUT TWO HOURS OR SO...
SEE YA!
TWO HOURS?!
MIWA, PLEASE GO AND BUY SOME TEA.
PHEW
RIGHT AWAY!
IF I HURRY, MAYBE I CAN GET A SELFIE WITH HIM!
VOOSH
TODO ARRIVES SAFELY AT THE VENUE.
WOULD IT BE OKAY TO REQUEST A TAKA-TAN BEAM?
SURE!♡ TAKA TAAAN! ☆
WOW...
TIME'S UP.

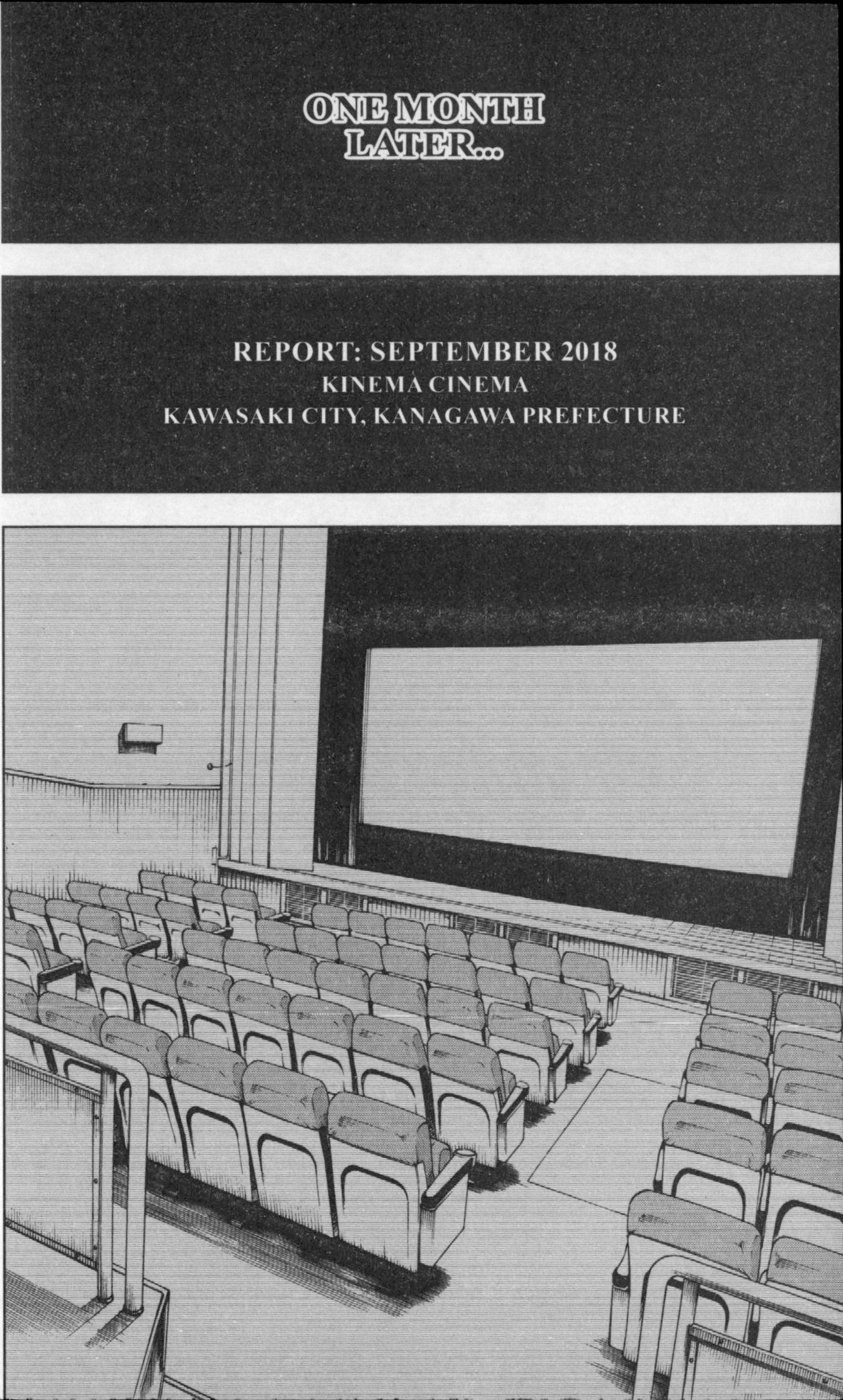
ONE MONTH LATER...
REPORT: SEPTEMBER 2018
KINEMA CINEMA
KAWASAKI CITY, KANAGAWA PREFECTURE

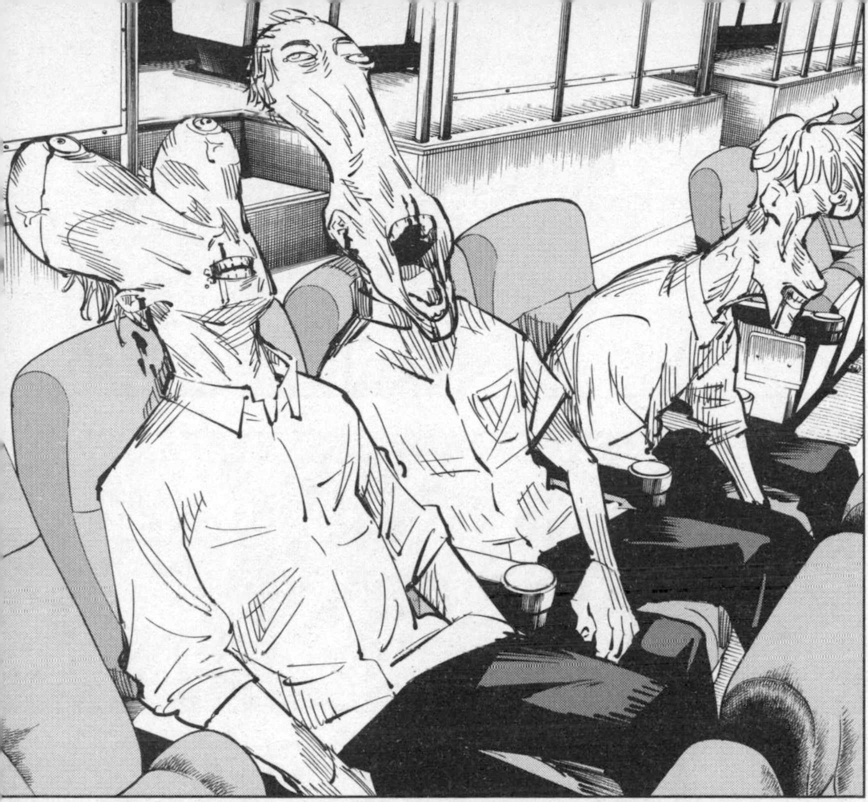

AFTER THE MOVIE FINISHED,
THE DEFORMED CORPSES OF THREE HIGH SCHOOL
BOYS WERE FOUND BY THE THEATER STAFF.

CAUSE OF DEATH:
INCREASE OF PRESSURE TO THE
BRAIN AND ASPHYXIATION DUE
TO CRANIAL DEFORMATION.

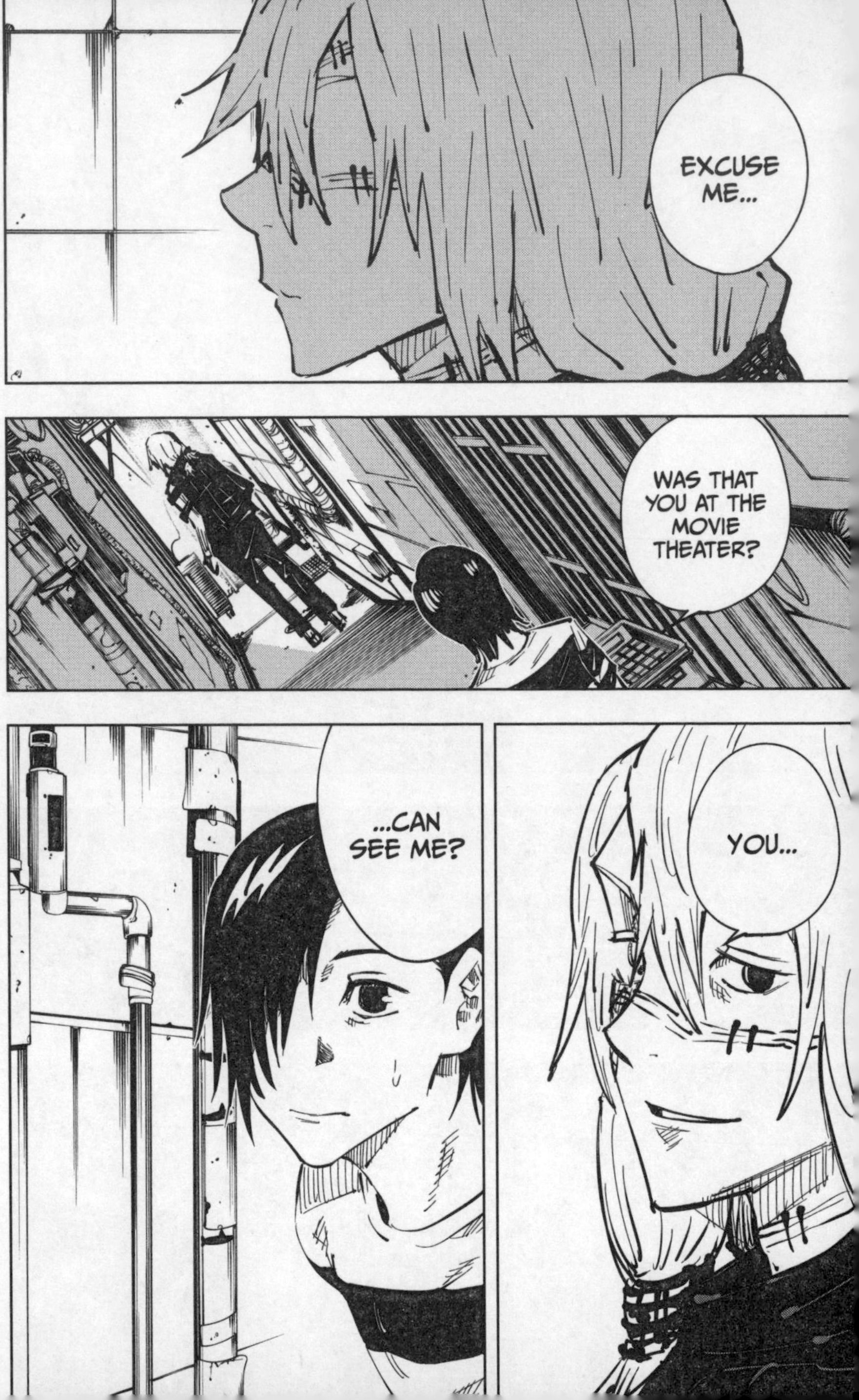
EXCUSE ME...
WAS THAT YOU AT THE MOVIE THEATER?
YOU...
...CAN SEE ME?

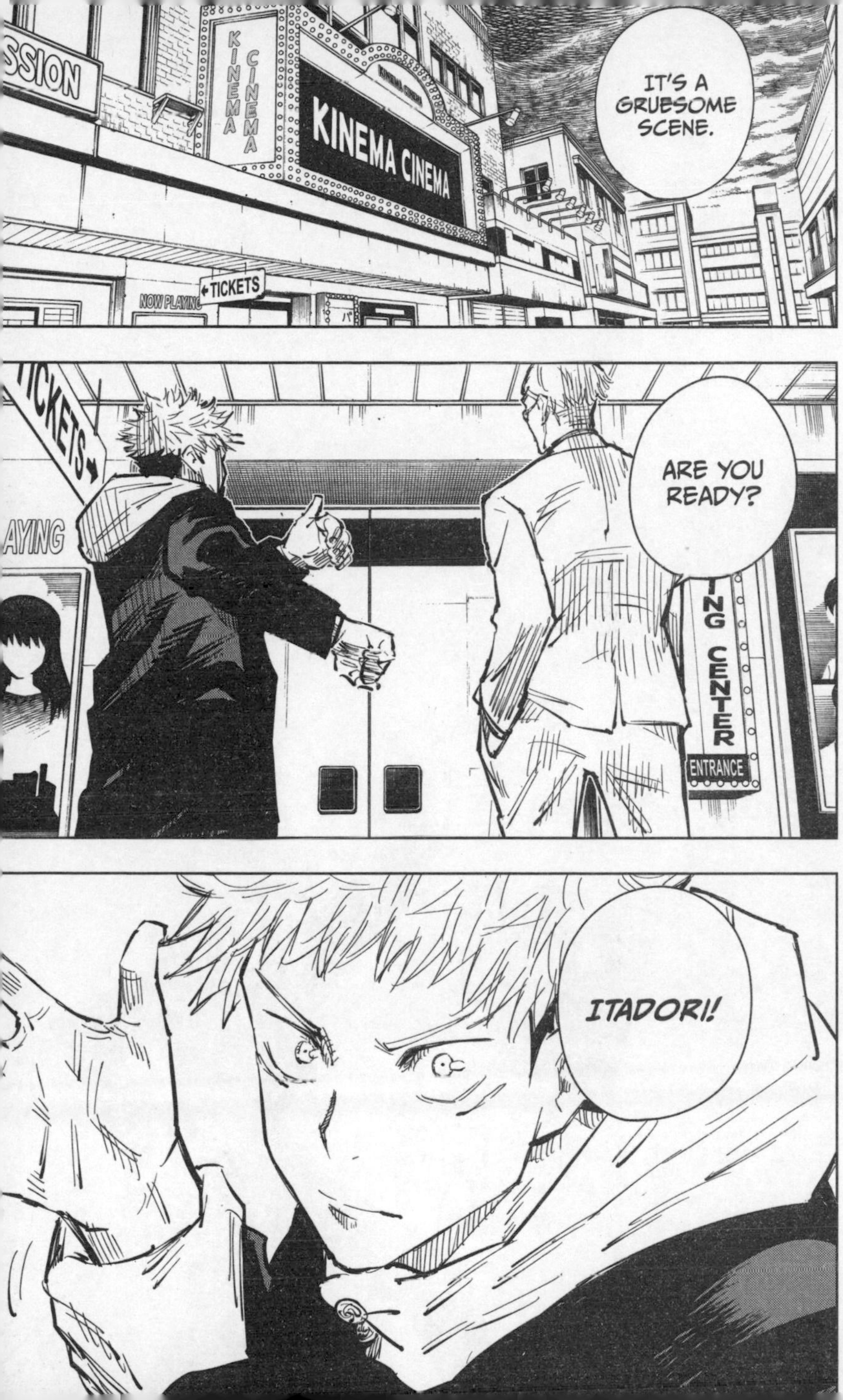
IT'S A GRUESOME SCENE.
KINEMA CINEMA
KINEMA CINEMA
SSION
TICKETS
NOW PLAYING
ARE YOU READY?
NG CENTER
ENTRANCE
TICKETS
AYING
ITADORI!

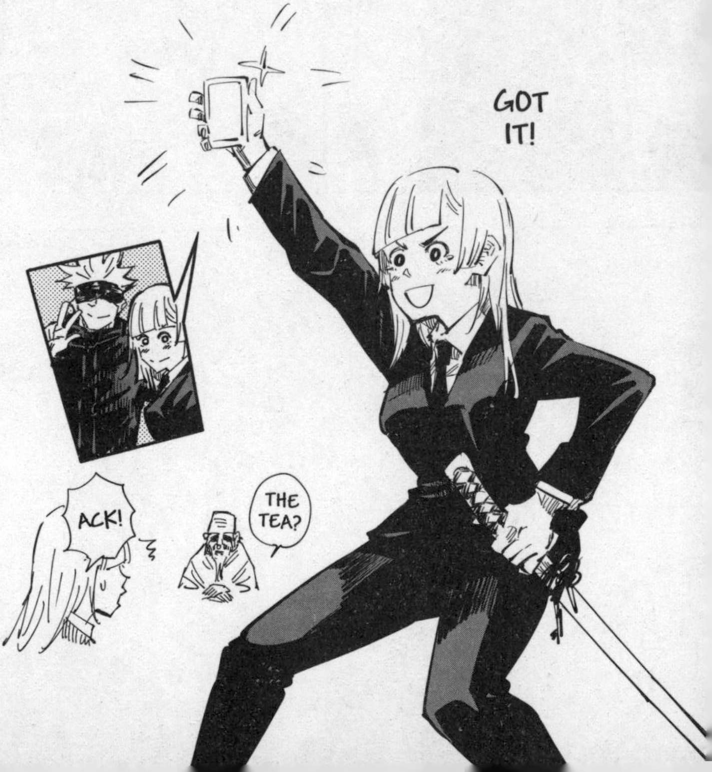
GOT IT!
THE TEA?
ACK!

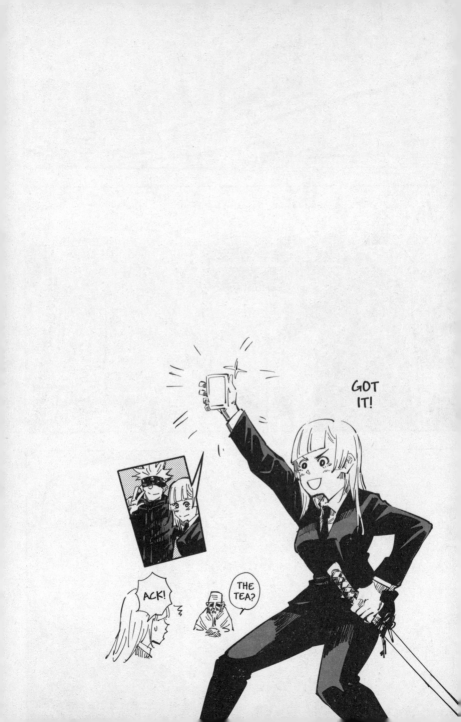

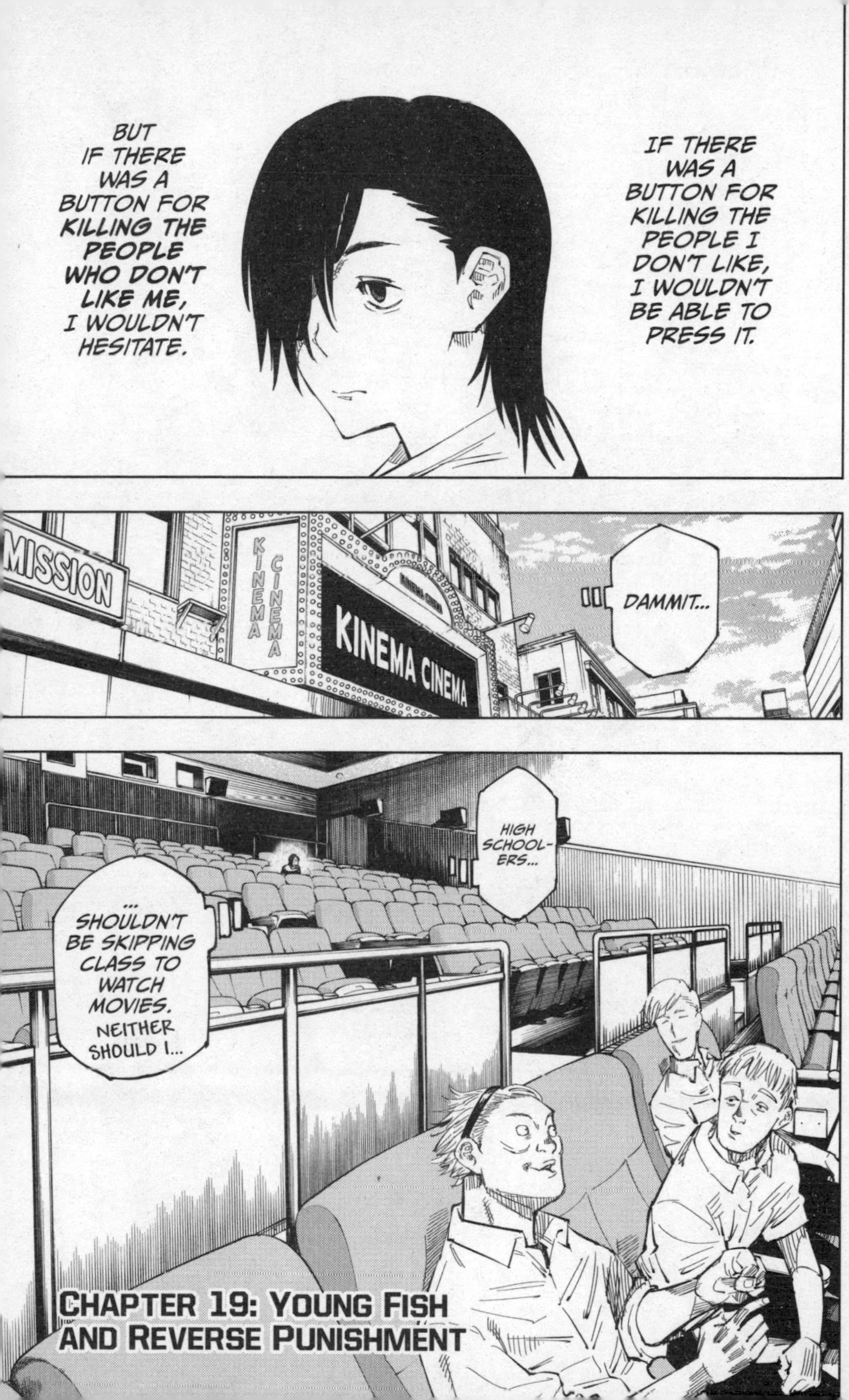
IF THERE WAS A BUTTON FOR KILLING THE PEOPLE I DON'T LIKE, I WOULDN'T BE ABLE TO PRESS IT.
BUT IF THERE WAS A BUTTON FOR KILLING THE PEOPLE WHO DON'T LIKE ME, I WOULDN'T HESITATE.
DAMMIT...
KINEMA CINEMA
KINEMA CINEMA
MISSION
HIGH SCHOOLERS...
...SHOULDN'T BE SKIPPING CLASS TO WATCH MOVIES. NEITHER SHOULD I...
CHAPTER 19: YOUNG FISH AND REVERSE PUNISHMENT

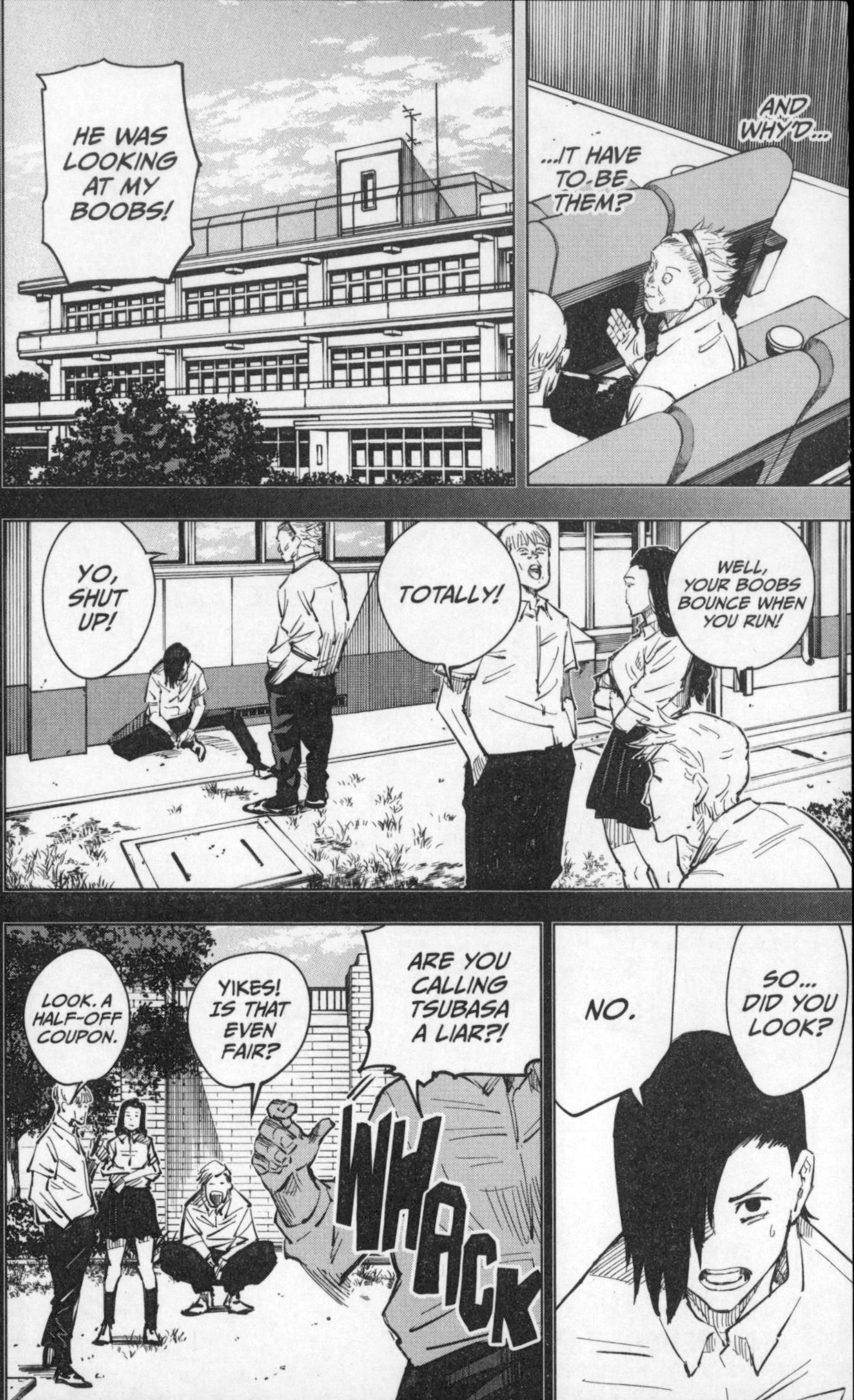
AND WHY'D...
...IT HAVE TO BE THEM?
HE WAS LOOKING AT MY BOOBS!
WELL, YOUR BOOBS BOUNCE WHEN YOU RUN!
TOTALLY!
YO, SHUT UP!
SO... DID YOU LOOK?
NO.
ARE YOU CALLING TSUBASA A LIAR?!
WHACK
YIKES! IS THAT EVEN FAIR?
LOOK. A HALF-OFF COUPON.

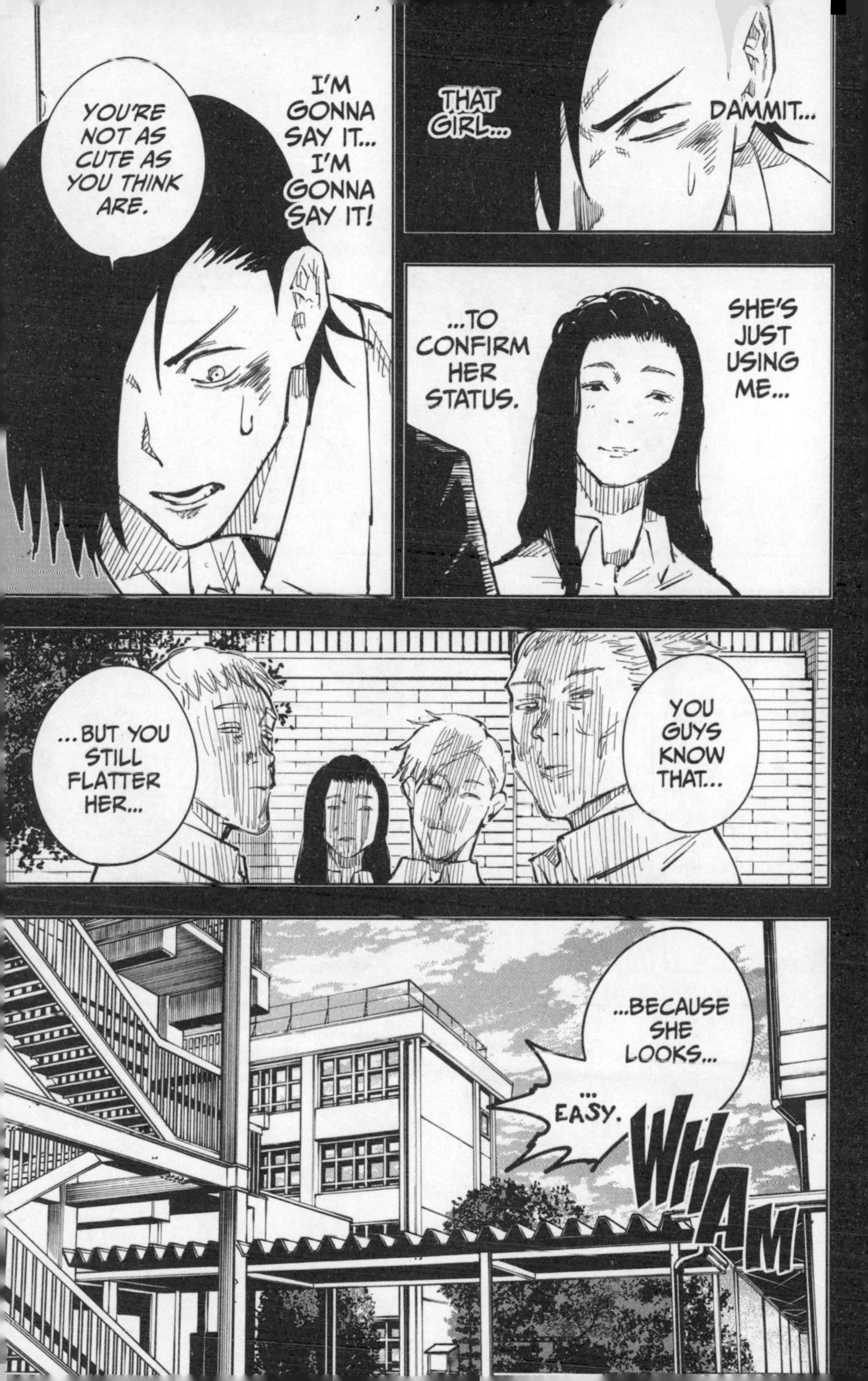
DAMMIT...
THAT GIRL...
SHE'S JUST USING ME...
...TO CONFIRM HER STATUS.
I'M GONNA SAY IT... I'M GONNA SAY IT!
YOU'RE NOT AS CUTE AS YOU THINK ARE.
YOU GUYS KNOW THAT...
...BUT YOU STILL FLATTER HER...
...BECAUSE SHE LOOKS...
...EASY.
WHAM

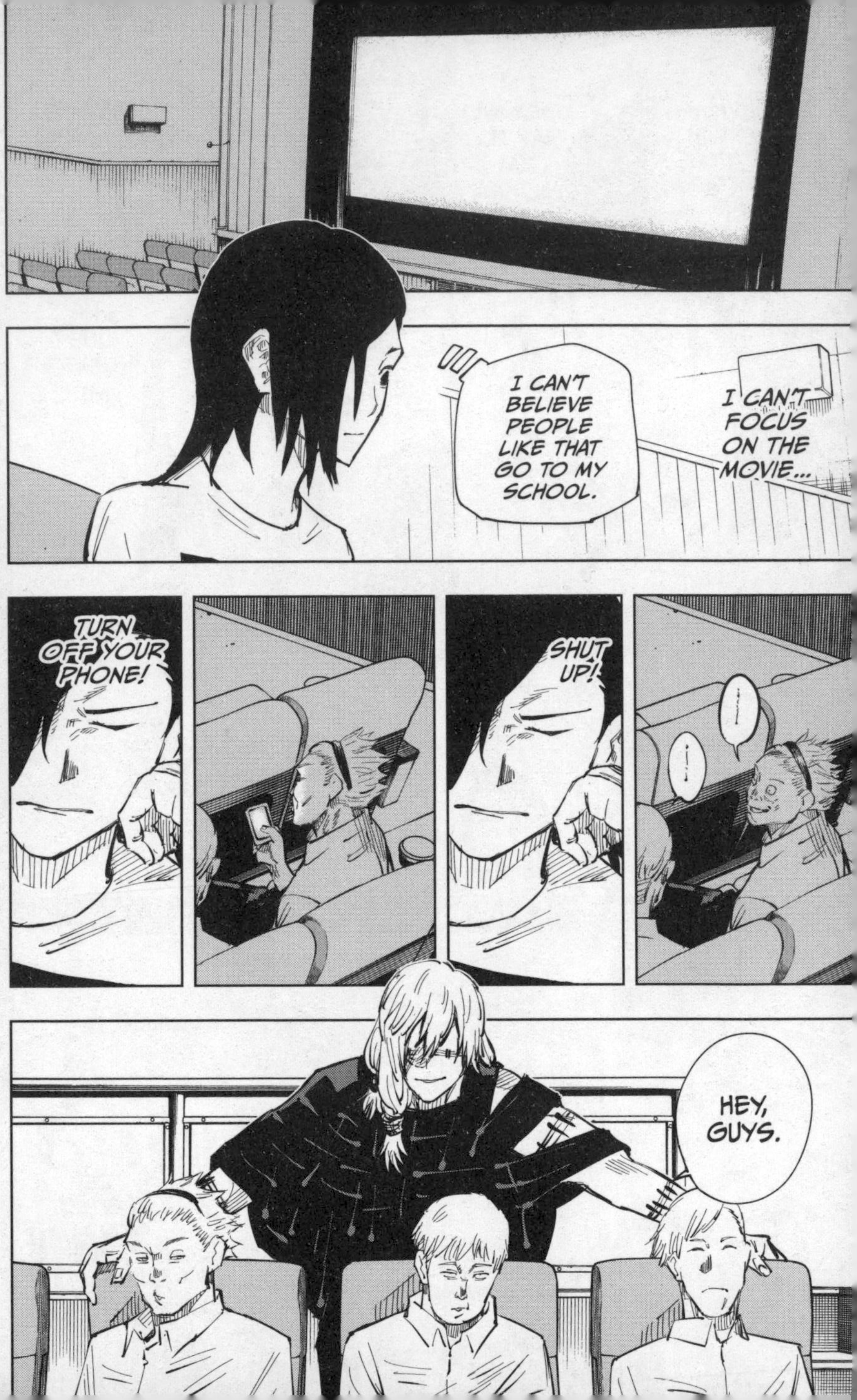
I CAN'T FOCUS ON THE MOVIE...
I CAN'T BELIEVE PEOPLE LIKE THAT GO TO MY SCHOOL.
SHUT UP!
TURN OFF YOUR PHONE!
HEY, GUYS.

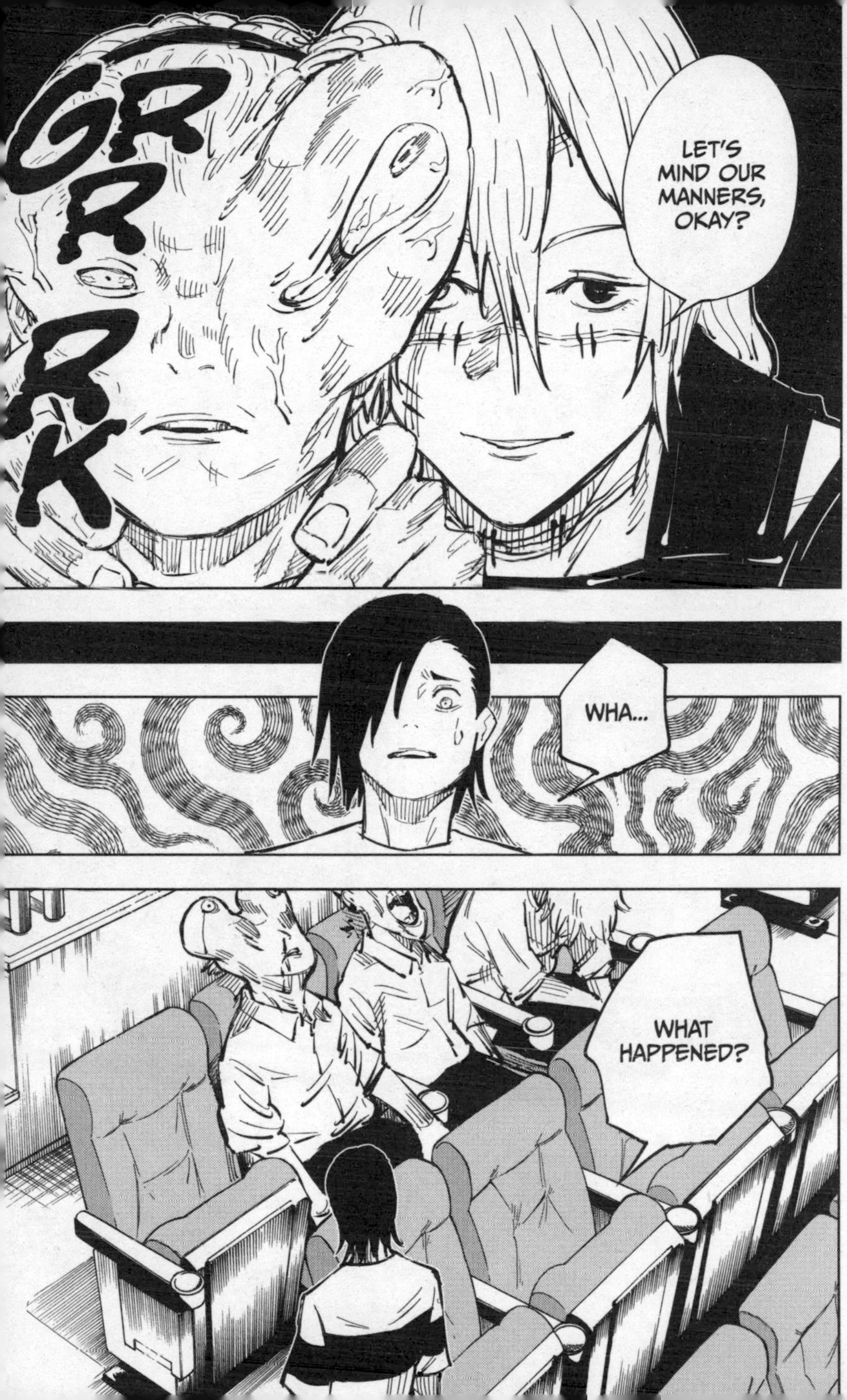
LET'S MIND OUR MANNERS, OKAY?
GRRRK
WHA...
WHAT HAPPENED?

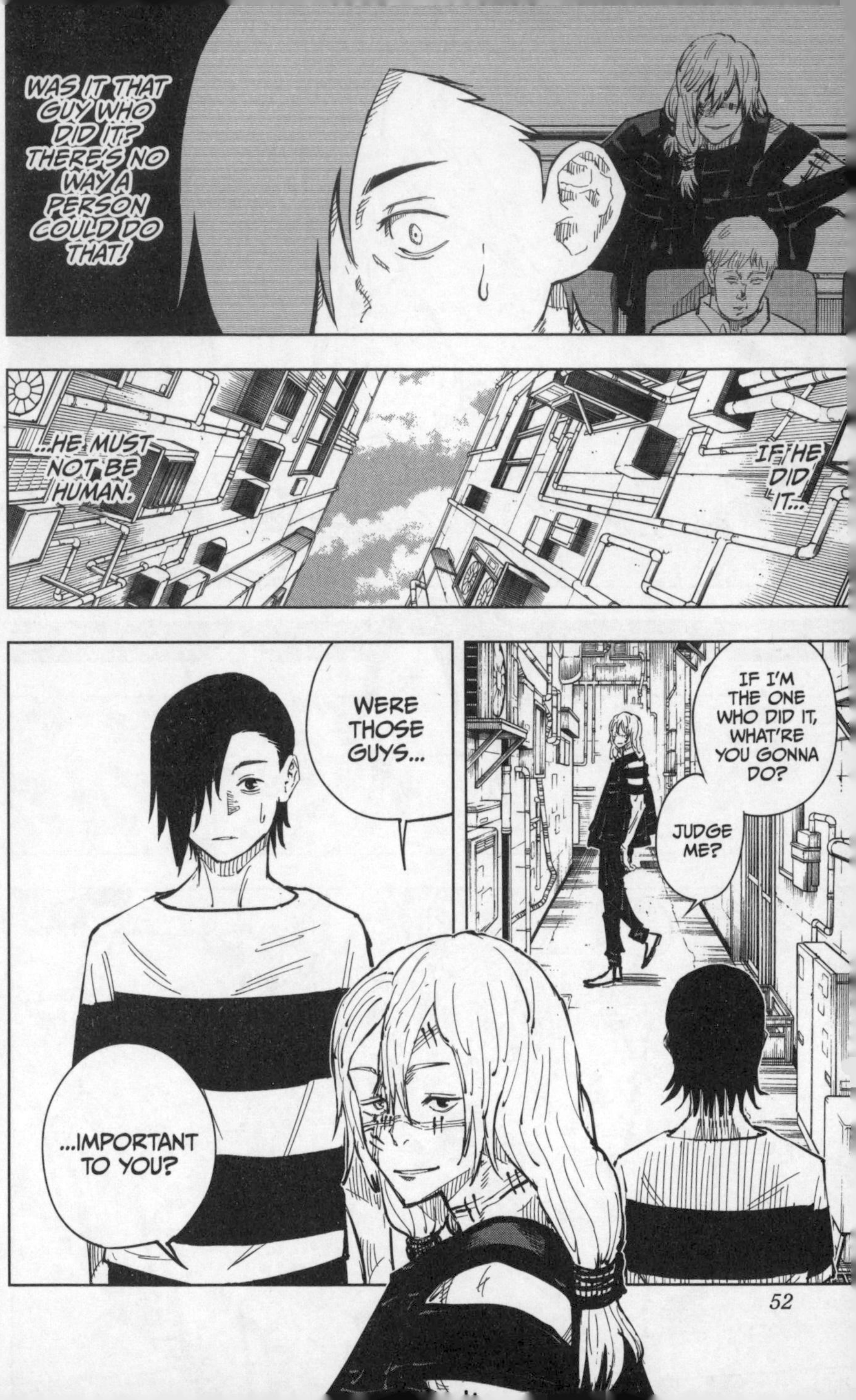
WAS IT THAT GUY WHO DID IT? THERE'S NO WAY A PERSON COULD DO THAT!
IF HE DID IT...
...HE MUST NOT BE HUMAN.
IF I'M THE ONE WHO DID IT, WHAT'RE YOU GONNA DO?
JUDGE ME?
WERE THOSE GUYS...
...IMPORTANT TO YOU?

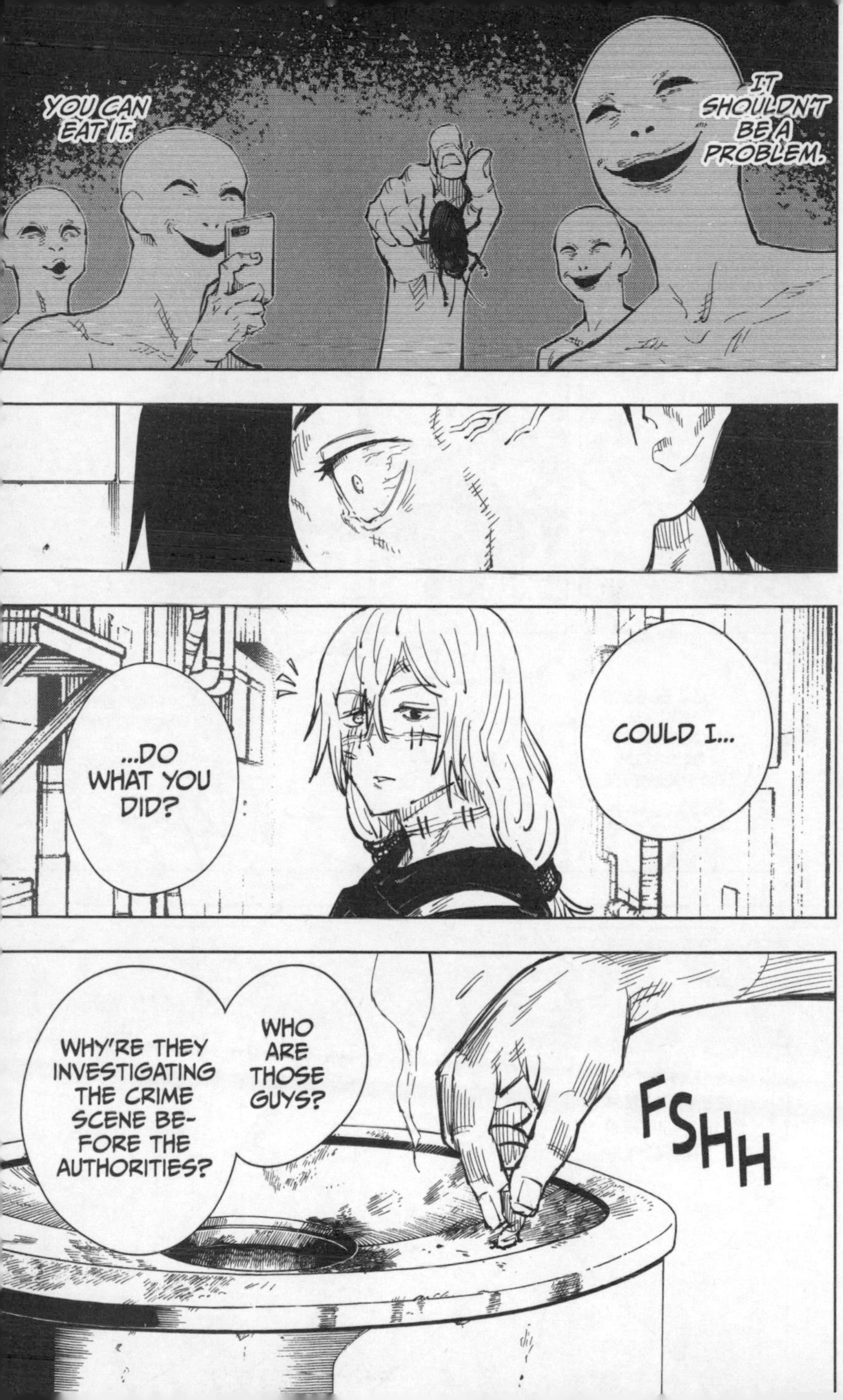
IT SHOULDN'T BE A PROBLEM.
YOU CAN EAT IT.
COULD I...
...DO WHAT YOU DID?
WHO ARE THOSE GUYS?
WHY'RE THEY INVESTIGATING THE CRIME SCENE BE- FORE THE AUTHORITIES?
FSHH

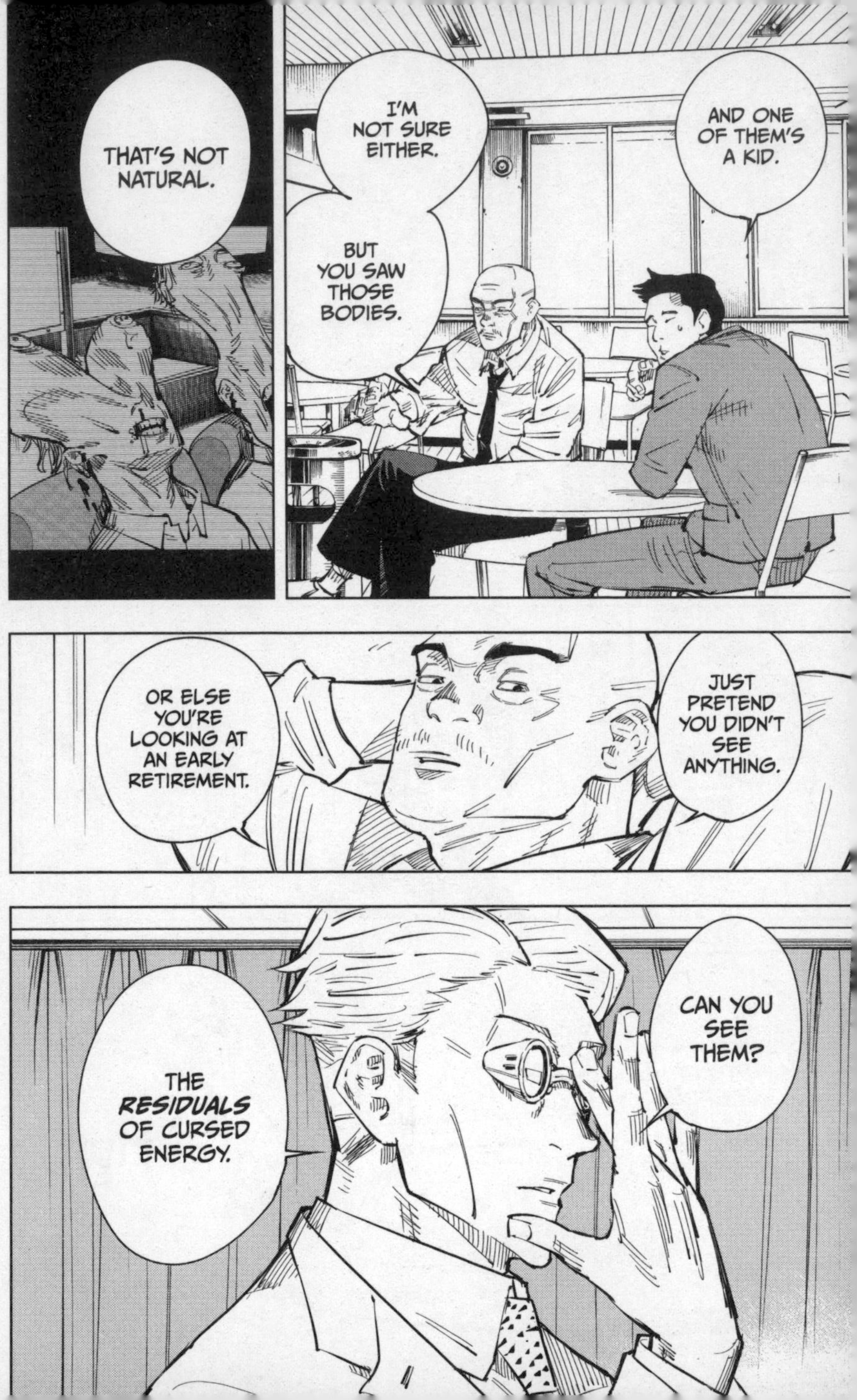
AND ONE OF THEM'S A KID.
I'M NOT SURE EITHER.
BUT YOU SAW THOSE BODIES.
THAT'S NOT NATURAL.
JUST PRETEND YOU DIDN'T SEE ANYTHING.
OR ELSE YOU'RE LOOKING AT AN EARLY RETIREMENT.
CAN YOU SEE THEM?
THE *RESIDUALS* OF CURSED ENERGY.

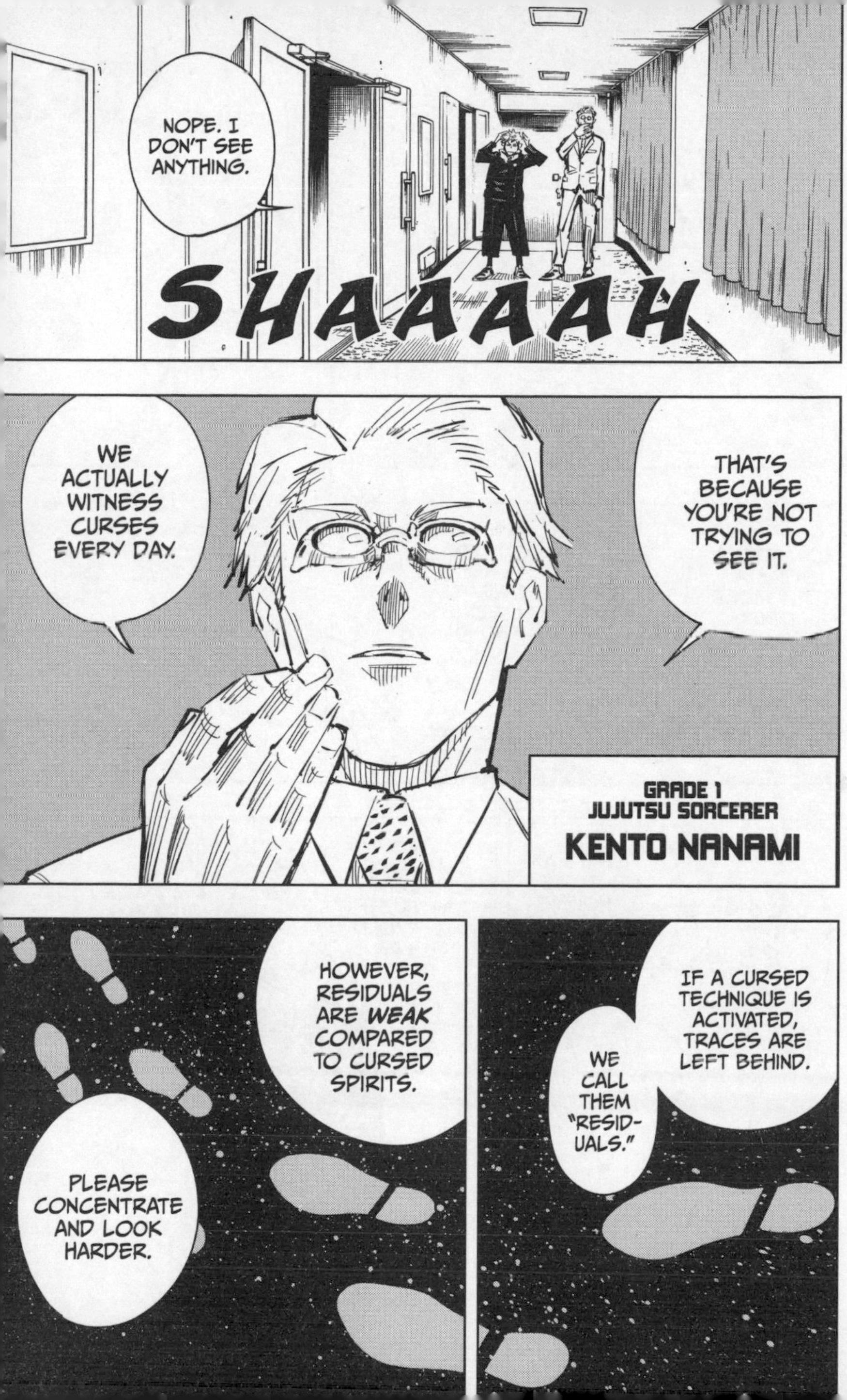
NOPE. I DON'T SEE ANYTHING.
SHAAAAH
THAT'S BECAUSE YOU'RE NOT TRYING TO SEE IT.
WE ACTUALLY WITNESS CURSES EVERY DAY.
GRADE 1 JUJUTSU SORCERER
KENTO NANAMI
IF A CURSED TECHNIQUE IS ACTIVATED, TRACES ARE LEFT BEHIND.
WE CALL THEM "RESID-UALS."
HOWEVER, RESIDUALS ARE WEAK COMPARED TO CURSED SPIRITS.
PLEASE CONCENTRATE AND LOOK HARDER.

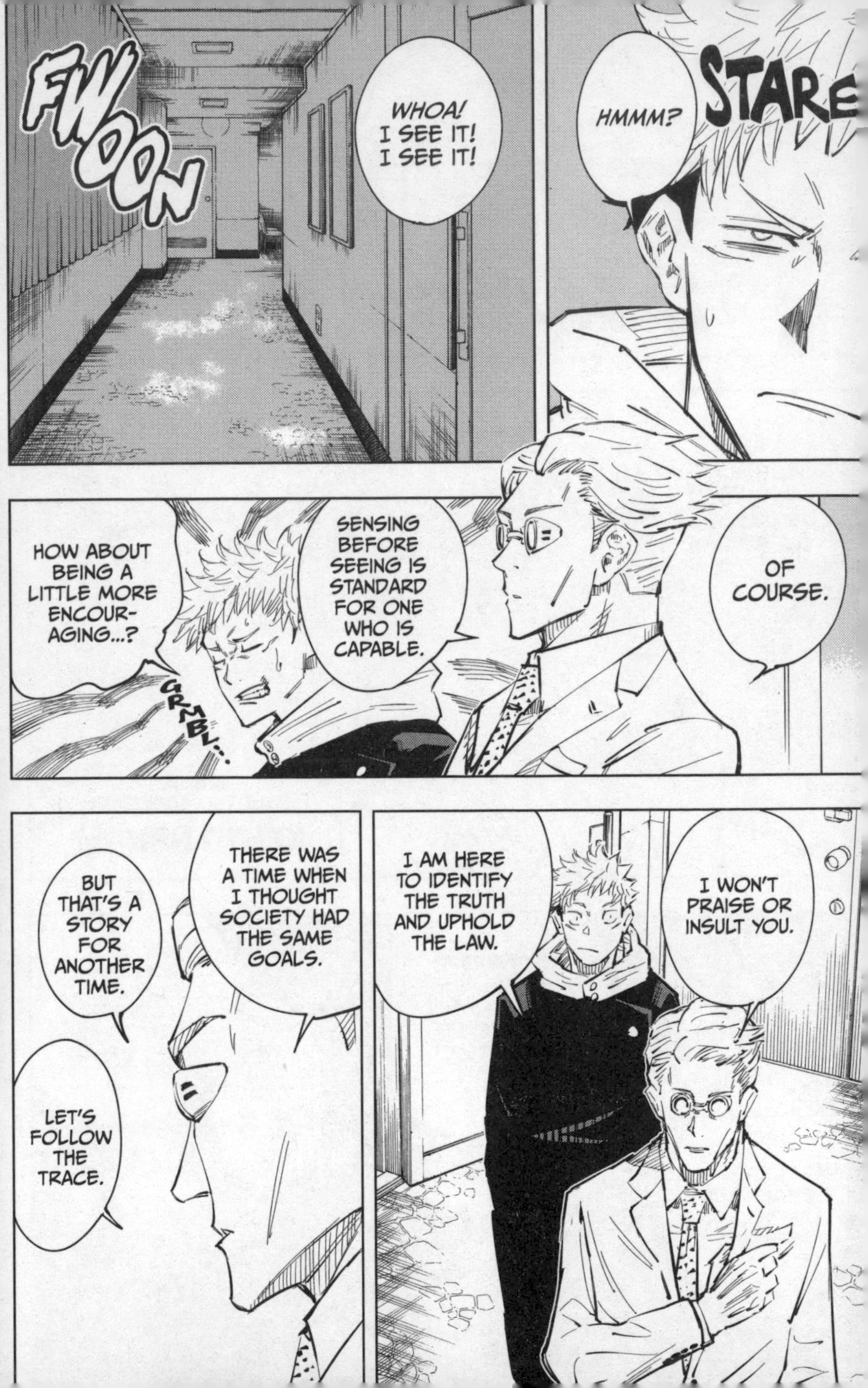
HMMM?
STARE
WHOA! I SEE IT! I SEE IT!
FWOON
OF COURSE.
SENSING BEFORE SEEING IS STANDARD FOR ONE WHO IS CAPABLE.
HOW ABOUT BEING A LITTLE MORE ENCOUR-AGING...?
GRMBL...
I WON'T PRAISE OR INSULT YOU.
I AM HERE TO IDENTIFY THE TRUTH AND UPHOLD THE LAW.
THERE WAS A TIME WHEN I THOUGHT SOCIETY HAD THE SAME GOALS.
BUT THAT'S A STORY FOR ANOTHER TIME.
LET'S FOLLOW THE TRACE.

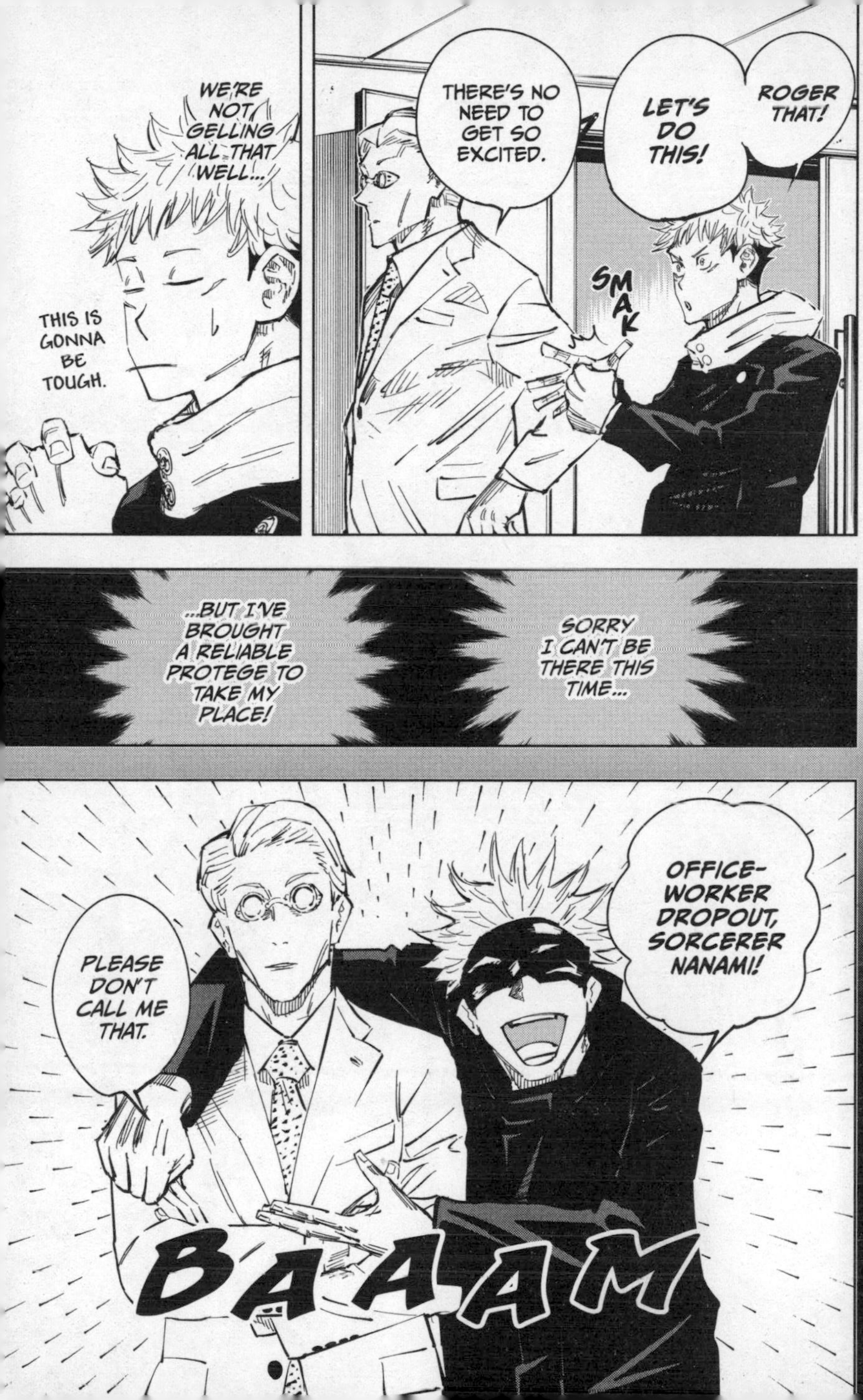
ROGER THAT!
LET'S DO THIS!
THERE'S NO NEED TO GET SO EXCITED.
SMAK
WE'RE NOT GELLING ALL THAT WELL...
THIS IS GONNA BE TOUGH.
SORRY I CAN'T BE THERE THIS TIME...
...BUT I'VE BROUGHT A RELIABLE PROTEGE TO TAKE MY PLACE!
OFFICE-WORKER DROPOUT, SORCERER NANAMI!
PLEASE DON'T CALL ME THAT.
BAAAM

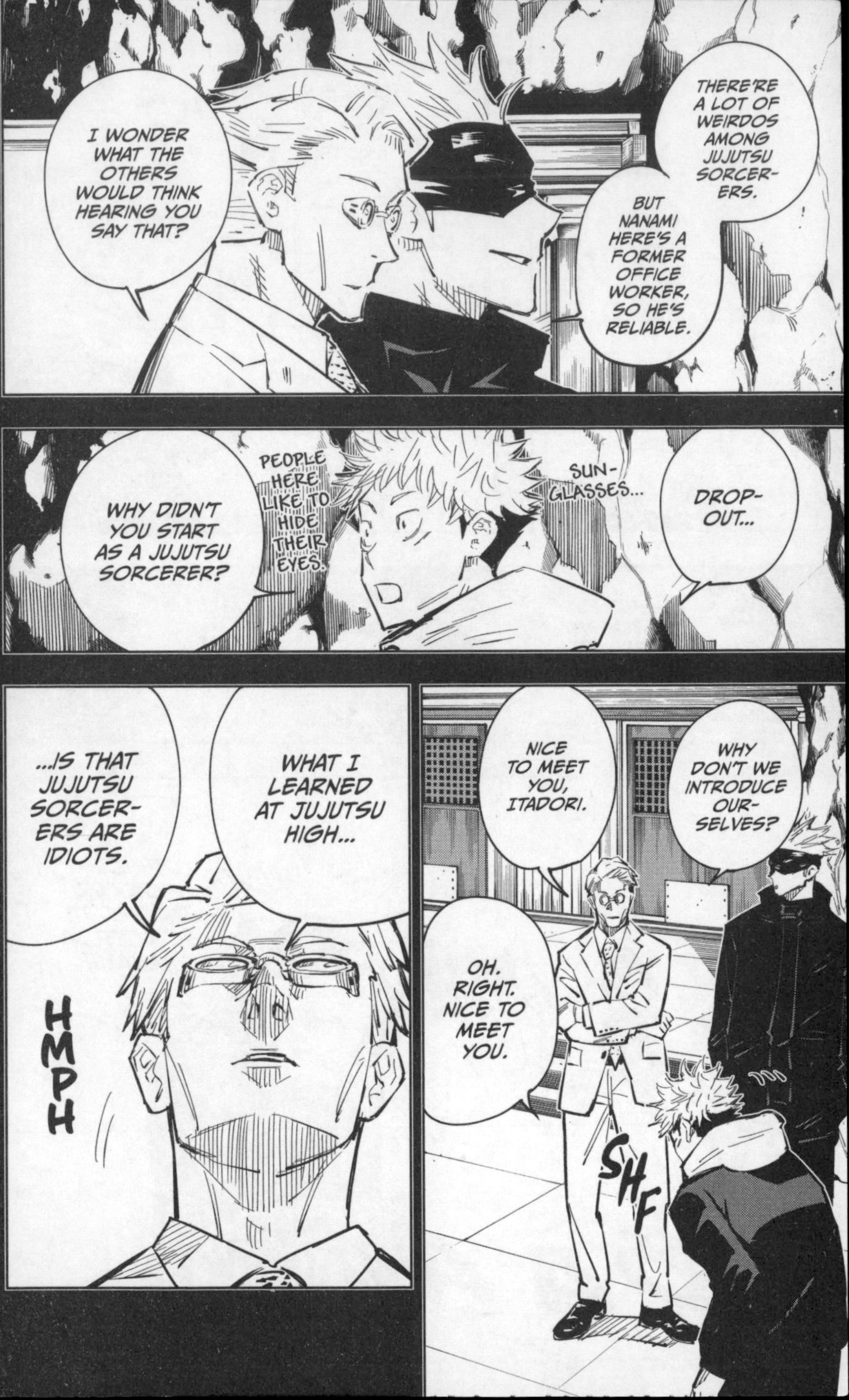
THERE'RE A LOT OF WEIRDOS AMONG JUJUTSU SORCERERS.
BUT NANAMI HERE'S A FORMER OFFICE WORKER, SO HE'S RELIABLE.
I WONDER WHAT THE OTHERS WOULD THINK HEARING YOU SAY THAT?
DROP-OUT...
SUN-GLASSES...
PEOPLE HERE LIKE TO HIDE THEIR EYES.
WHY DIDN'T YOU START AS A JUJUTSU SORCERER?
WHY DON'T WE INTRODUCE OURSELVES?
NICE TO MEET YOU, ITADORI.
OH. RIGHT. NICE TO MEET YOU.
SHF
WHAT I LEARNED AT JUJUTSU HIGH...
...IS THAT JUJUTSU SORCERERS ARE IDIOTS.
HMPH

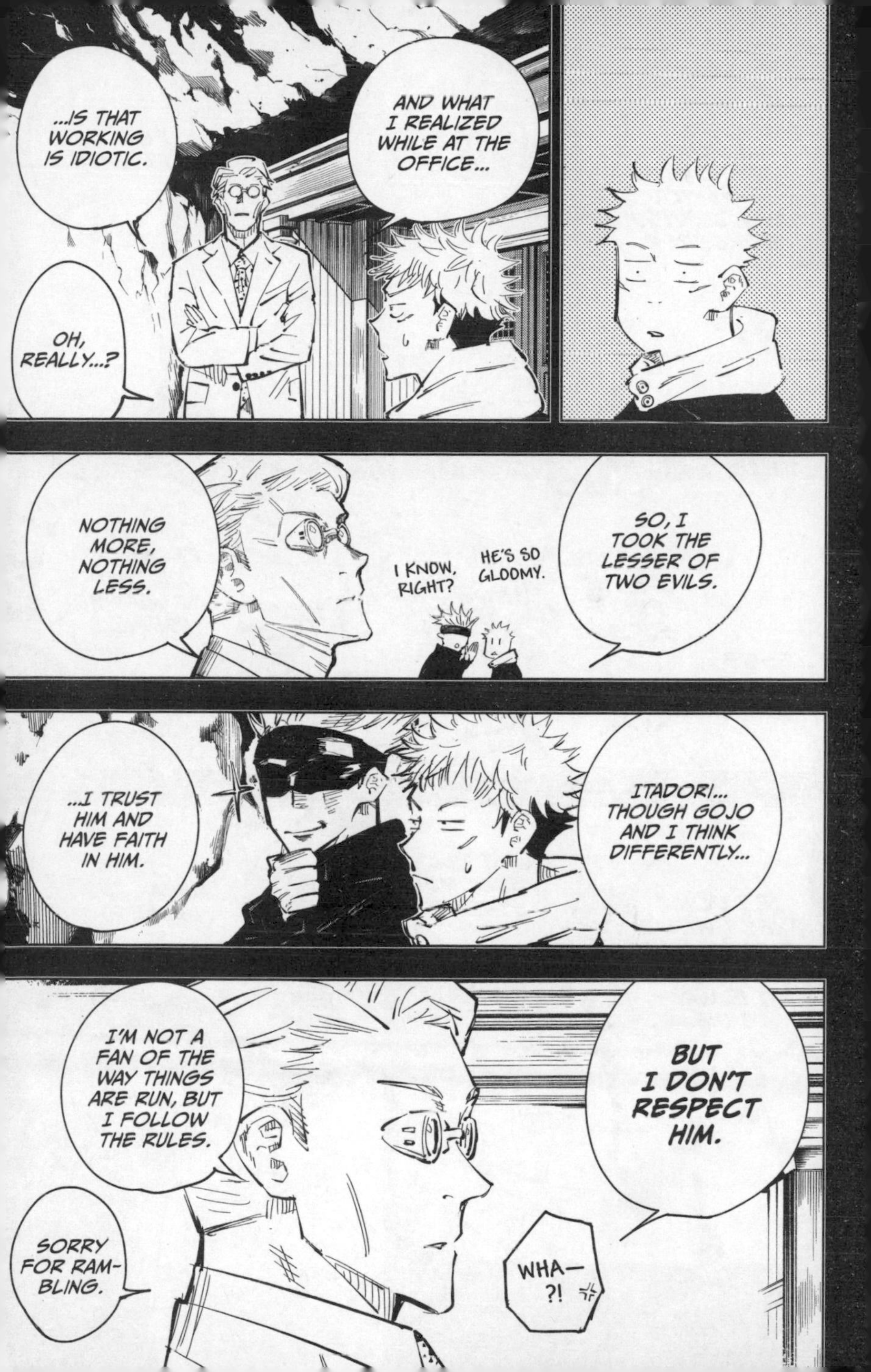
AND WHAT I REALIZED WHILE AT THE OFFICE...
...IS THAT WORKING IS IDIOTIC.
OH, REALLY...?
SO, I TOOK THE LESSER OF TWO EVILS.
HE'S SO GLOOMY.
I KNOW, RIGHT?
NOTHING MORE, NOTHING LESS.
ITADORI... THOUGH GOJO AND I THINK DIFFERENTLY...
...I TRUST HIM AND HAVE FAITH IN HIM.
BUT I DON'T RESPECT HIM.
I'M NOT A FAN OF THE WAY THINGS ARE RUN, BUT I FOLLOW THE RULES.
WHA—?!
SORRY FOR RAMBLING.

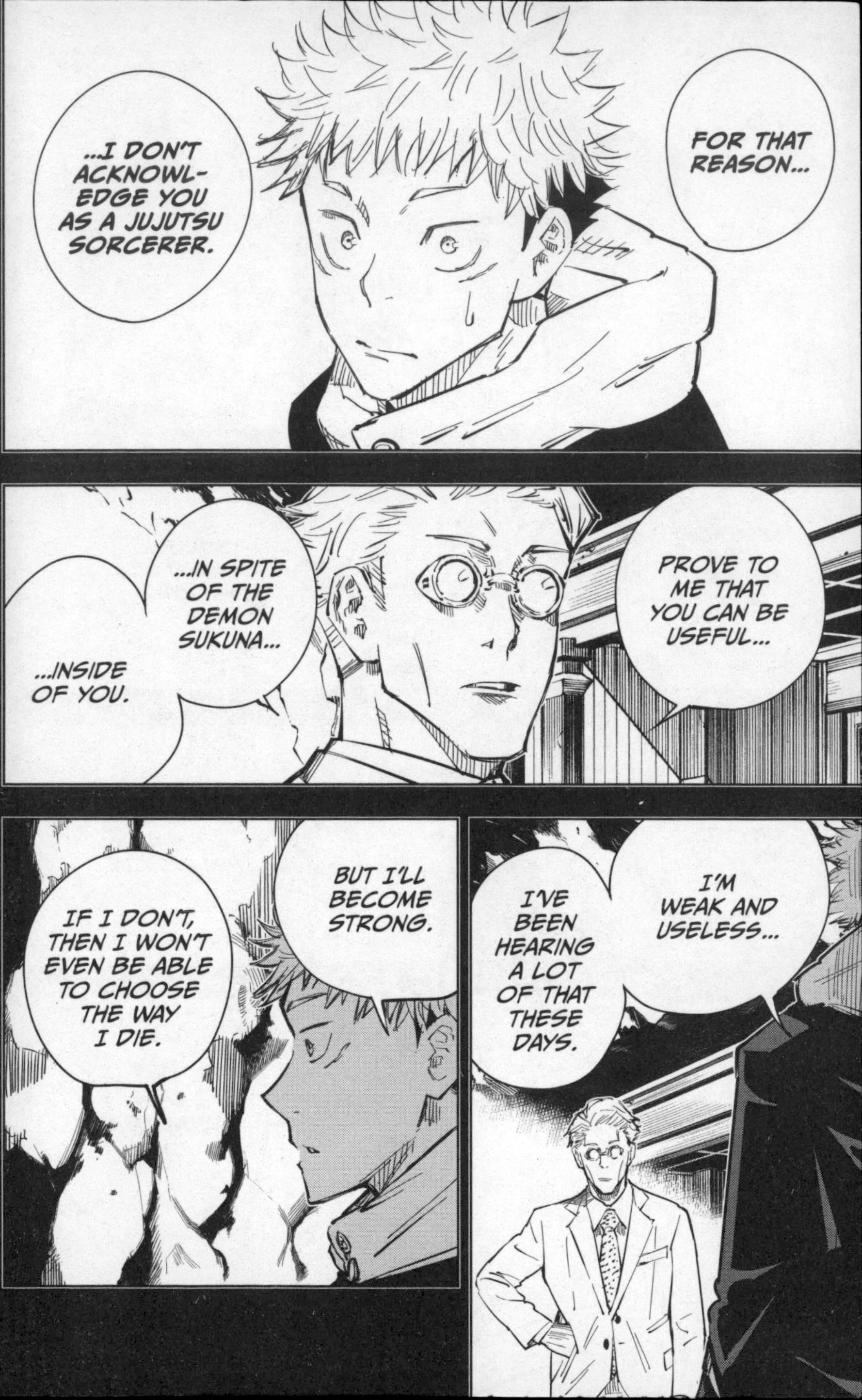
FOR THAT REASON...
...I DON'T ACKNOWL-EDGE YOU AS A JUJUTSU SORCERER.
PROVE TO ME THAT YOU CAN BE USEFUL...
...IN SPITE OF THE DEMON SUKUNA...
...INSIDE OF YOU.
I'M WEAK AND USELESS...
I'VE BEEN HEARING A LOT OF THAT THESE DAYS.
BUT I'LL BECOME STRONG.
IF I DON'T, THEN I WON'T EVEN BE ABLE TO CHOOSE THE WAY I DIE.

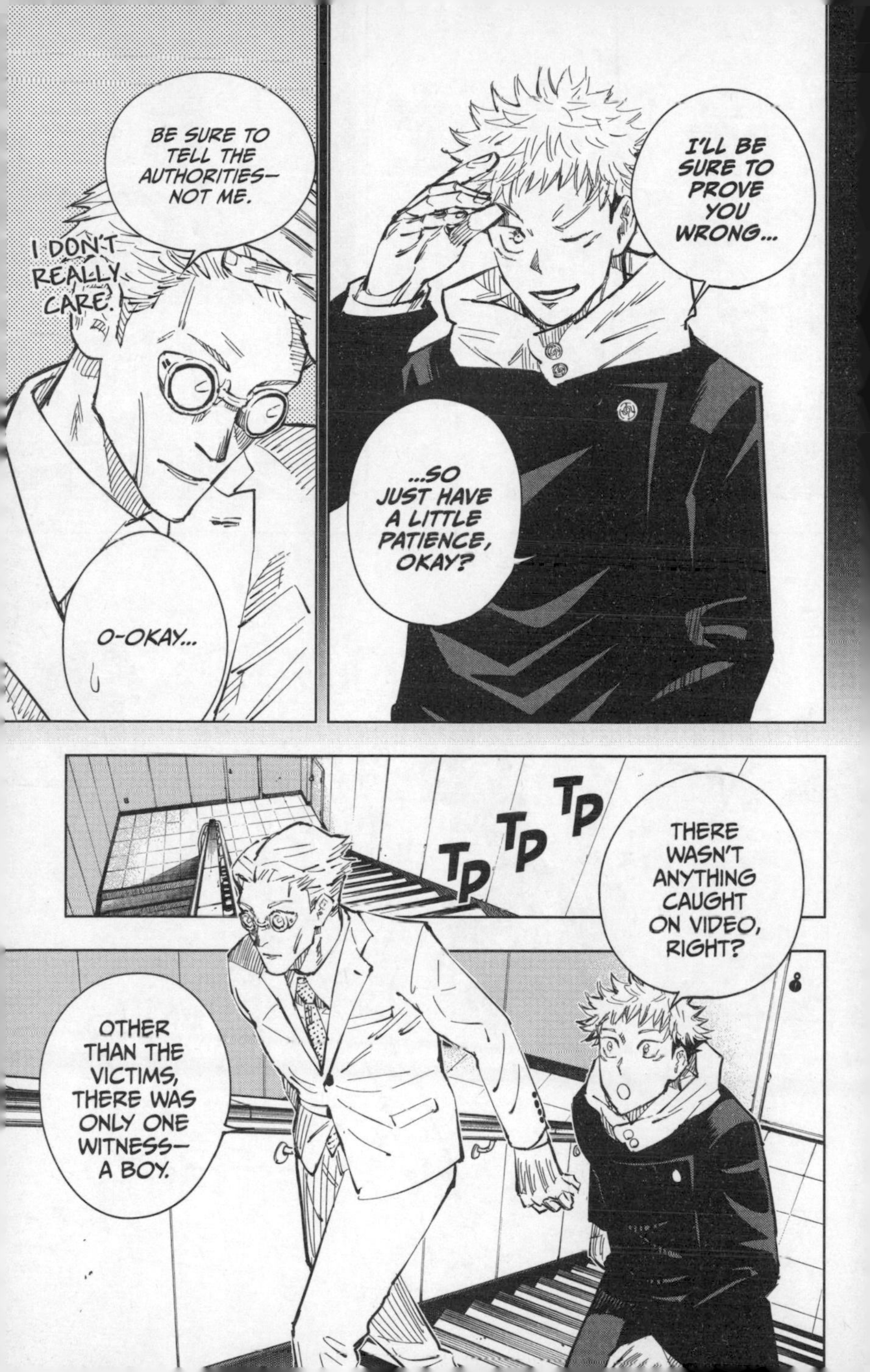
I'LL BE SURE TO PROVE YOU WRONG...
...SO JUST HAVE A LITTLE PATIENCE, OKAY?
BE SURE TO TELL THE AUTHORITIES— NOT ME.
I DON'T REALLY CARE.
O-OKAY...
TP TP TP
THERE WASN'T ANYTHING CAUGHT ON VIDEO, RIGHT?
OTHER THAN THE VICTIMS, THERE WAS ONLY ONE WITNESS— A BOY.

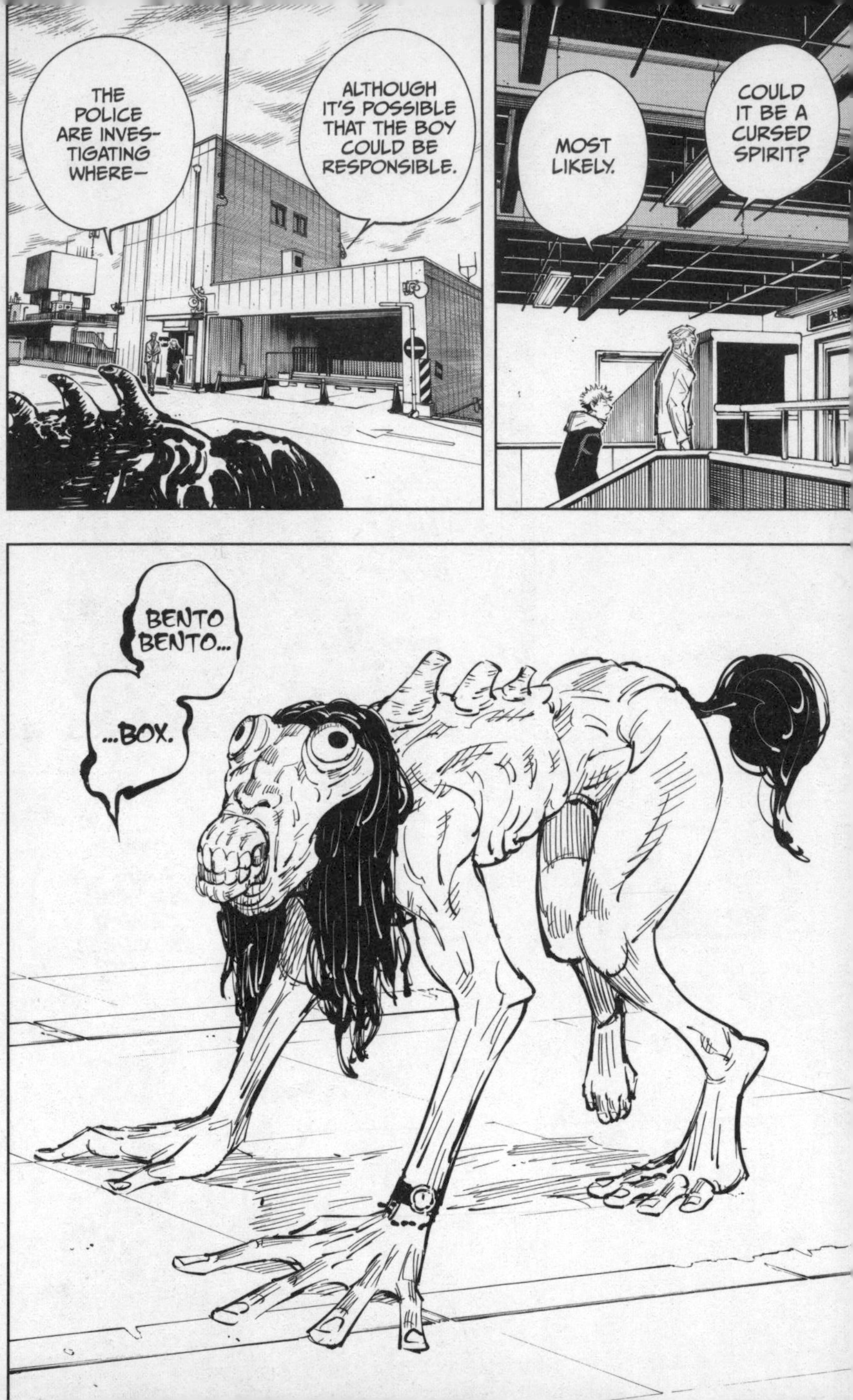

COULD IT BE A CURSED SPIRIT?
MOST LIKELY.
ALTHOUGH IT'S POSSIBLE THAT THE BOY COULD BE RESPONSIBLE.
THE POLICE ARE INVES-TIGATING WHERE—
BENTO BENTO...
...BOX.

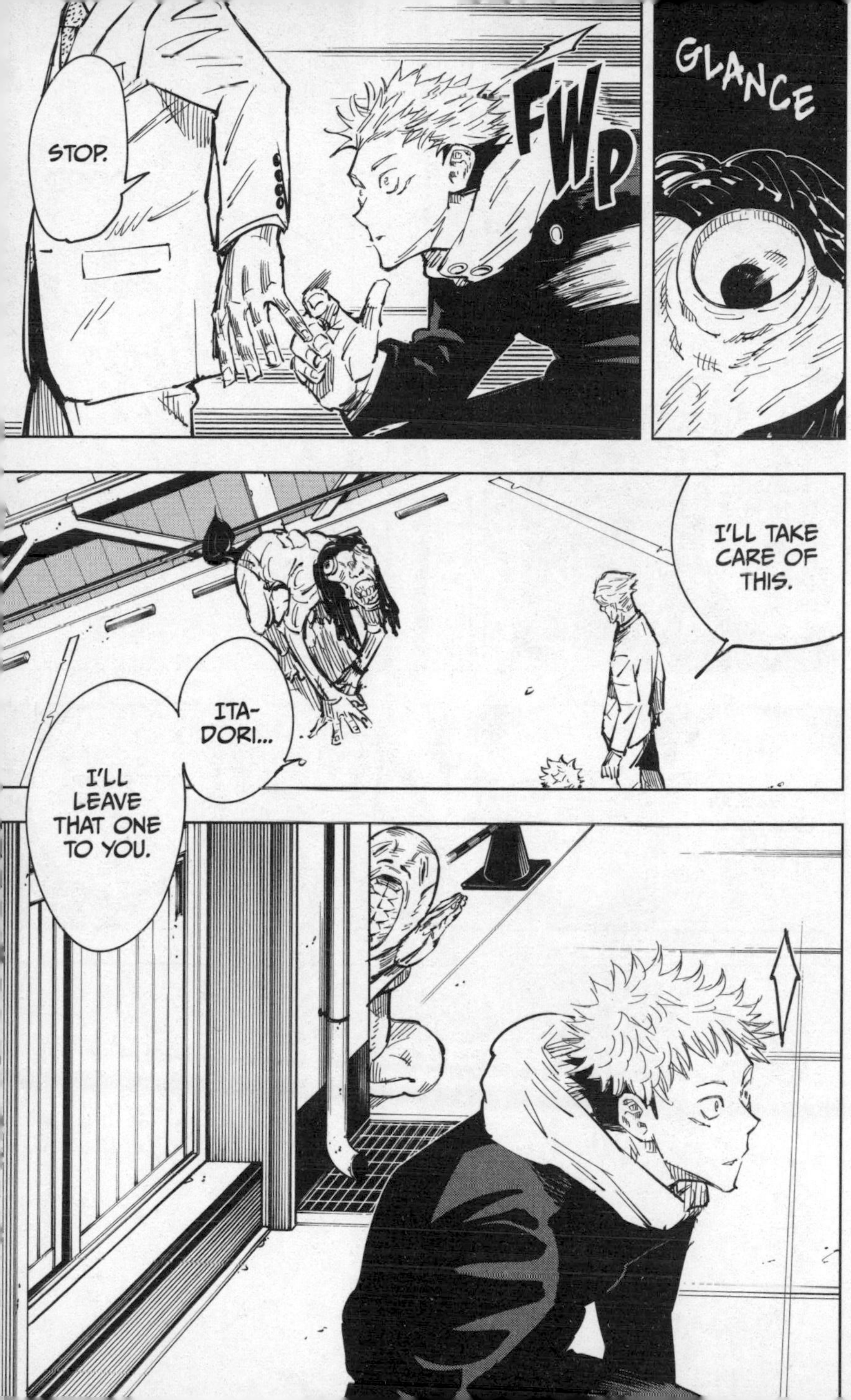
GLANCE
FWP
STOP.
I'LL TAKE CARE OF THIS.
ITA-DORI...
I'LL LEAVE THAT ONE TO YOU.

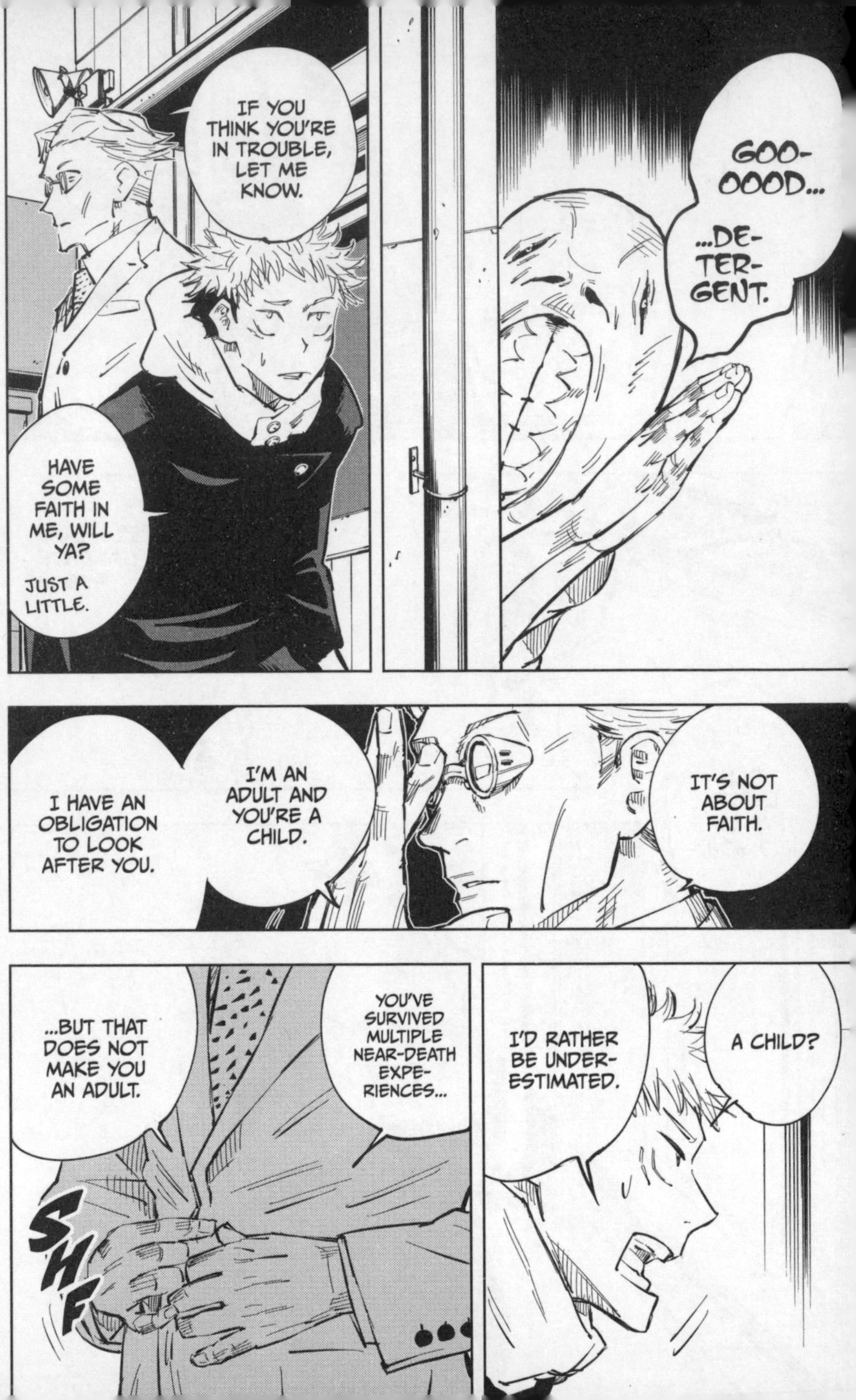
GOO-OOOD...
...DE-TER-GENT.
IF YOU THINK YOU'RE IN TROUBLE, LET ME KNOW.
HAVE SOME FAITH IN ME, WILL YA?
JUST A LITTLE.
IT'S NOT ABOUT FAITH.
I'M AN ADULT AND YOU'RE A CHILD.
I HAVE AN OBLIGATION TO LOOK AFTER YOU.
A CHILD?
I'D RATHER BE UNDER-ESTIMATED.
YOU'VE SURVIVED MULTIPLE NEAR-DEATH EXPE-RIENCES...
...BUT THAT DOES NOT MAKE YOU AN ADULT.
SHF

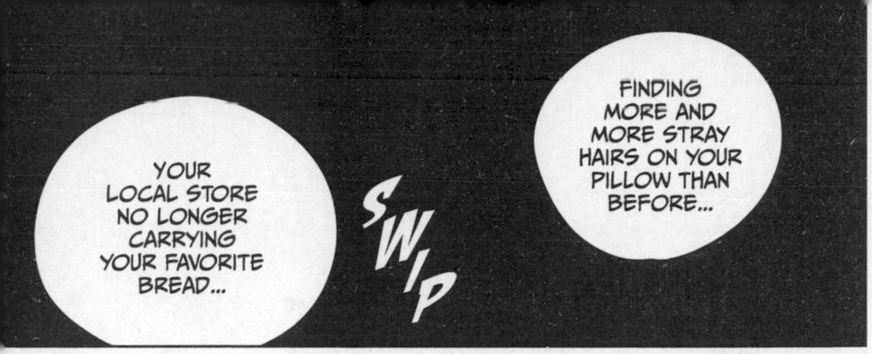
FINDING MORE AND MORE STRAY HAIRS ON YOUR PILLOW THAN BEFORE...
SWIP
YOUR LOCAL STORE NO LONGER CARRYING YOUR FAVORITE BREAD...
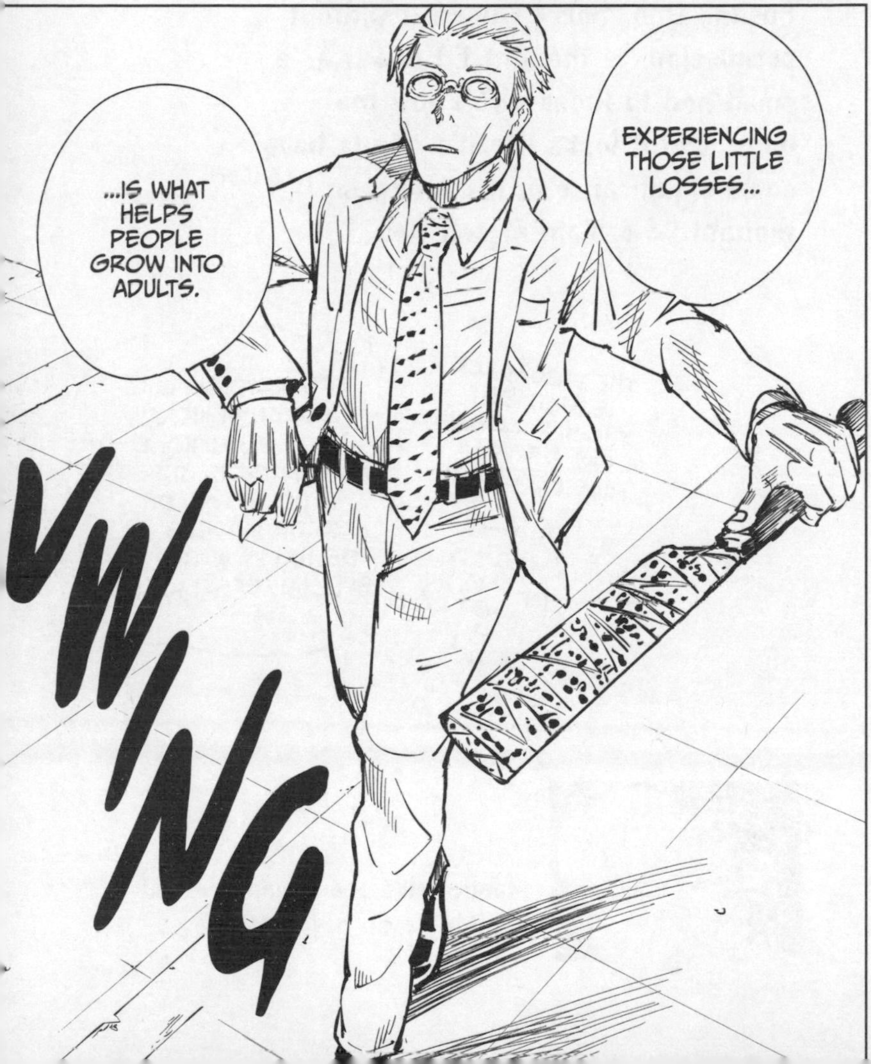
EXPERIENCING THOSE LITTLE LOSSES...
...IS WHAT HELPS PEOPLE GROW INTO ADULTS.
VWING

The word "residuals" was taken from a book by the same name written by Fuyumi Ono. Sorry I used it without permission... I thought I'd use it as a small nod to those who know the book. But it looks like it's gonna have some significance in the story, so I thought I'd explain myself now.

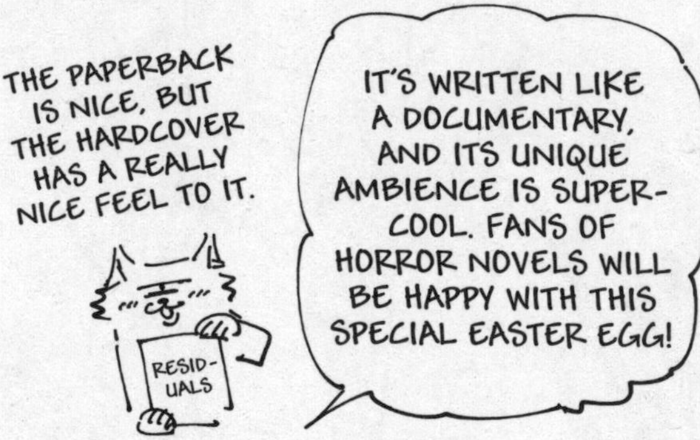

IT'S WRITTEN LIKE A DOCUMENTARY, AND ITS UNIQUE AMBIENCE IS SUPER-COOL. FANS OF HORROR NOVELS WILL BE HAPPY WITH THIS SPECIAL EASTER EGG!
THE PAPERBACK IS NICE, BUT THE HARDCOVER HAS A REALLY NICE FEEL TO IT.
RESID-UALS

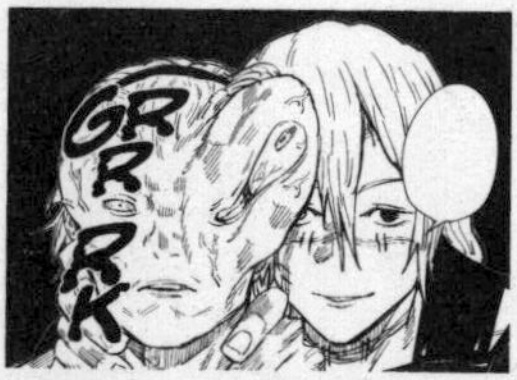

GRRRK

Mahito talks about manners, but he didn't even pay the tab.

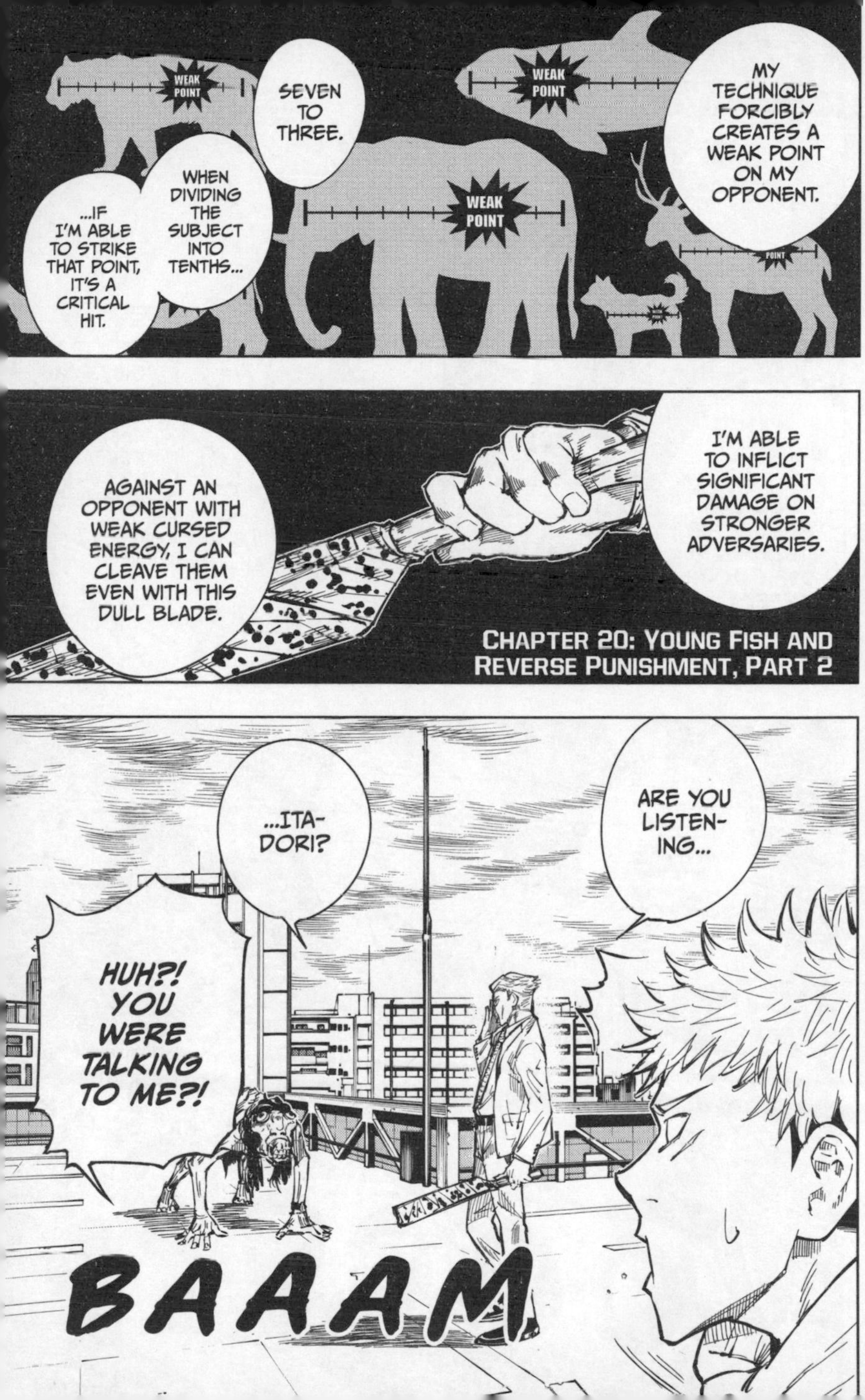
MY TECHNIQUE FORCIBLY CREATES A WEAK POINT ON MY OPPONENT.
WEAK POINT
SEVEN TO THREE.
WEAK POINT
POINT
WEAK POINT
WHEN DIVIDING THE SUBJECT INTO TENTHS...
...IF I'M ABLE TO STRIKE THAT POINT, IT'S A CRITICAL HIT.
I'M ABLE TO INFLICT SIGNIFICANT DAMAGE ON STRONGER ADVERSARIES.
AGAINST AN OPPONENT WITH WEAK CURSED ENERGY, I CAN CLEAVE THEM EVEN WITH THIS DULL BLADE.
CHAPTER 20: YOUNG FISH AND REVERSE PUNISHMENT, PART 2
ARE YOU LISTEN-ING...
...ITA-DORI?
HUH?! YOU WERE TALKING TO ME?!
BAAAM

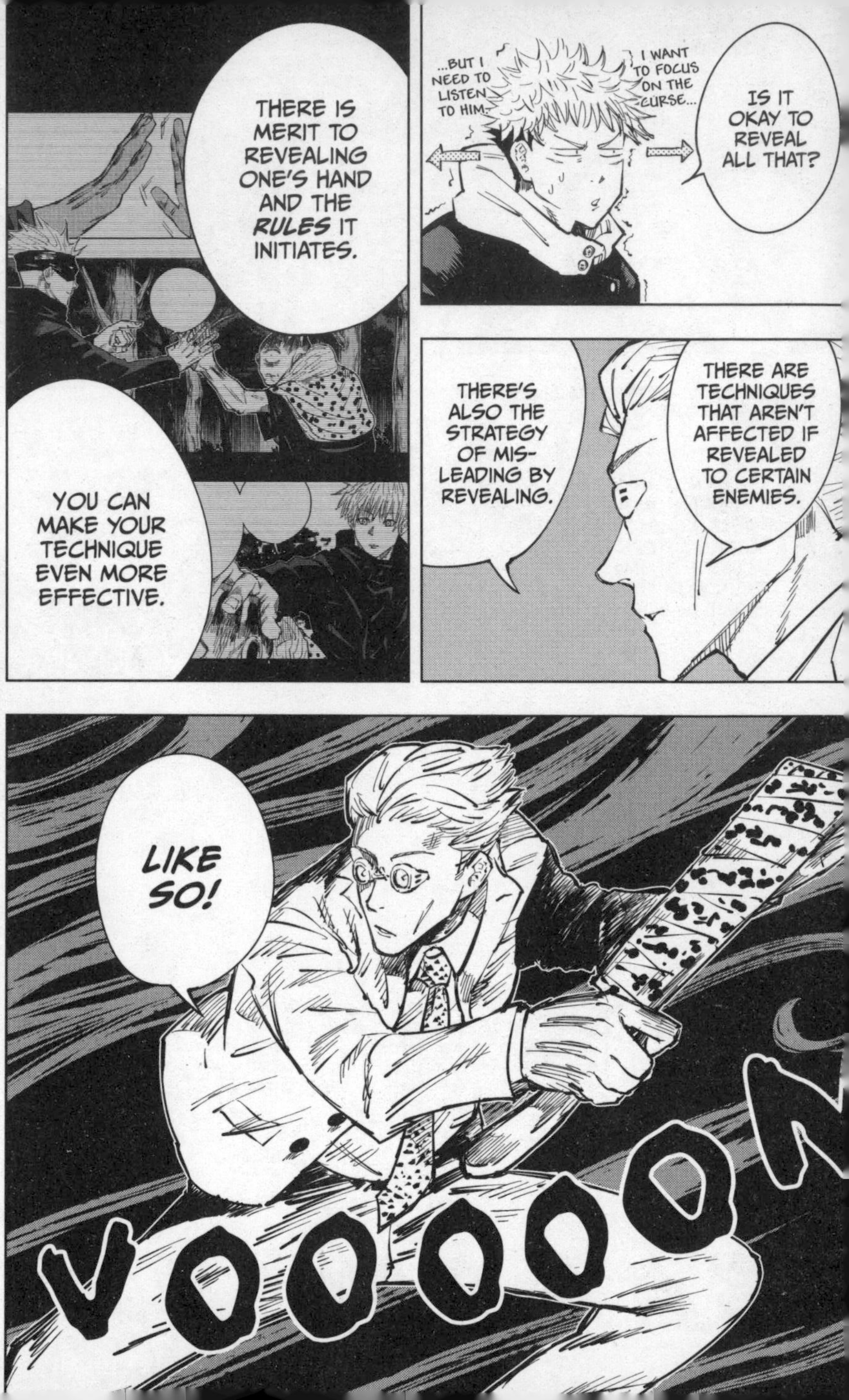
IS IT OKAY TO REVEAL ALL THAT?
I WANT TO FOCUS ON THE CURSE...
...BUT I NEED TO LISTEN TO HIM.
THERE ARE TECHNIQUES THAT AREN'T AFFECTED IF REVEALED TO CERTAIN ENEMIES.
THERE'S ALSO THE STRATEGY OF MIS-LEADING BY REVEALING.
THERE IS MERIT TO REVEALING ONE'S HAND AND THE *RULES* IT INITIATES.
YOU CAN MAKE YOUR TECHNIQUE EVEN MORE EFFECTIVE.
LIKE SO!
VOOOOON

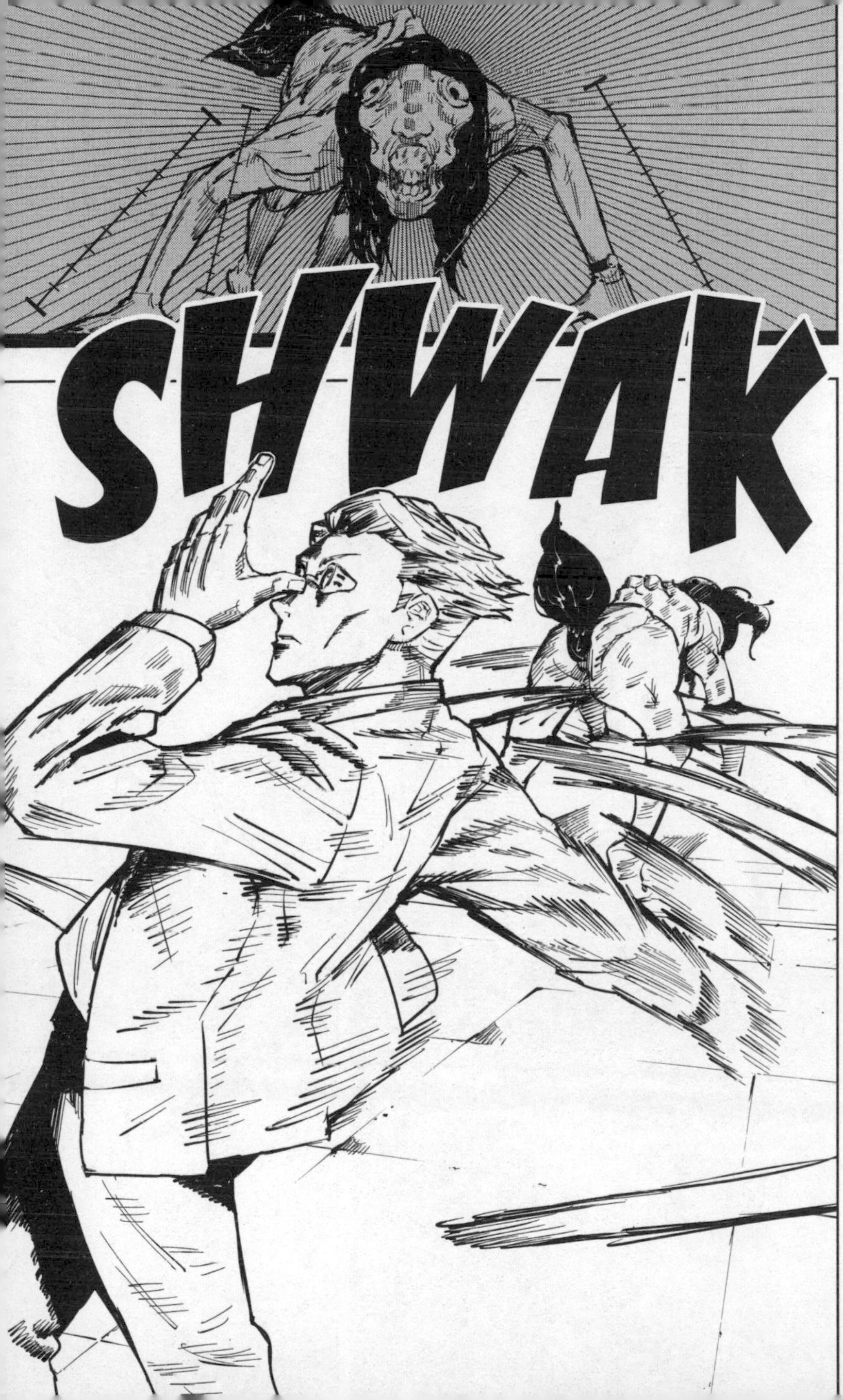
SHWAK

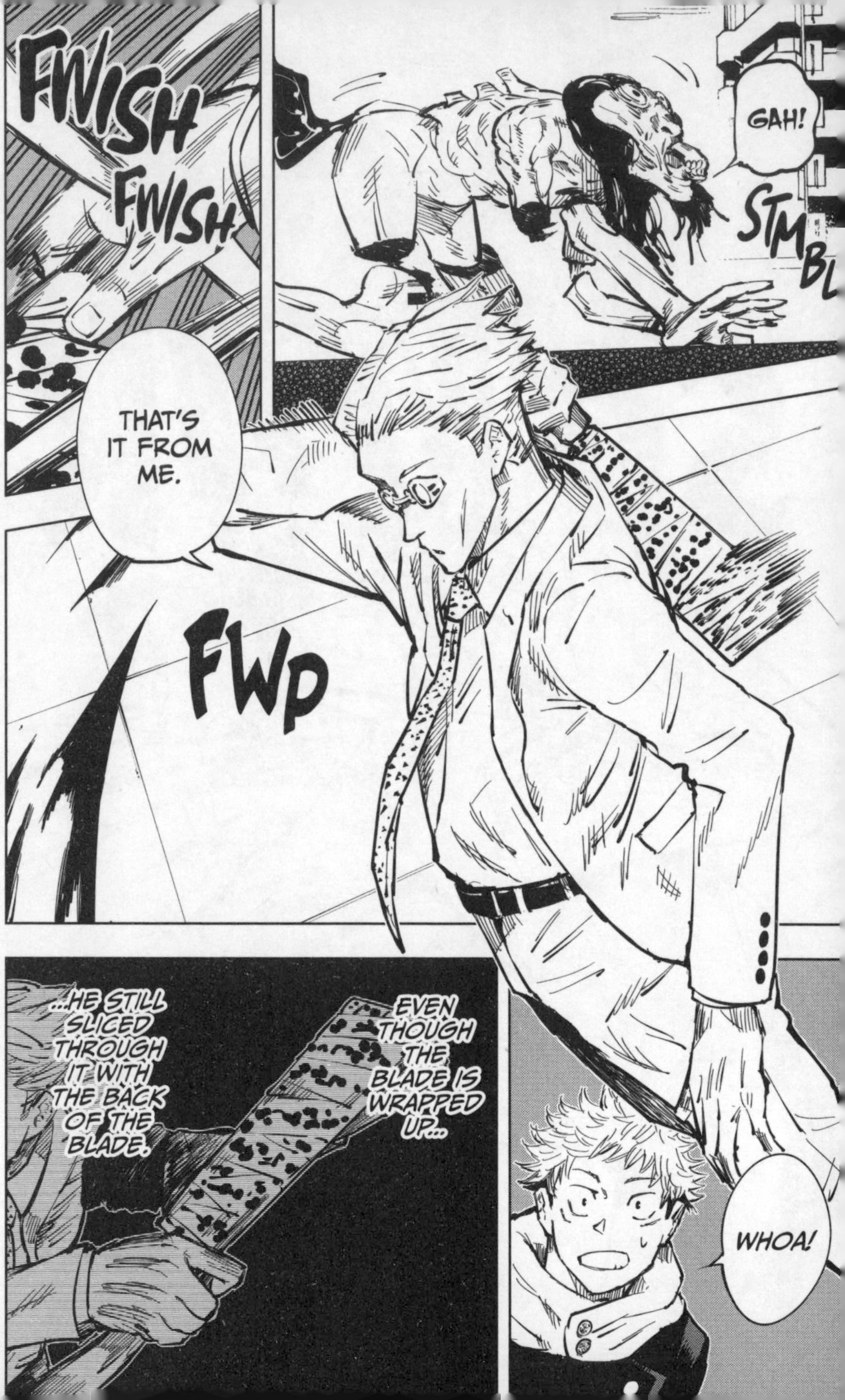
GAH!
STMBL
FWISH
FWISH
THAT'S IT FROM ME.
FWP
WHOA!
EVEN THOUGH THE BLADE IS WRAPPED UP...
...HE STILL SLICED THROUGH IT WITH THE BACK OF THE BLADE.

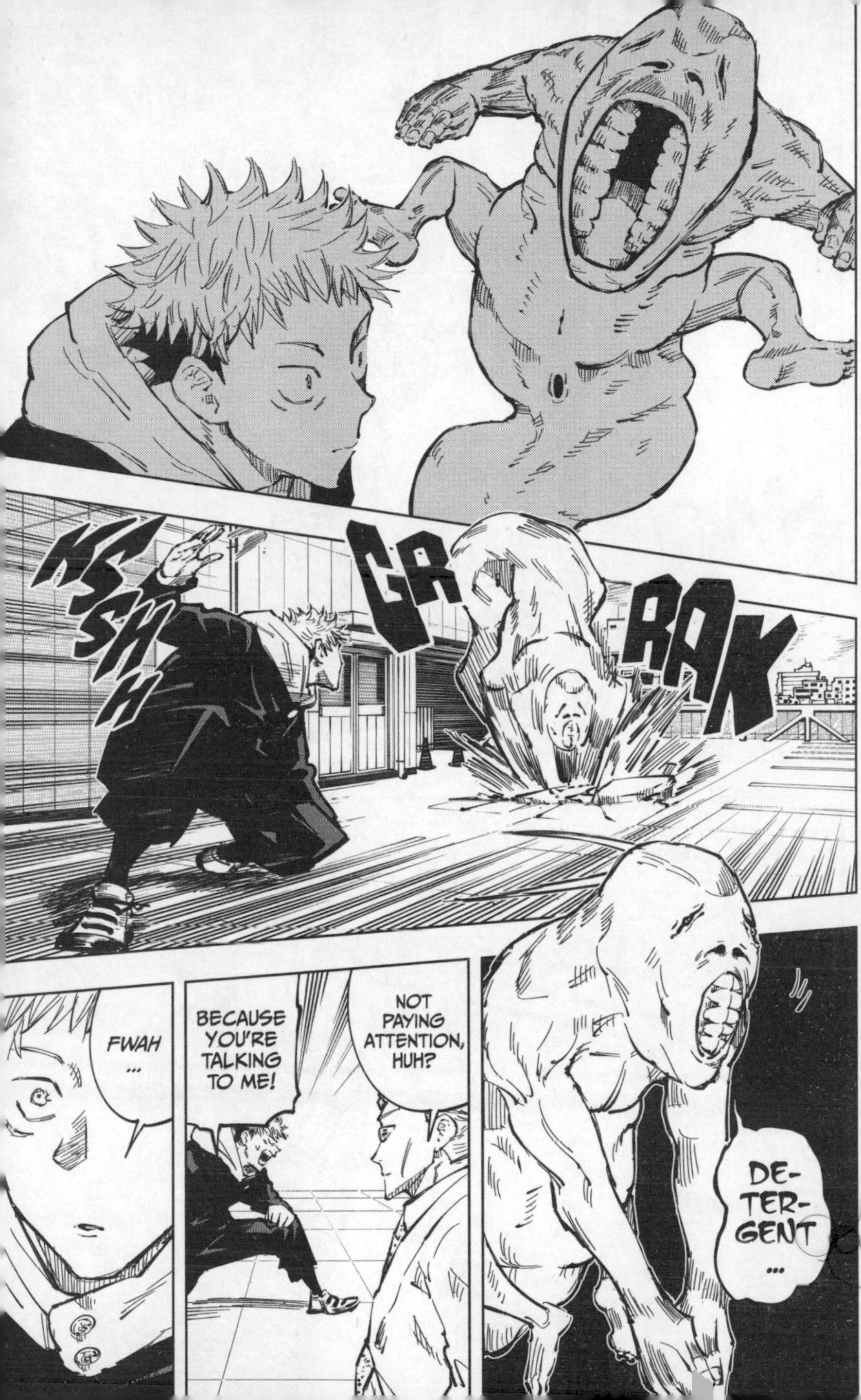
GRRAK
KSHSHH
DE-TER-GENT ...
NOT PAYING ATTENTION, HUH?
BECAUSE YOU'RE TALKING TO ME!
FWAH ...

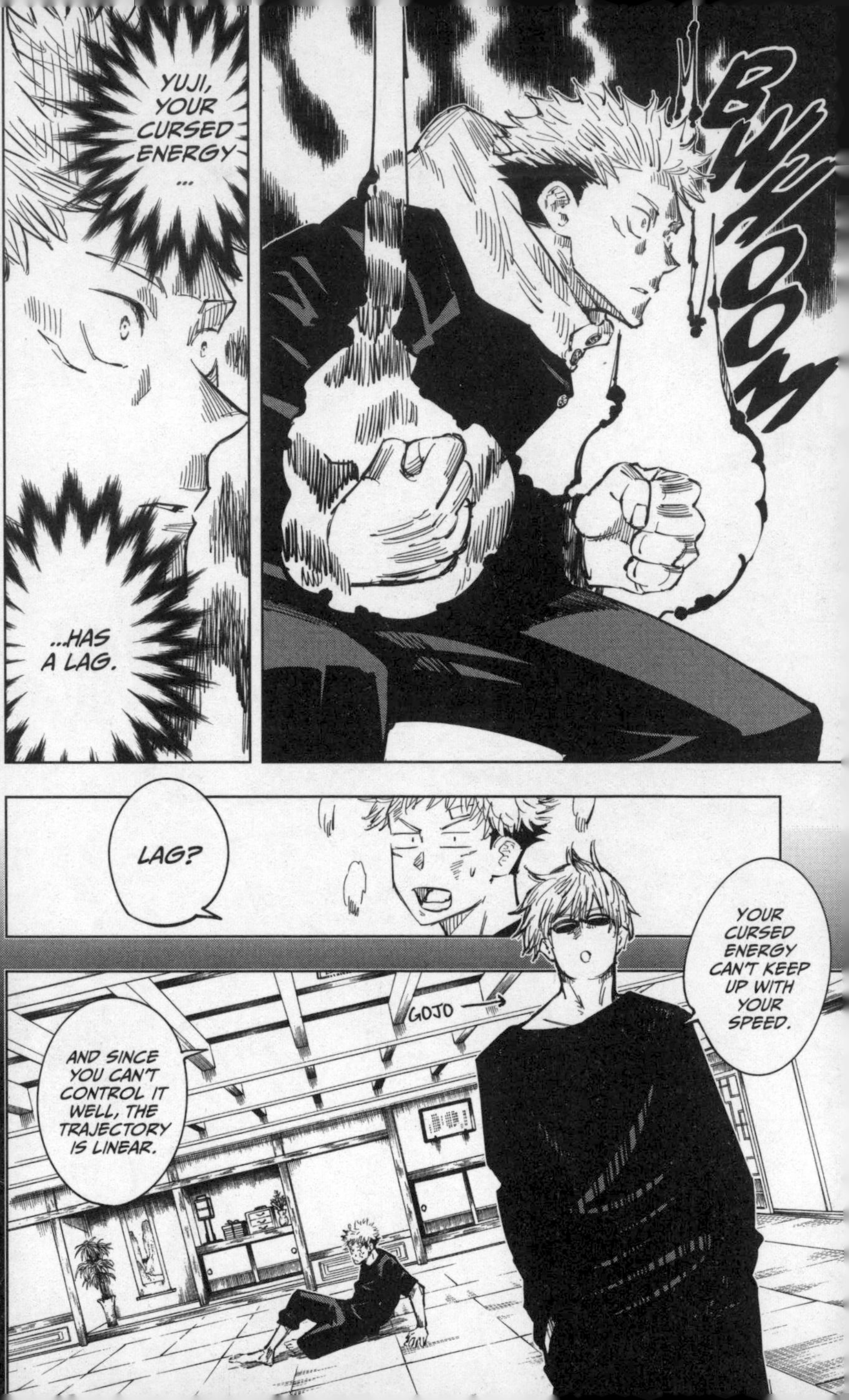
BWHOOM
YUJI, YOUR CURSED ENERGY ...
...HAS A LAG.
LAG?
YOUR CURSED ENERGY CAN'T KEEP UP WITH YOUR SPEED.
GOJO
AND SINCE YOU CAN'T CONTROL IT WELL, THE TRAJECTORY IS LINEAR.

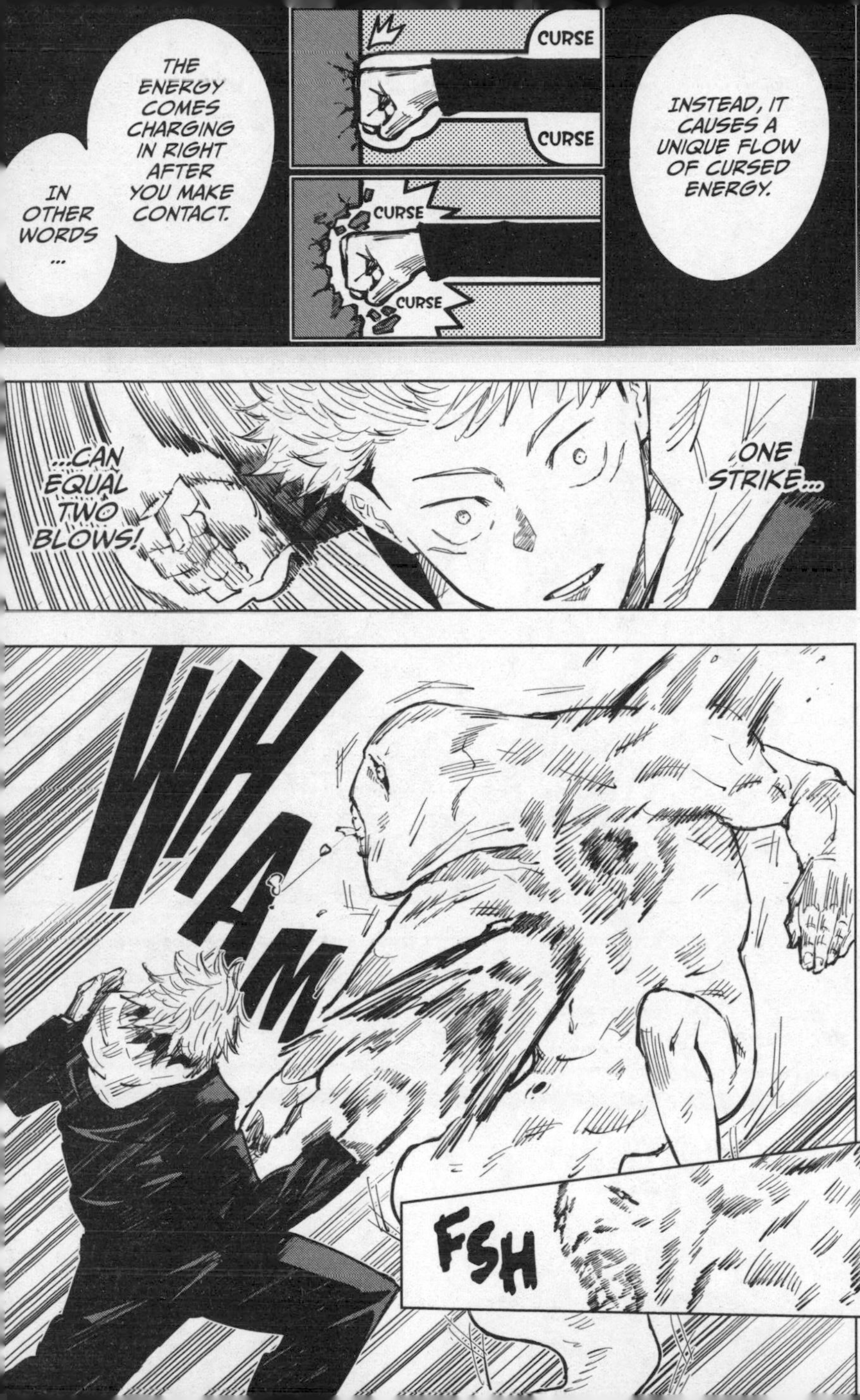
INSTEAD, IT CAUSES A UNIQUE FLOW OF CURSED ENERGY.
CURSE
CURSE
CURSE
CURSE
THE ENERGY COMES CHARGING IN RIGHT AFTER YOU MAKE CONTACT.
IN OTHER WORDS ...
ONE STRIKE...
...CAN EQUAL TWO BLOWS!
WHAM
FSH

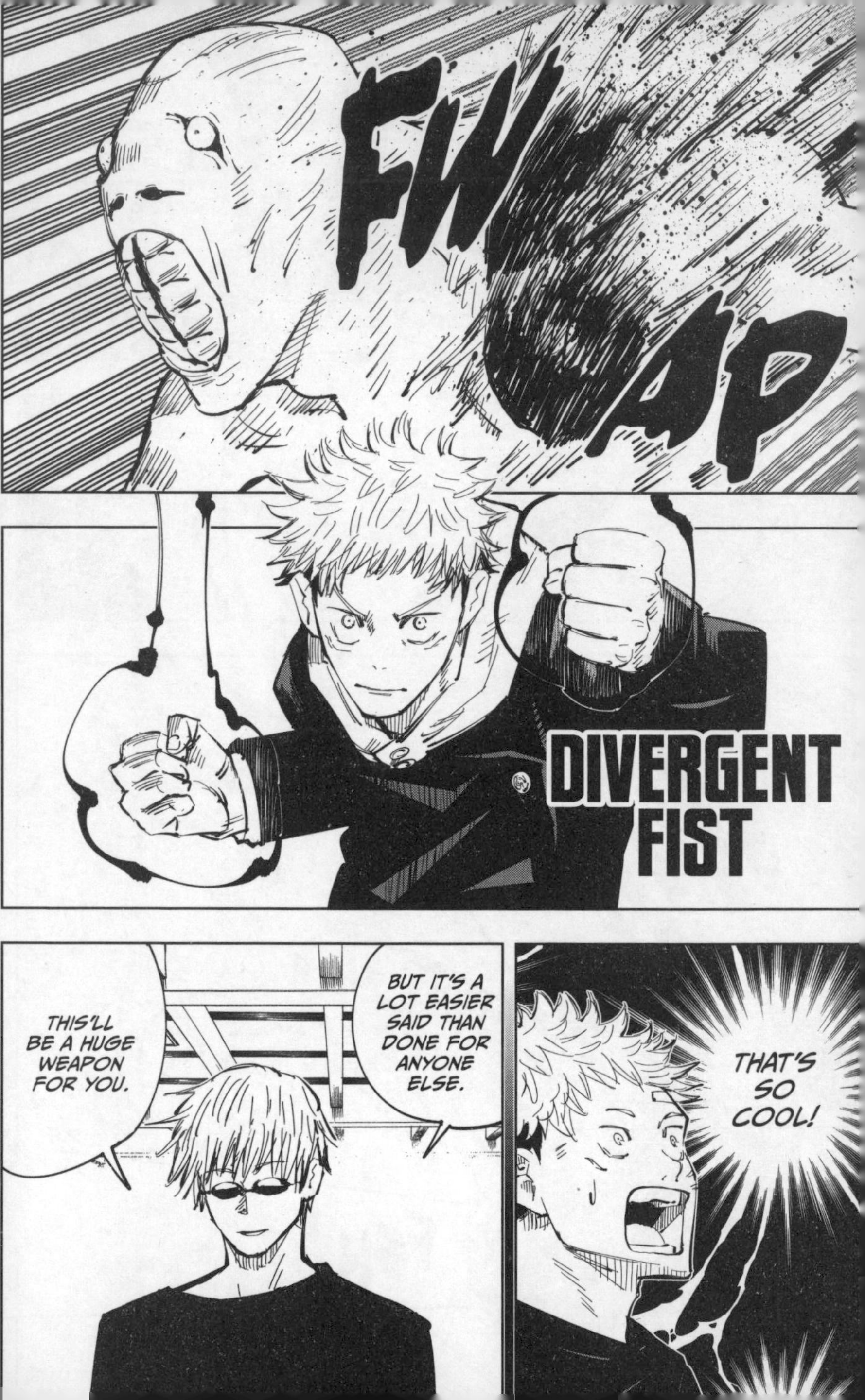
FWAP
DIVERGENT FIST
THAT'S SO COOL!
BUT IT'S A LOT EASIER SAID THAN DONE FOR ANYONE ELSE.
THIS'LL BE A HUGE WEAPON FOR YOU.

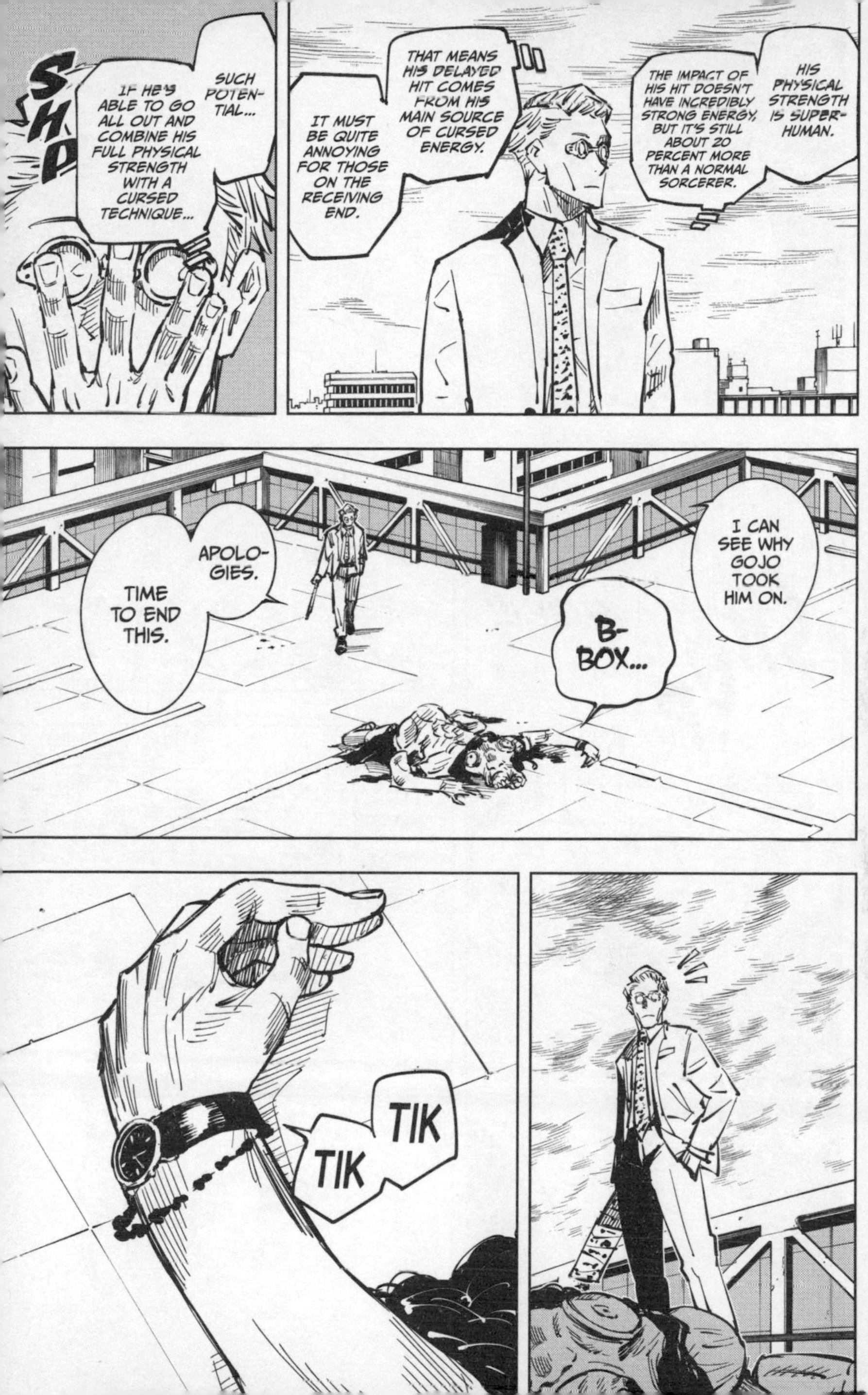
HIS PHYSICAL STRENGTH IS SUPER-HUMAN.
THE IMPACT OF HIS HIT DOESN'T HAVE INCREDIBLY STRONG ENERGY, BUT IT'S STILL ABOUT 20 PERCENT MORE THAN A NORMAL SORCERER.
THAT MEANS HIS DELAYED HIT COMES FROM HIS MAIN SOURCE OF CURSED ENERGY.
IT MUST BE QUITE ANNOYING FOR THOSE ON THE RECEIVING END.
SUCH POTENTIAL...
IF HE'S ABLE TO GO ALL OUT AND COMBINE HIS FULL PHYSICAL STRENGTH WITH A CURSED TECHNIQUE...
SHP
I CAN SEE WHY GOJO TOOK HIM ON.
B-BOX...
APOLOGIES.
TIME TO END THIS.
TIK
TIK

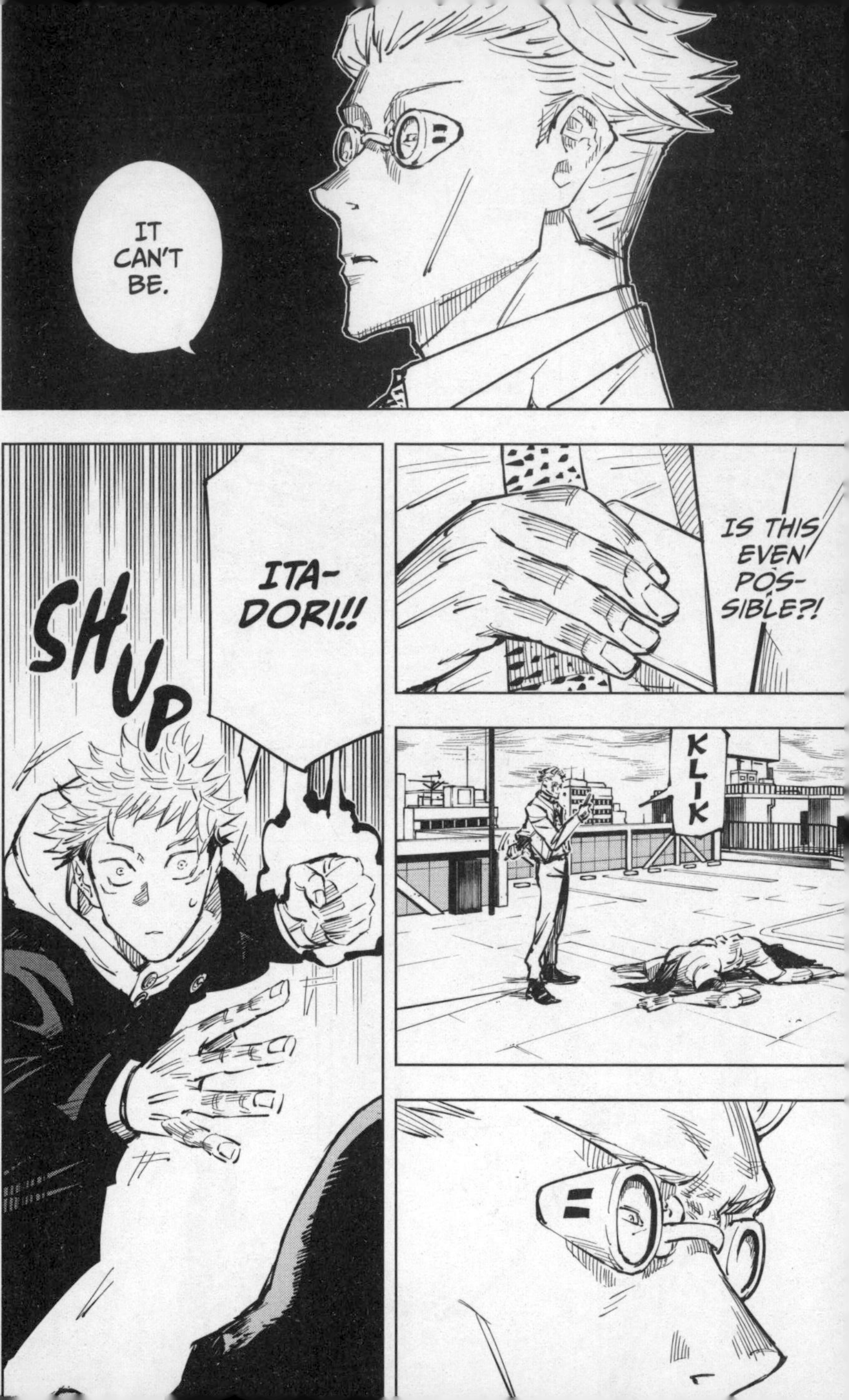
IT CAN'T BE.
IS THIS EVEN POS-SIBLE?!
KLIK
ITA-DORI!!
SHUP

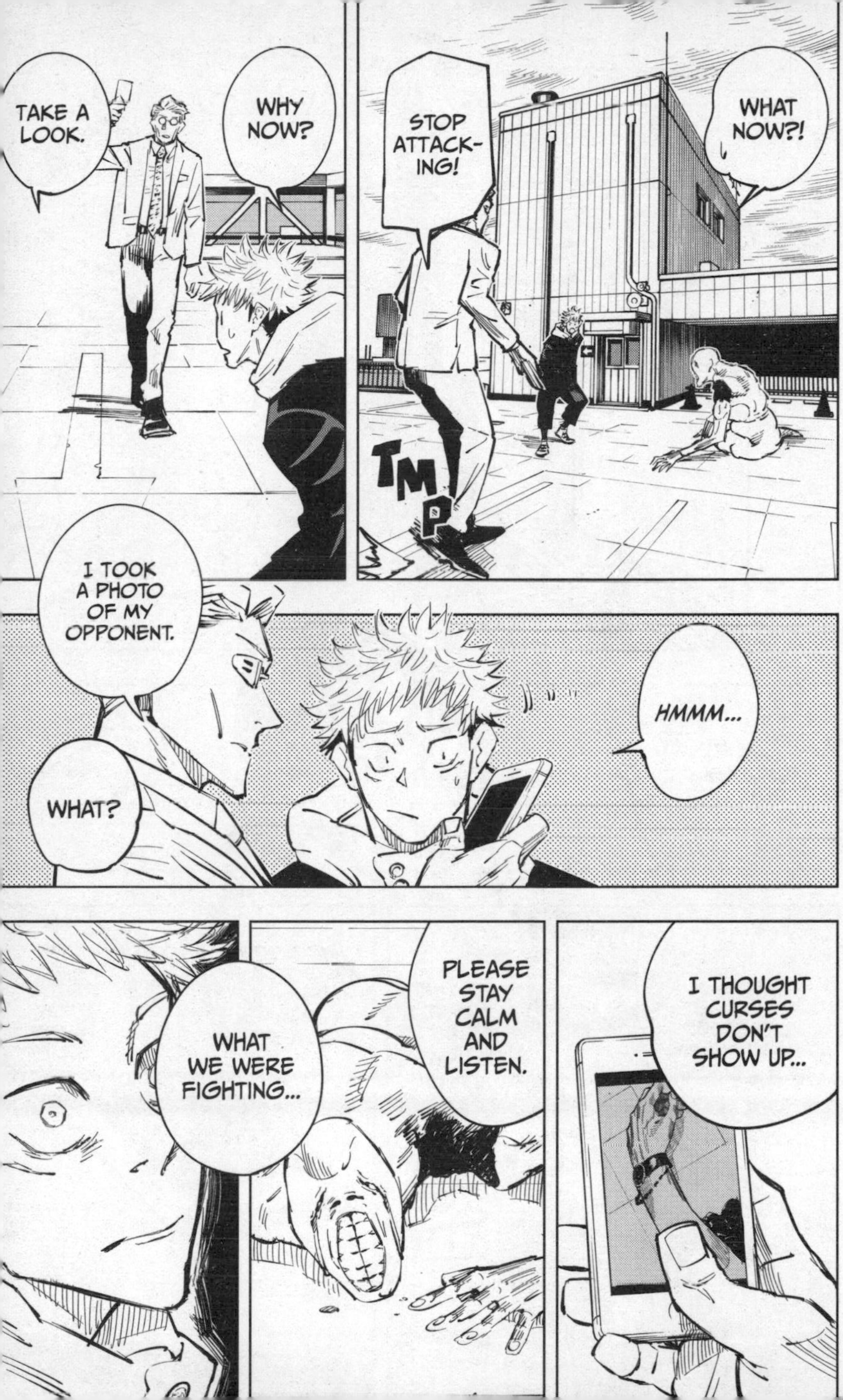
WHAT NOW?!
STOP ATTACKING!
TMP
WHY NOW?
TAKE A LOOK.
I TOOK A PHOTO OF MY OPPONENT.
HMMM...
WHAT?
I THOUGHT CURSES DON'T SHOW UP...
PLEASE STAY CALM AND LISTEN.
WHAT WE WERE FIGHTING...

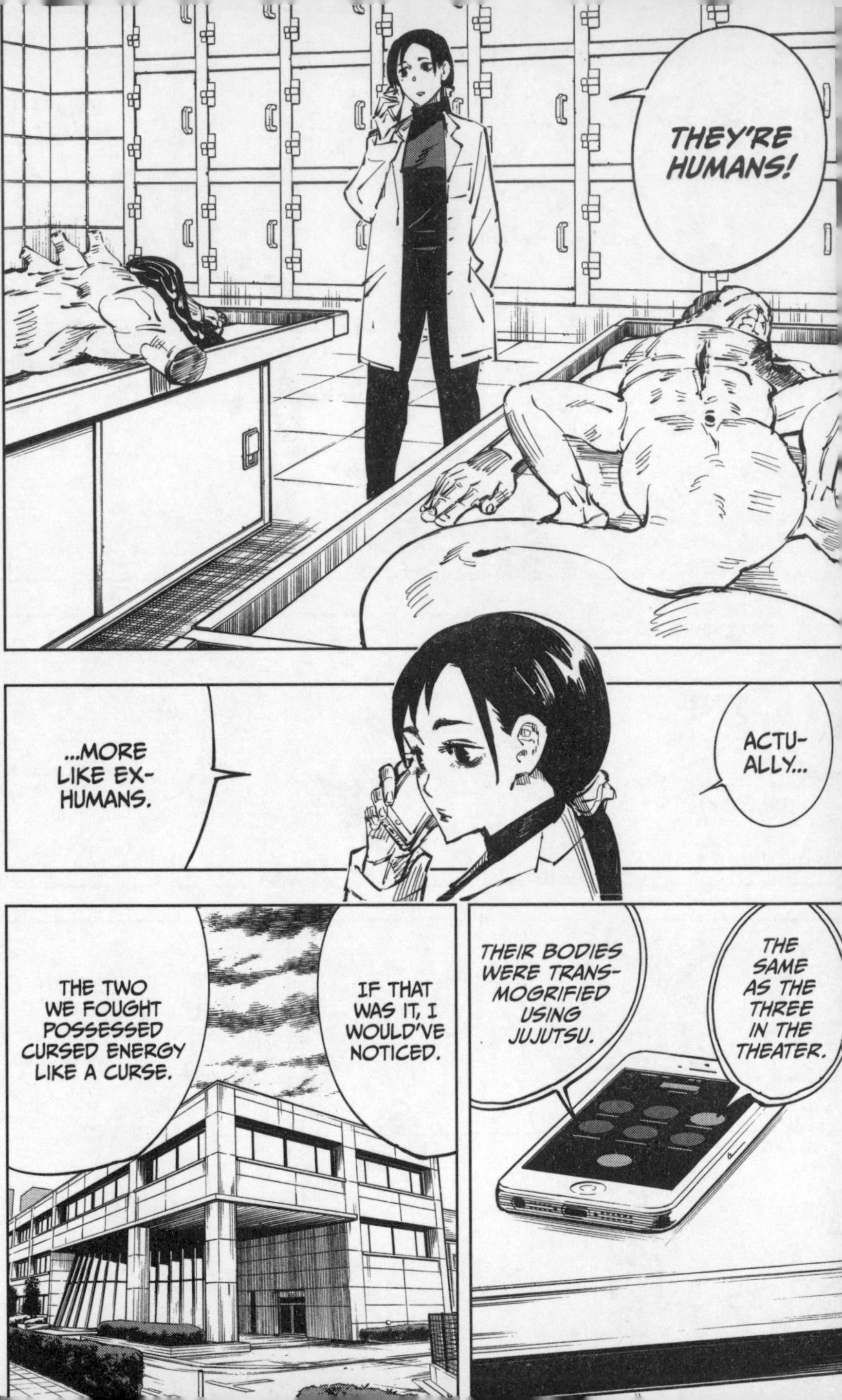
THEY'RE HUMANS!
ACTU-ALLY...
...MORE LIKE EX-HUMANS.
THE SAME AS THE THREE IN THE THEATER.
THEIR BODIES WERE TRANS-MOGRIFIED USING JUJUTSU.
IF THAT WAS IT, I WOULD'VE NOTICED.
THE TWO WE FOUGHT POSSESSED CURSED ENERGY LIKE A CURSE.

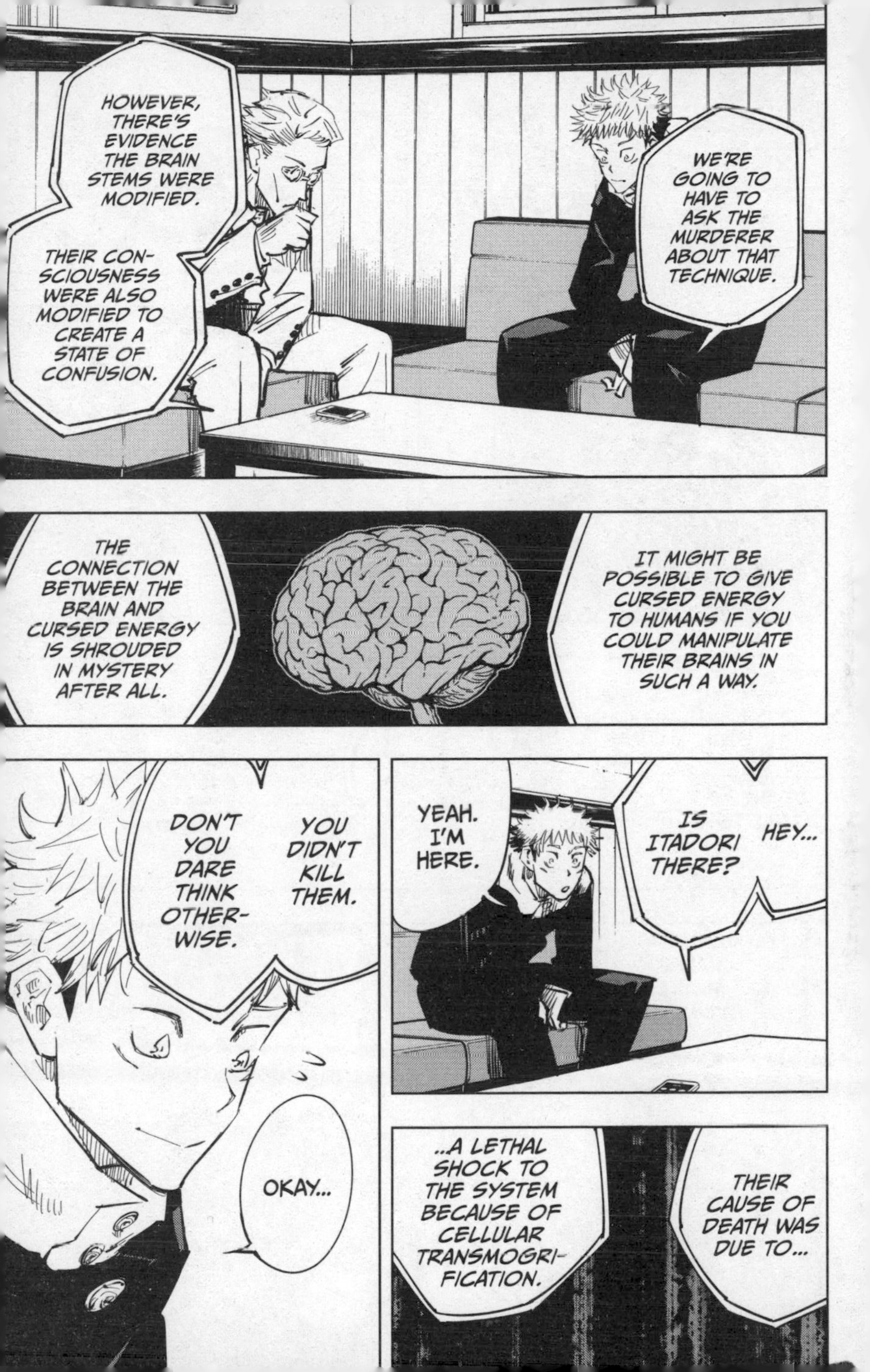
HOWEVER, THERE'S EVIDENCE THE BRAIN STEMS WERE MODIFIED.
THEIR CONSCIOUSNESS WERE ALSO MODIFIED TO CREATE A STATE OF CONFUSION.
WE'RE GOING TO HAVE TO ASK THE MURDERER ABOUT THAT TECHNIQUE.
IT MIGHT BE POSSIBLE TO GIVE CURSED ENERGY TO HUMANS IF YOU COULD MANIPULATE THEIR BRAINS IN SUCH A WAY.
THE CONNECTION BETWEEN THE BRAIN AND CURSED ENERGY IS SHROUDED IN MYSTERY AFTER ALL.
HEY...
IS ITADORI THERE?
YEAH. I'M HERE.
THEIR CAUSE OF DEATH WAS DUE TO...
...A LETHAL SHOCK TO THE SYSTEM BECAUSE OF CELLULAR TRANSMOGRIFICATION.
YOU DIDN'T KILL THEM.
DON'T YOU DARE THINK OTHERWISE.
OKAY...

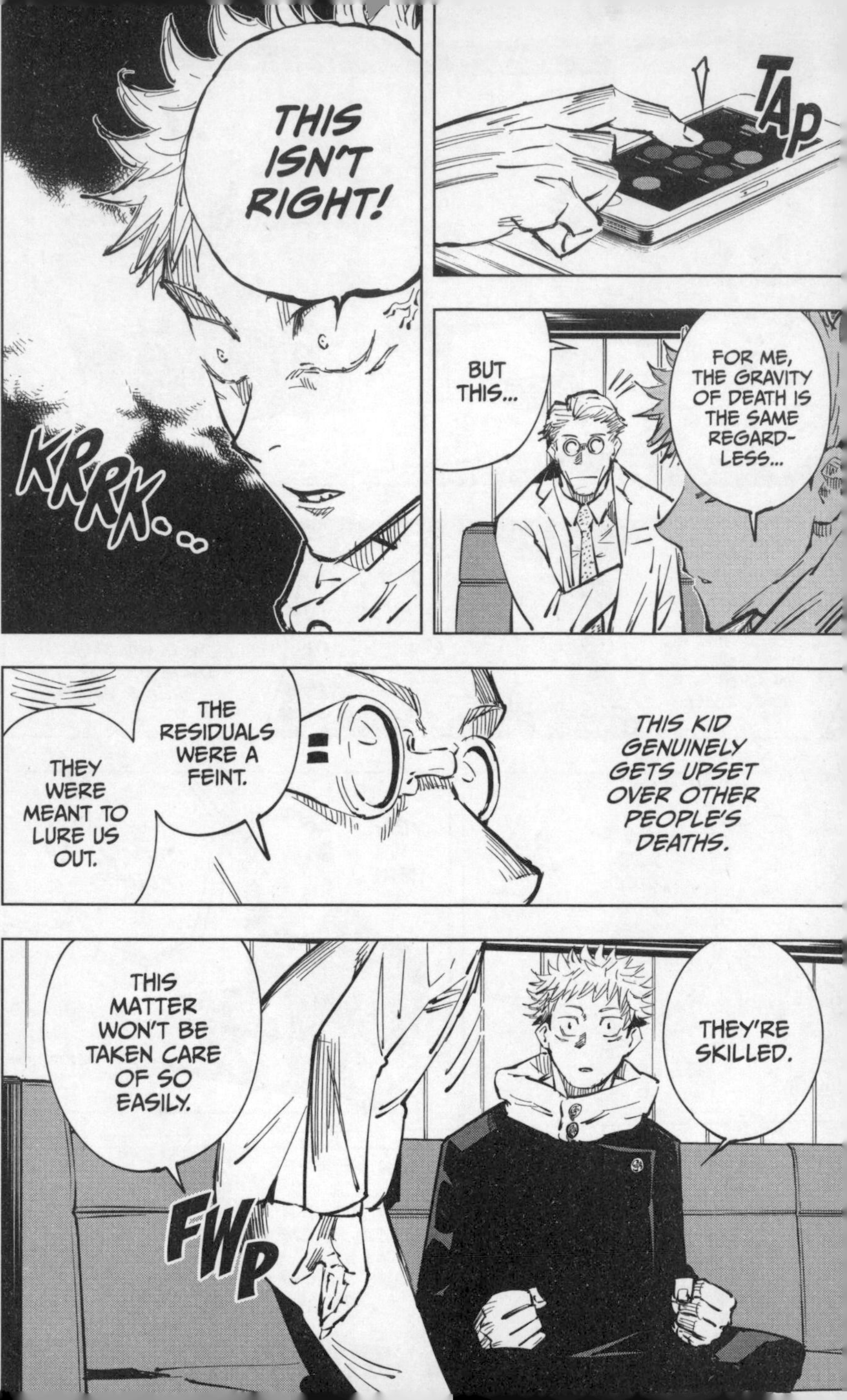
TAP
FOR ME, THE GRAVITY OF DEATH IS THE SAME REGARDLESS...
BUT THIS...
THIS ISN'T RIGHT!
KRRK...
THIS KID GENUINELY GETS UPSET OVER OTHER PEOPLE'S DEATHS.
THE RESIDUALS WERE A FEINT.
THEY WERE MEANT TO LURE US OUT.
THEY'RE SKILLED.
THIS MATTER WON'T BE TAKEN CARE OF SO EASILY.
FWP

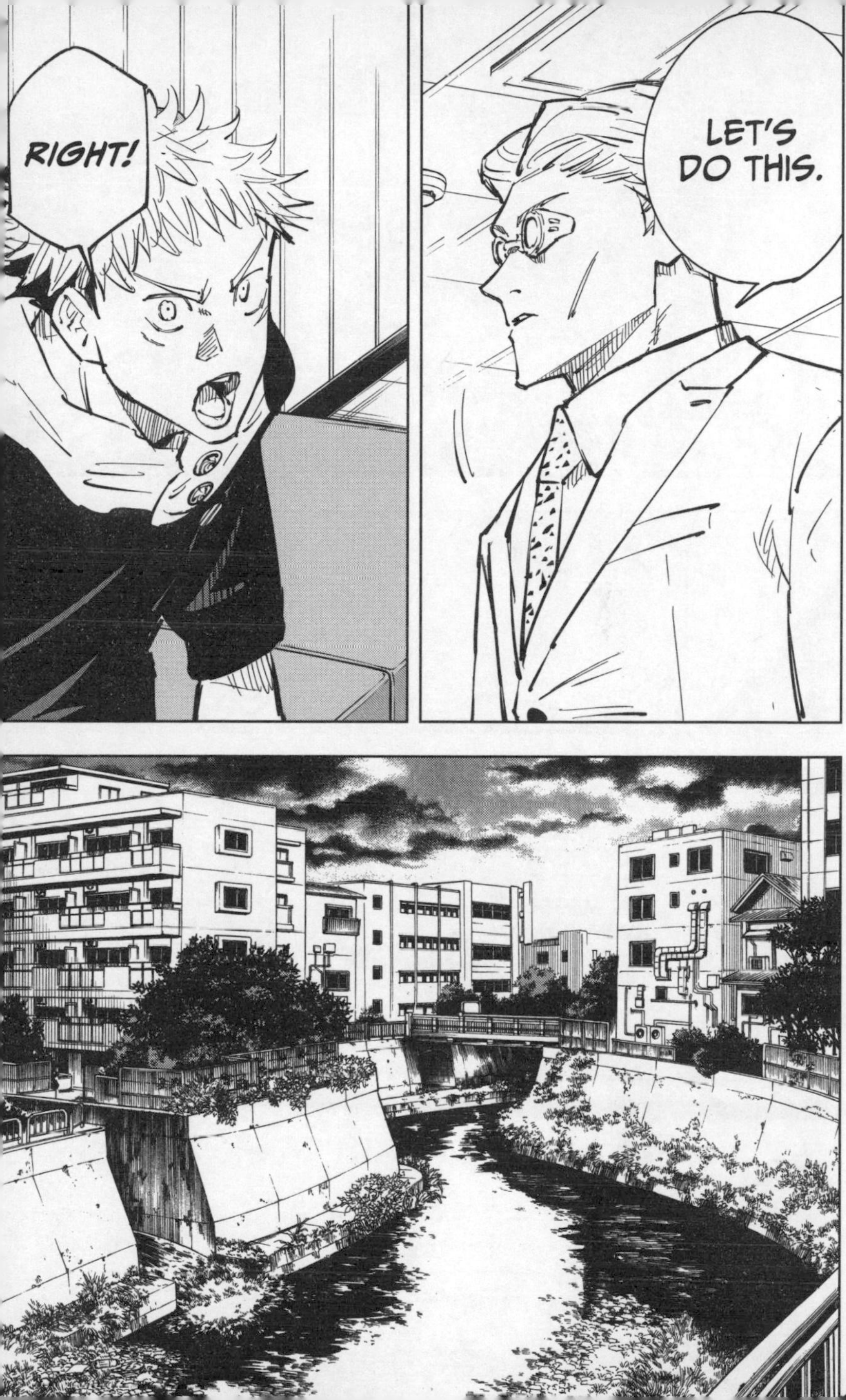
LET'S DO THIS.
RIGHT!

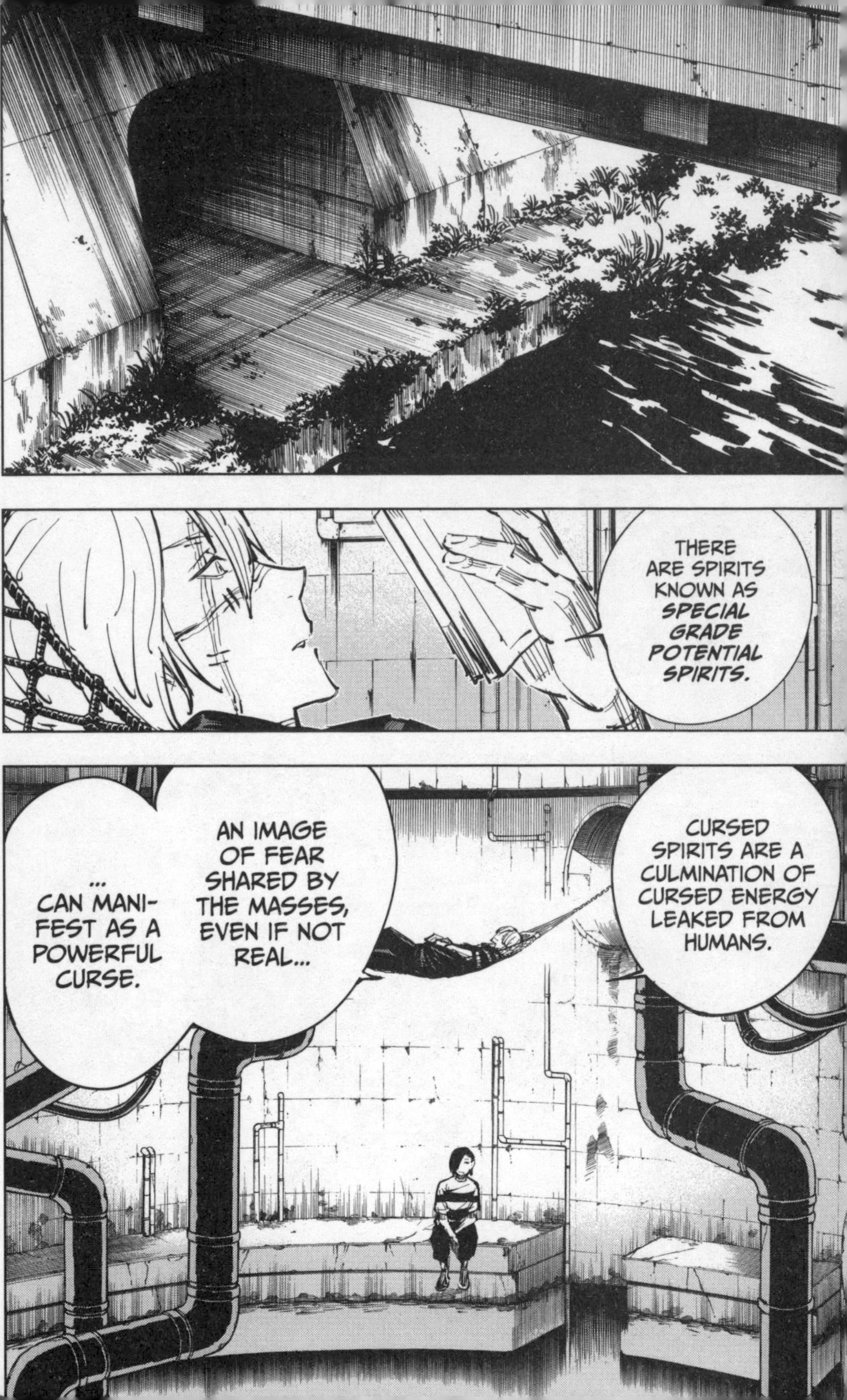
THERE ARE SPIRITS KNOWN AS SPECIAL GRADE POTENTIAL SPIRITS.
CURSED SPIRITS ARE A CULMINATION OF CURSED ENERGY LEAKED FROM HUMANS.
AN IMAGE OF FEAR SHARED BY THE MASSES, EVEN IF NOT REAL...
...CAN MANIFEST AS A POWERFUL CURSE.

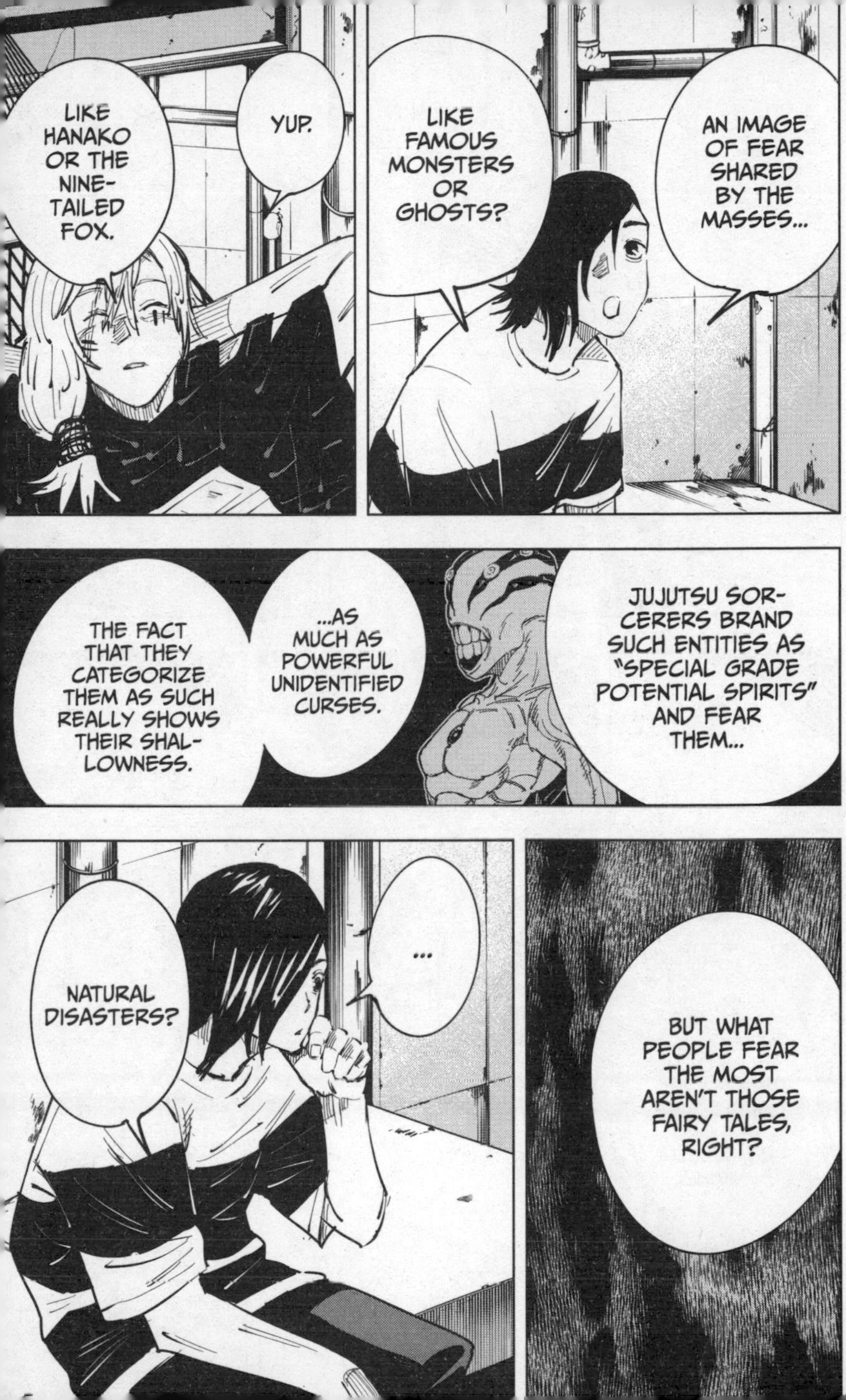
AN IMAGE OF FEAR SHARED BY THE MASSES...
LIKE FAMOUS MONSTERS OR GHOSTS?
YUP.
LIKE HANAKO OR THE NINE-TAILED FOX.
JUJUTSU SORCERERS BRAND SUCH ENTITIES AS "SPECIAL GRADE POTENTIAL SPIRITS" AND FEAR THEM...
...AS MUCH AS POWERFUL UNIDENTIFIED CURSES.
THE FACT THAT THEY CATEGORIZE THEM AS SUCH REALLY SHOWS THEIR SHALLOWNESS.
BUT WHAT PEOPLE FEAR THE MOST AREN'T THOSE FAIRY TALES, RIGHT?
...
NATURAL DISASTERS?

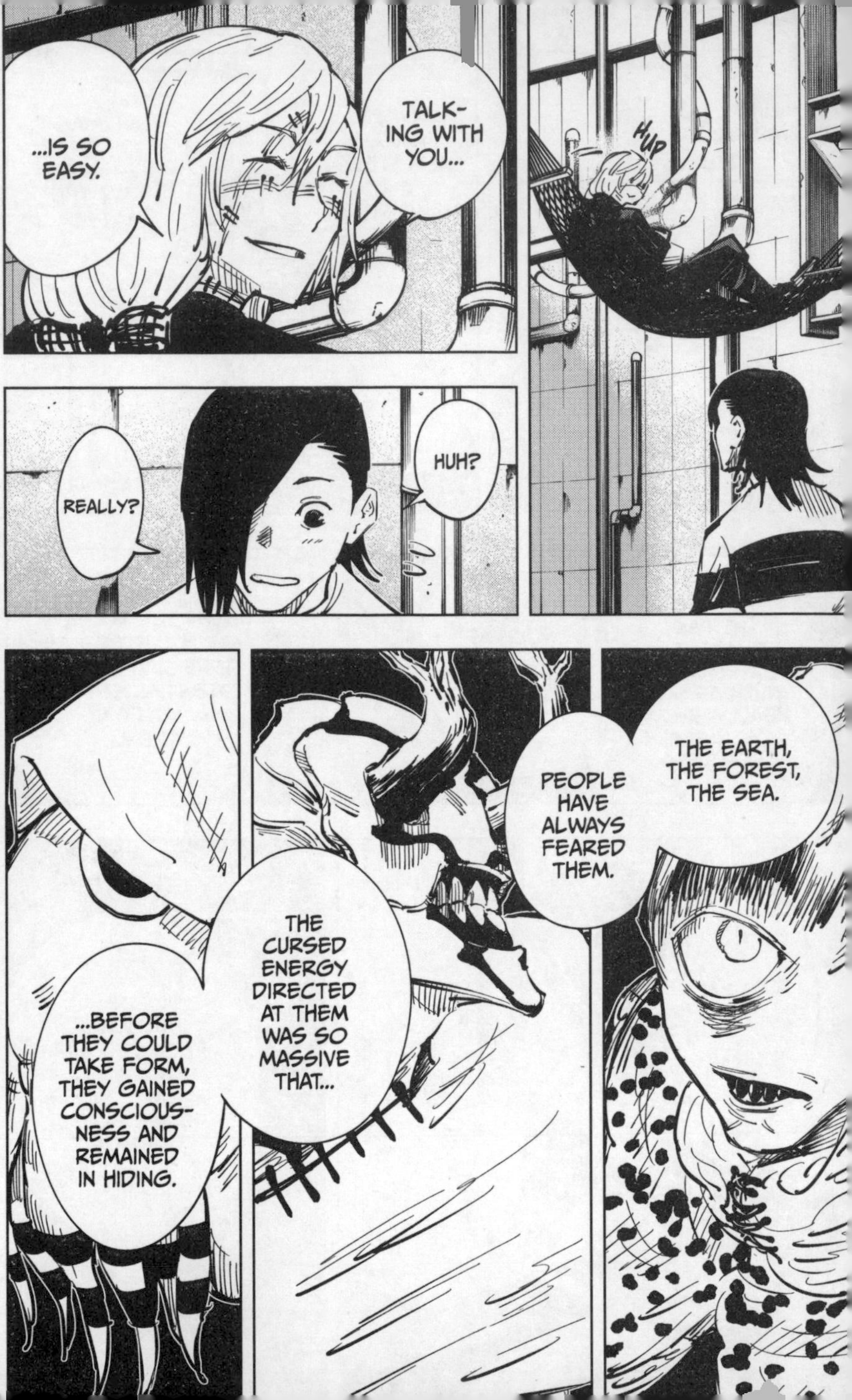
HUP
TALK-ING WITH YOU...
...IS SO EASY.
HUH?
REALLY?
THE EARTH, THE FOREST, THE SEA.
PEOPLE HAVE ALWAYS FEARED THEM.
THE CURSED ENERGY DIRECTED AT THEM WAS SO MASSIVE THAT...
...BEFORE THEY COULD TAKE FORM, THEY GAINED CONSCIOUS-NESS AND REMAINED IN HIDING.

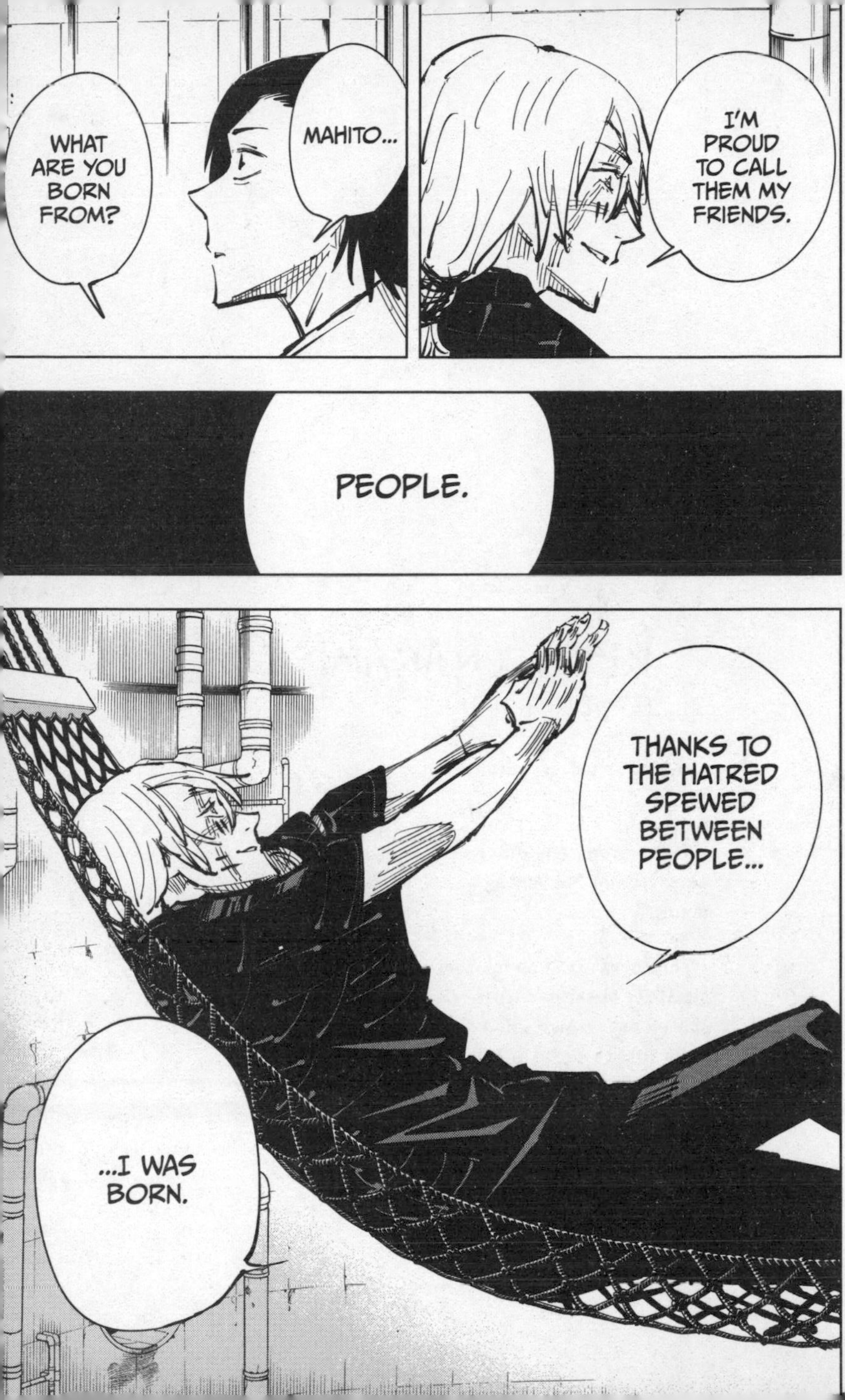
I'M PROUD TO CALL THEM MY FRIENDS.
MAHITO...
WHAT ARE YOU BORN FROM?
PEOPLE.
THANKS TO THE HATRED SPEWED BETWEEN PEOPLE...
...I WAS BORN.

KENTO NANAMI
(27 YEARS OLD)

• His maternal grandfather is Danish.

• There aren't any other sorcerers in Nanami's family.

• Sorcerers wear sunglasses to stealthily observe curses. Curses can be aggressive when they know they're being watched. (Gojo has a separate reason.)

• He loves bread and is a foodie.

• He's 184 centimeters tall.

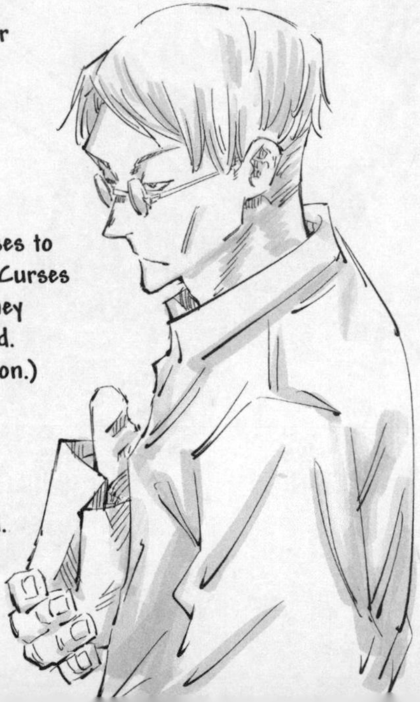

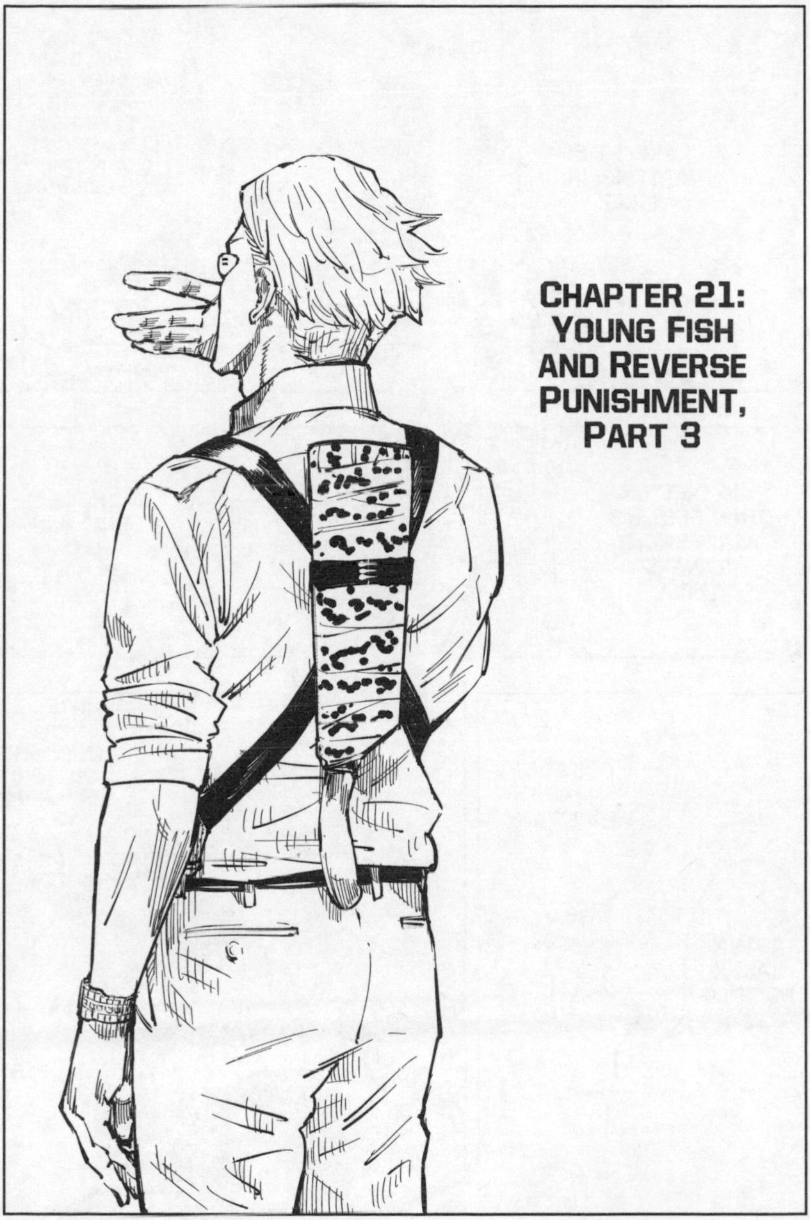
CHAPTER 21:
YOUNG FISH
AND REVERSE
PUNISHMENT,
PART 3

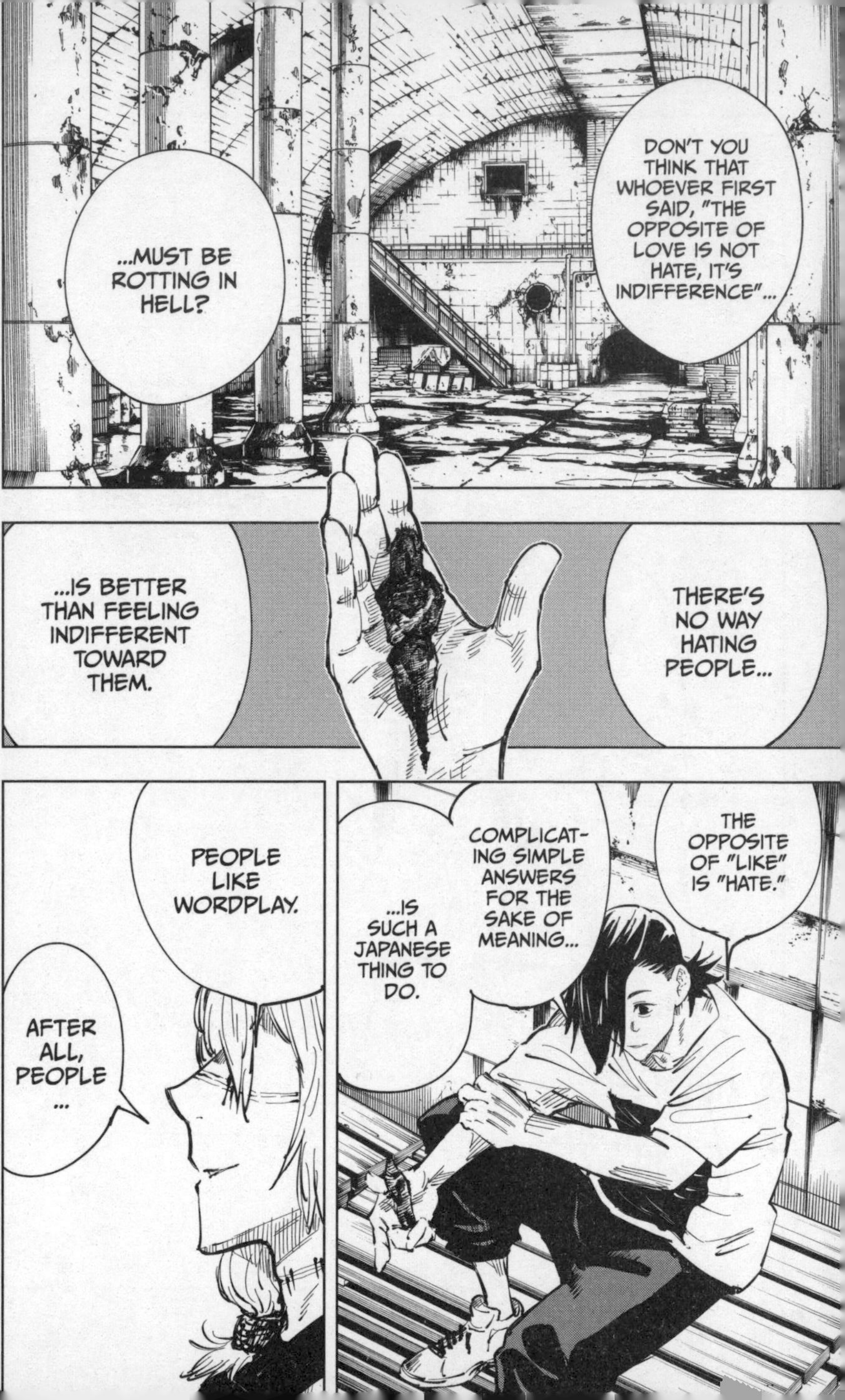
DON'T YOU THINK THAT WHOEVER FIRST SAID, "THE OPPOSITE OF LOVE IS NOT HATE, IT'S INDIFFERENCE"...
...MUST BE ROTTING IN HELL?
THERE'S NO WAY HATING PEOPLE...
...IS BETTER THAN FEELING INDIFFERENT TOWARD THEM.
THE OPPOSITE OF "LIKE" IS "HATE."
COMPLICATING SIMPLE ANSWERS FOR THE SAKE OF MEANING...
...IS SUCH A JAPANESE THING TO DO.
PEOPLE LIKE WORDPLAY.
AFTER ALL, PEOPLE ...

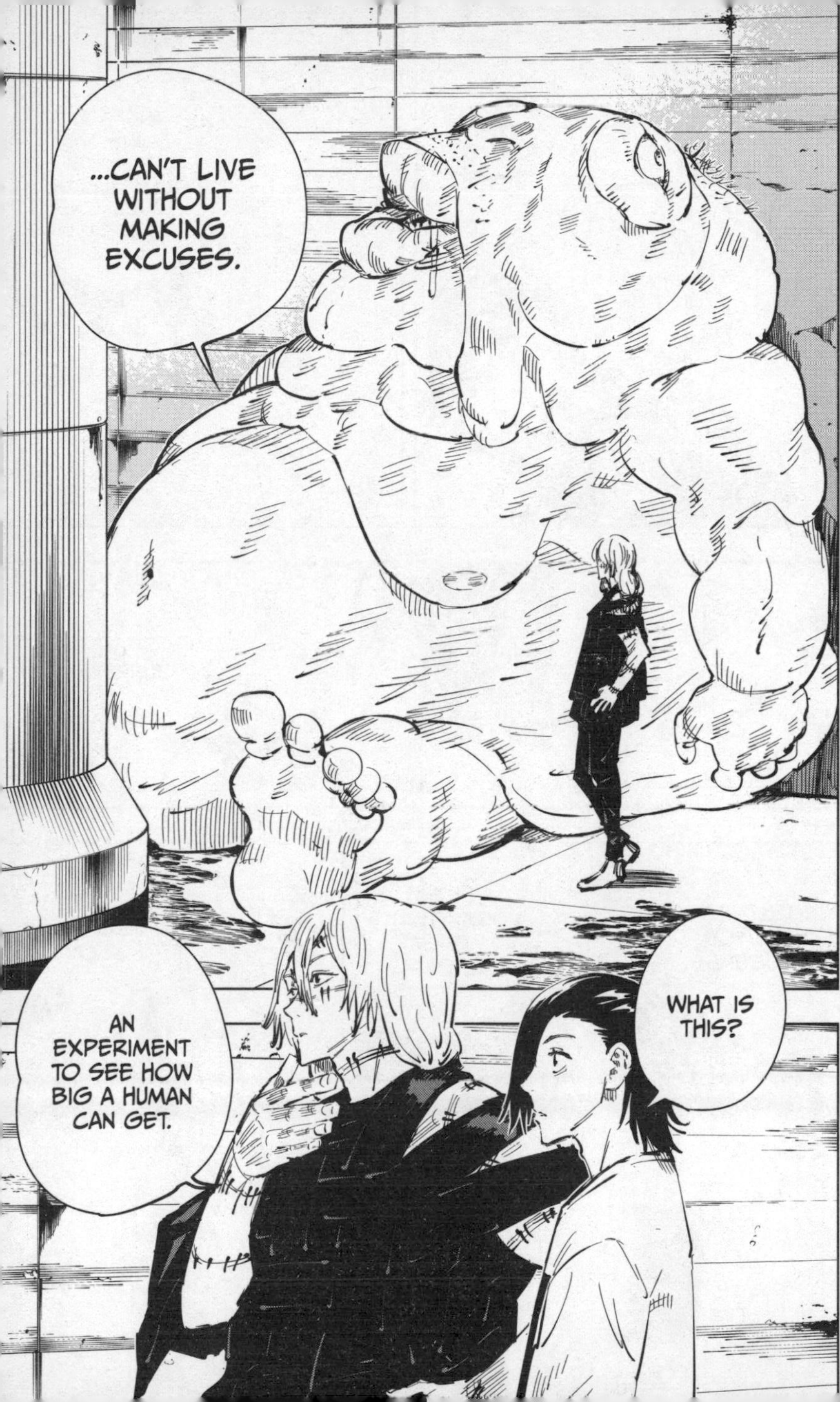
...CAN'T LIVE WITHOUT MAKING EXCUSES.
WHAT IS THIS?
AN EXPERIMENT TO SEE HOW BIG A HUMAN CAN GET.

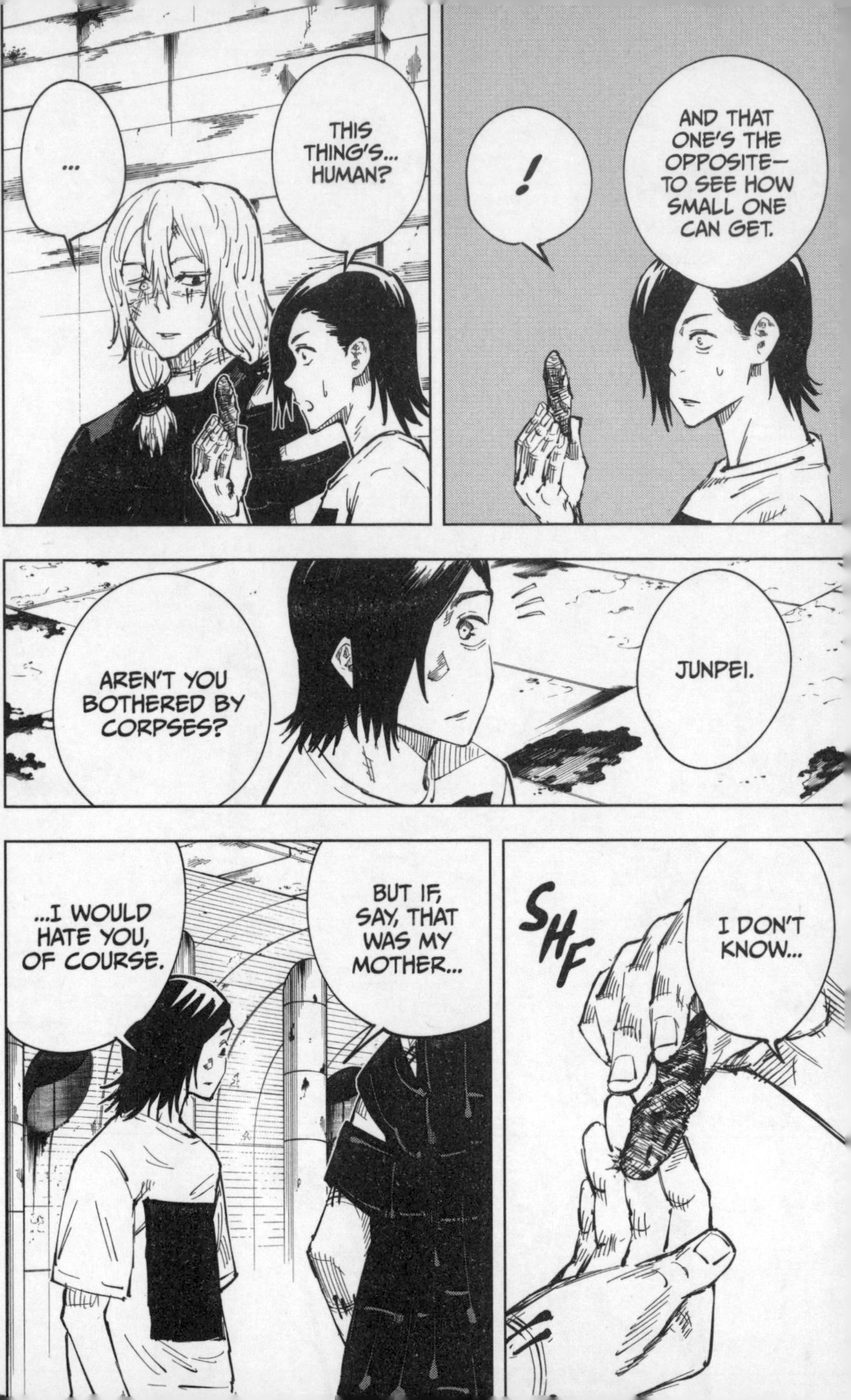
AND THAT ONE'S THE OPPOSITE— TO SEE HOW SMALL ONE CAN GET.
!
THIS THING'S... HUMAN?
...
JUNPEI.
AREN'T YOU BOTHERED BY CORPSES?
I DON'T KNOW...
SHF
BUT IF, SAY, THAT WAS MY MOTHER...
...I WOULD HATE YOU, OF COURSE.

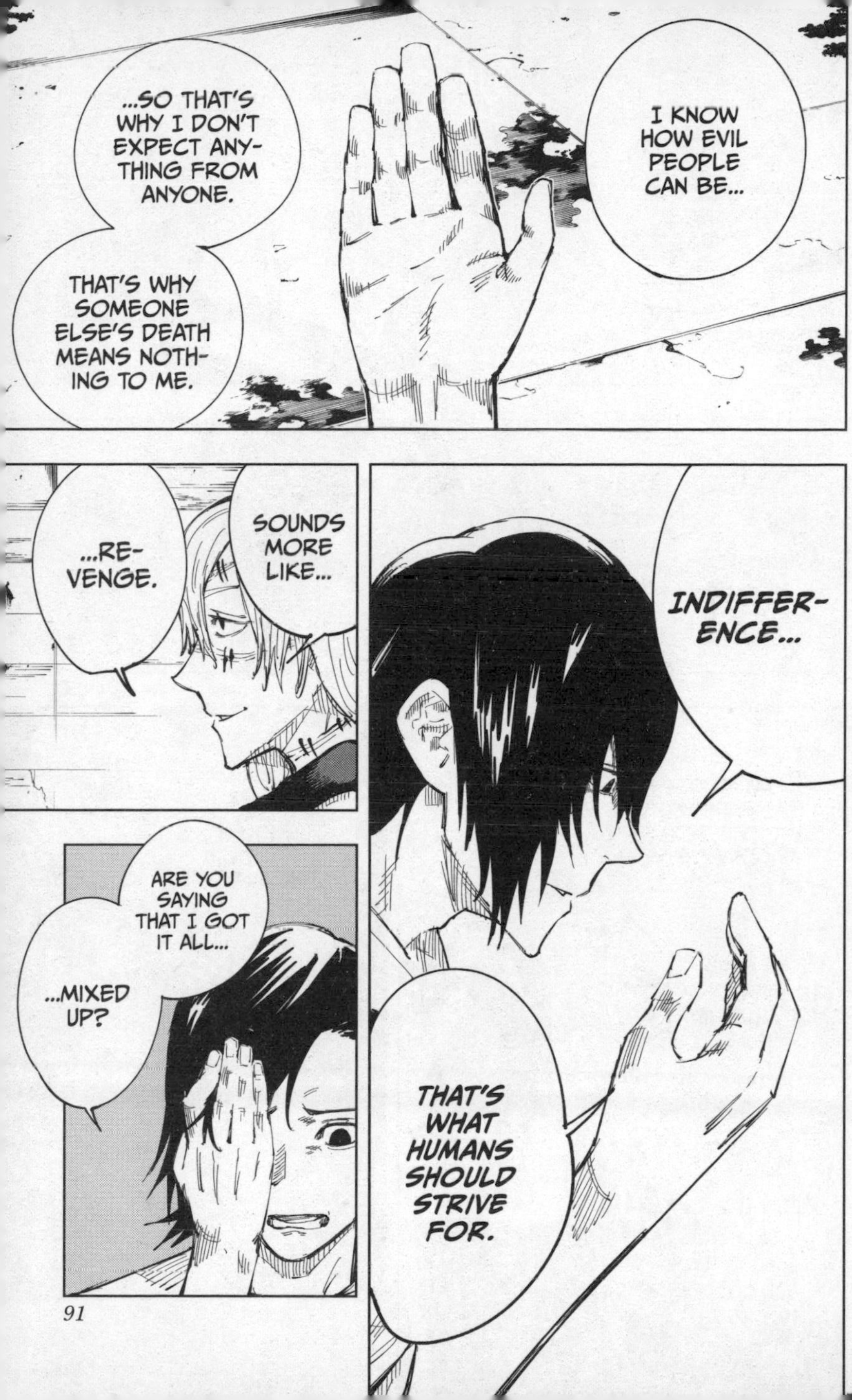
I KNOW HOW EVIL PEOPLE CAN BE...
...SO THAT'S WHY I DON'T EXPECT ANYTHING FROM ANYONE.
THAT'S WHY SOMEONE ELSE'S DEATH MEANS NOTHING TO ME.
INDIFFERENCE...
THAT'S WHAT HUMANS SHOULD STRIVE FOR.
SOUNDS MORE LIKE...
...REVENGE.
ARE YOU SAYING THAT I GOT IT ALL...
...MIXED UP?

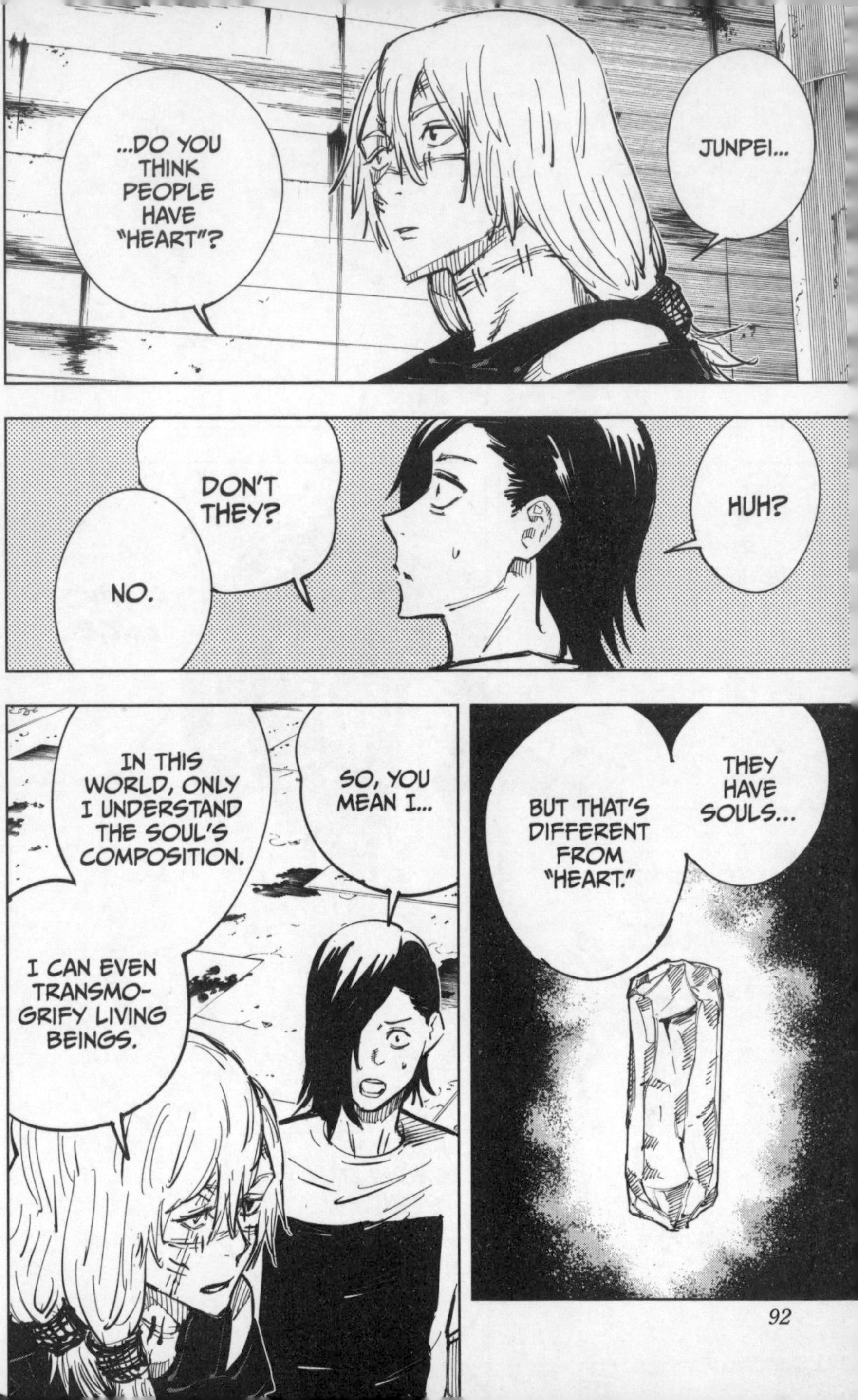
JUNPEI...
...DO YOU THINK PEOPLE HAVE "HEART"?
HUH?
DON'T THEY?
NO.
THEY HAVE SOULS...
BUT THAT'S DIFFERENT FROM "HEART."
SO, YOU MEAN I...
IN THIS WORLD, ONLY I UNDERSTAND THE SOUL'S COMPOSITION.
I CAN EVEN TRANSMO-GRIFY LIVING BEINGS.

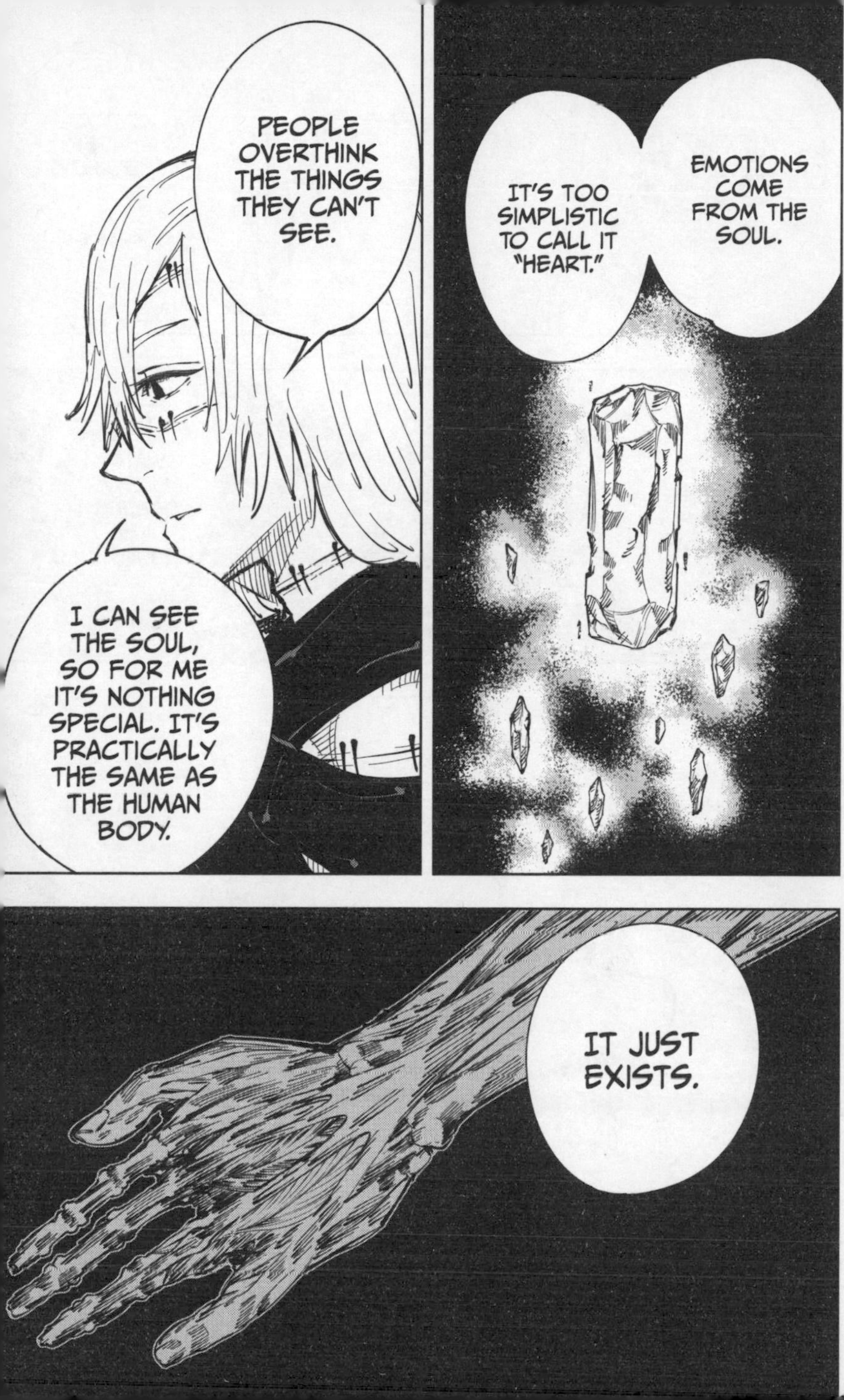
EMOTIONS COME FROM THE SOUL.
IT'S TOO SIMPLISTIC TO CALL IT "HEART."
PEOPLE OVERTHINK THE THINGS THEY CAN'T SEE.
I CAN SEE THE SOUL, SO FOR ME IT'S NOTHING SPECIAL. IT'S PRACTICALLY THE SAME AS THE HUMAN BODY.
IT JUST EXISTS.

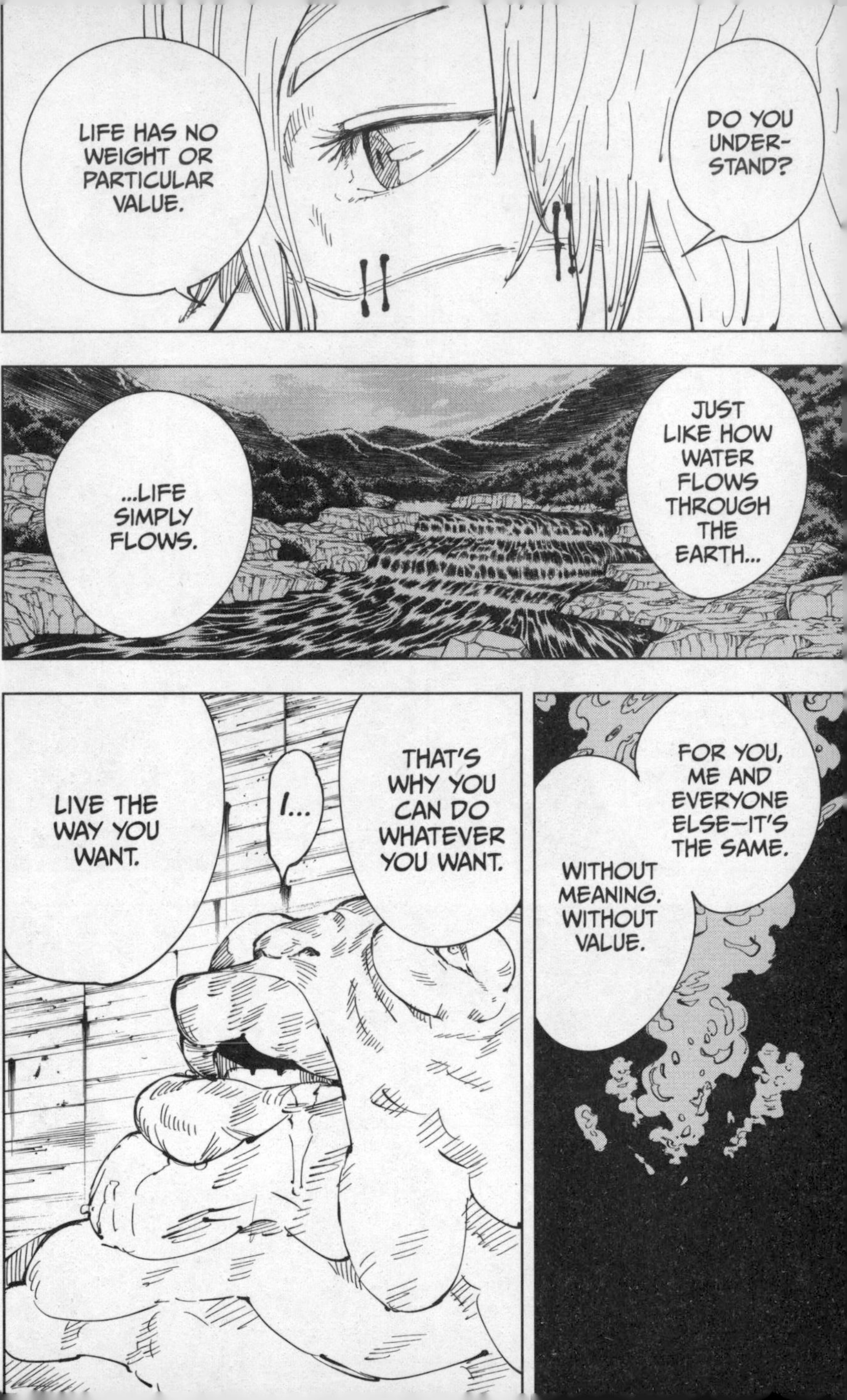
DO YOU UNDER-STAND?
LIFE HAS NO WEIGHT OR PARTICULAR VALUE.
JUST LIKE HOW WATER FLOWS THROUGH THE EARTH...
...LIFE SIMPLY FLOWS.
FOR YOU, ME AND EVERYONE ELSE—IT'S THE SAME.
WITHOUT MEANING. WITHOUT VALUE.
THAT'S WHY YOU CAN DO WHATEVER YOU WANT.
I...
LIVE THE WAY YOU WANT.

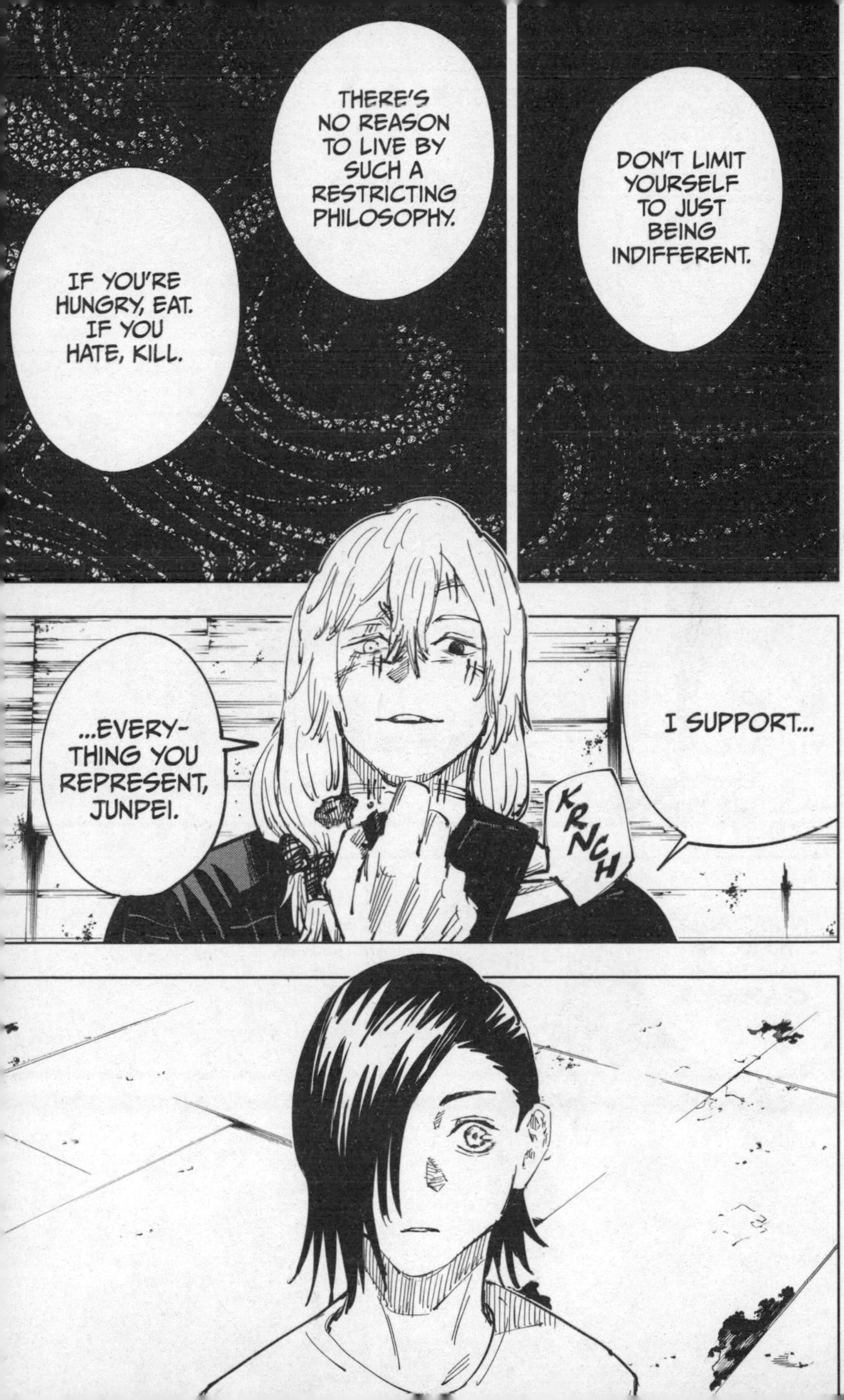
DON'T LIMIT YOURSELF TO JUST BEING INDIFFERENT.
THERE'S NO REASON TO LIVE BY SUCH A RESTRICTING PHILOSOPHY.
IF YOU'RE HUNGRY, EAT. IF YOU HATE, KILL.
I SUPPORT...
KRNCH
...EVERY-THING YOU REPRESENT, JUNPEI.

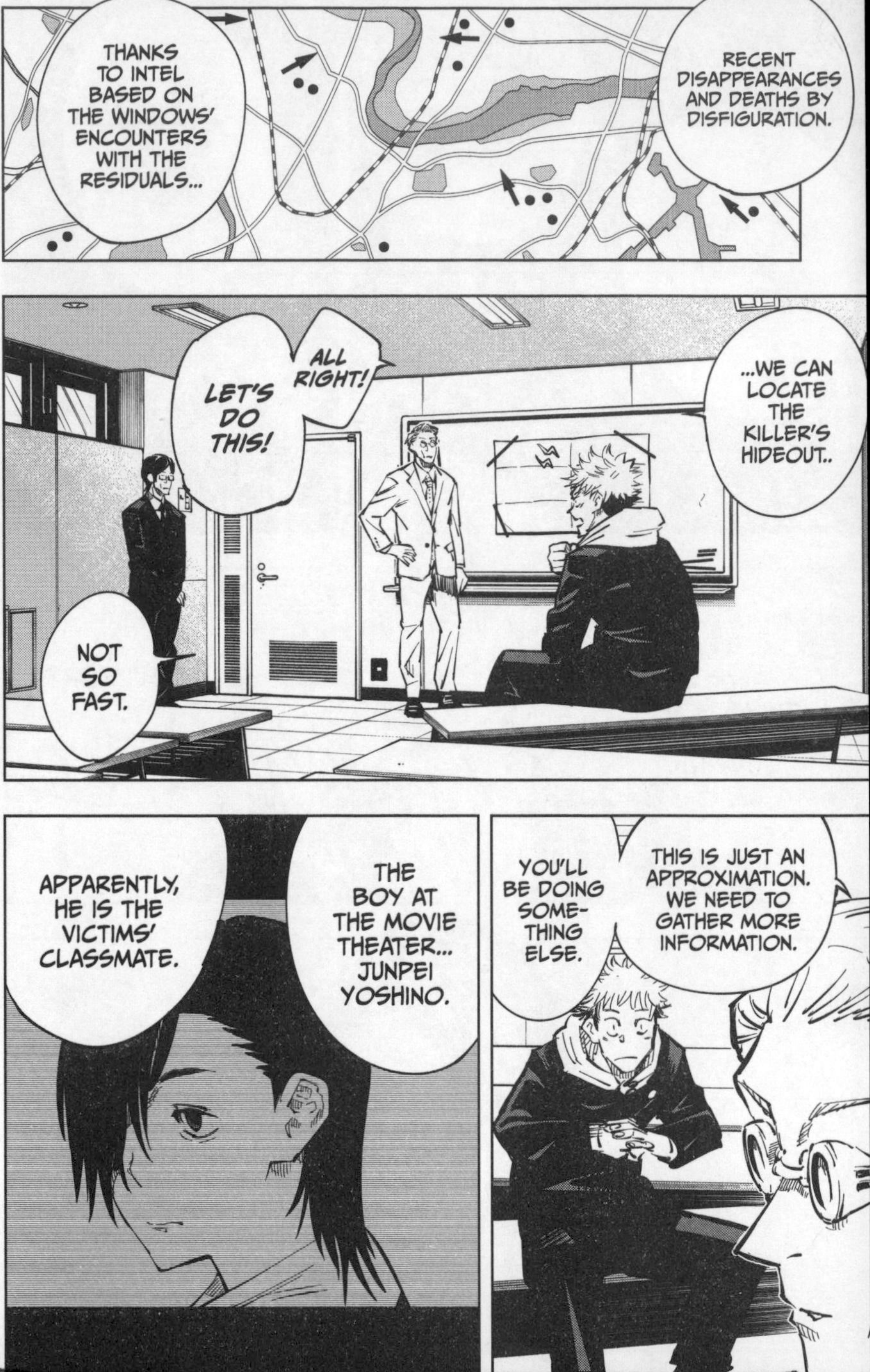
RECENT DISAPPEARANCES AND DEATHS BY DISFIGURATION.
THANKS TO INTEL BASED ON THE WINDOWS' ENCOUNTERS WITH THE RESIDUALS...
...WE CAN LOCATE THE KILLER'S HIDEOUT..
ALL RIGHT!
LET'S DO THIS!
NOT SO FAST.
THIS IS JUST AN APPROXIMATION. WE NEED TO GATHER MORE INFORMATION.
YOU'LL BE DOING SOME-THING ELSE.
THE BOY AT THE MOVIE THEATER... JUNPEI YOSHINO.
APPARENTLY, HE IS THE VICTIMS' CLASSMATE.

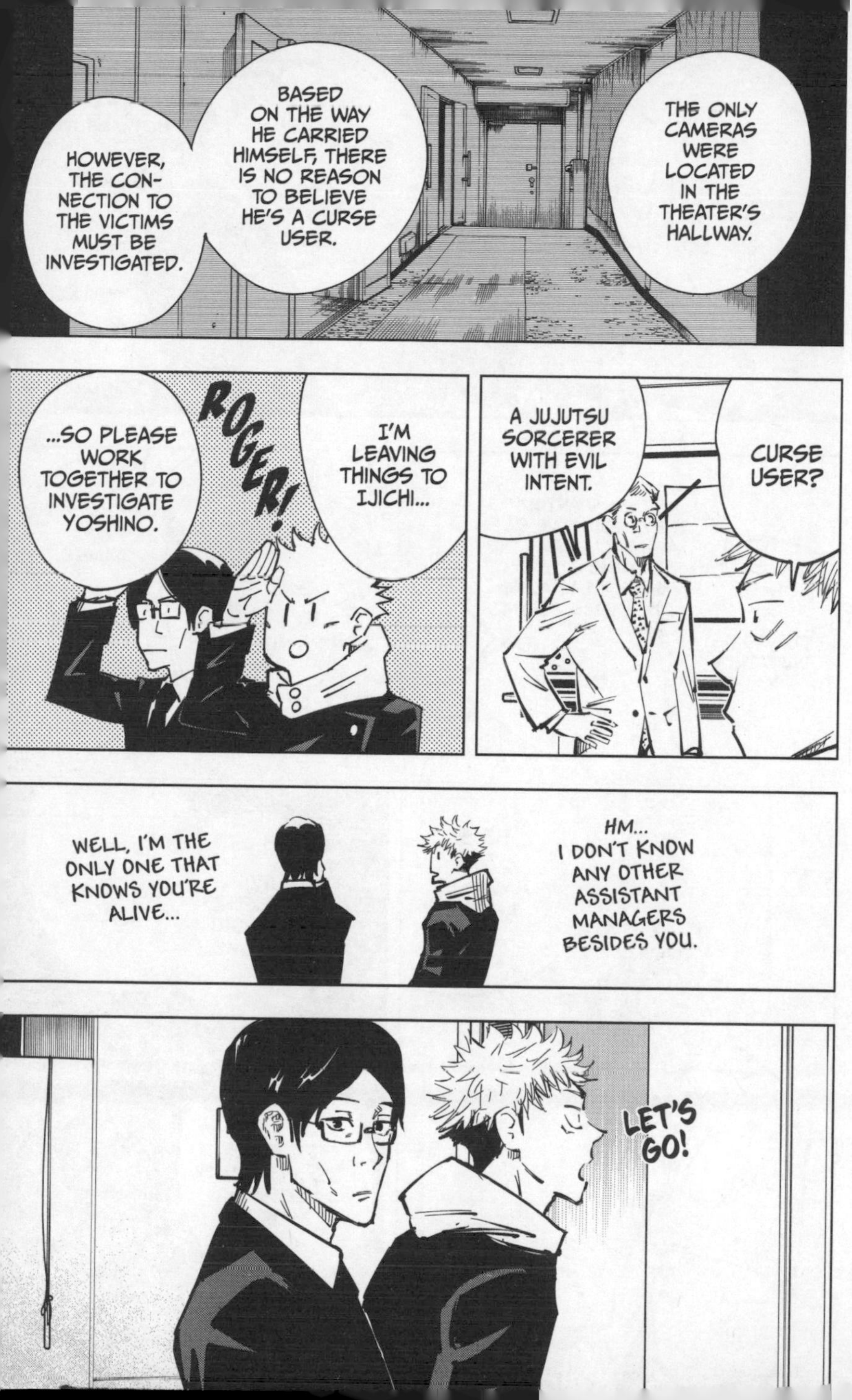
THE ONLY CAMERAS WERE LOCATED IN THE THEATER'S HALLWAY.
BASED ON THE WAY HE CARRIED HIMSELF, THERE IS NO REASON TO BELIEVE HE'S A CURSE USER.
HOWEVER, THE CONNECTION TO THE VICTIMS MUST BE INVESTIGATED.
CURSE USER?
A JUJUTSU SORCERER WITH EVIL INTENT.
I'M LEAVING THINGS TO IJICHI...
...SO PLEASE WORK TOGETHER TO INVESTIGATE YOSHINO.
ROGER!
HM... I DON'T KNOW ANY OTHER ASSISTANT MANAGERS BESIDES YOU.
WELL, I'M THE ONLY ONE THAT KNOWS YOU'RE ALIVE...
LET'S GO!

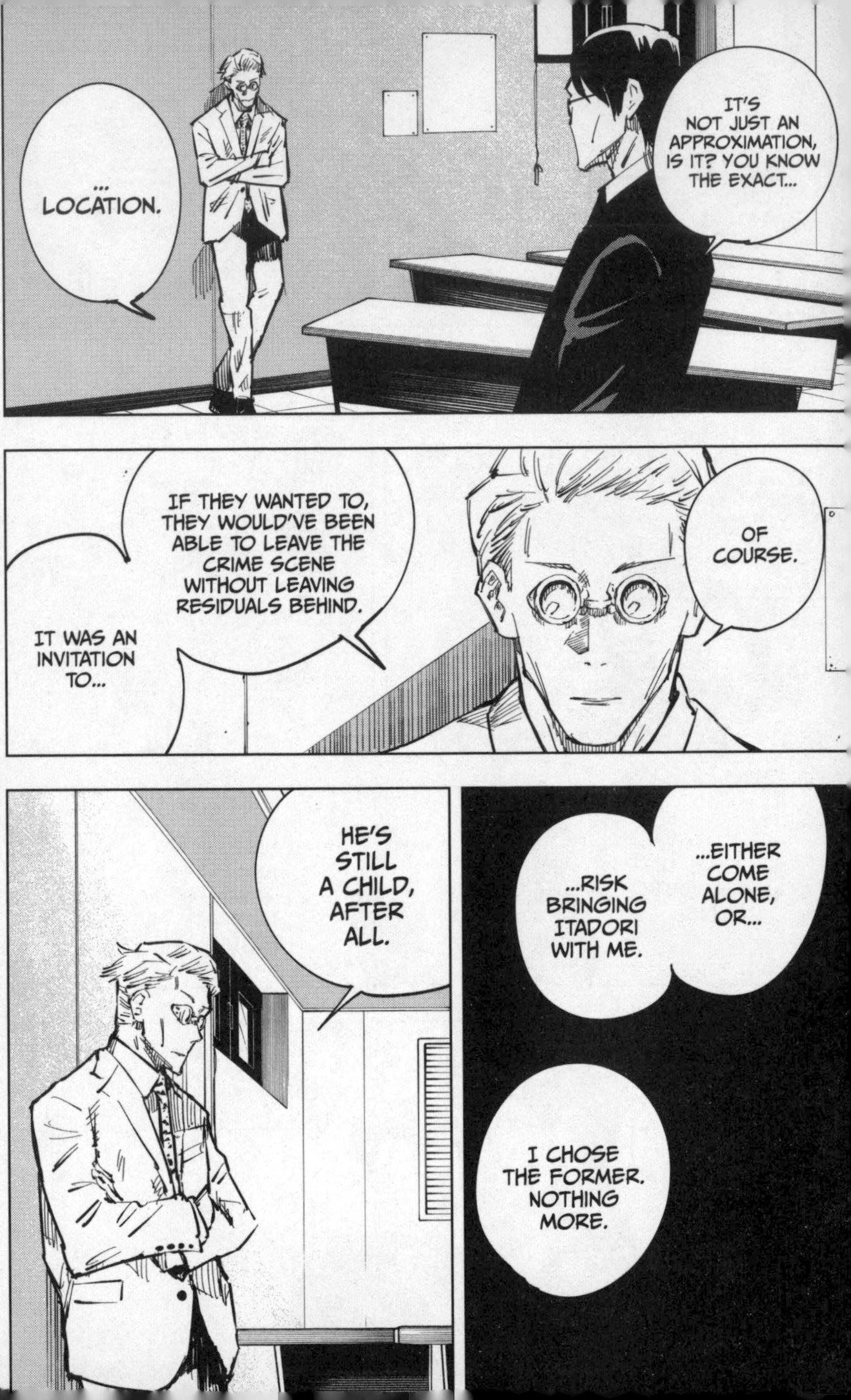
IT'S NOT JUST AN APPROXIMATION, IS IT? YOU KNOW THE EXACT...
... LOCATION.
OF COURSE.
IF THEY WANTED TO, THEY WOULD'VE BEEN ABLE TO LEAVE THE CRIME SCENE WITHOUT LEAVING RESIDUALS BEHIND.
IT WAS AN INVITATION TO...
...EITHER COME ALONE, OR...
...RISK BRINGING ITADORI WITH ME.
I CHOSE THE FORMER. NOTHING MORE.
HE'S STILL A CHILD, AFTER ALL.

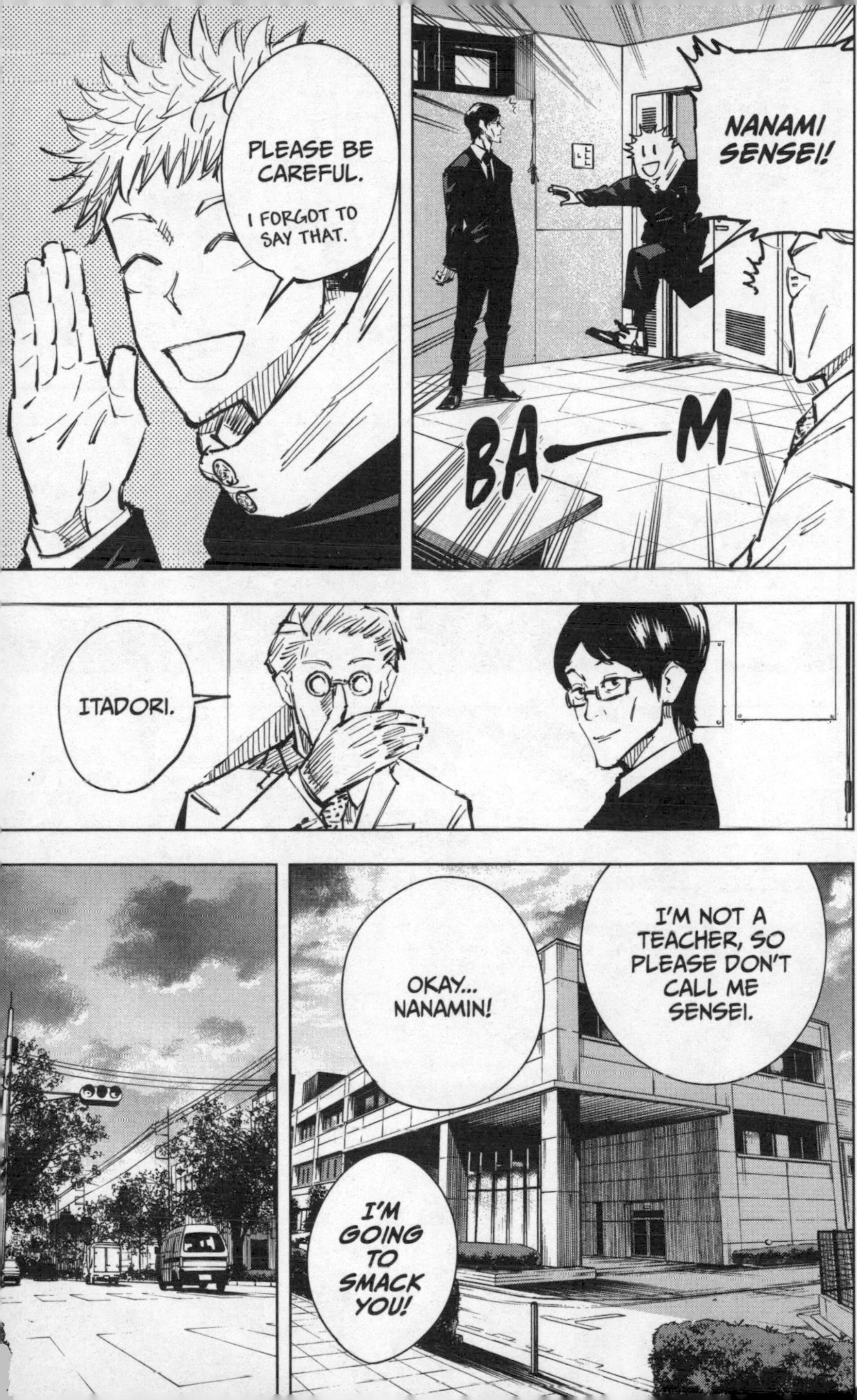
NANAMI SENSEI!
BA—M
PLEASE BE CAREFUL.
I FORGOT TO SAY THAT.
ITADORI.
I'M NOT A TEACHER, SO PLEASE DON'T CALL ME SENSEI.
OKAY... NANAMIN!
I'M GOING TO SMACK YOU!

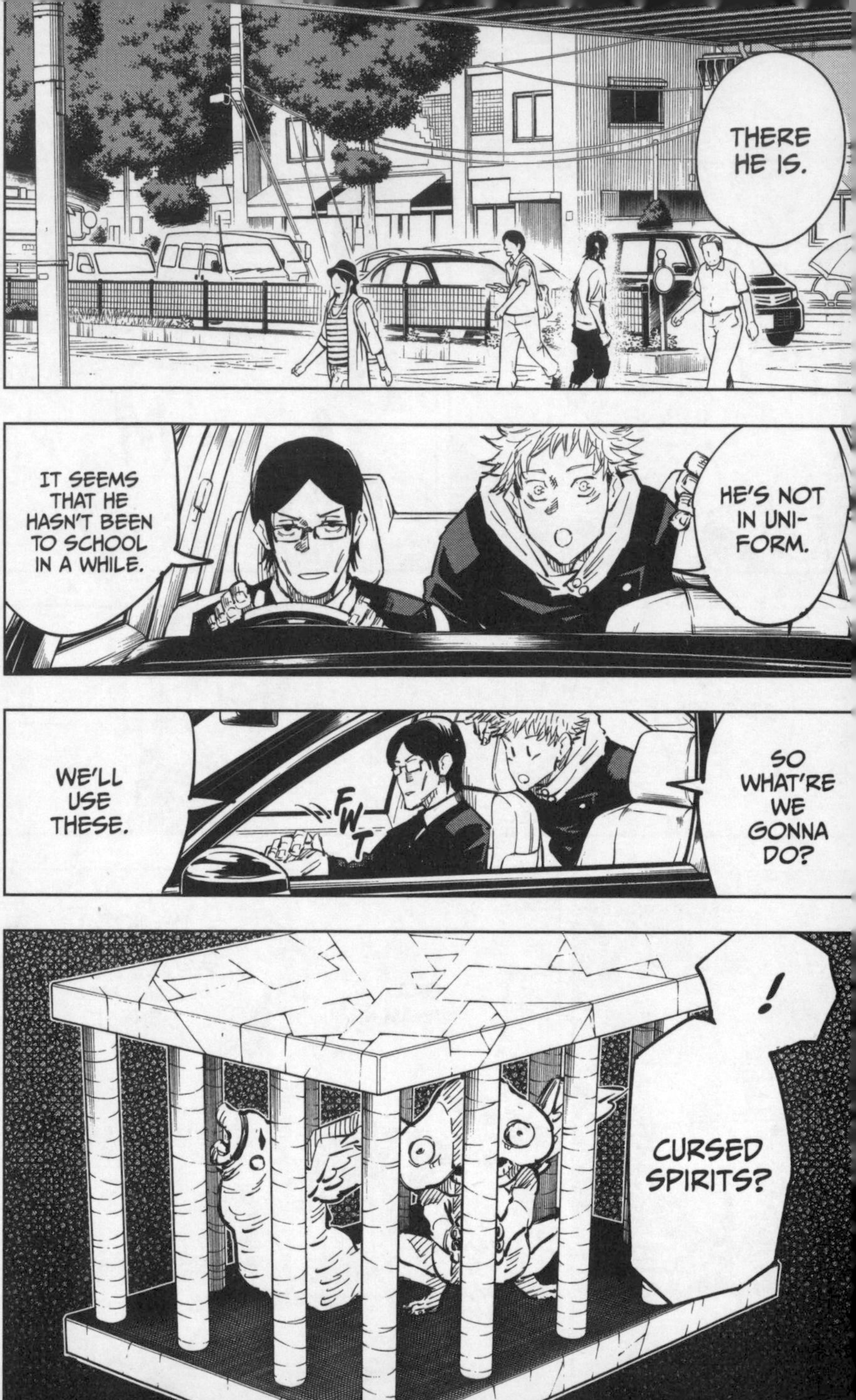
THERE HE IS.
HE'S NOT IN UNI-FORM.
IT SEEMS THAT HE HASN'T BEEN TO SCHOOL IN A WHILE.
SO WHAT'RE WE GONNA DO?
FWT
WE'LL USE THESE.
!
CURSED SPIRITS?

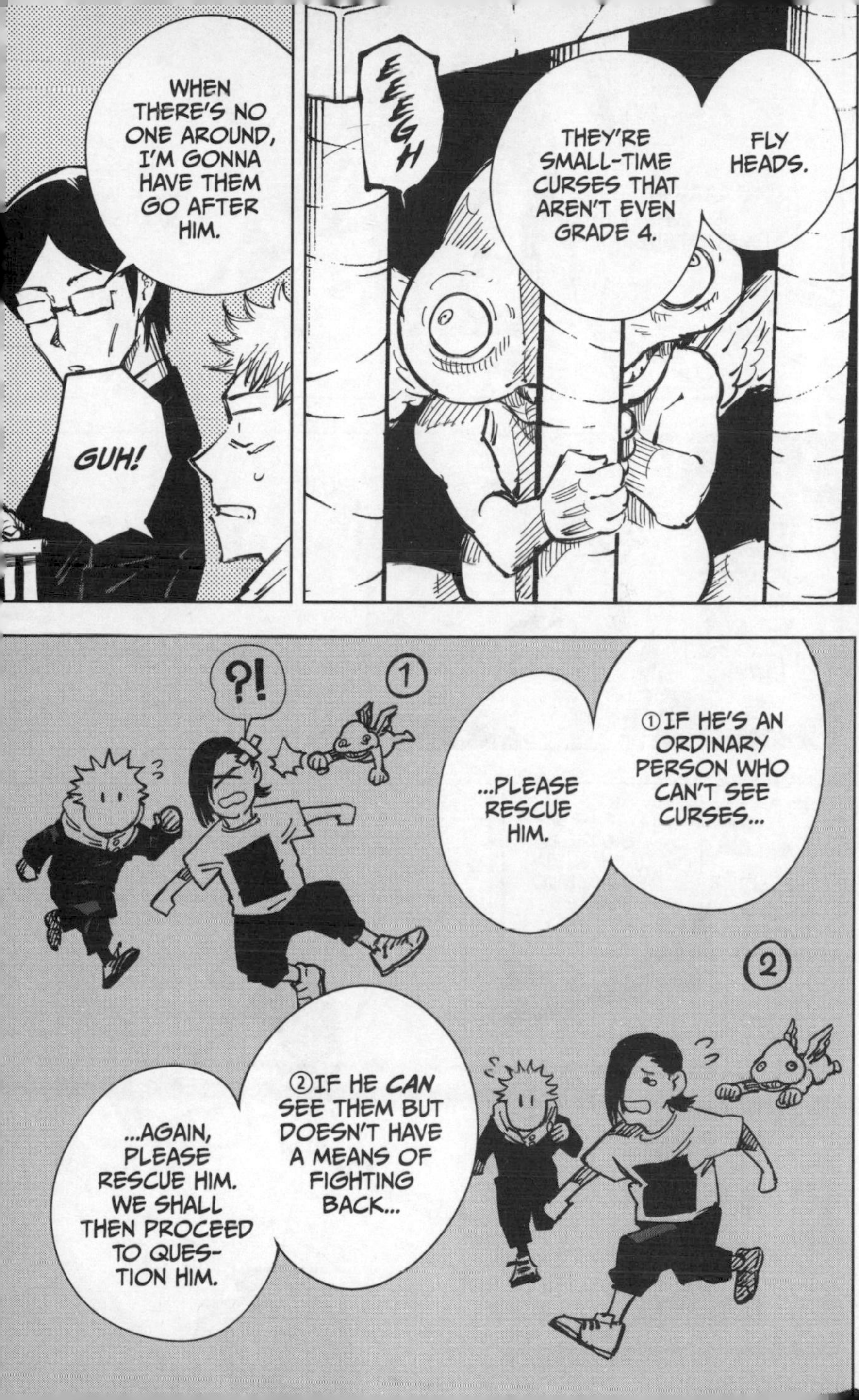
FLY HEADS.
THEY'RE SMALL-TIME CURSES THAT AREN'T EVEN GRADE 4.
EEEGH
WHEN THERE'S NO ONE AROUND, I'M GONNA HAVE THEM GO AFTER HIM.
GUH!
①IF HE'S AN ORDINARY PERSON WHO CAN'T SEE CURSES...
...PLEASE RESCUE HIM.
①
?!
②
②IF HE *CAN* SEE THEM BUT DOESN'T HAVE A MEANS OF FIGHTING BACK...
...AGAIN, PLEASE RESCUE HIM. WE SHALL THEN PROCEED TO QUES-TION HIM.

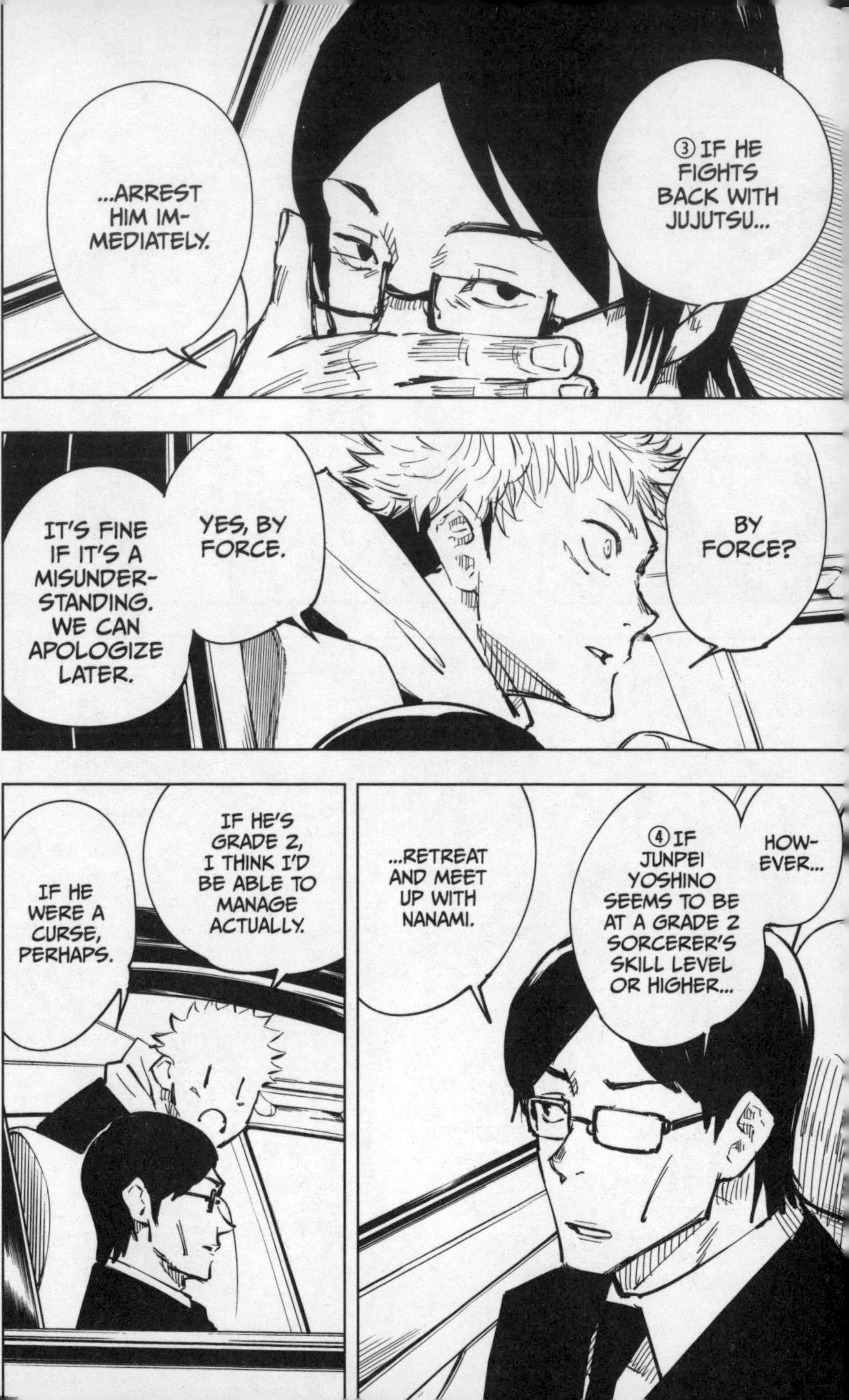
③ IF HE FIGHTS BACK WITH JUJUTSU...
...ARREST HIM IM-MEDIATELY.
BY FORCE?
YES, BY FORCE.
IT'S FINE IF IT'S A MISUNDER-STANDING. WE CAN APOLOGIZE LATER.
HOW-EVER...
④ IF JUNPEI YOSHINO SEEMS TO BE AT A GRADE 2 SORCERER'S SKILL LEVEL OR HIGHER...
...RETREAT AND MEET UP WITH NANAMI.
IF HE'S GRADE 2, I THINK I'D BE ABLE TO MANAGE ACTUALLY.
IF HE WERE A CURSE, PERHAPS.

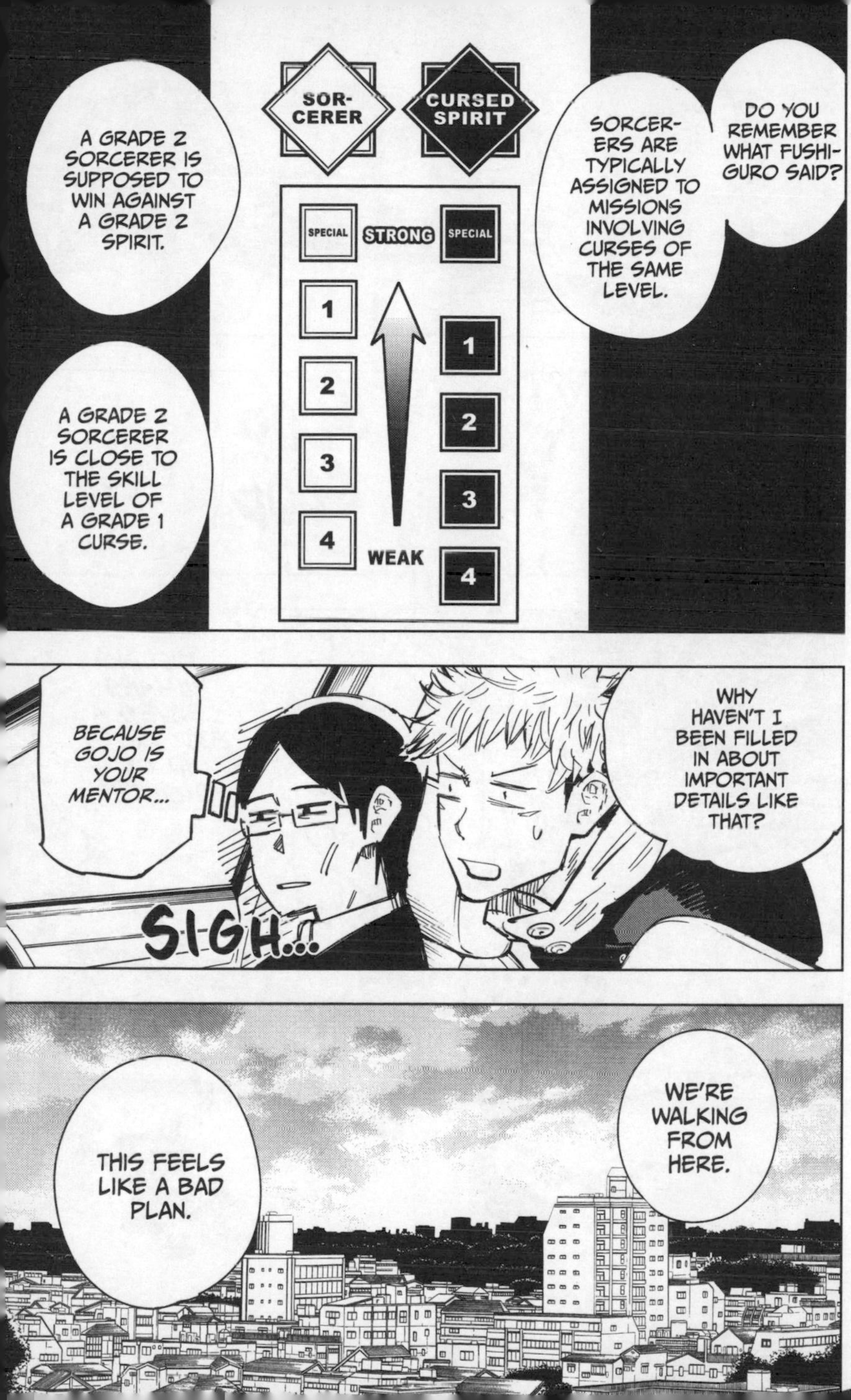
DO YOU REMEMBER WHAT FUSHIGURO SAID?
SORCERERS ARE TYPICALLY ASSIGNED TO MISSIONS INVOLVING CURSES OF THE SAME LEVEL.
SORCERER
CURSED SPIRIT
SPECIAL
STRONG
SPECIAL
1
1
2
2
3
3
4
WEAK
4
A GRADE 2 SORCERER IS SUPPOSED TO WIN AGAINST A GRADE 2 SPIRIT.
A GRADE 2 SORCERER IS CLOSE TO THE SKILL LEVEL OF A GRADE 1 CURSE.
WHY HAVEN'T I BEEN FILLED IN ABOUT IMPORTANT DETAILS LIKE THAT?
BECAUSE GOJO IS YOUR MENTOR...
SIGH...
WE'RE WALKING FROM HERE.
THIS FEELS LIKE A BAD PLAN.

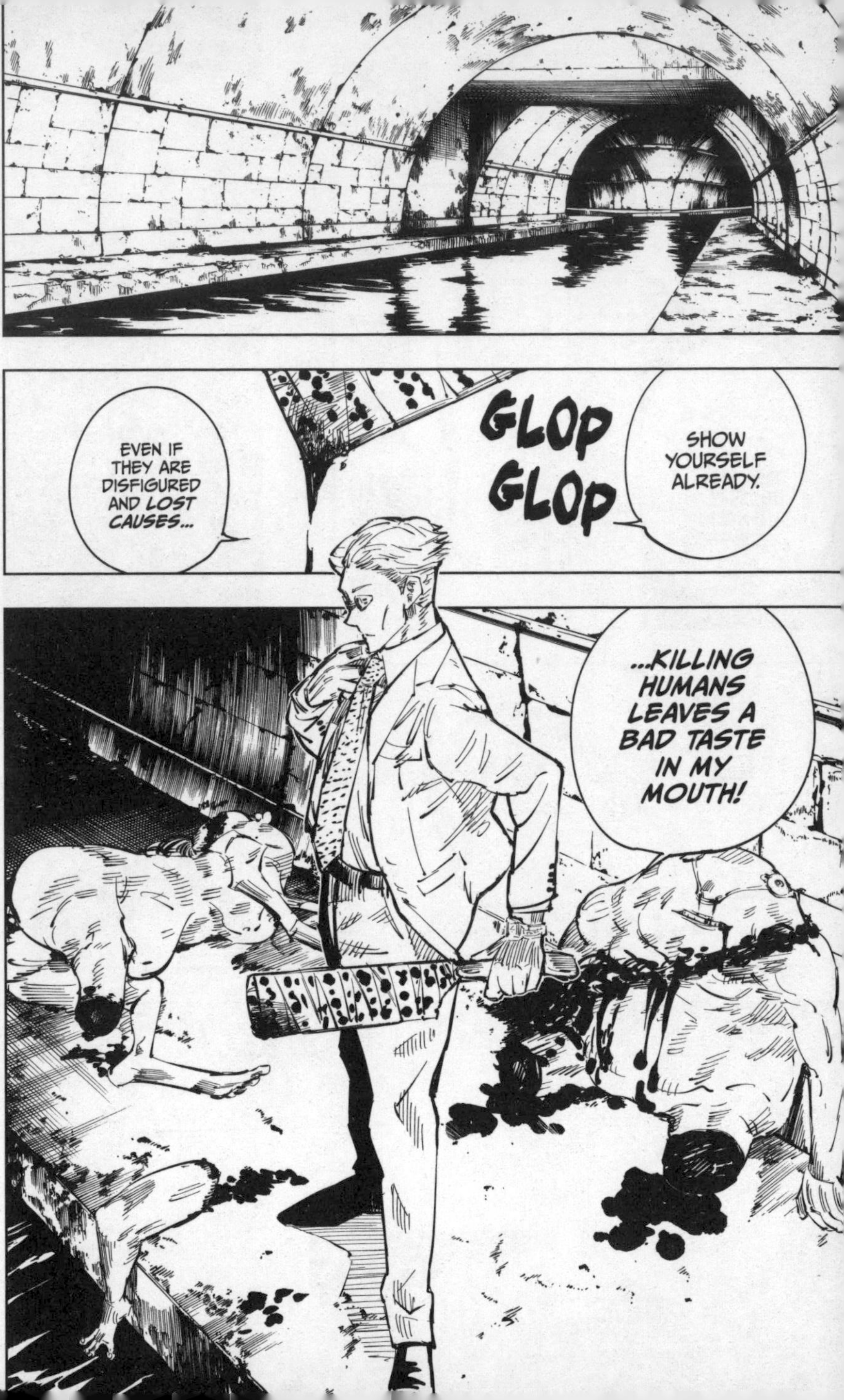
SHOW YOURSELF ALREADY.
GLOP GLOP
EVEN IF THEY ARE DISFIGURED AND LOST CAUSES...
...KILLING HUMANS LEAVES A BAD TASTE IN MY MOUTH!

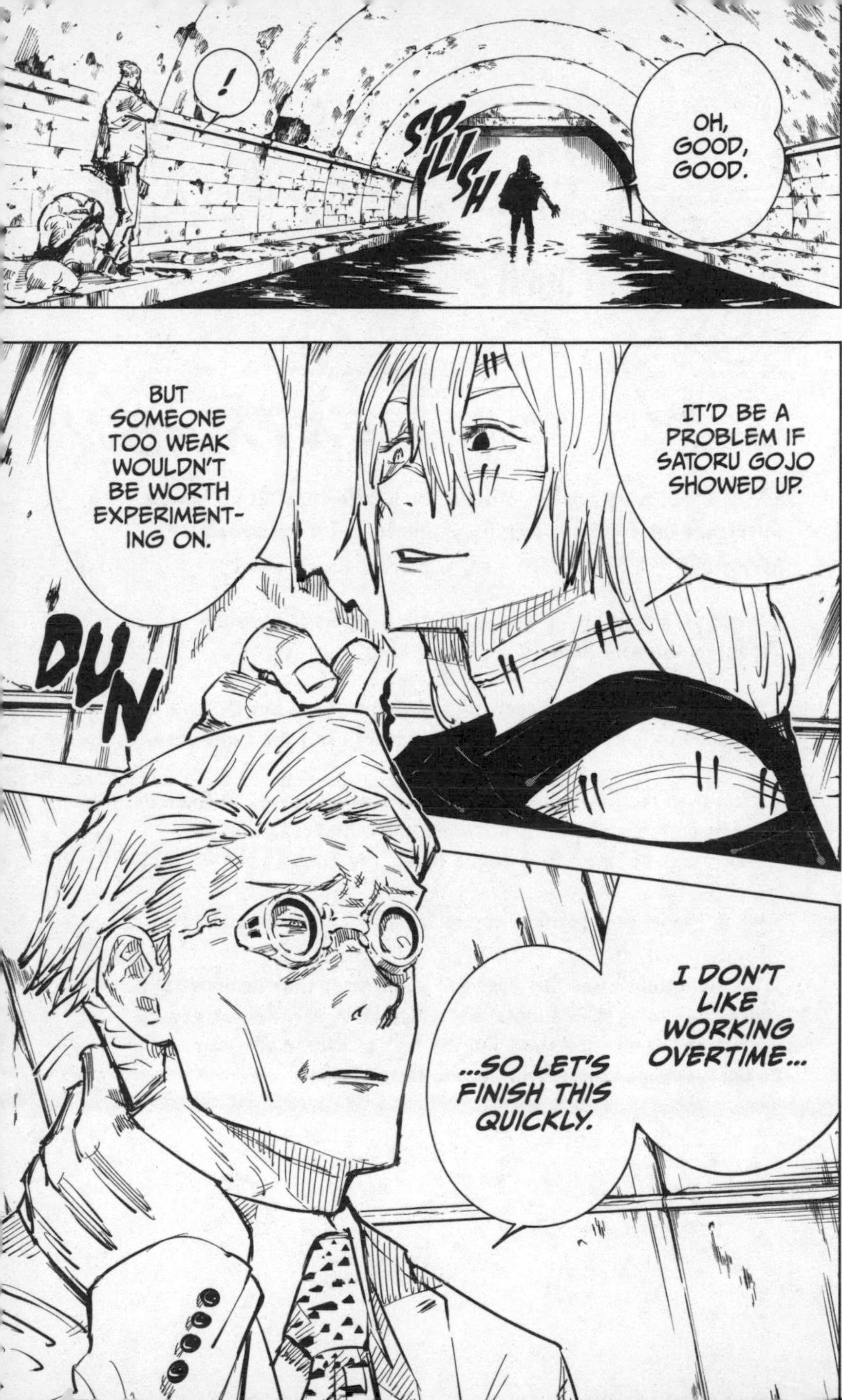
OH, GOOD, GOOD.
SPLISH
!
IT'D BE A PROBLEM IF SATORU GOJO SHOWED UP.
BUT SOMEONE TOO WEAK WOULDN'T BE WORTH EXPERIMENTING ON.
DUN
I DON'T LIKE WORKING OVERTIME...
...SO LET'S FINISH THIS QUICKLY.

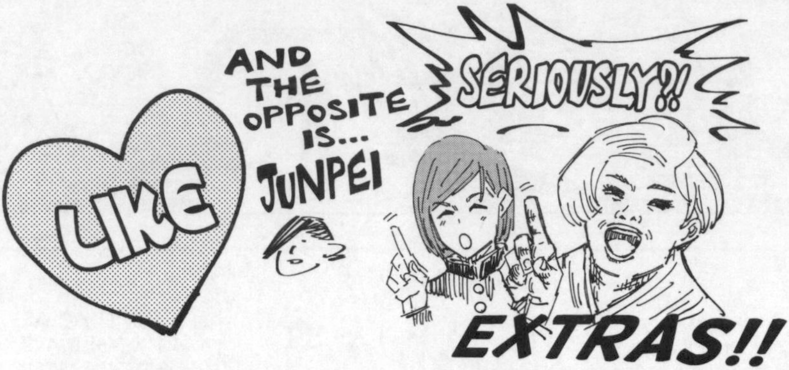
LIKE
AND THE OPPOSITE IS...
JUNPEI
SERIOUSLY?!
EXTRAS!!

• "The opposite of love is not hate, it's indifference." It's a phrase uttered by the super-moody Junpei that's had me stressed for several months now.

• Some people, including my editor, claim it wasn't someone Japanese who said that.

• Somebody who wasn't Japanese stated that there are multiple definitions of love, so "indifference" is most likely the right word.

• I feel like "love" is a word Japanese people don't use all the time, so perhaps that's why the phrase became widespread with the casual usage of "like." And maybe that's why Junpei used it, right?

• What Junpei says perhaps comes from this misunderstanding.

• The thing that I was the most sad about wasn't my inability to convey this concept in a more understandable way. Rather, several friends and family now think I'm the type of person who can't even do basic Google research to get the facts straight.

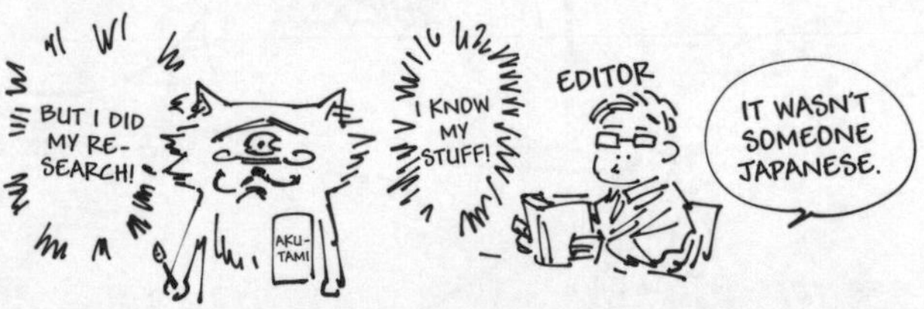
IT WASN'T SOMEONE JAPANESE.
EDITOR
I KNOW MY STUFF!
BUT I DID MY RE-SEARCH!
AKU-TAMI

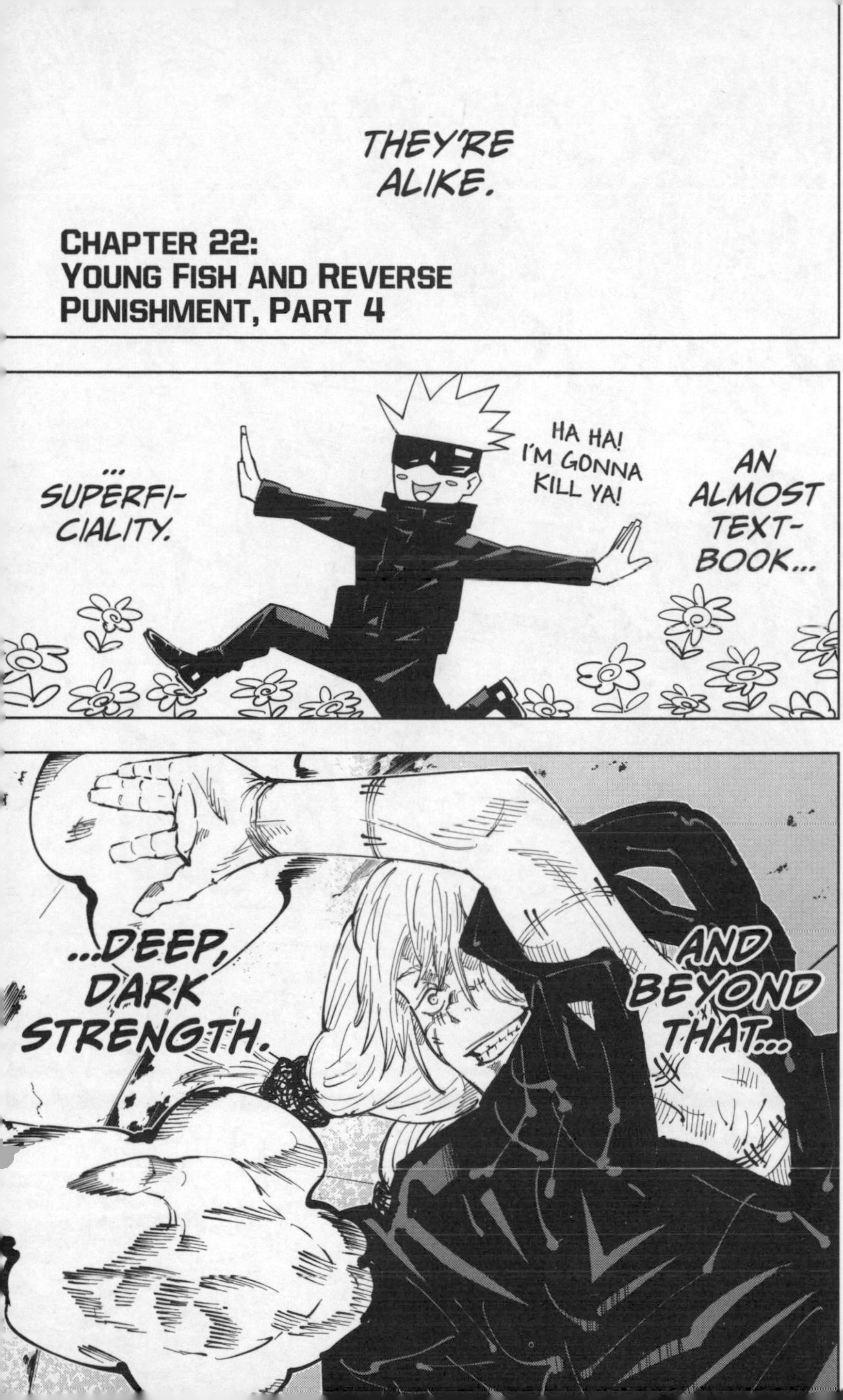
THEY'RE ALIKE.
CHAPTER 22: YOUNG FISH AND REVERSE PUNISHMENT, PART 4
AN ALMOST TEXTBOOK...
HA HA! I'M GONNA KILL YA!
...SUPERFICIALITY.
AND BEYOND THAT...
...DEEP, DARK STRENGTH.

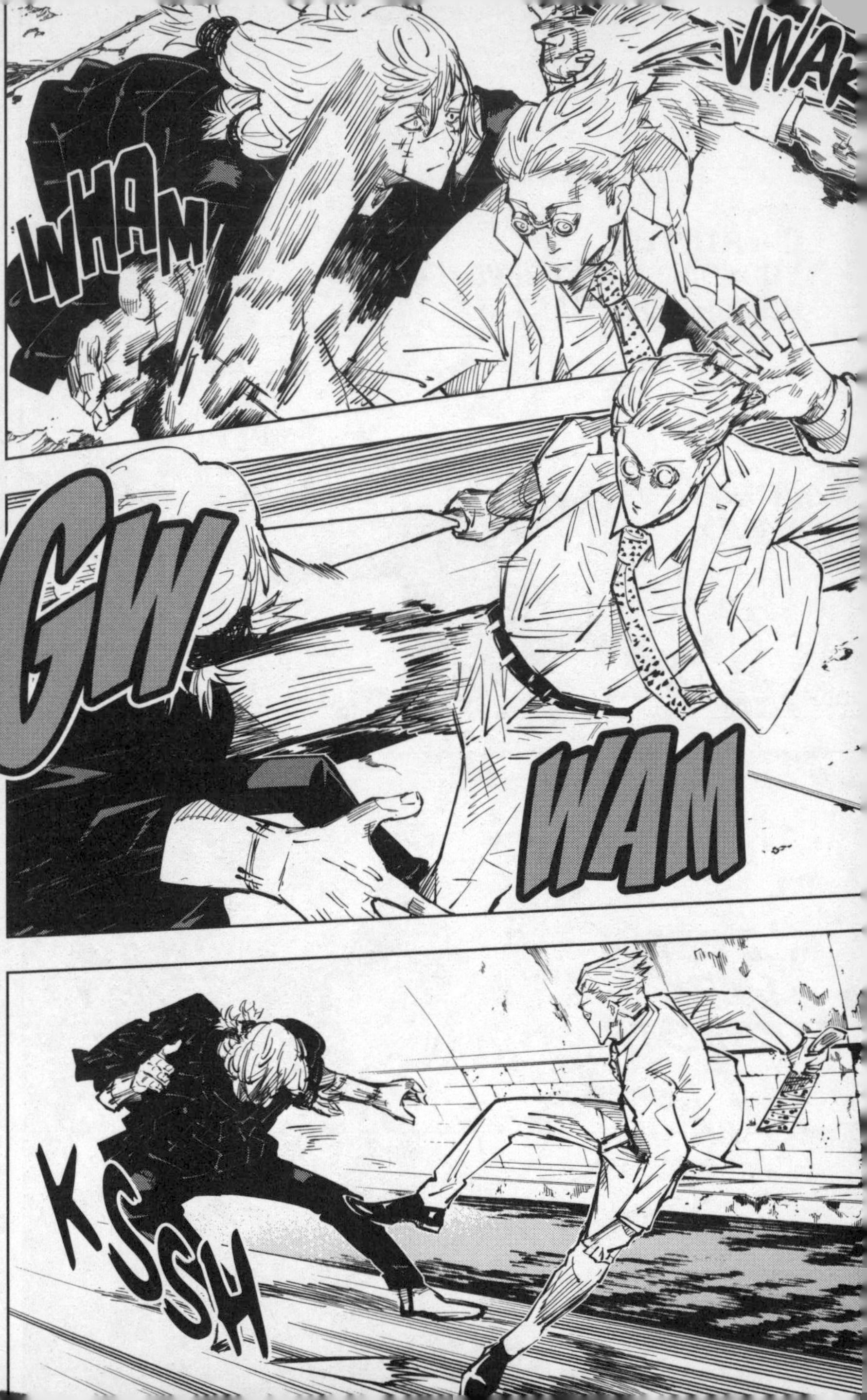
WHAM
GW
WAM
KSSH

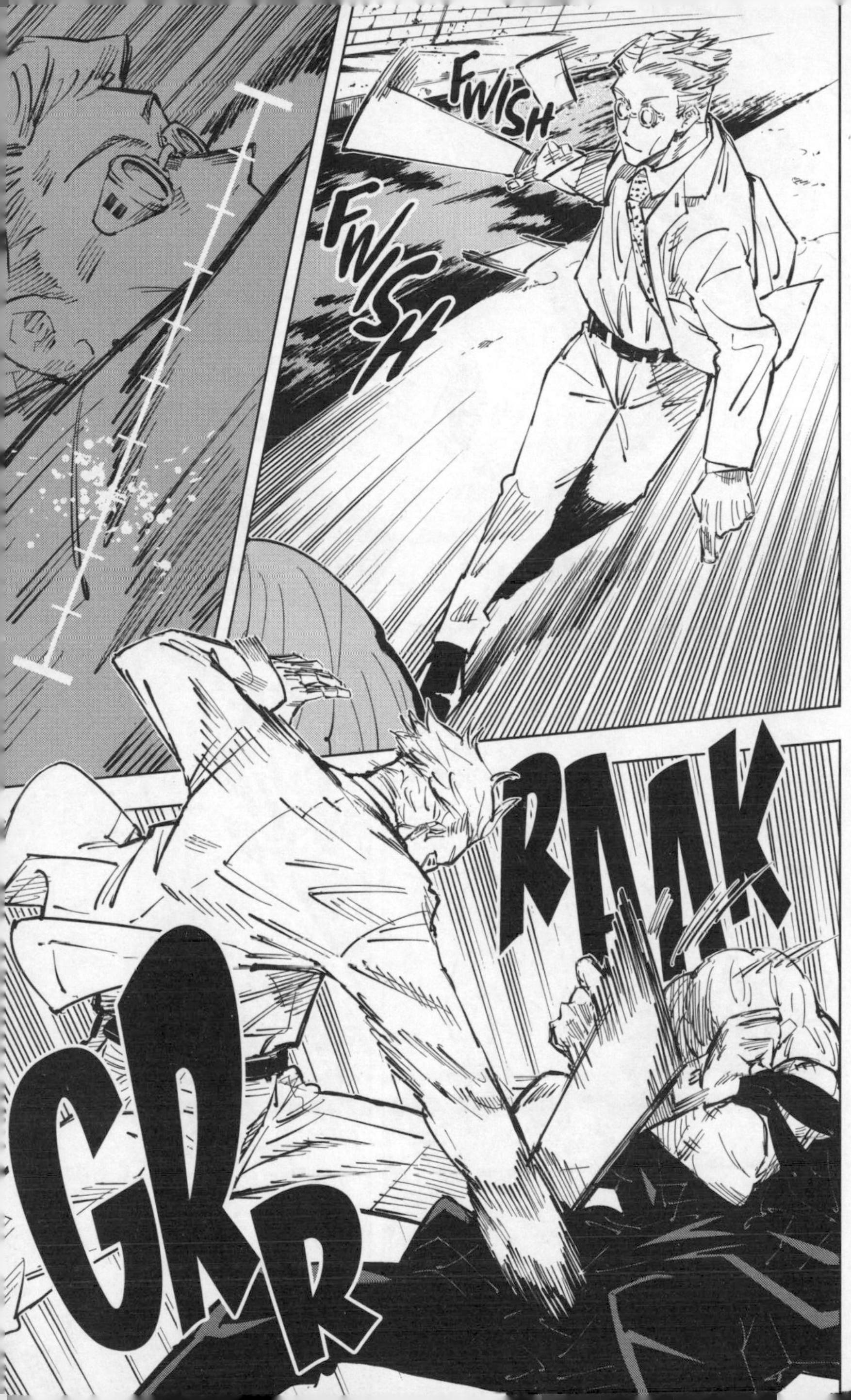
FWISH
FWISH
RAAK
GRR

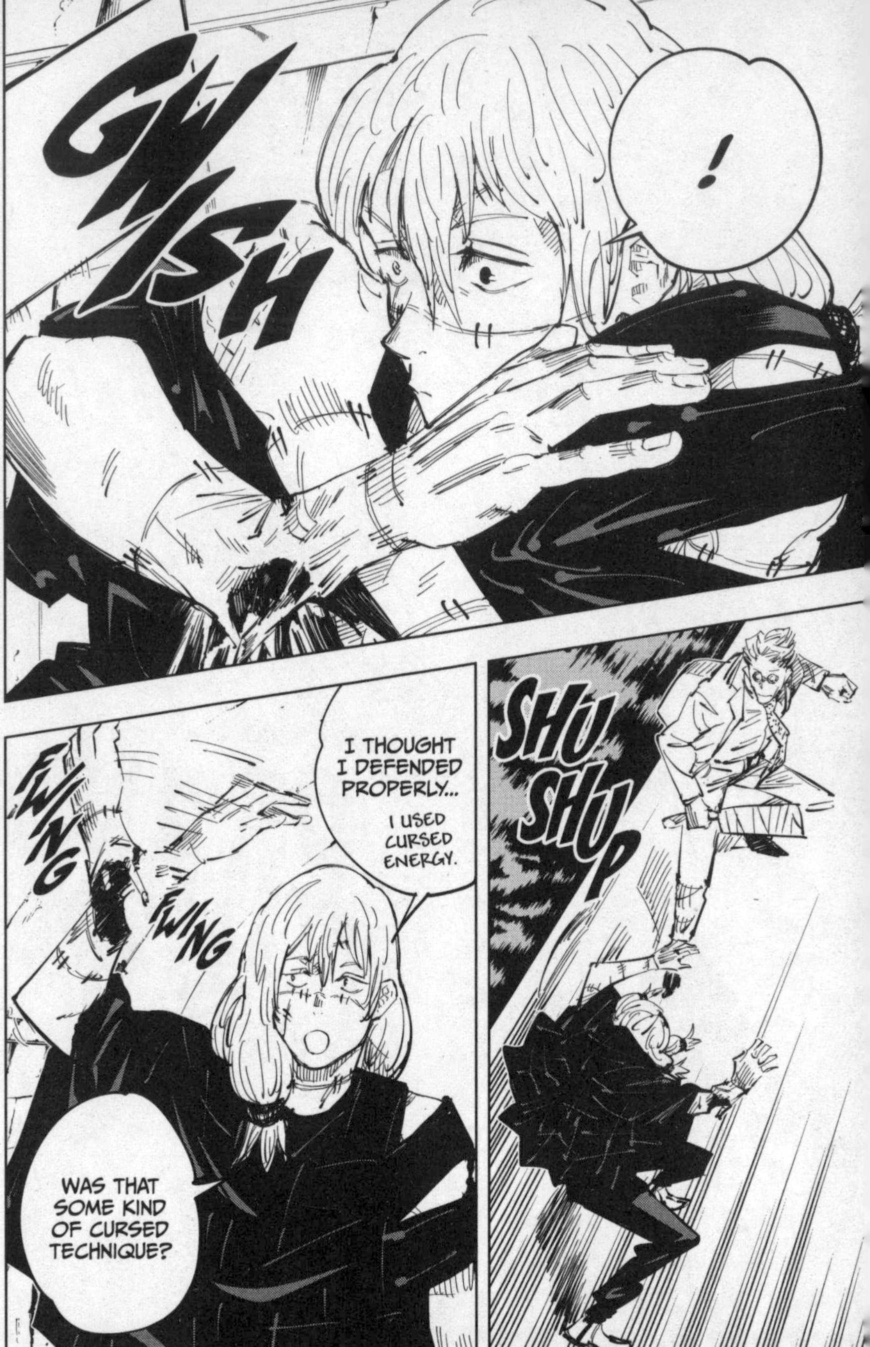
!
GWISH
SHU SHUP
I THOUGHT I DEFENDED PROPERLY...
I USED CURSED ENERGY.
FWING FWING
WAS THAT SOME KIND OF CURSED TECHNIQUE?

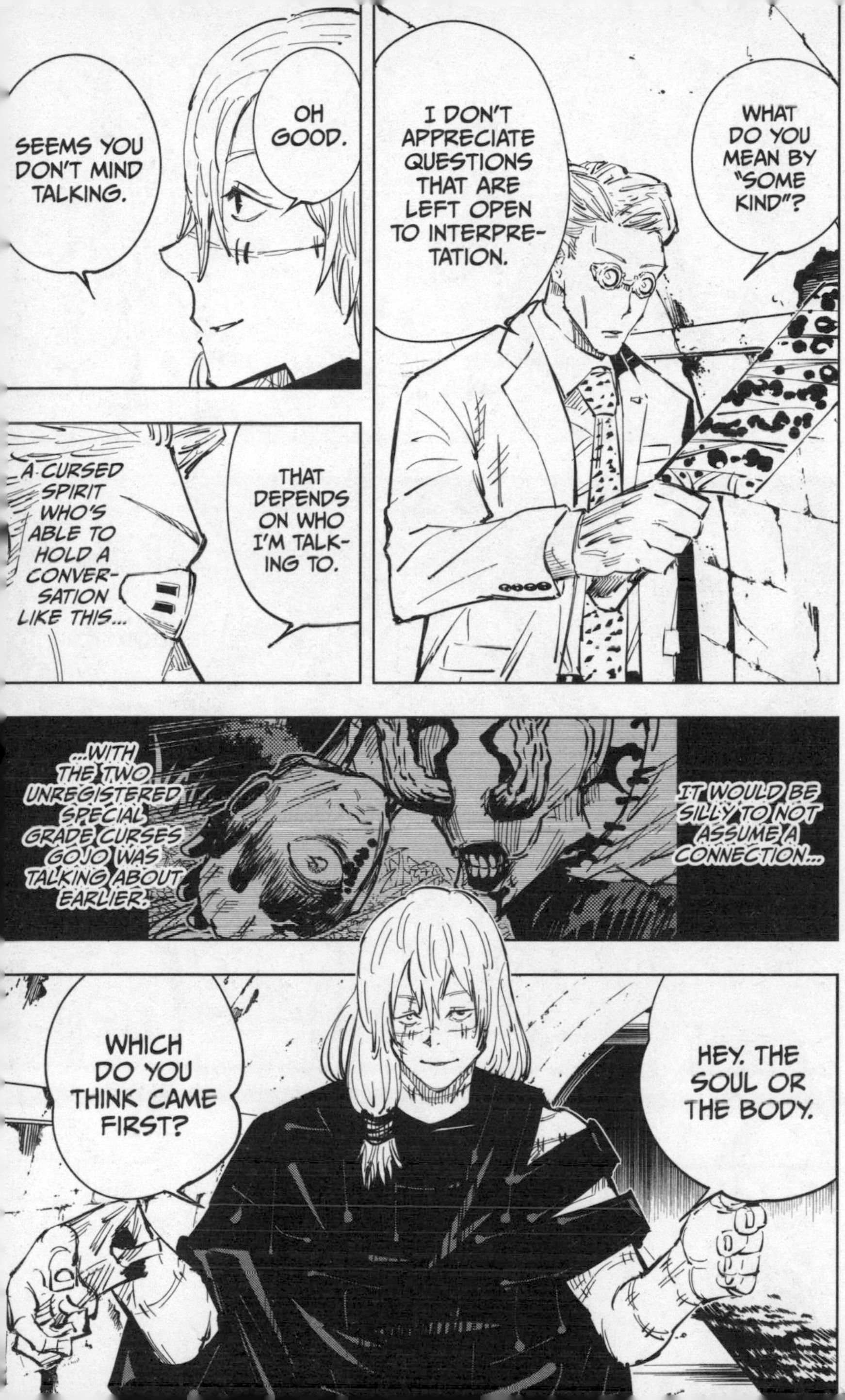
WHAT DO YOU MEAN BY "SOME KIND"?
I DON'T APPRECIATE QUESTIONS THAT ARE LEFT OPEN TO INTERPRETATION.
OH GOOD.
SEEMS YOU DON'T MIND TALKING.
THAT DEPENDS ON WHO I'M TALKING TO.
A CURSED SPIRIT WHO'S ABLE TO HOLD A CONVERSATION LIKE THIS...
IT WOULD BE SILLY TO NOT ASSUME A CONNECTION...
...WITH THE TWO UNREGISTERED SPECIAL GRADE CURSES GOJO WAS TALKING ABOUT EARLIER.
HEY. THE SOUL OR THE BODY.
WHICH DO YOU THINK CAME FIRST?

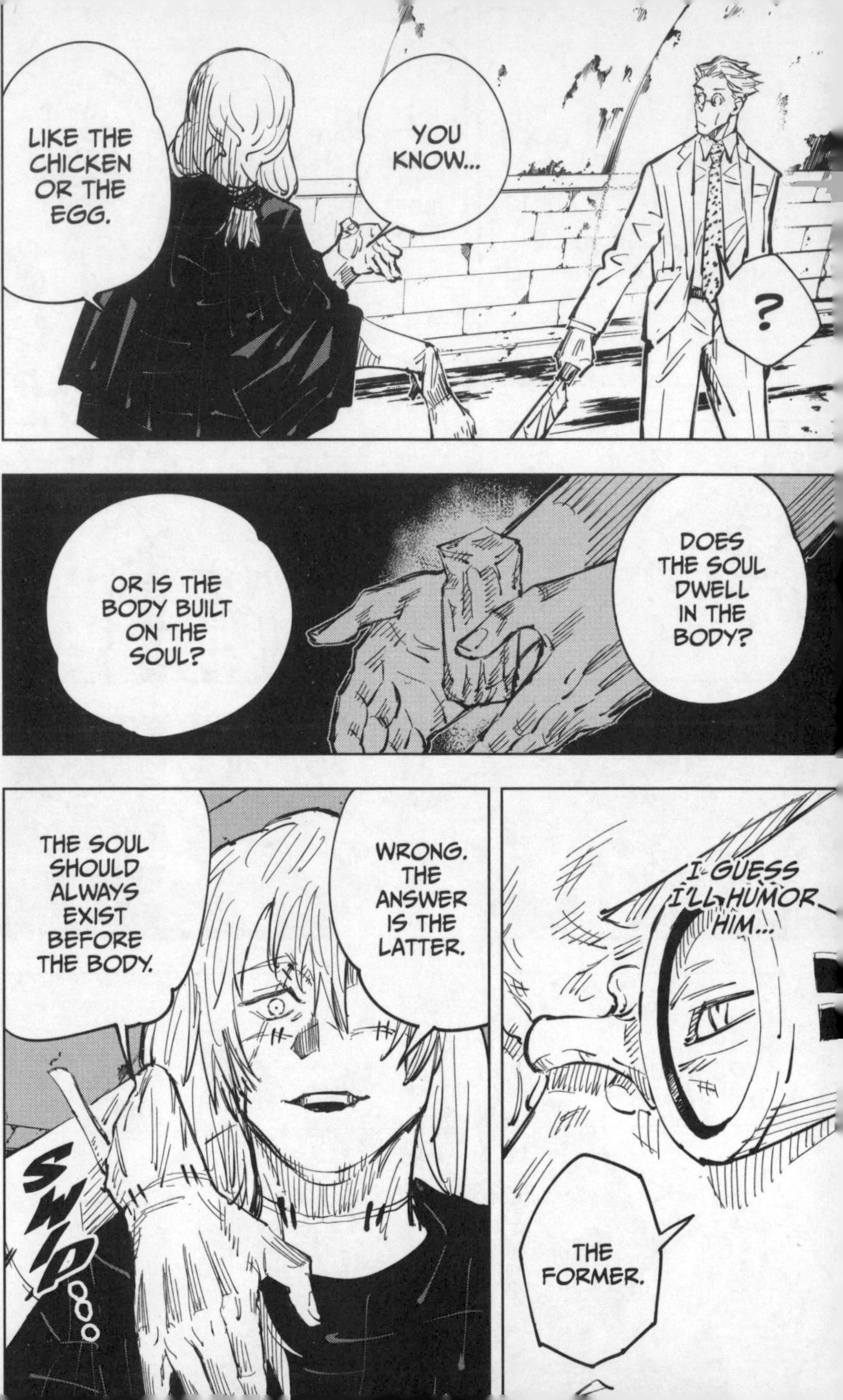
YOU KNOW...
LIKE THE CHICKEN OR THE EGG.
?
DOES THE SOUL DWELL IN THE BODY?
OR IS THE BODY BUILT ON THE SOUL?
I GUESS I'LL HUMOR HIM...
THE FORMER.
WRONG. THE ANSWER IS THE LATTER.
THE SOUL SHOULD ALWAYS EXIST BEFORE THE BODY.
SWIP

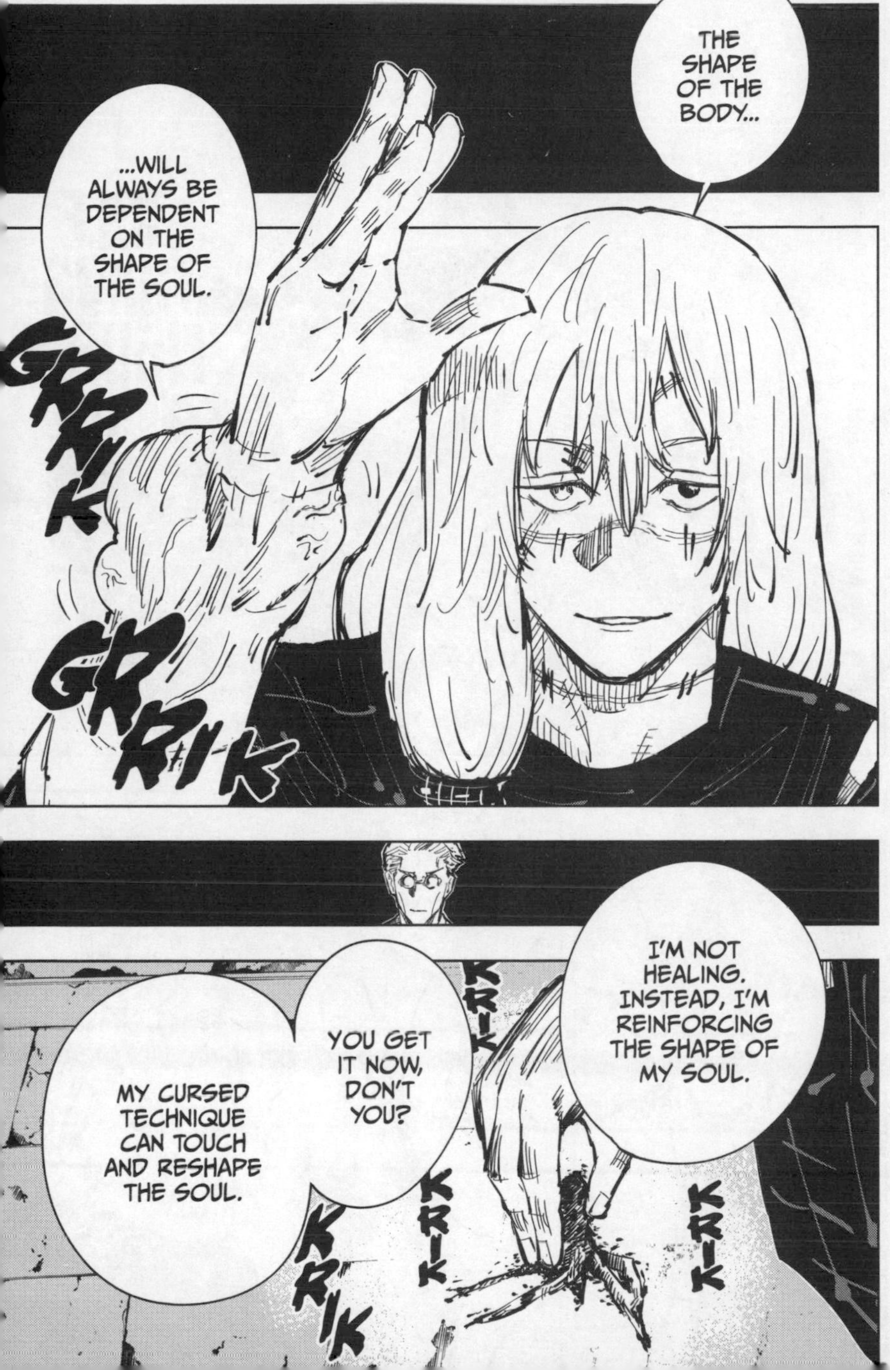
THE SHAPE OF THE BODY...
...WILL ALWAYS BE DEPENDENT ON THE SHAPE OF THE SOUL.
GRRIK
GRRIK
I'M NOT HEALING. INSTEAD, I'M REINFORCING THE SHAPE OF MY SOUL.
KRIK
KRIK
YOU GET IT NOW, DON'T YOU?
KRIK
MY CURSED TECHNIQUE CAN TOUCH AND RESHAPE THE SOUL.
KRIK
KRIK

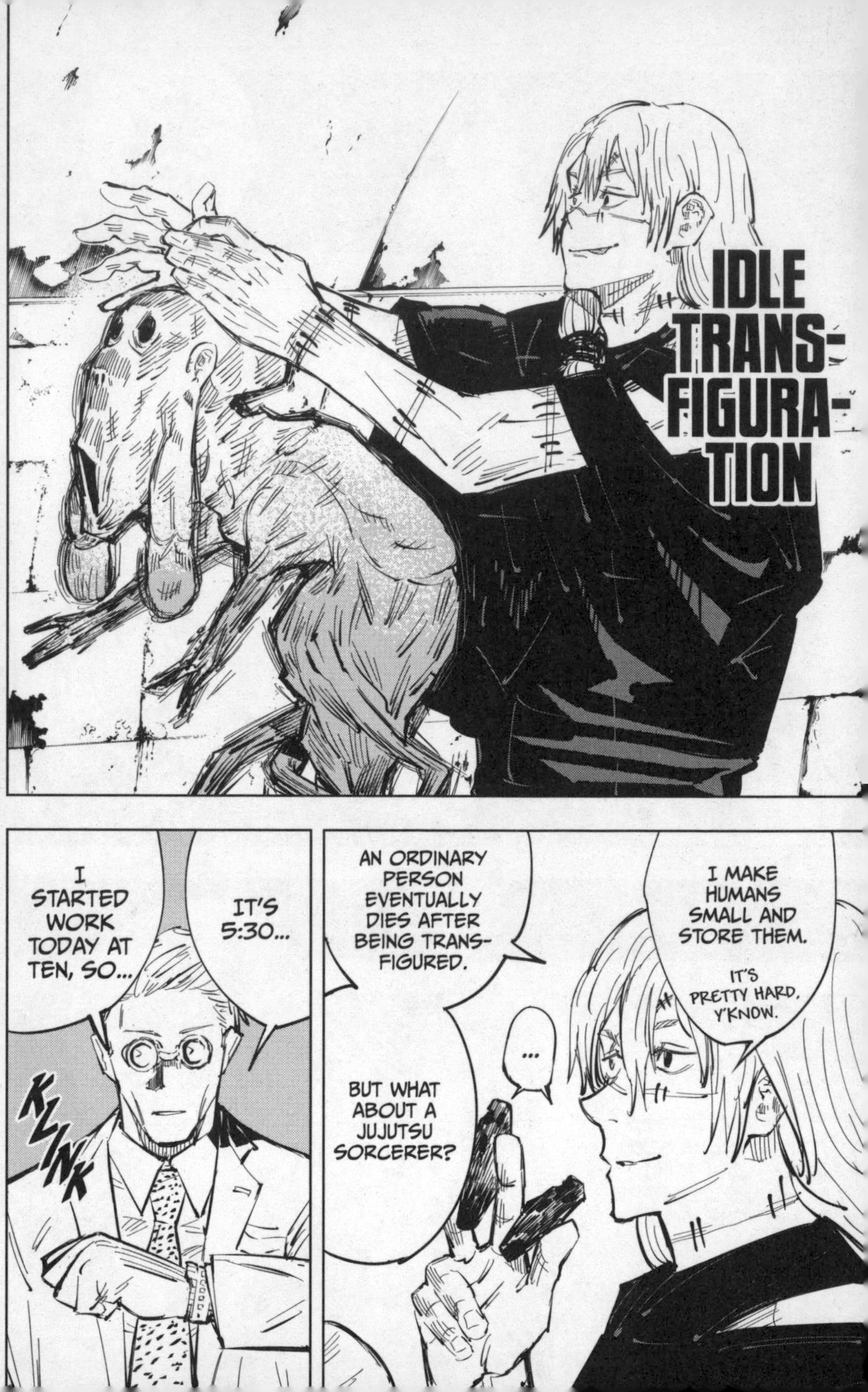
IDLE TRANSFIGURATION
I MAKE HUMANS SMALL AND STORE THEM.
IT'S PRETTY HARD, Y'KNOW.
AN ORDINARY PERSON EVENTUALLY DIES AFTER BEING TRANSFIGURED.
...
BUT WHAT ABOUT A JUJUTSU SORCERER?
IT'S 5:30...
I STARTED WORK TODAY AT TEN, SO...
KLINK

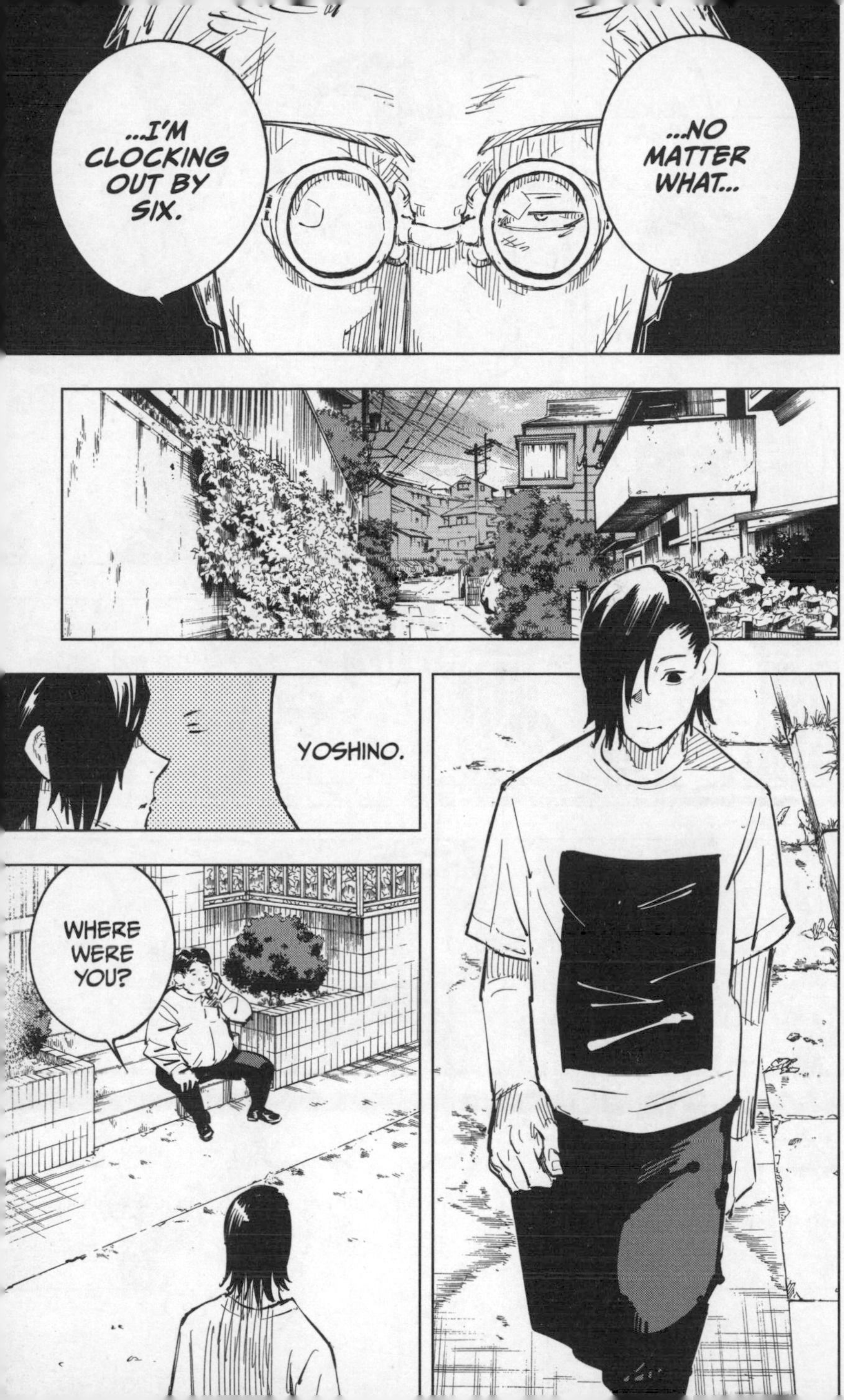
...NO MATTER WHAT...
...I'M CLOCKING OUT BY SIX.
YOSHINO.
WHERE WERE YOU?

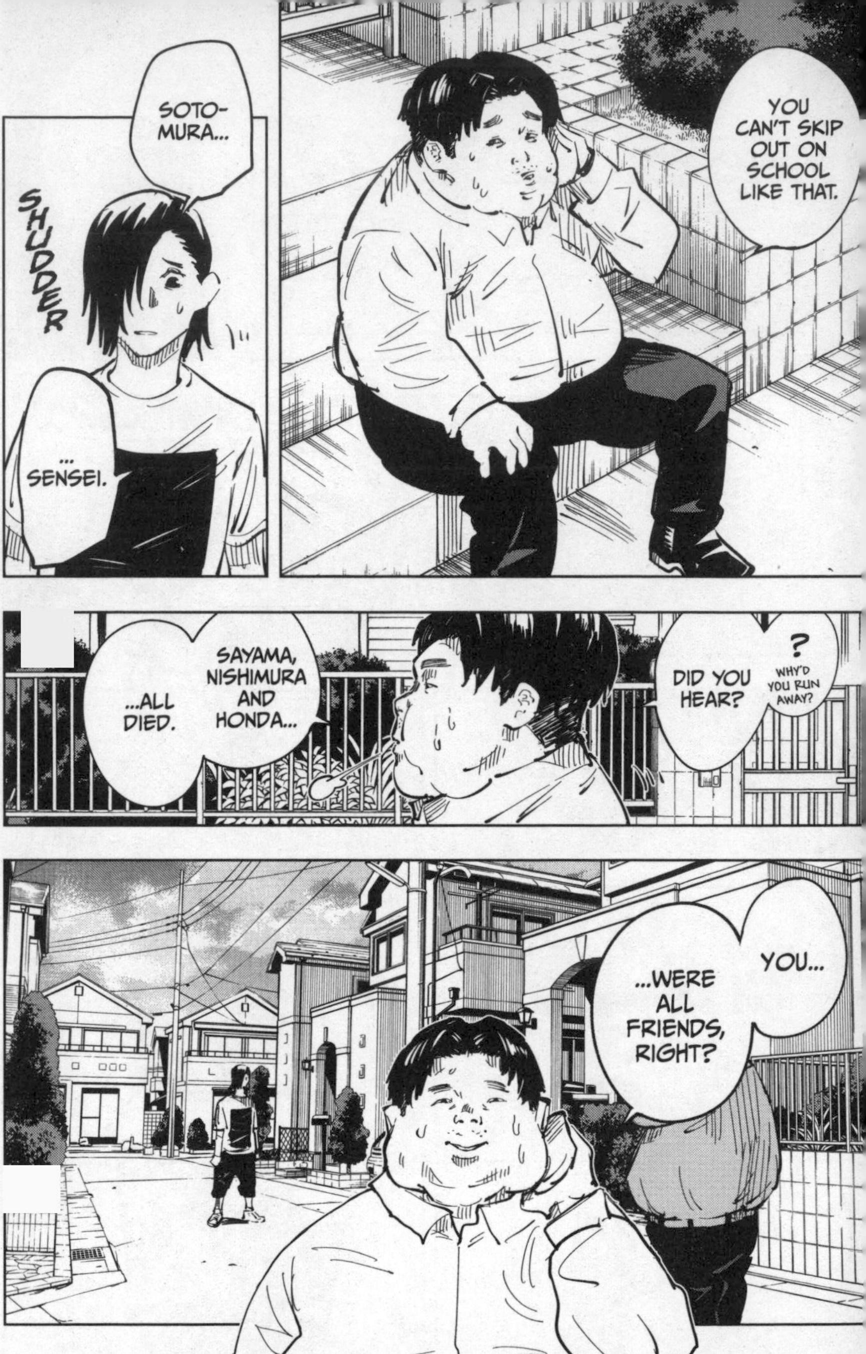
YOU CAN'T SKIP OUT ON SCHOOL LIKE THAT.
SOTO-MURA...
SHUDDER
...SENSEI.
?
WHY'D YOU RUN AWAY?
DID YOU HEAR?
SAYAMA, NISHIMURA AND HONDA...
...ALL DIED.
YOU...
...WERE ALL FRIENDS, RIGHT?

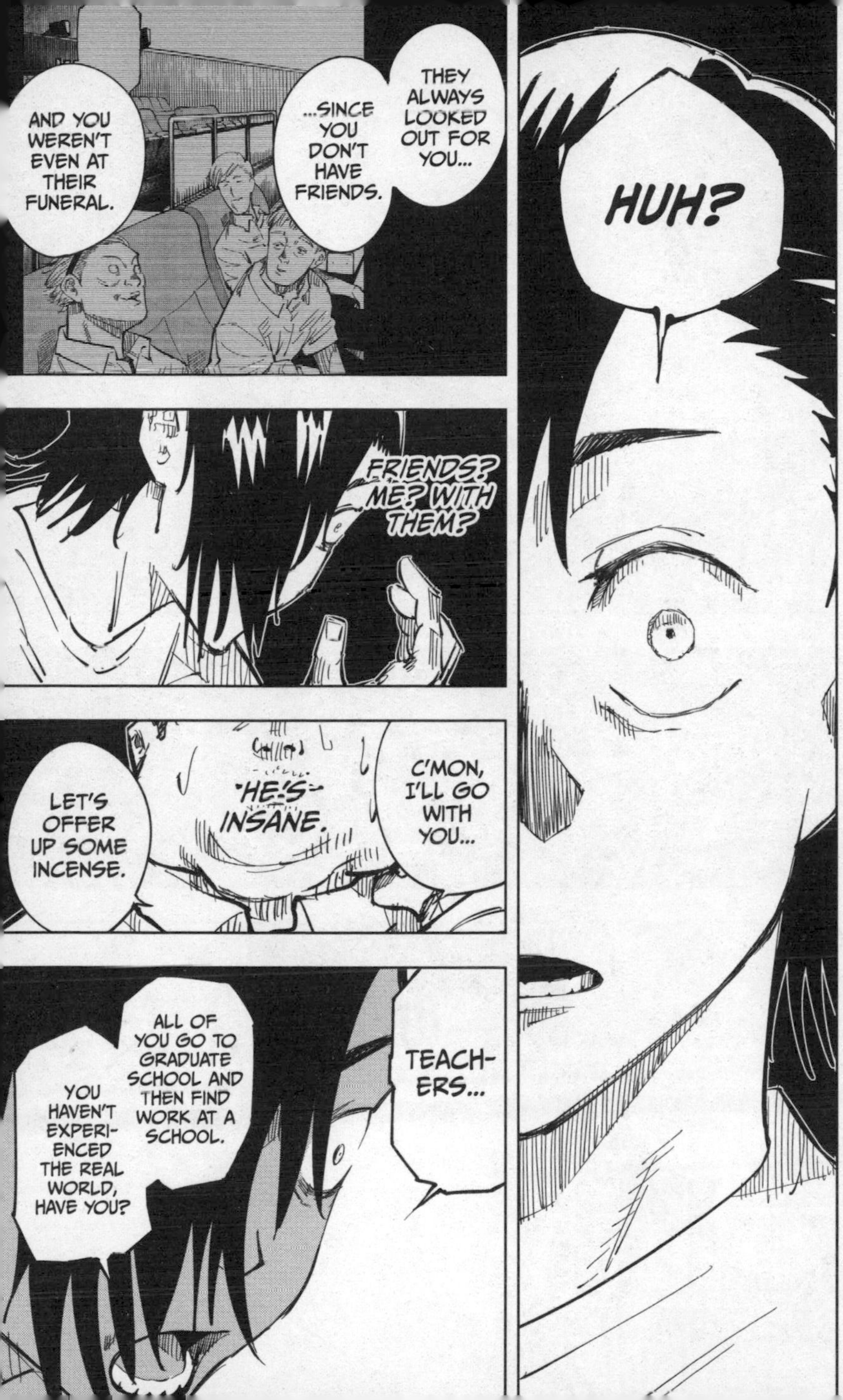
HUH?
THEY ALWAYS LOOKED OUT FOR YOU...
...SINCE YOU DON'T HAVE FRIENDS.
AND YOU WEREN'T EVEN AT THEIR FUNERAL.
FRIENDS? ME? WITH THEM?
C'MON, I'LL GO WITH YOU...
HE'S INSANE.
LET'S OFFER UP SOME INCENSE.
TEACHERS...
ALL OF YOU GO TO GRADUATE SCHOOL AND THEN FIND WORK AT A SCHOOL.
YOU HAVEN'T EXPERIENCED THE REAL WORLD, HAVE YOU?

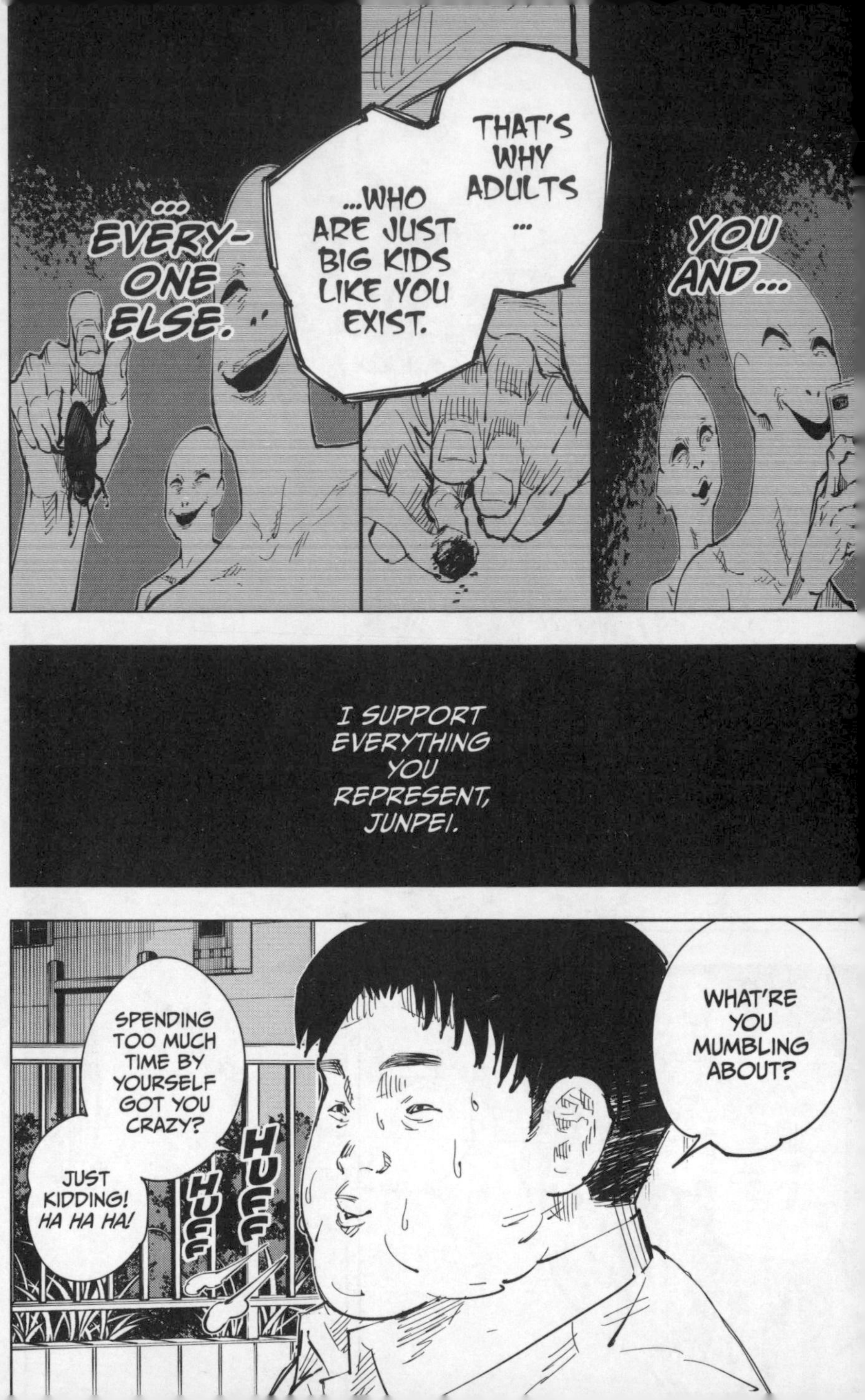
YOU AND...
THAT'S WHY ADULTS ...
...WHO ARE JUST BIG KIDS LIKE YOU EXIST.
...EVERY-ONE ELSE.
I SUPPORT EVERYTHING YOU REPRESENT, JUNPEI.
WHAT'RE YOU MUMBLING ABOUT?
SPENDING TOO MUCH TIME BY YOURSELF GOT YOU CRAZY?
HUFF
HUFF
JUST KIDDING! HA HA HA!

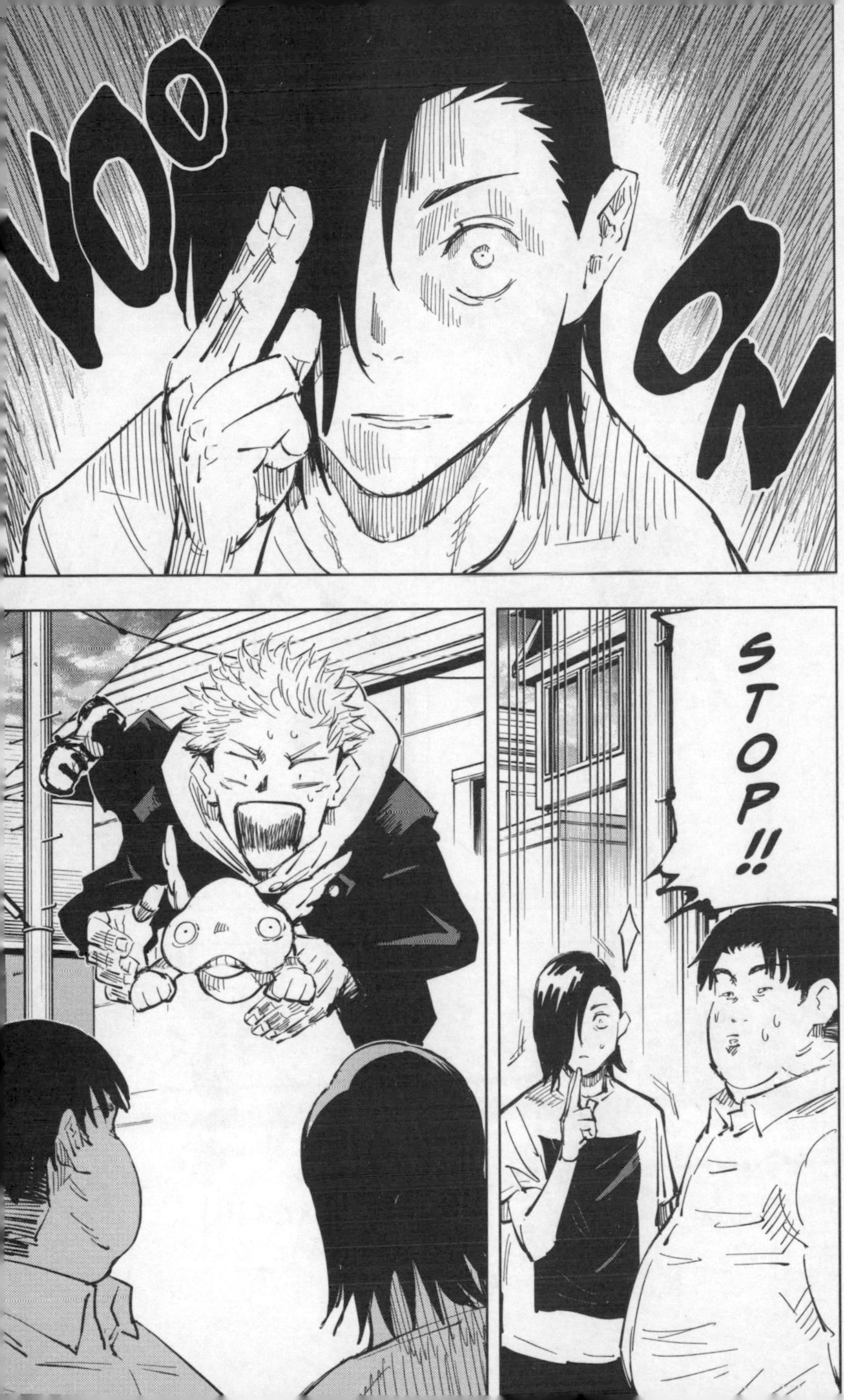
VOOOOM
STOP!!

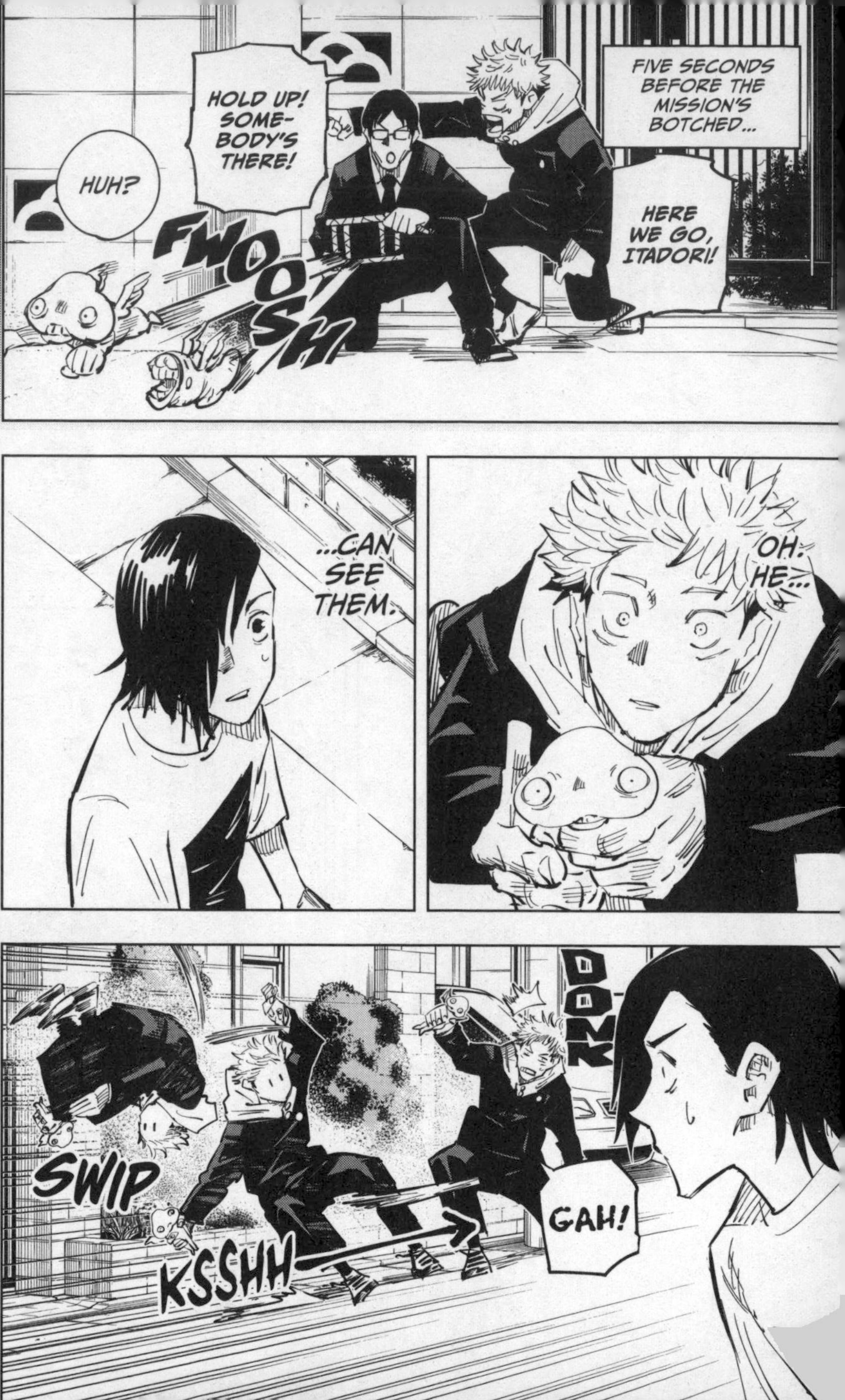
FIVE SECONDS BEFORE THE MISSION'S BOTCHED...
HERE WE GO, ITADORI!
HOLD UP! SOME-BODY'S THERE!
HUH?
FWOOSH
OH. HE...
...CAN SEE THEM.
DOMK
GAH!
SWIP
KSSHH

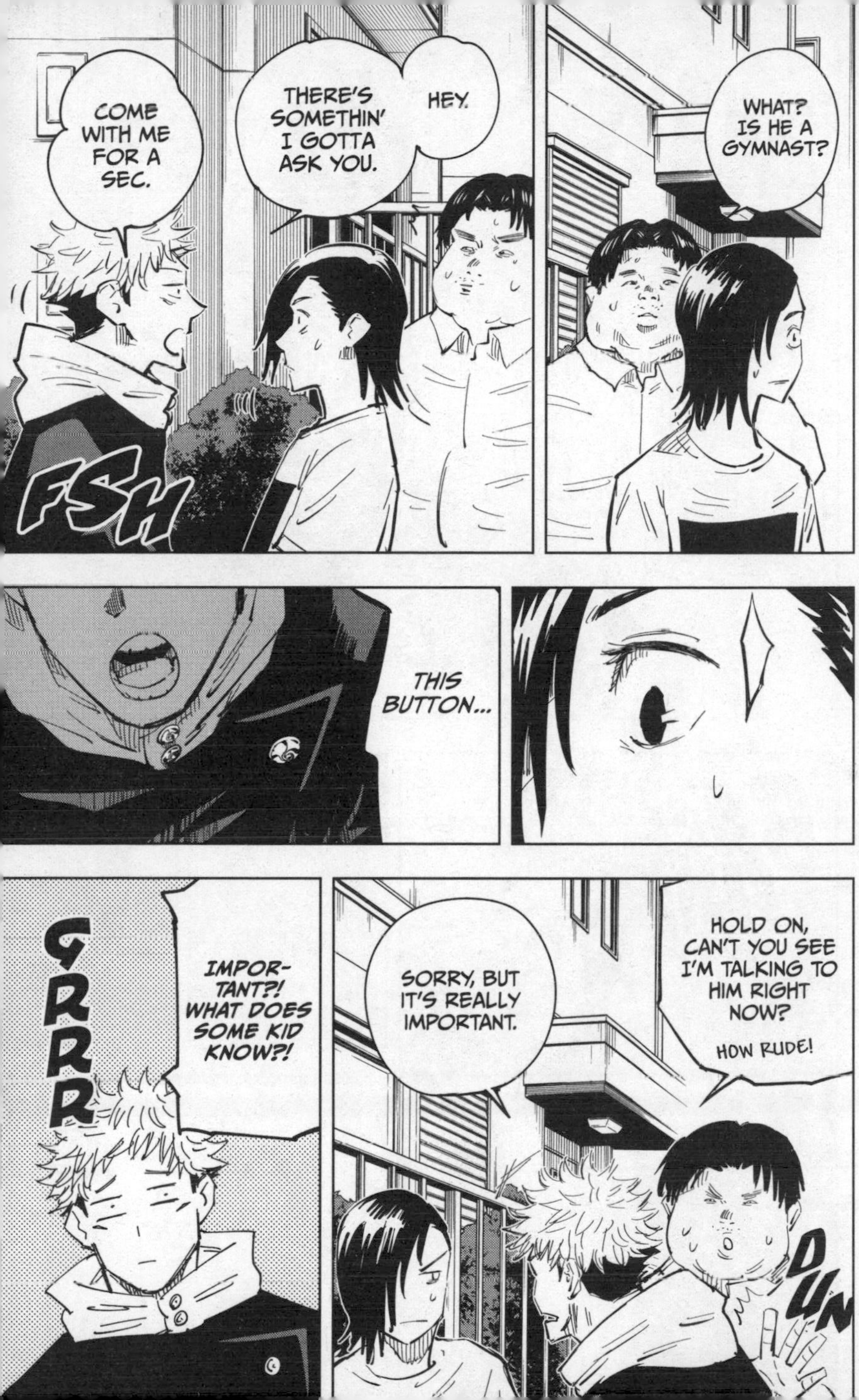
WHAT? IS HE A GYMNAST?
HEY.
THERE'S SOMETHIN' I GOTTA ASK YOU.
COME WITH ME FOR A SEC.
FSH
THIS BUTTON...
HOLD ON, CAN'T YOU SEE I'M TALKING TO HIM RIGHT NOW?
HOW RUDE!
SORRY, BUT IT'S REALLY IMPORTANT.
DUN
IMPOR-TANT?! WHAT DOES SOME KID KNOW?!
GRRR

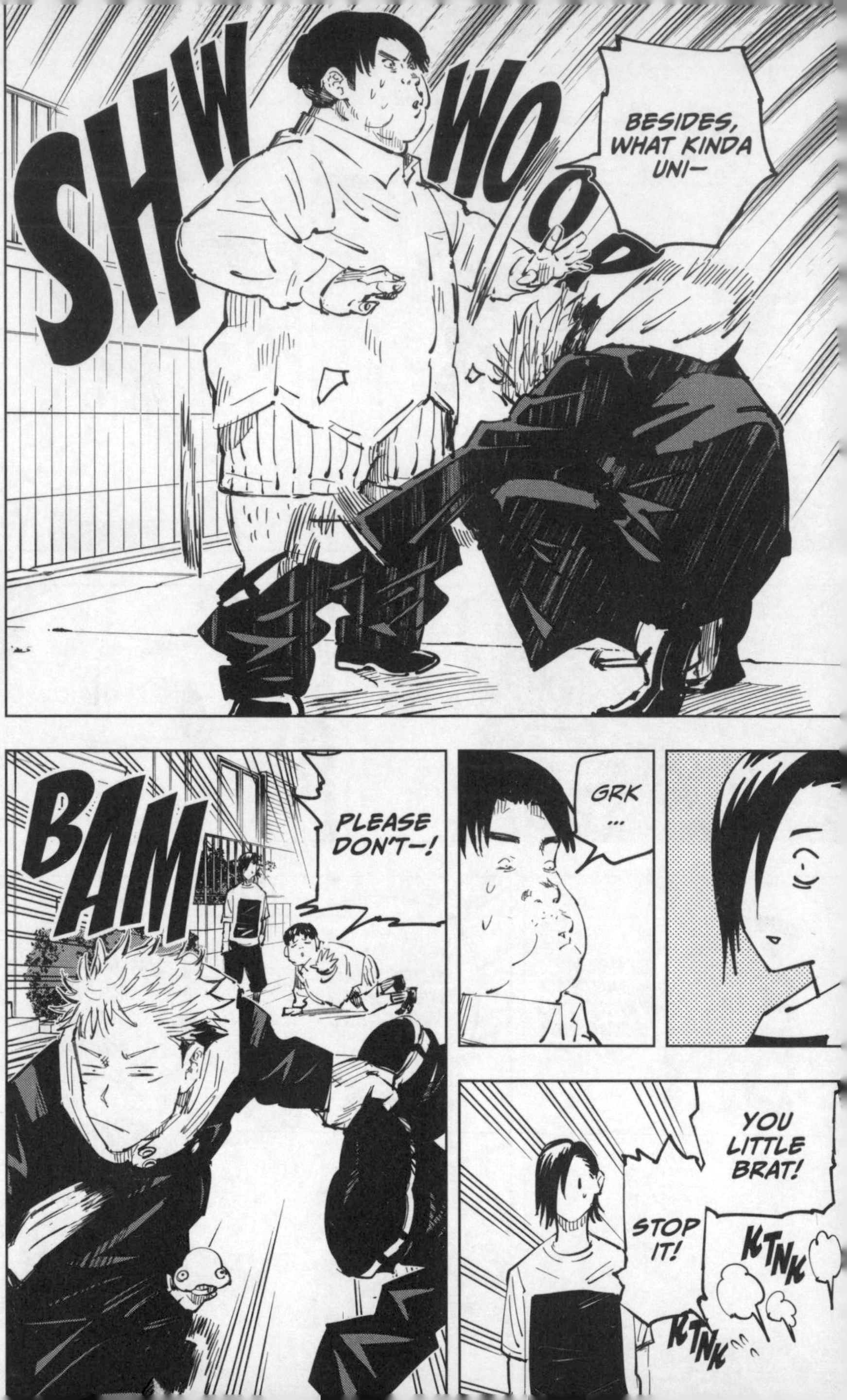
SHW
WOOO
BESIDES, WHAT KINDA UNI—
GRK ...
YOU LITTLE BRAT!
STOP IT!
KTNK
KTNK
BAM
PLEASE DON'T—!

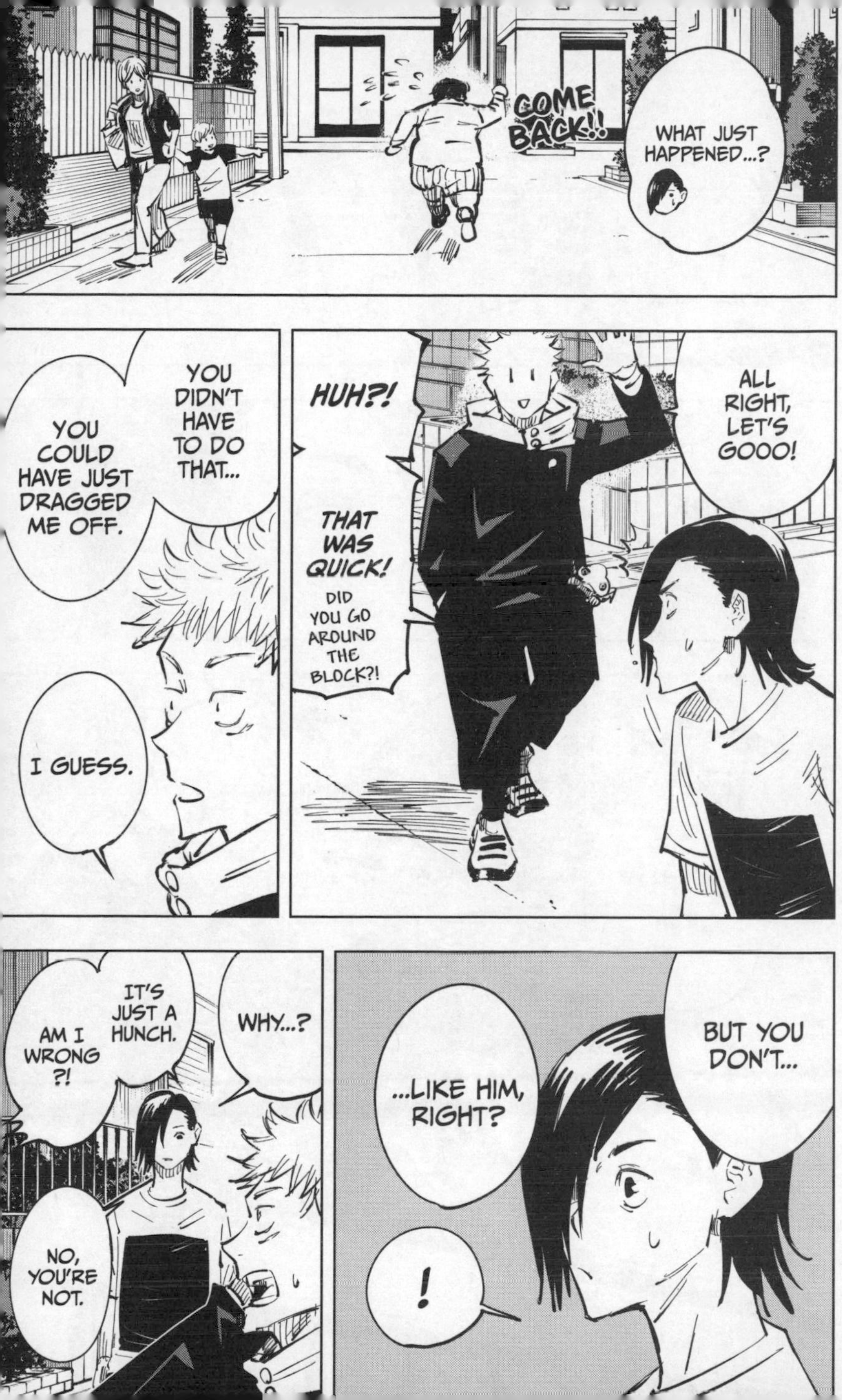
WHAT JUST HAPPENED...?
COME BACK!!
ALL RIGHT, LET'S GOOO!
HUH?!
THAT WAS QUICK! DID YOU GO AROUND THE BLOCK?!
YOU DIDN'T HAVE TO DO THAT...
YOU COULD HAVE JUST DRAGGED ME OFF.
I GUESS.
BUT YOU DON'T...
...LIKE HIM, RIGHT?
!
WHY...?
IT'S JUST A HUNCH.
AM I WRONG?!
NO, YOU'RE NOT.

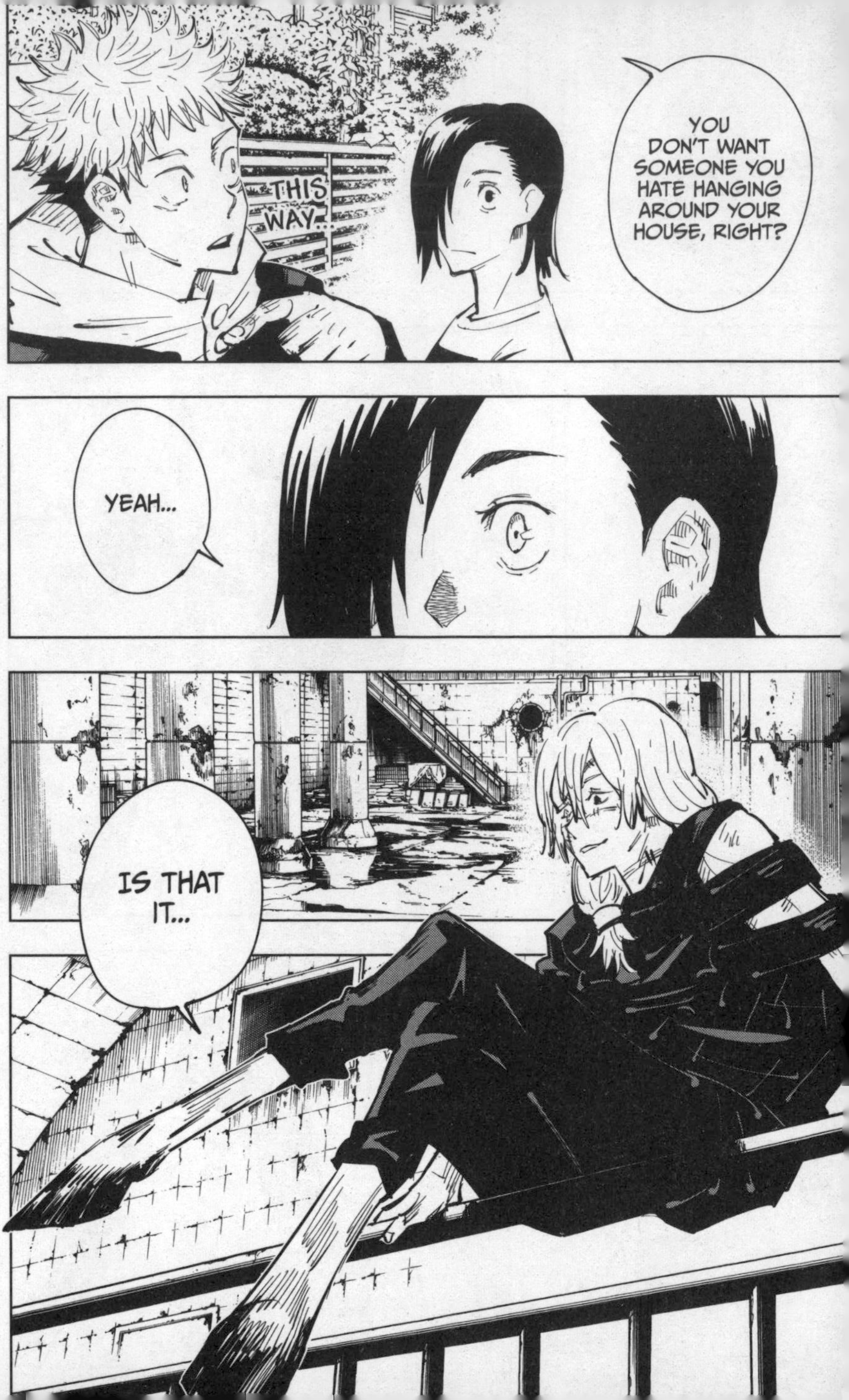
YOU DON'T WANT SOMEONE YOU HATE HANGING AROUND YOUR HOUSE, RIGHT?
THIS WAY...
YEAH...
IS THAT IT...

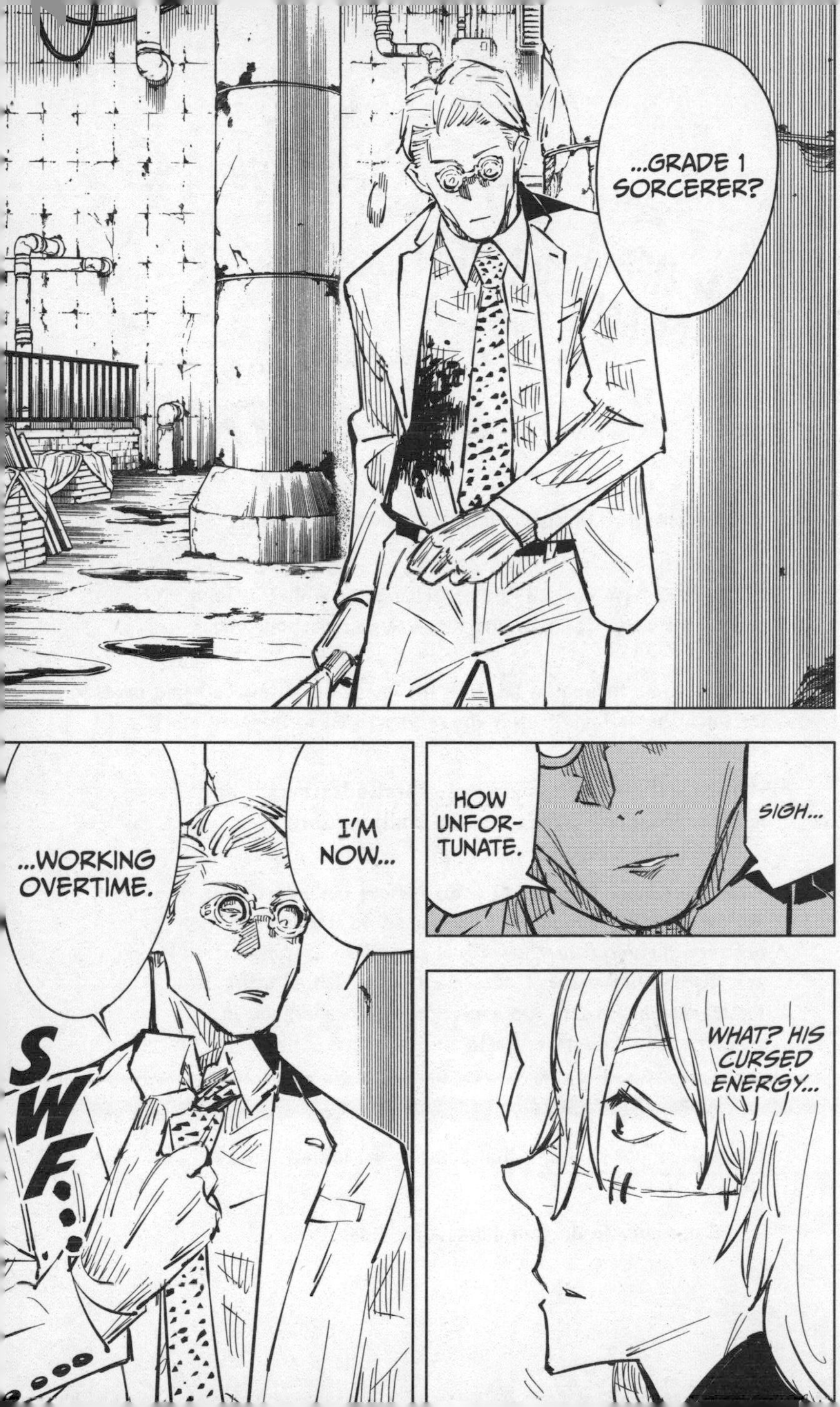
...GRADE 1 SORCERER?
SIGH...
HOW UNFOR-TUNATE.
WHAT? HIS CURSED ENERGY...
I'M NOW...
...WORKING OVERTIME.
SWF...

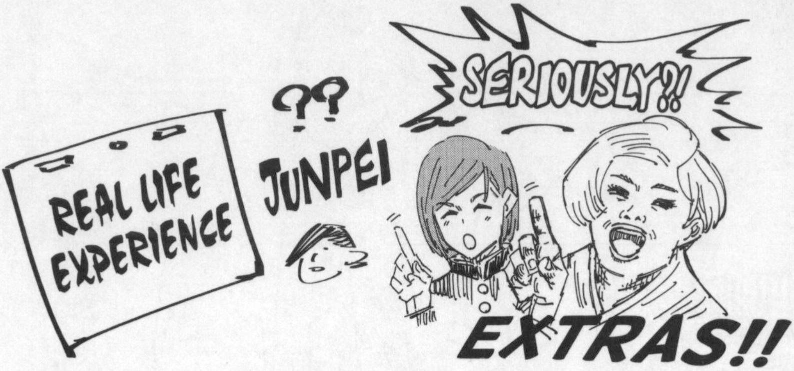
SERIOUSLY?!
EXTRAS!!
JUNPEI
REAL LIFE EXPERIENCE

• The problem child of this book, Junpei, is at it again.

• "Teachers have no real-life experience! Take that!" Along with pulling his pants down, saying that was so irresponsible!

• Teachers go through a lot, with the low pay and always being pressed for time. Please look it up if you're interested in learning more.

• There are lots of strange people besides teachers. I don't have much confidence. I wasn't a model student either...

• In high school, I once had some history homework over the summer. I didn't spend a single second on it and ended up not even turning it in. Plus, I had completely forgotten that I actually had homework. I was called to the school office and the teacher asked me, "Do you know why I called you in?" In response, I made a face like this:

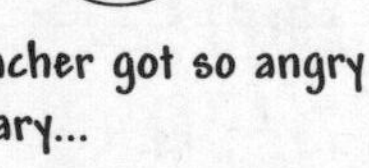

The teacher got so angry that I nearly wet myself. That was scary...

Remember to do your homework, kids...

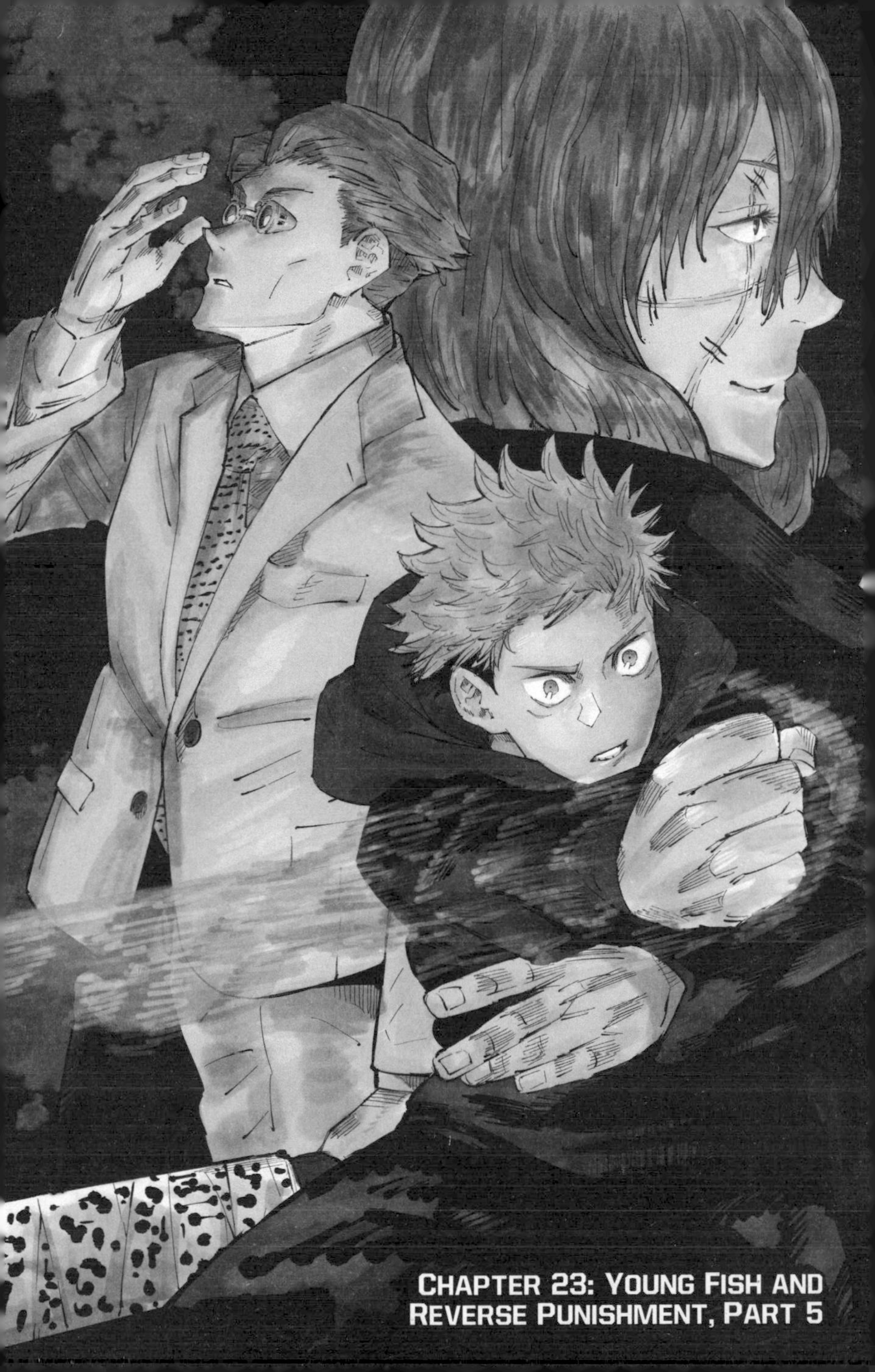

Chapter 23: Young Fish and Reverse Punishment, Part 5

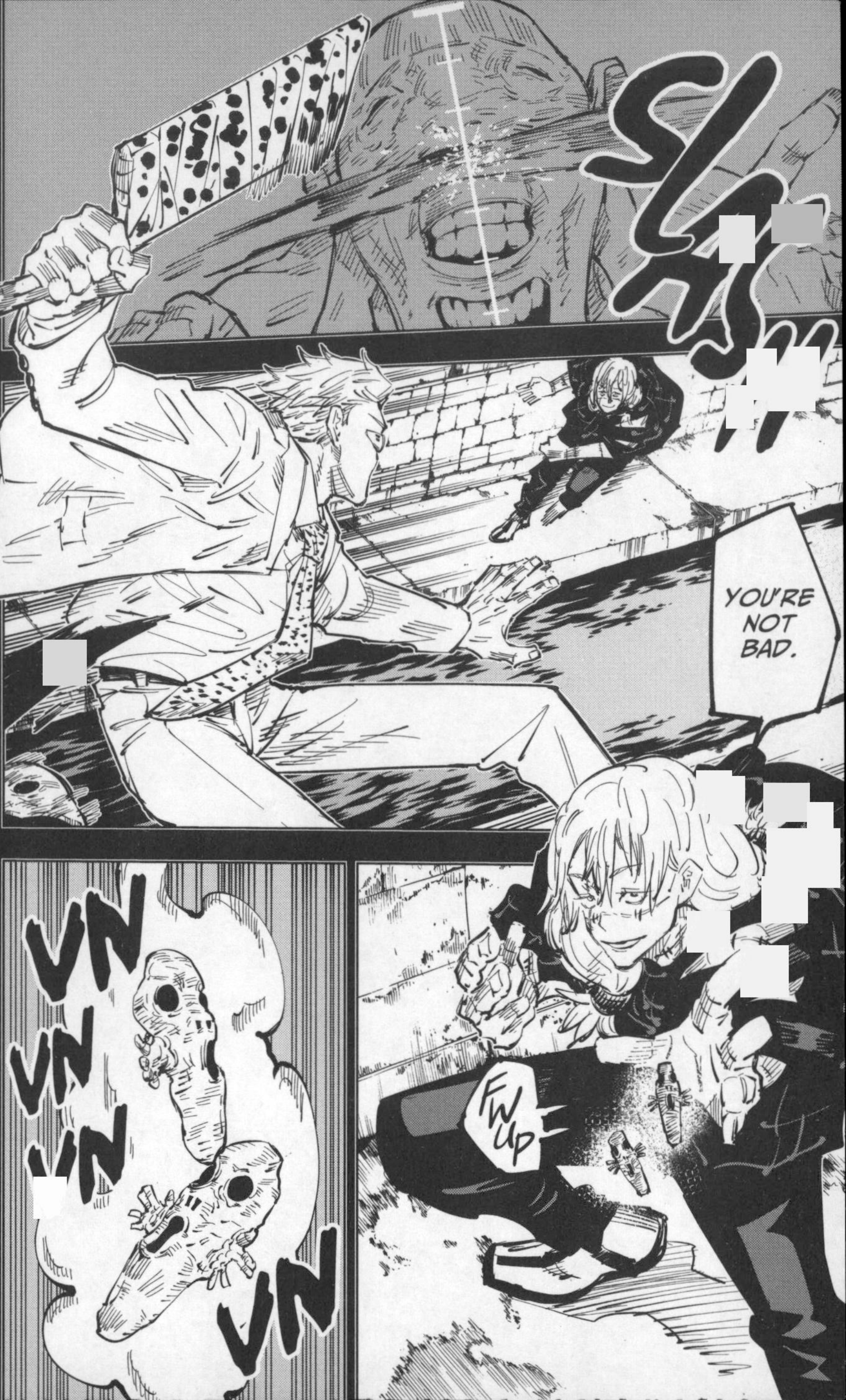
YOU'RE NOT BAD.
FWUP
VN
VN
VN
VN
VN

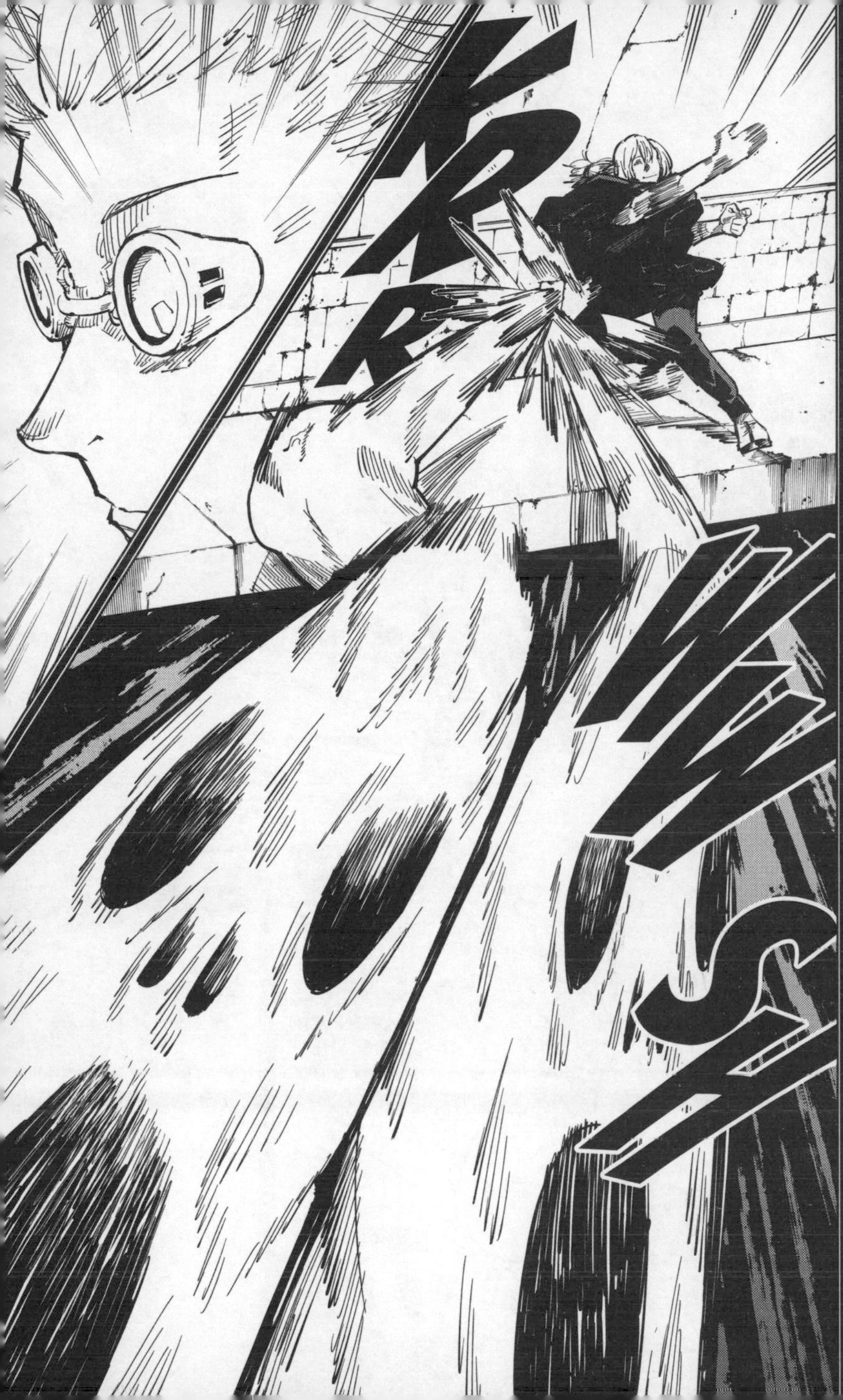
KRR

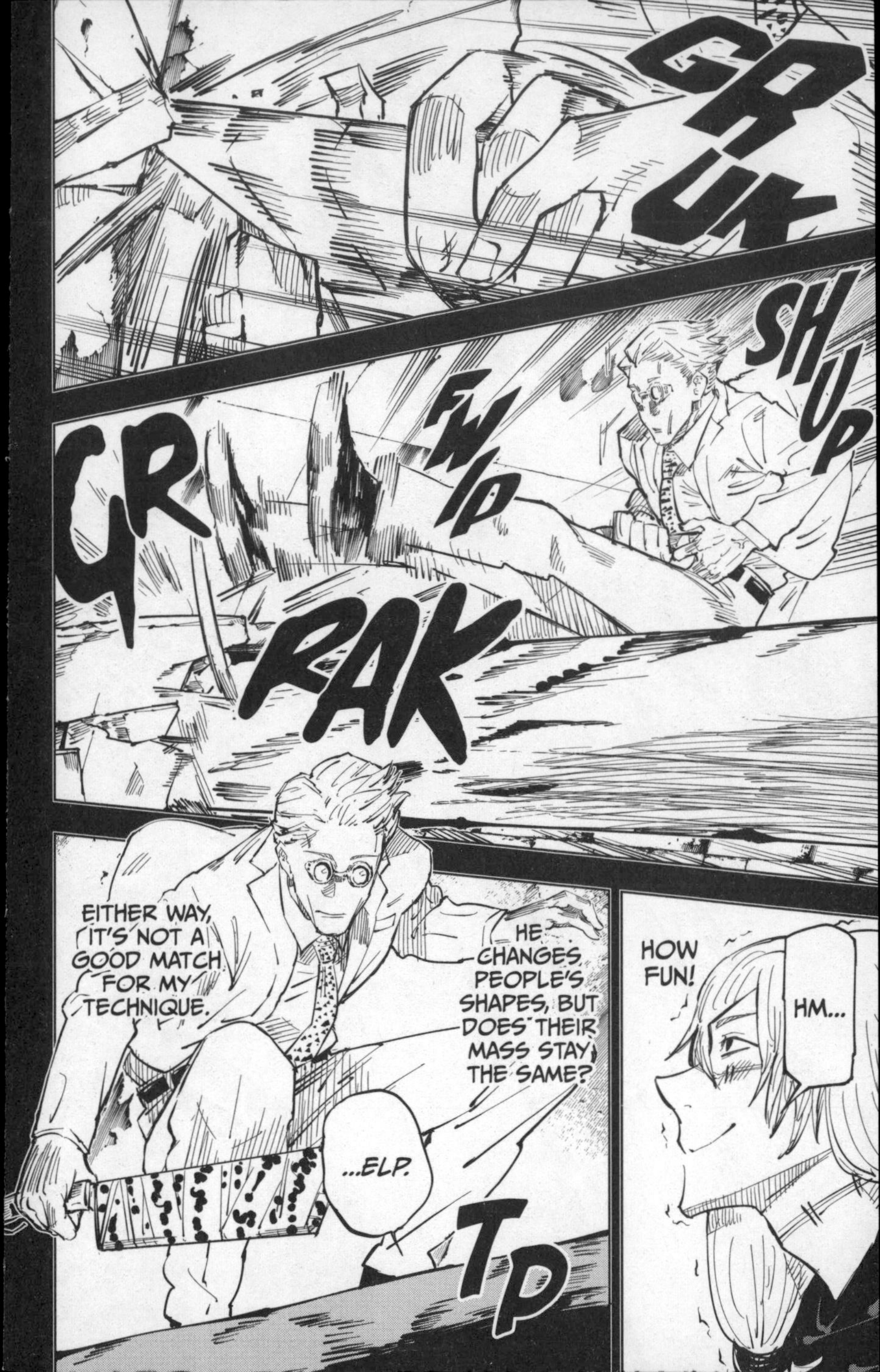
GRUK
SHUP
FWIP
GRRAK
HM...
HOW FUN!
HE CHANGES PEOPLE'S SHAPES, BUT DOES THEIR MASS STAY THE SAME?
EITHER WAY, IT'S NOT A GOOD MATCH FOR MY TECHNIQUE.
...ELP.
TP

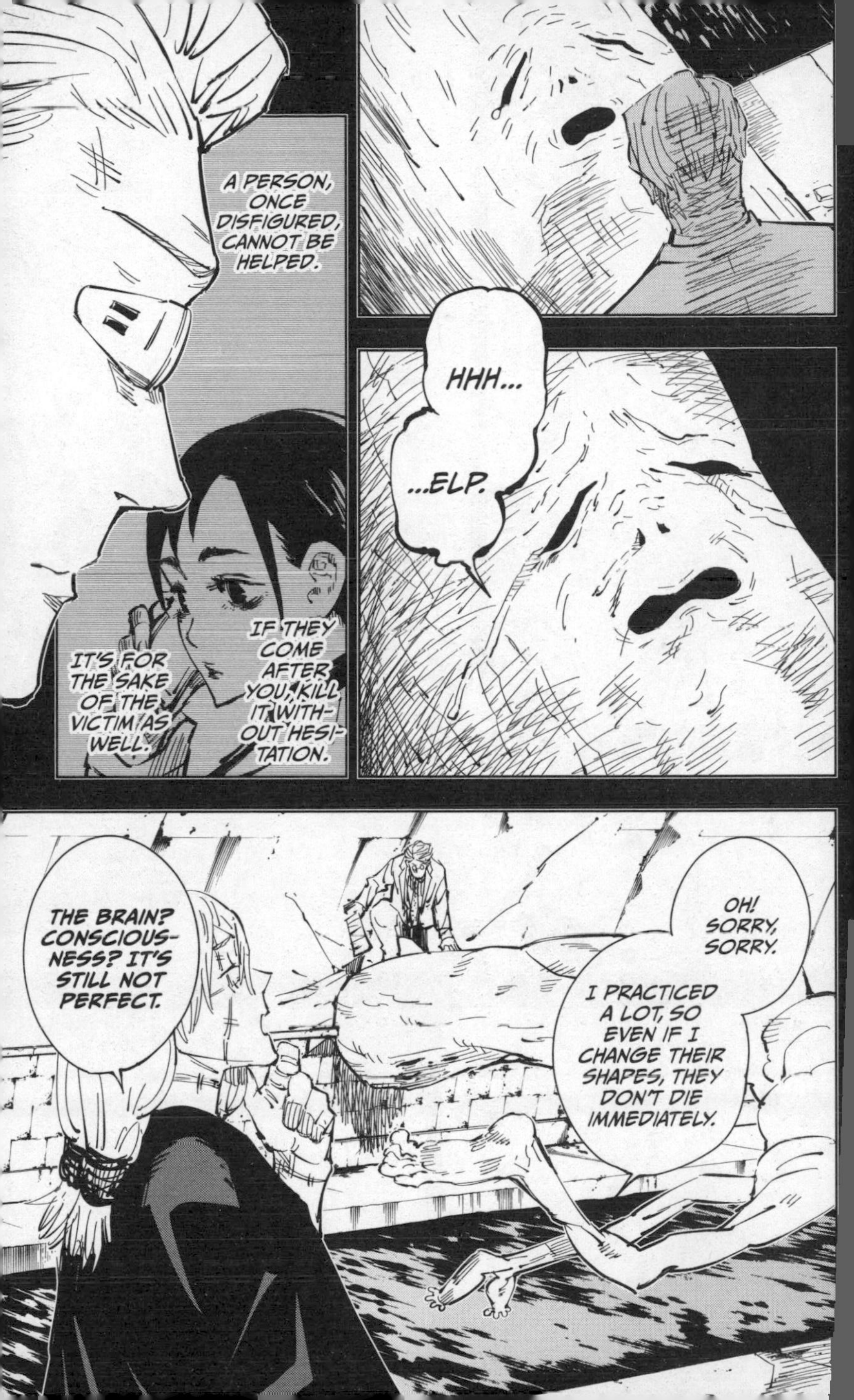
HHH...
...ELP.
A PERSON, ONCE DISFIGURED, CANNOT BE HELPED.
IF THEY COME AFTER YOU, KILL IT WITH-OUT HESI-TATION.
IT'S FOR THE SAKE OF THE VICTIM AS WELL.
OH! SORRY, SORRY.
I PRACTICED A LOT, SO EVEN IF I CHANGE THEIR SHAPES, THEY DON'T DIE IMMEDIATELY.
THE BRAIN? CONSCIOUS-NESS? IT'S STILL NOT PERFECT.

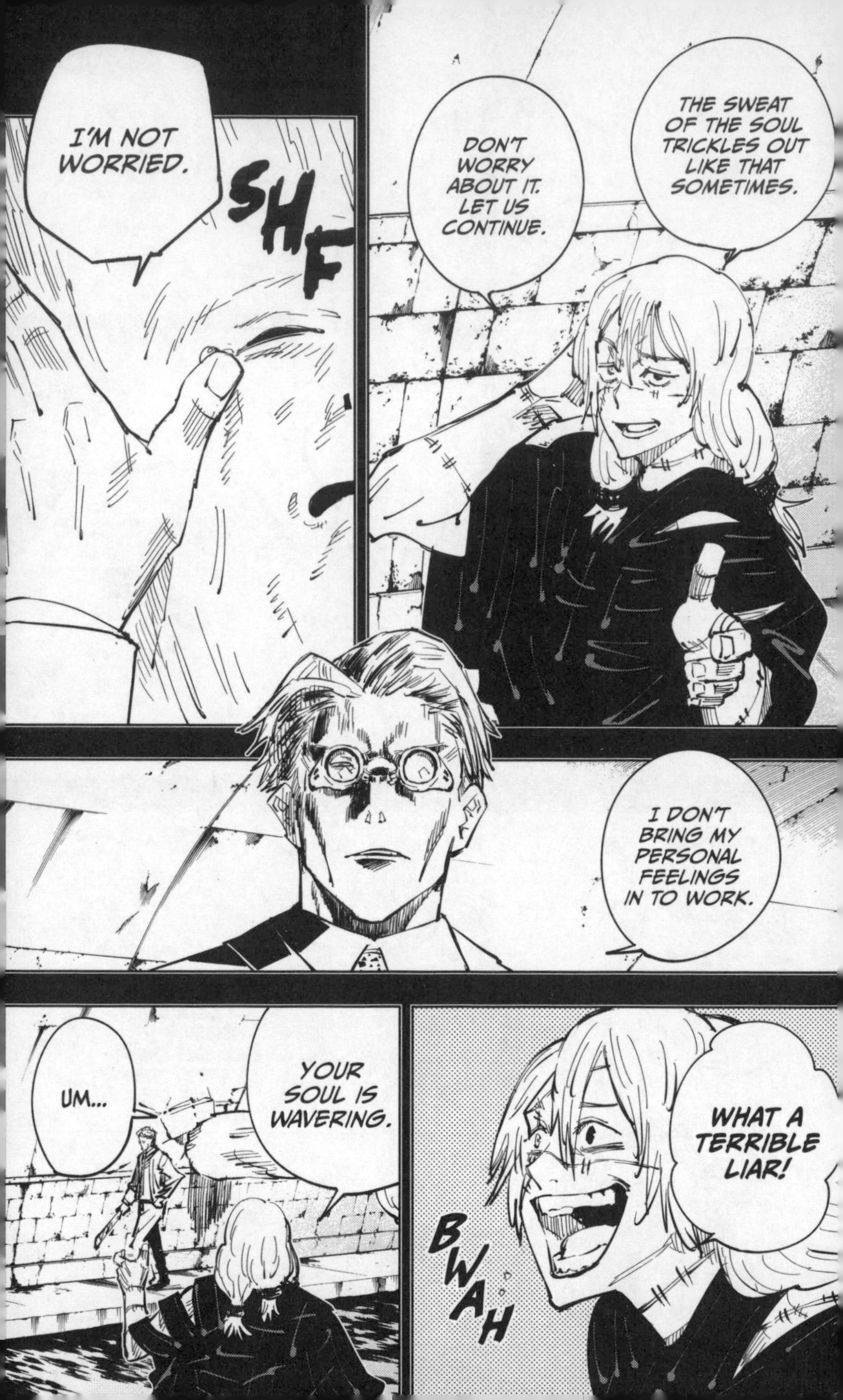
THE SWEAT OF THE SOUL TRICKLES OUT LIKE THAT SOMETIMES.
DON'T WORRY ABOUT IT. LET US CONTINUE.
I'M NOT WORRIED.
SHF
I DON'T BRING MY PERSONAL FEELINGS IN TO WORK.
WHAT A TERRIBLE LIAR!
BWAH
YOUR SOUL IS WAVERING.
UM...

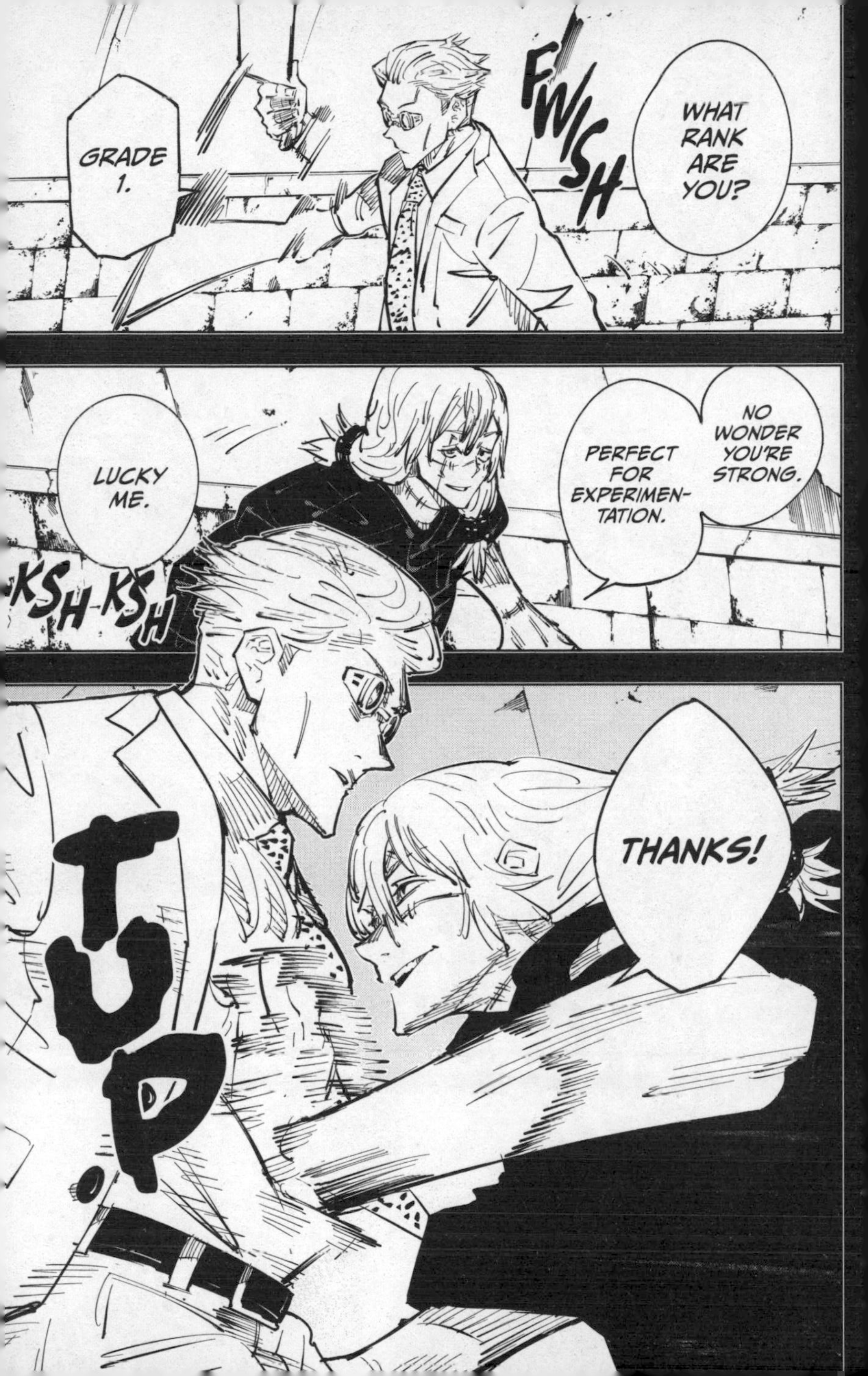
WHAT RANK ARE YOU?
FWISH
GRADE 1.
NO WONDER YOU'RE STRONG.
PERFECT FOR EXPERIMENTATION.
LUCKY ME.
KSH-KSH
THANKS!
TUP

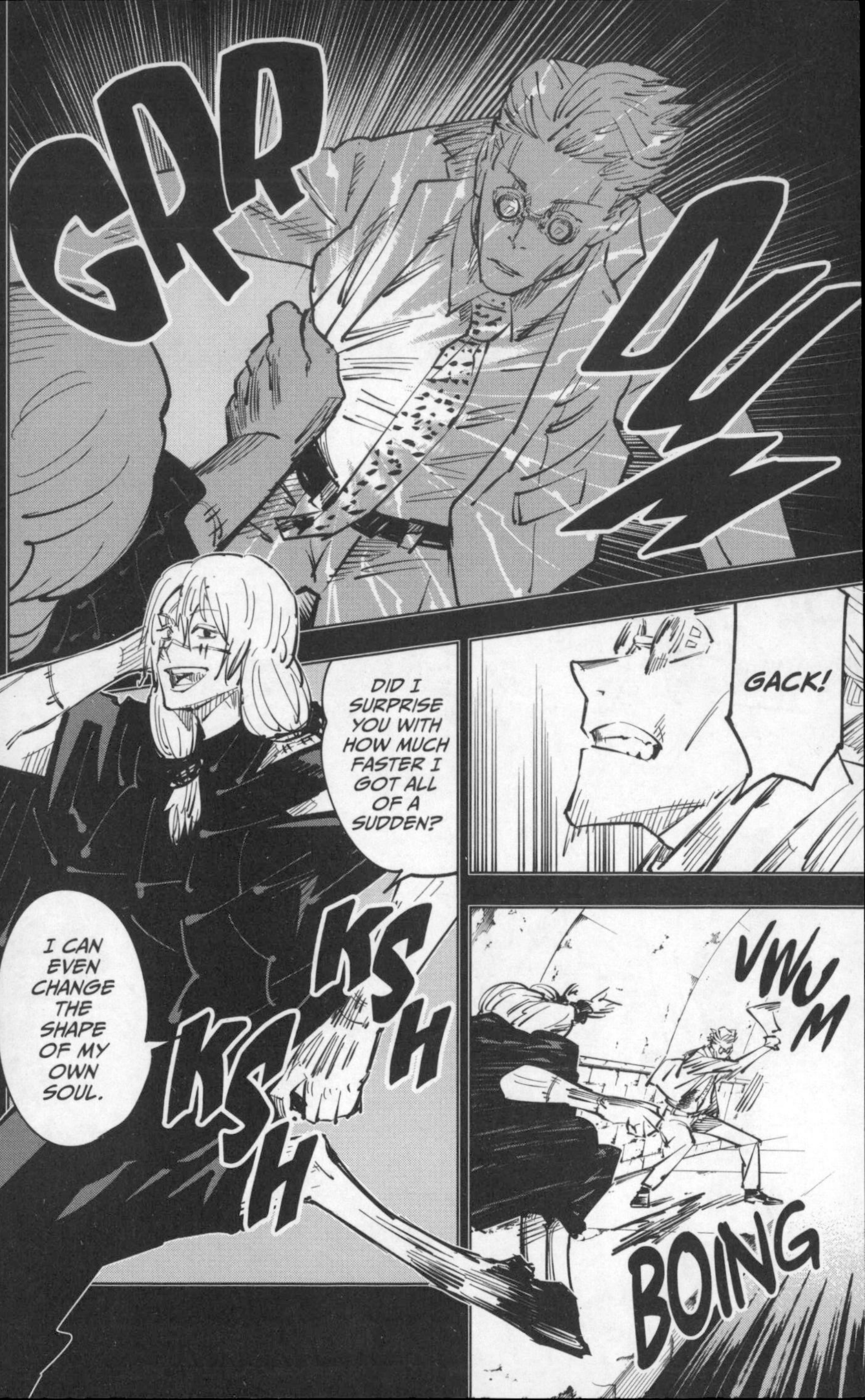
GRR
GACK!
VWUM
BOING
DID I SURPRISE YOU WITH HOW MUCH FASTER I GOT ALL OF A SUDDEN?
I CAN EVEN CHANGE THE SHAPE OF MY OWN SOUL.
KSH
KSH

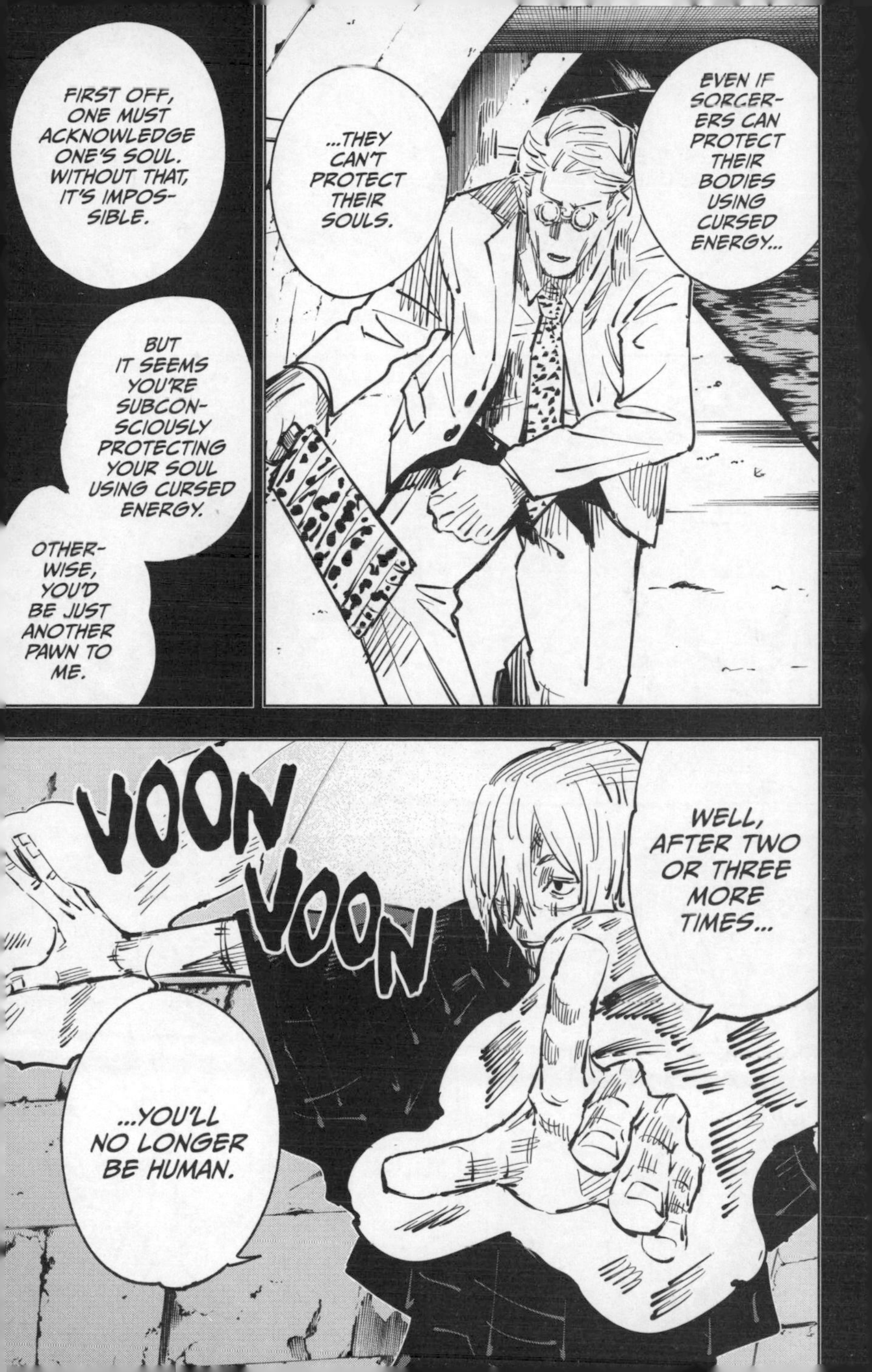
EVEN IF SORCERERS CAN PROTECT THEIR BODIES USING CURSED ENERGY...
...THEY CAN'T PROTECT THEIR SOULS.
FIRST OFF, ONE MUST ACKNOWLEDGE ONE'S SOUL. WITHOUT THAT, IT'S IMPOSSIBLE.
BUT IT SEEMS YOU'RE SUBCONSCIOUSLY PROTECTING YOUR SOUL USING CURSED ENERGY.
OTHERWISE, YOU'D BE JUST ANOTHER PAWN TO ME.
WELL, AFTER TWO OR THREE MORE TIMES...
VOON VOON
...YOU'LL NO LONGER BE HUMAN.

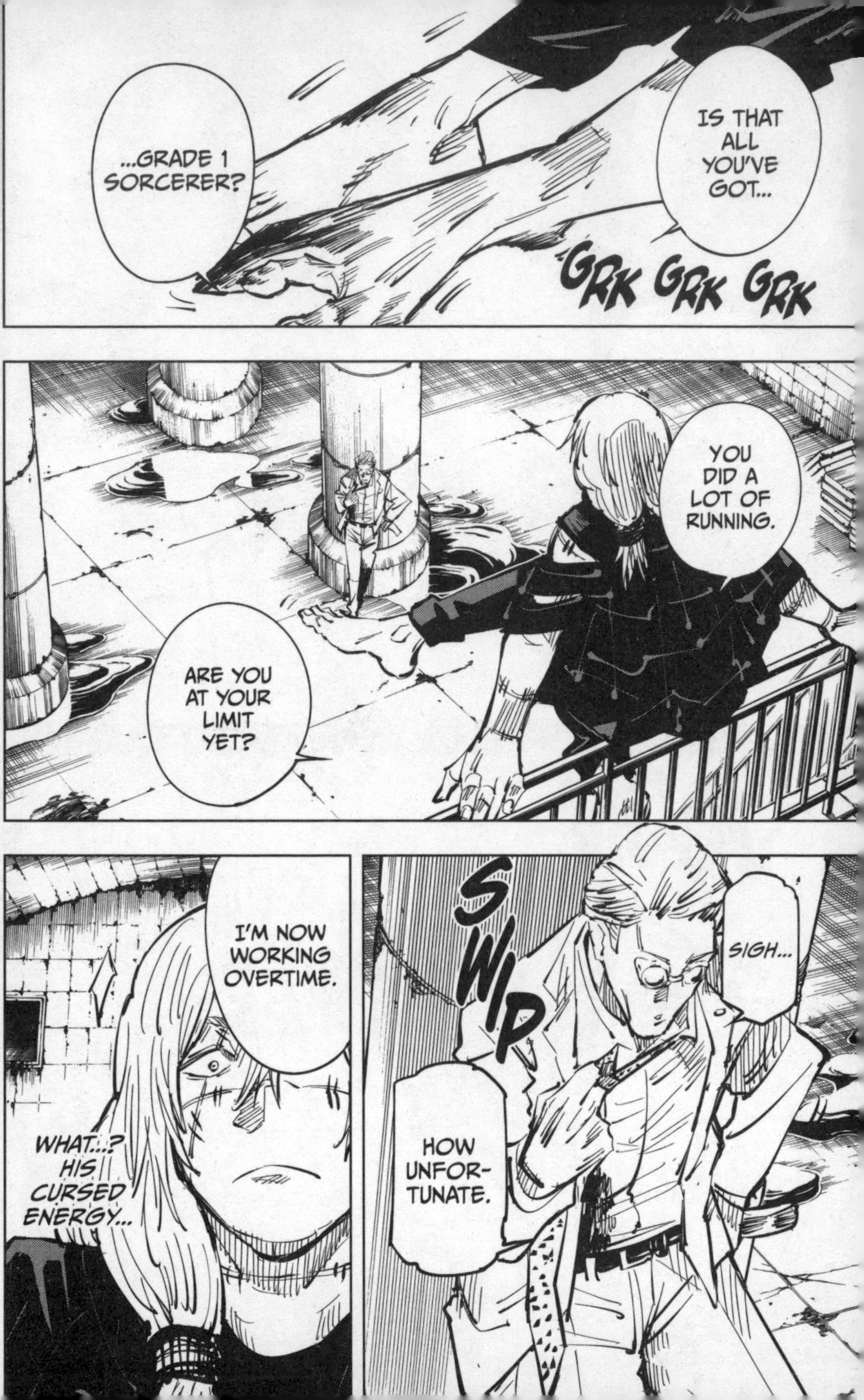
IS THAT ALL YOU'VE GOT...
GRK GRK GRK
...GRADE 1 SORCERER?
YOU DID A LOT OF RUNNING.
ARE YOU AT YOUR LIMIT YET?
SIGH...
SWIP
HOW UNFORTUNATE.
I'M NOW WORKING OVERTIME.
WHAT...? HIS CURSED ENERGY...

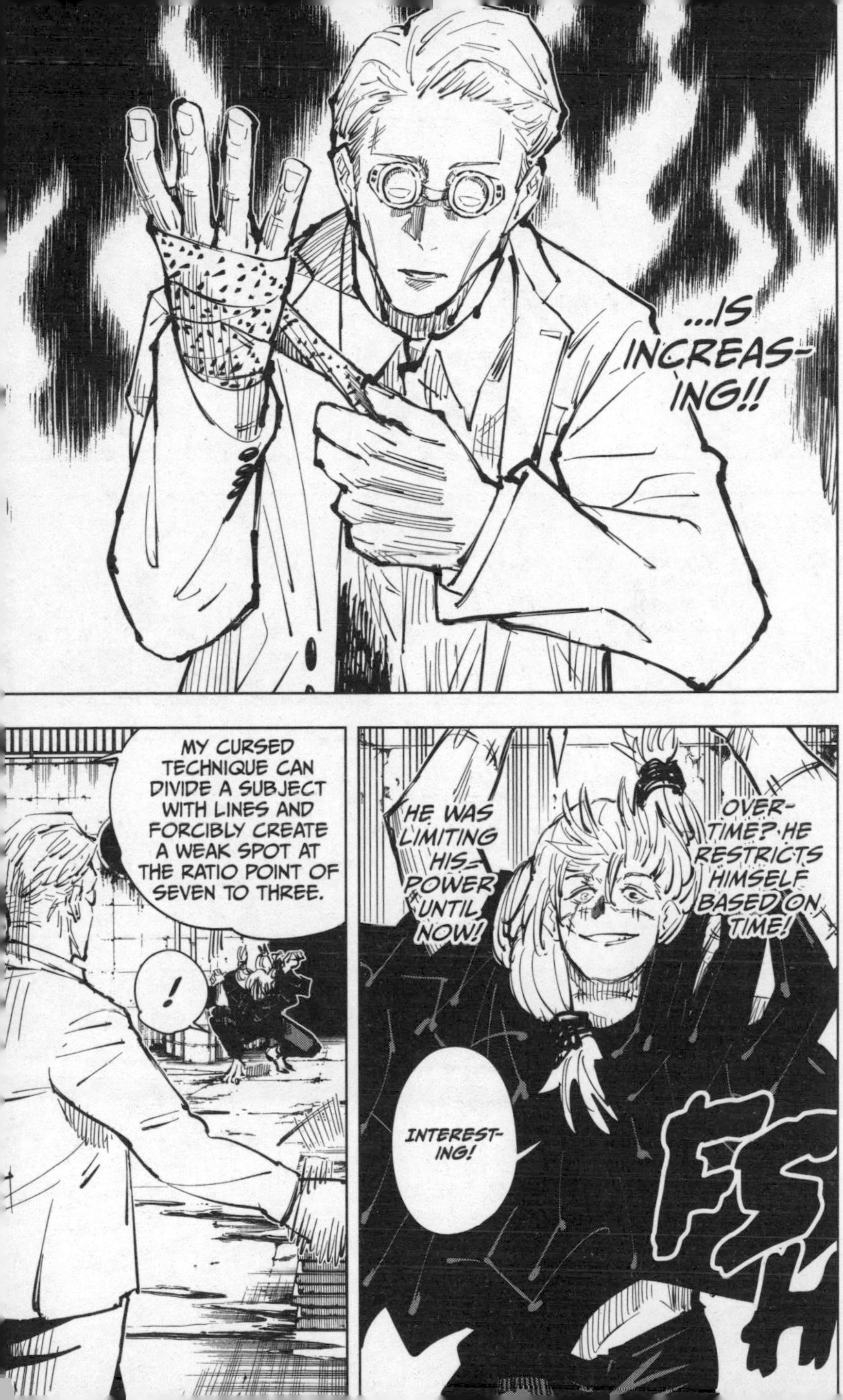
...IS INCREAS-ING!!
OVER-TIME? HE RESTRICTS HIMSELF BASED ON TIME!
HE WAS LIMITING HIS POWER UNTIL NOW!
INTERESTING!
FS
MY CURSED TECHNIQUE CAN DIVIDE A SUBJECT WITH LINES AND FORCIBLY CREATE A WEAK SPOT AT THE RATIO POINT OF SEVEN TO THREE.
!

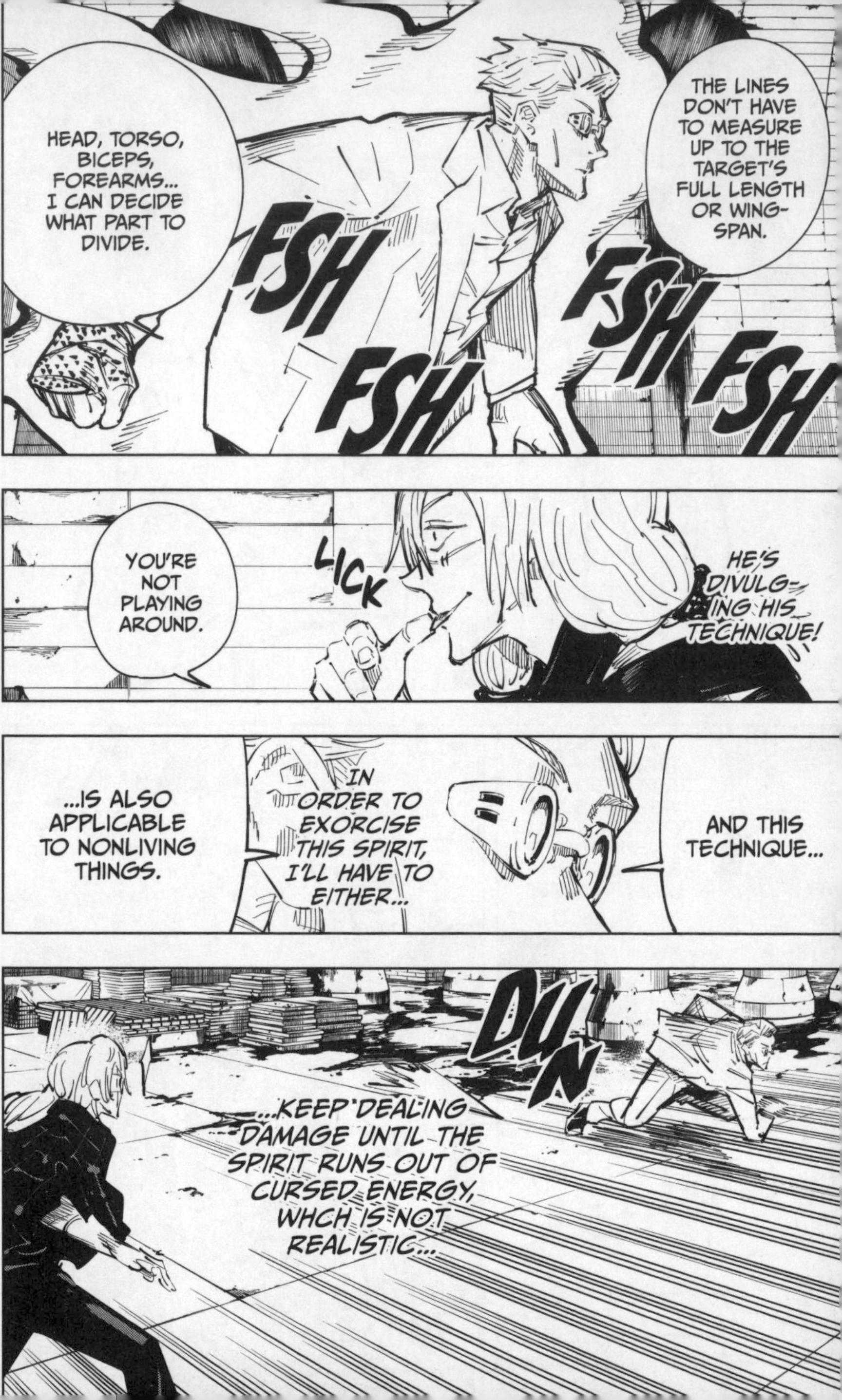
THE LINES DON'T HAVE TO MEASURE UP TO THE TARGET'S FULL LENGTH OR WING-SPAN.
FSH FSH
HEAD, TORSO, BICEPS, FOREARMS... I CAN DECIDE WHAT PART TO DIVIDE.
FSH FSH
HE'S DIVULGING HIS TECHNIQUE!
LICK
YOU'RE NOT PLAYING AROUND.
AND THIS TECHNIQUE...
IN ORDER TO EXORCISE THIS SPIRIT, I'LL HAVE TO EITHER...
...IS ALSO APPLICABLE TO NONLIVING THINGS.
DUN
...KEEP DEALING DAMAGE UNTIL THE SPIRIT RUNS OUT OF CURSED ENERGY, WHCH IS NOT REALISTIC...

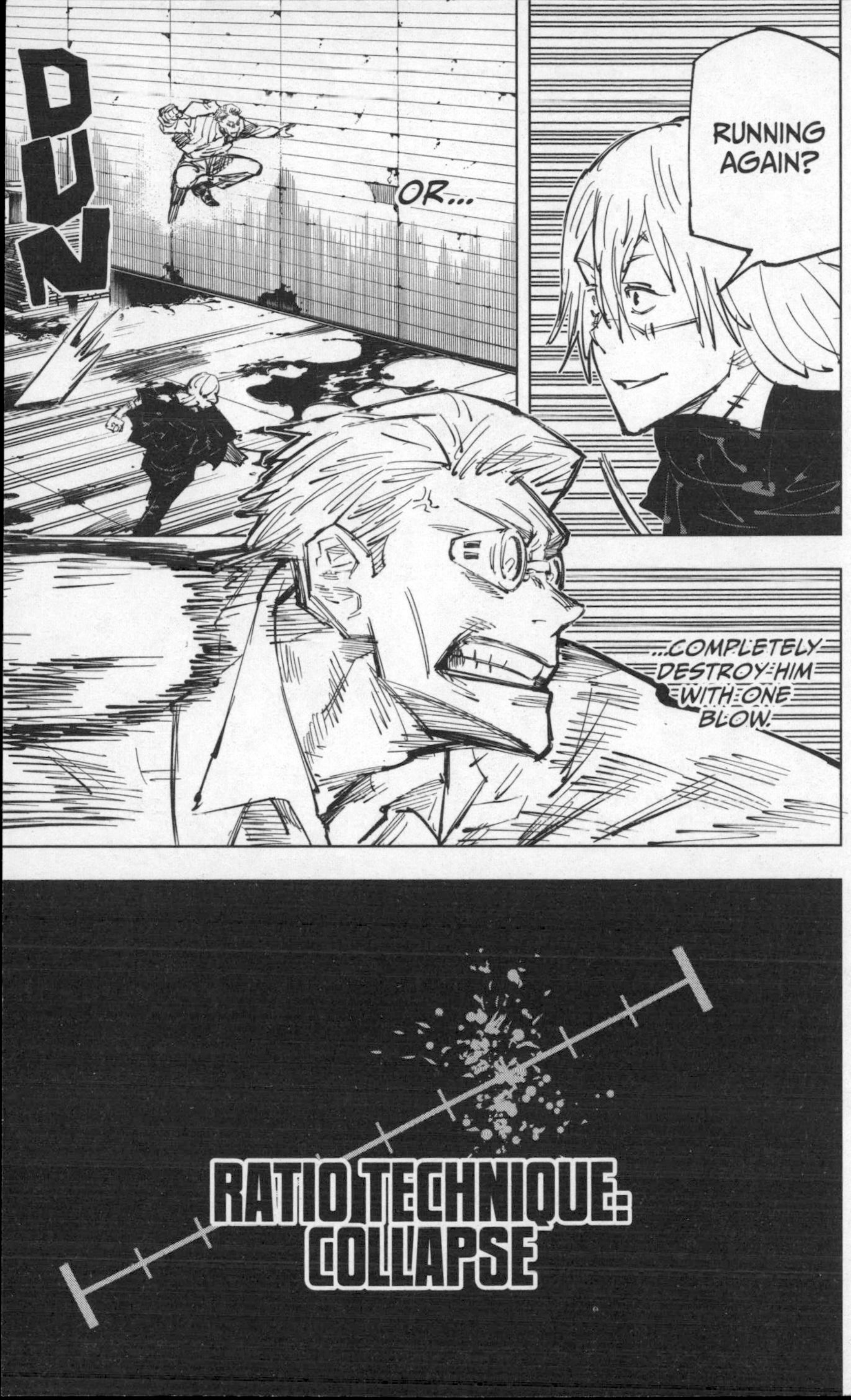
RUNNING AGAIN?
DUN
OR...
...COMPLETELY DESTROY HIM WITH ONE BLOW.
RATIO TECHNIQUE: COLLAPSE

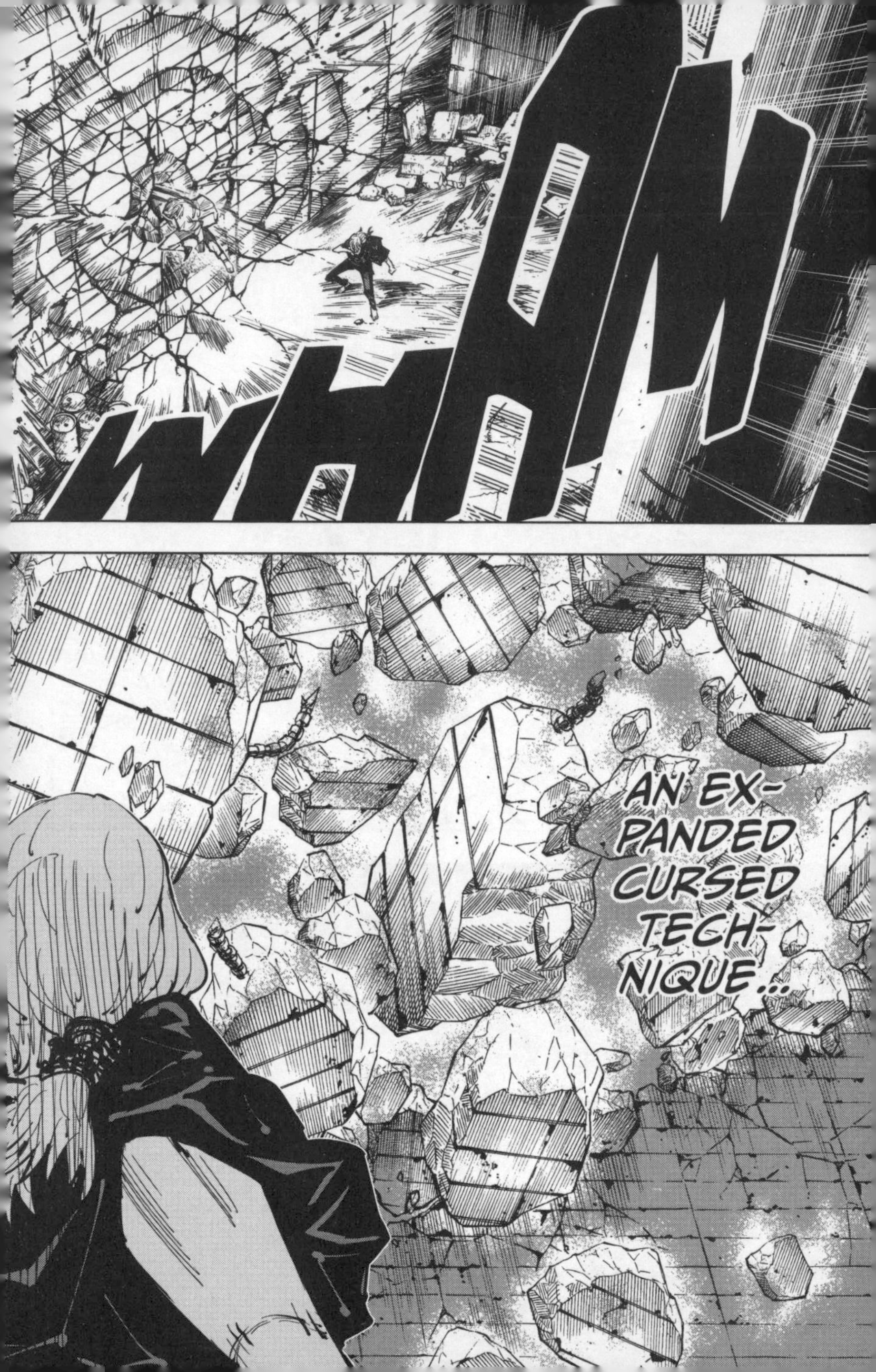
WHAM
AN EX-PANDED CURSED TECH-NIQUE...

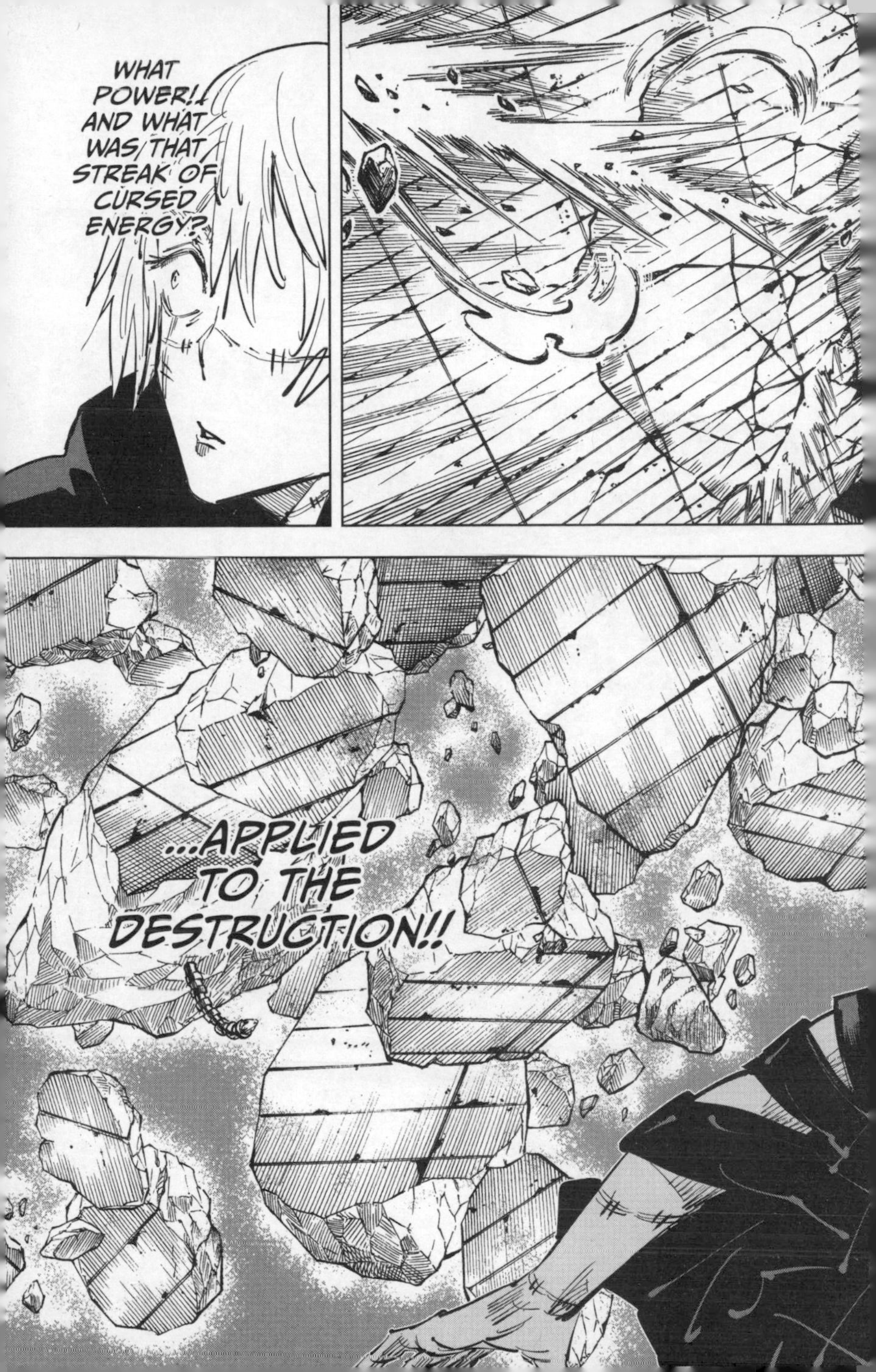
WHAT POWER!! AND WHAT WAS THAT STREAK OF CURSED ENERGY?
...APPLIED TO THE DESTRUCTION!!

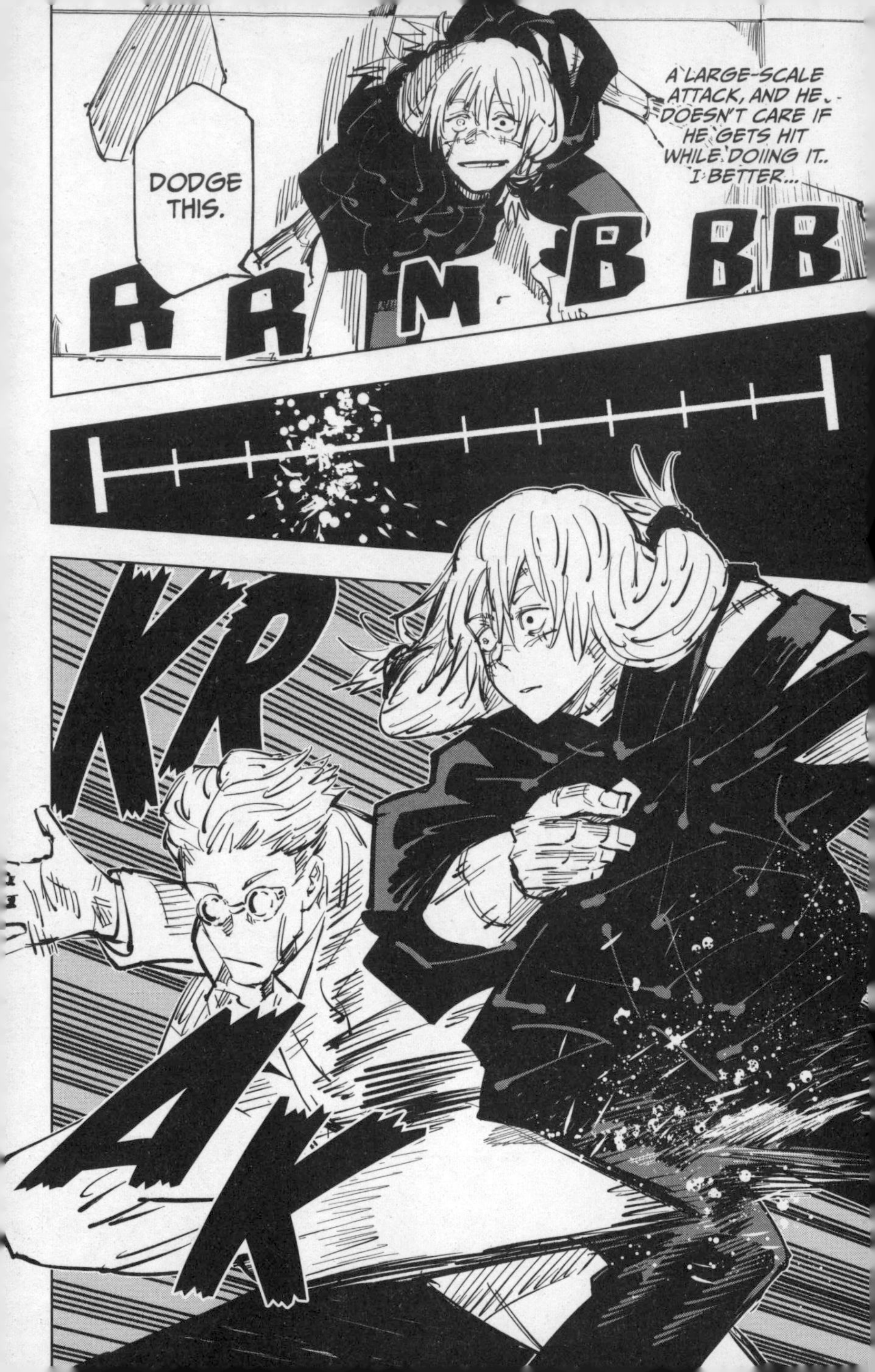
A LARGE-SCALE ATTACK, AND HE DOESN'T CARE IF HE GETS HIT WHILE DOIING IT.. I BETTER...
DODGE THIS.
RRMBBB
KRAK

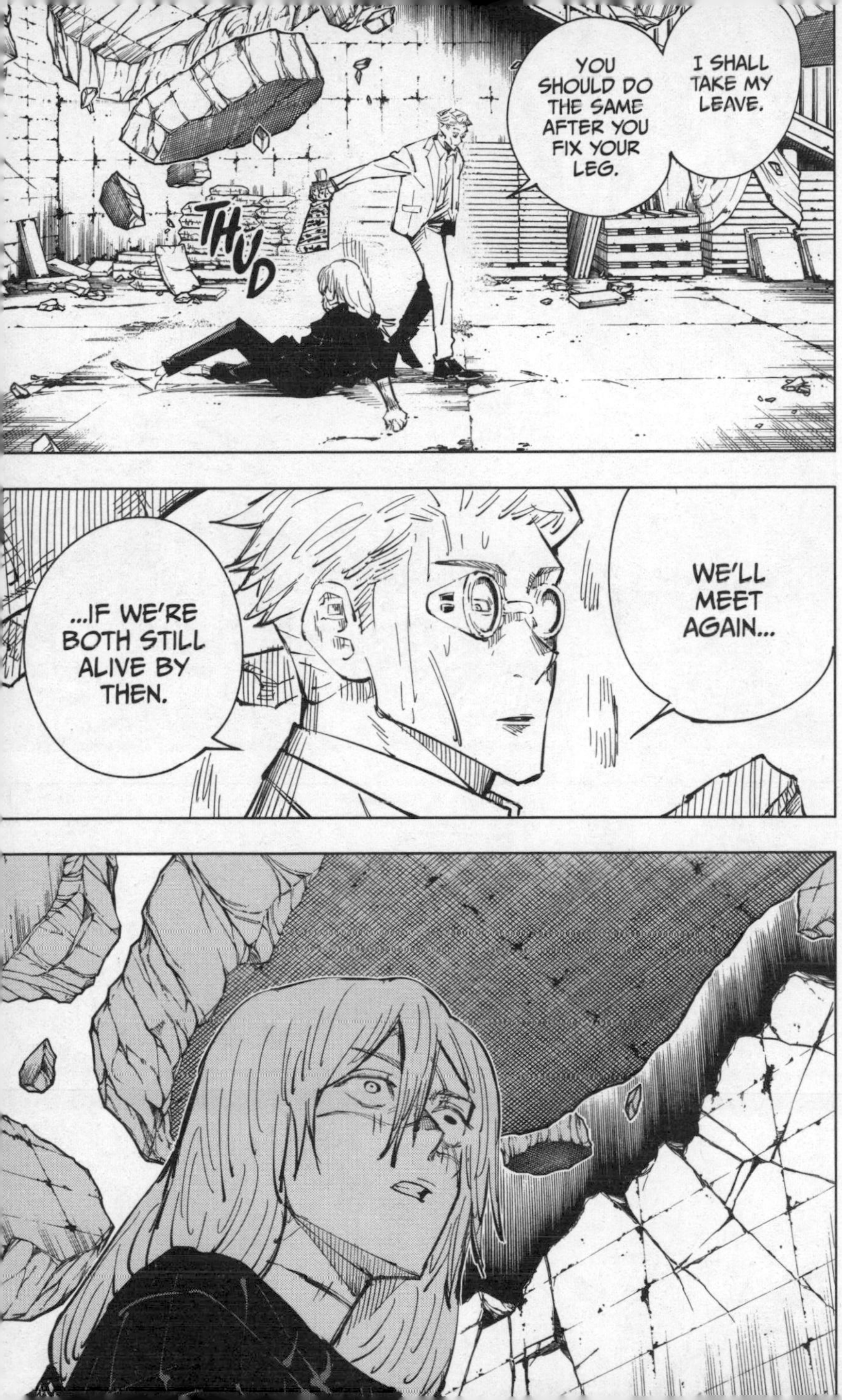
I SHALL TAKE MY LEAVE.
YOU SHOULD DO THE SAME AFTER YOU FIX YOUR LEG.
THUD
WE'LL MEET AGAIN...
...IF WE'RE BOTH STILL ALIVE BY THEN.

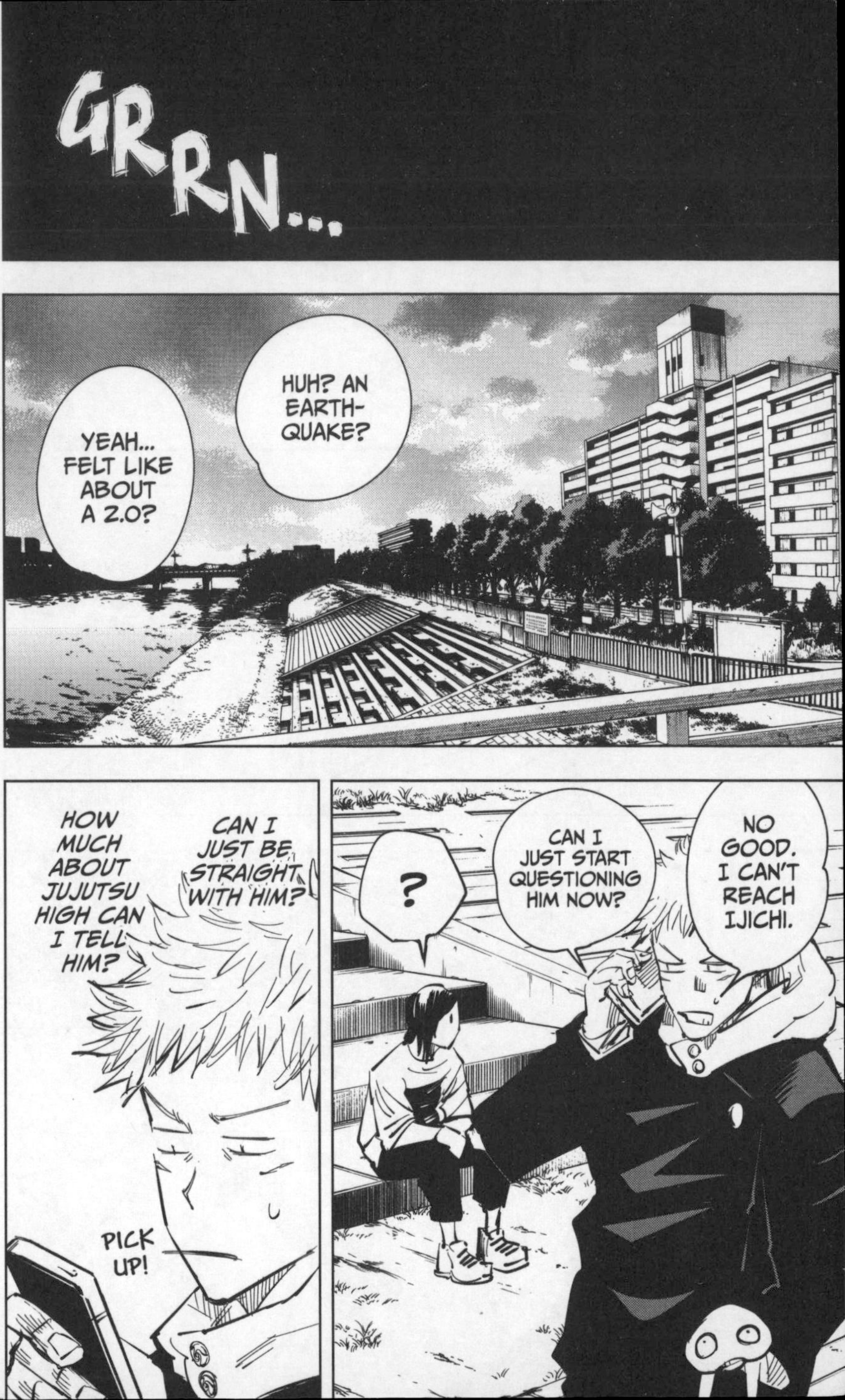
GRRN...
HUH? AN EARTH-QUAKE?
YEAH... FELT LIKE ABOUT A 2.0?
NO GOOD. I CAN'T REACH IJICHI.
CAN I JUST START QUESTIONING HIM NOW?
?
CAN I JUST BE STRAIGHT WITH HIM?
HOW MUCH ABOUT JUJUTSU HIGH CAN I TELL HIM?
PICK UP!

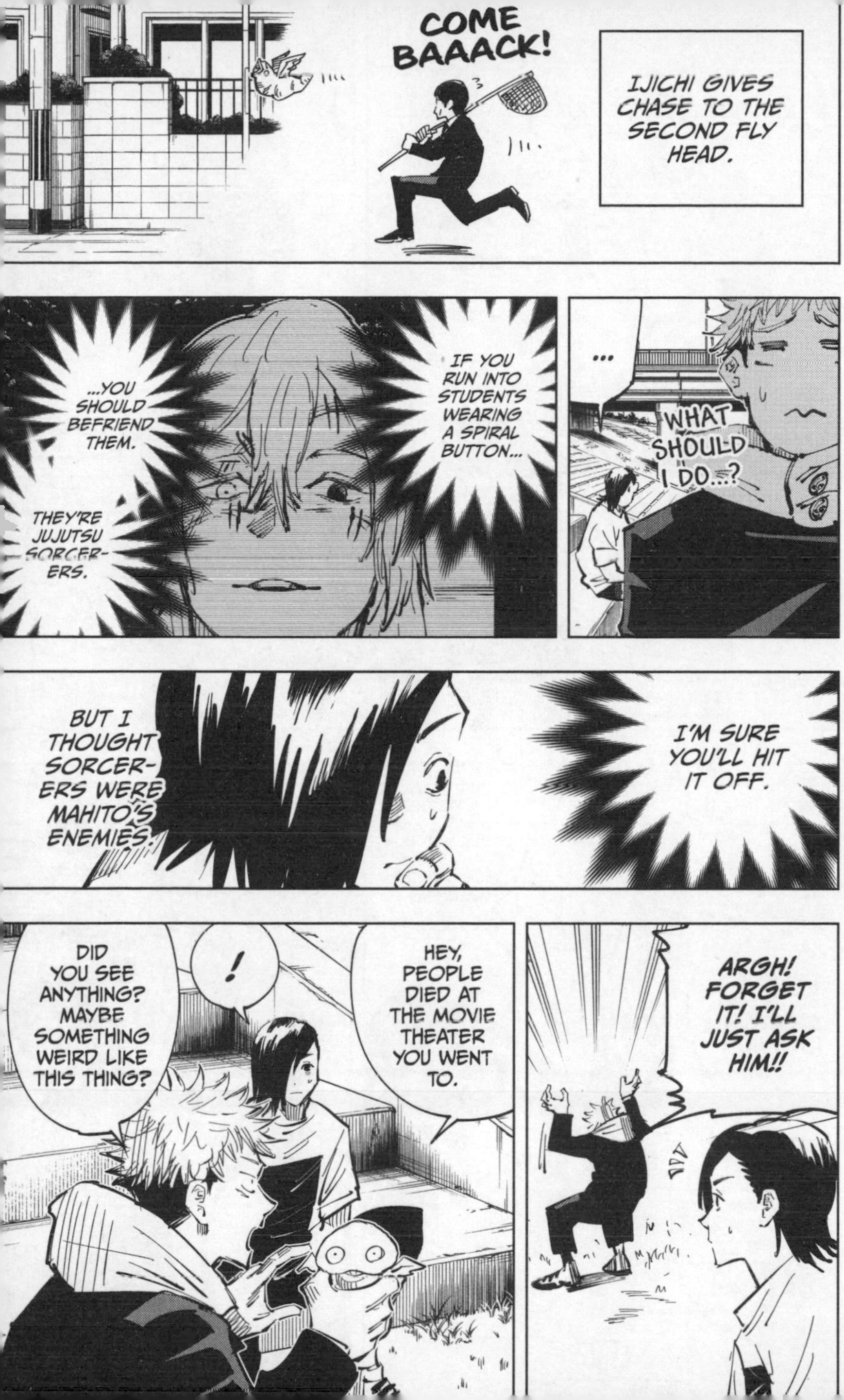
IJICHI GIVES CHASE TO THE SECOND FLY HEAD.
COME BAAACK!
...
WHAT SHOULD I DO...?
IF YOU RUN INTO STUDENTS WEARING A SPIRAL BUTTON...
...YOU SHOULD BEFRIEND THEM.
THEY'RE JUJUTSU SORCERERS.
I'M SURE YOU'LL HIT IT OFF.
BUT I THOUGHT SORCERERS WERE MAHITO'S ENEMIES.
ARGH! FORGET IT! I'LL JUST ASK HIM!!
HEY, PEOPLE DIED AT THE MOVIE THEATER YOU WENT TO.
!
DID YOU SEE ANYTHING? MAYBE SOMETHING WEIRD LIKE THIS THING?

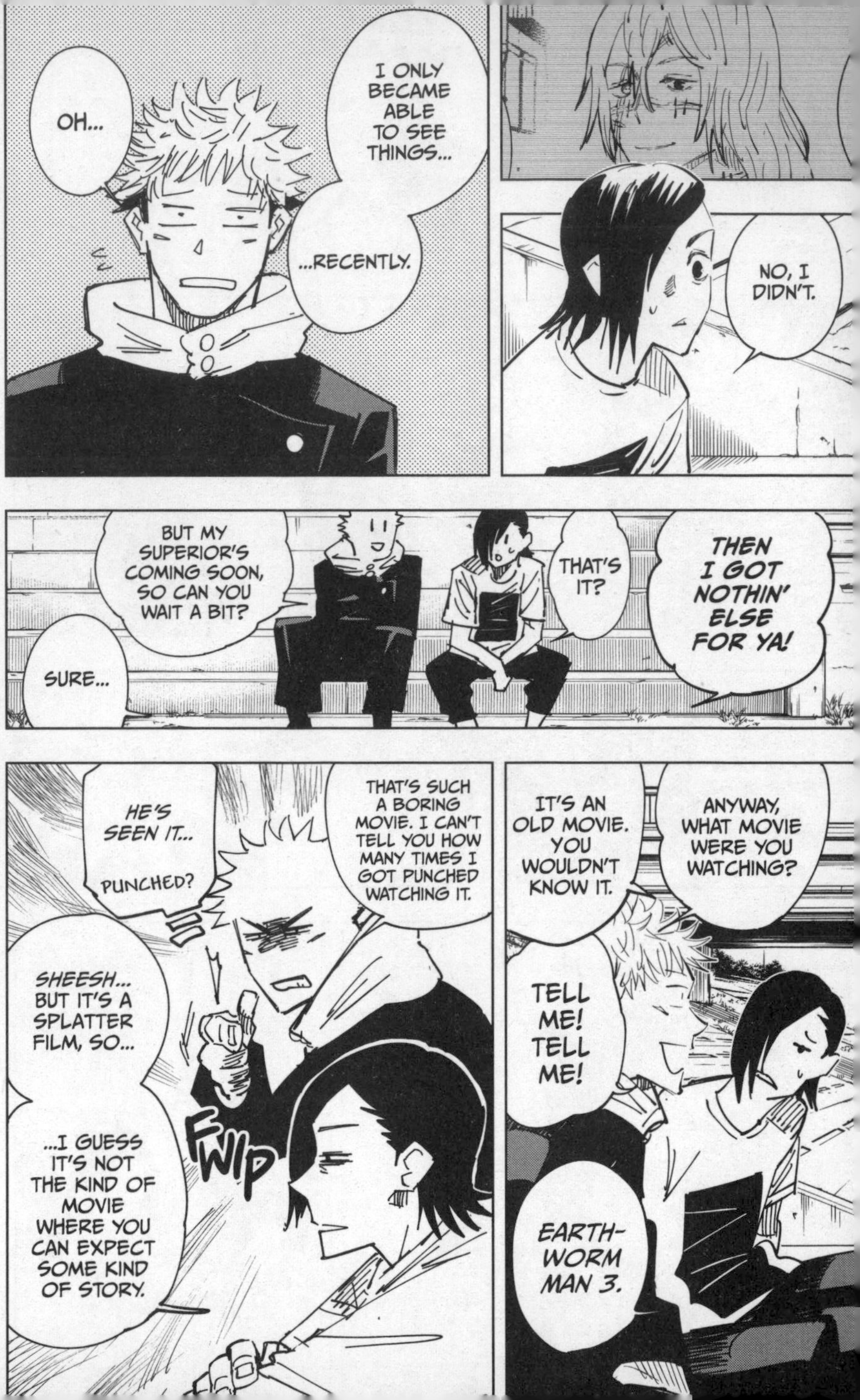
NO, I DIDN'T.
I ONLY BECAME ABLE TO SEE THINGS...
...RECENTLY.
OH...
THEN I GOT NOTHIN' ELSE FOR YA!
THAT'S IT?
BUT MY SUPERIOR'S COMING SOON, SO CAN YOU WAIT A BIT?
SURE...
ANYWAY, WHAT MOVIE WERE YOU WATCHING?
IT'S AN OLD MOVIE. YOU WOULDN'T KNOW IT.
TELL ME! TELL ME!
EARTH-WORM MAN 3.
THAT'S SUCH A BORING MOVIE. I CAN'T TELL YOU HOW MANY TIMES I GOT PUNCHED WATCHING IT.
HE'S SEEN IT...
PUNCHED?
FWIP
SHEESH... BUT IT'S A SPLATTER FILM, SO...
...I GUESS IT'S NOT THE KIND OF MOVIE WHERE YOU CAN EXPECT SOME KIND OF STORY.

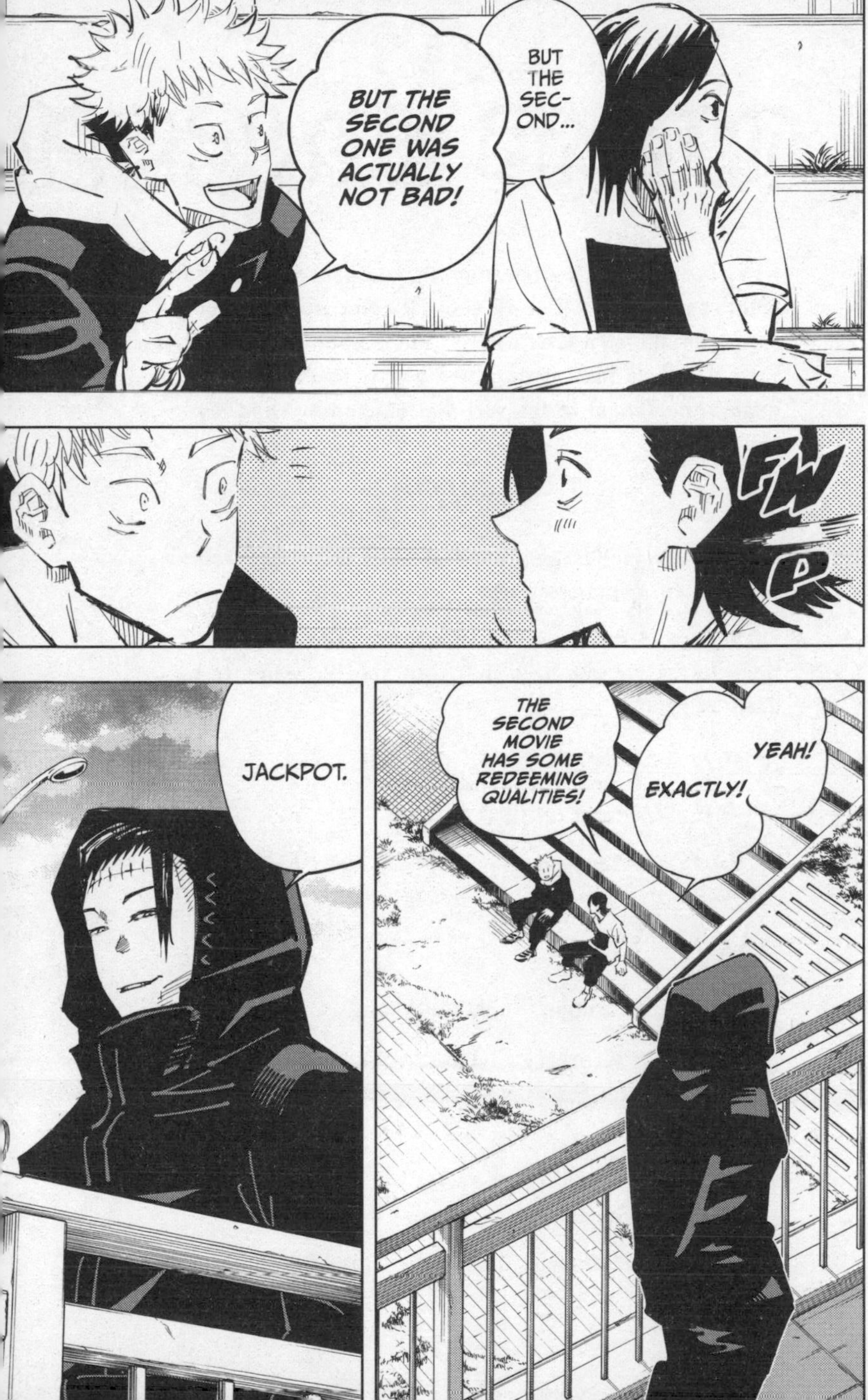
BUT THE SEC-OND...
BUT THE SECOND ONE WAS ACTUALLY NOT BAD!
FWP
YEAH! EXACTLY!
THE SECOND MOVIE HAS SOME REDEEMING QUALITIES!
JACKPOT.

THEME SONGS?!

• I've been told that Character Profile pages are sort of pointless, so fine! I'll show you! I'll come up with theme songs for the characters instead!! As soon as I said that, the side of me that wants other people to think I have good taste in music got in the way and started swaying my choices.

BUT!!

• I'm feeling jaded about a lot of stuff these days, so I'll just present my choices now.

• Goodbye to the me who wants to be liked by people! Hello to the me who says that...but actually wants to be liked by people.

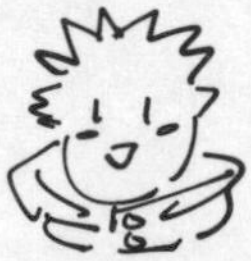

Itadori

• 9mm Parabellum Bullet - "Heart Ni Hi O Tsukete"

• Kuchiroro - "Itsuka Dokoka De"

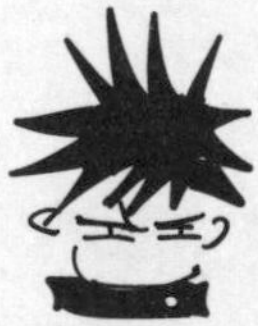

Fushiguro

• Uchujin - "Hakujitsumu"

• Weezer - "Island in the Sun"

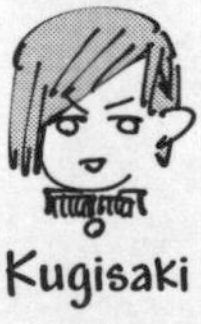

Kugisaki

• Sunny Day Service - "Seishun Kyosokyoku"

• Natsuko Nisshoku - "Ano Depaato"

Chapter 24: Young Fish and Reverse Punishment, Part 6

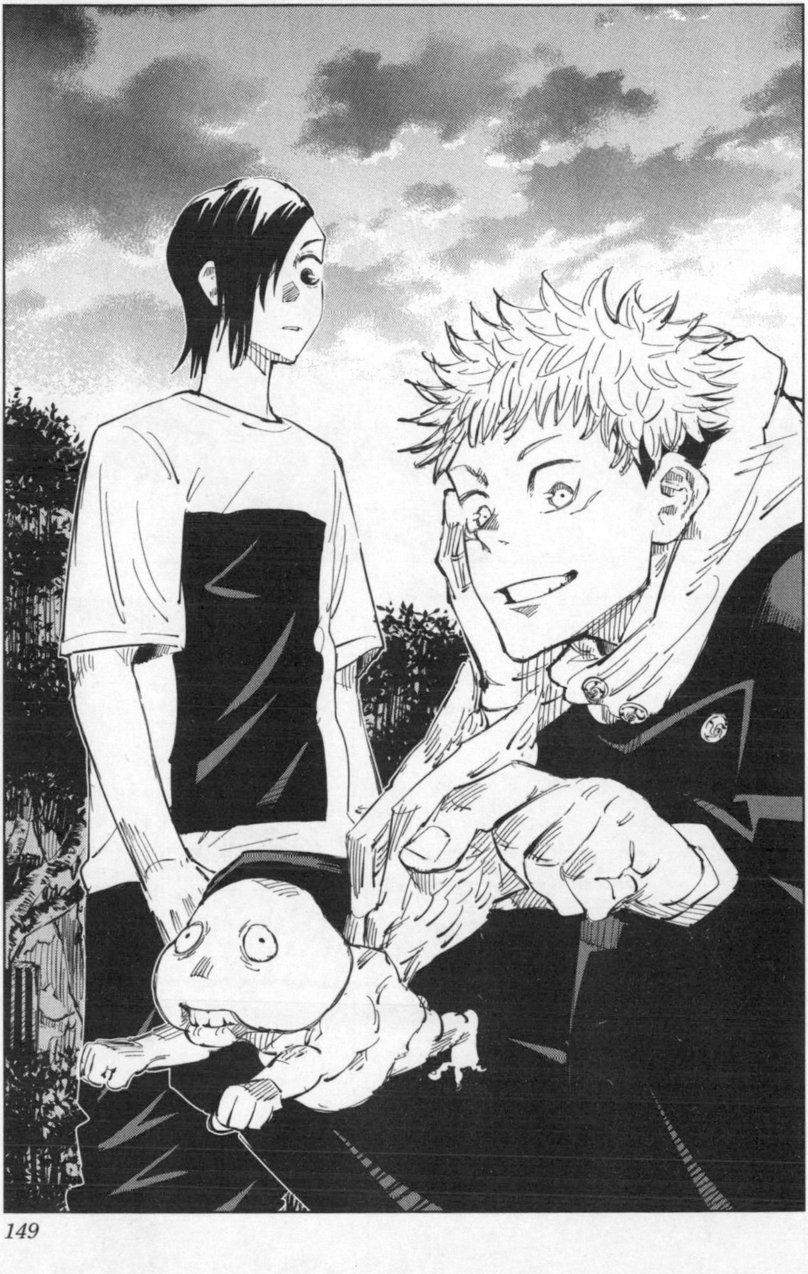

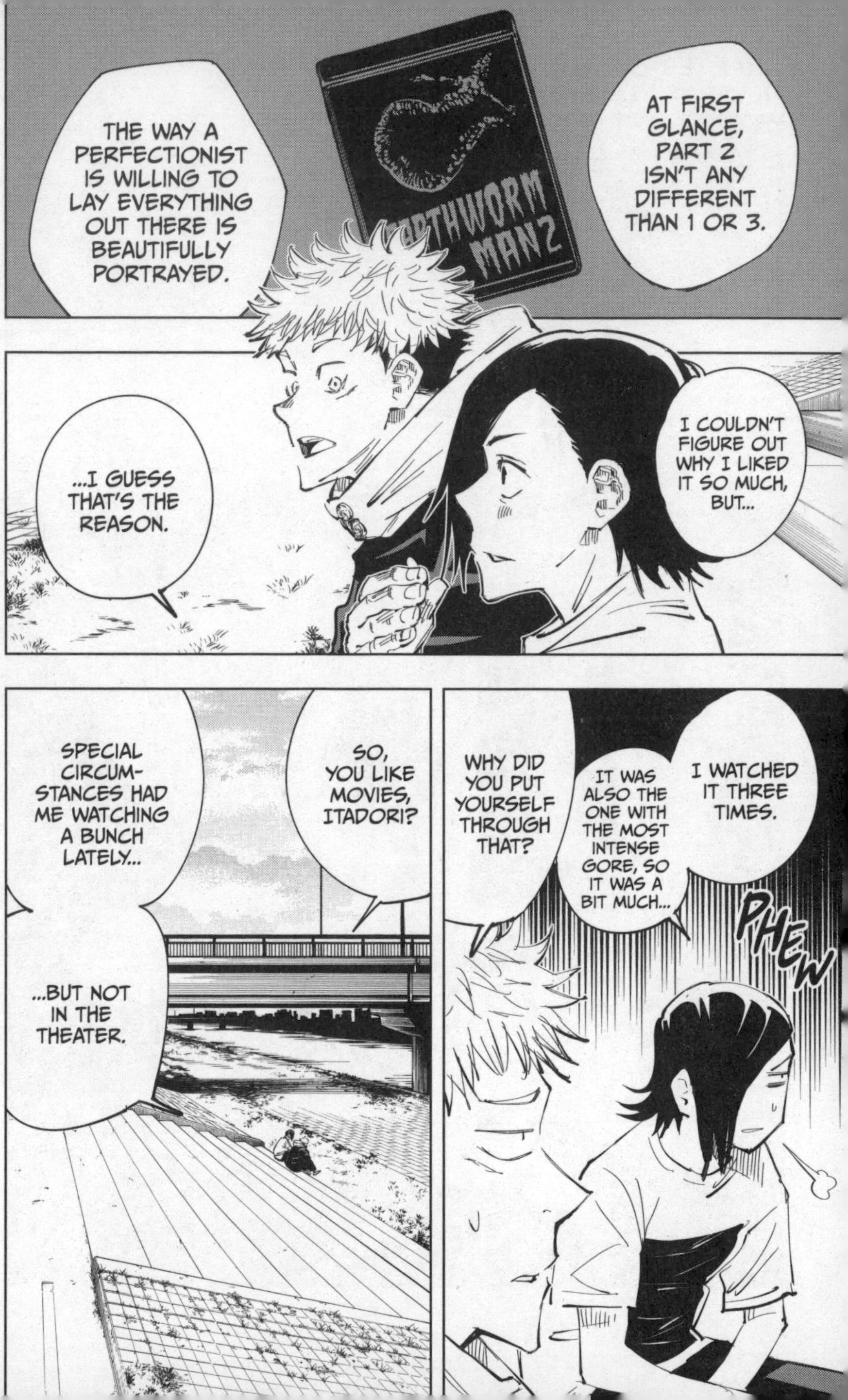
AT FIRST GLANCE, PART 2 ISN'T ANY DIFFERENT THAN 1 OR 3.
THE WAY A PERFECTIONIST IS WILLING TO LAY EVERYTHING OUT THERE IS BEAUTIFULLY PORTRAYED.
I COULDN'T FIGURE OUT WHY I LIKED IT SO MUCH, BUT...
...I GUESS THAT'S THE REASON.
I WATCHED IT THREE TIMES.
IT WAS ALSO THE ONE WITH THE MOST INTENSE GORE, SO IT WAS A BIT MUCH...
PHEW
WHY DID YOU PUT YOURSELF THROUGH THAT?
SO, YOU LIKE MOVIES, ITADORI?
SPECIAL CIRCUM-STANCES HAD ME WATCHING A BUNCH LATELY...
...BUT NOT IN THE THEATER.

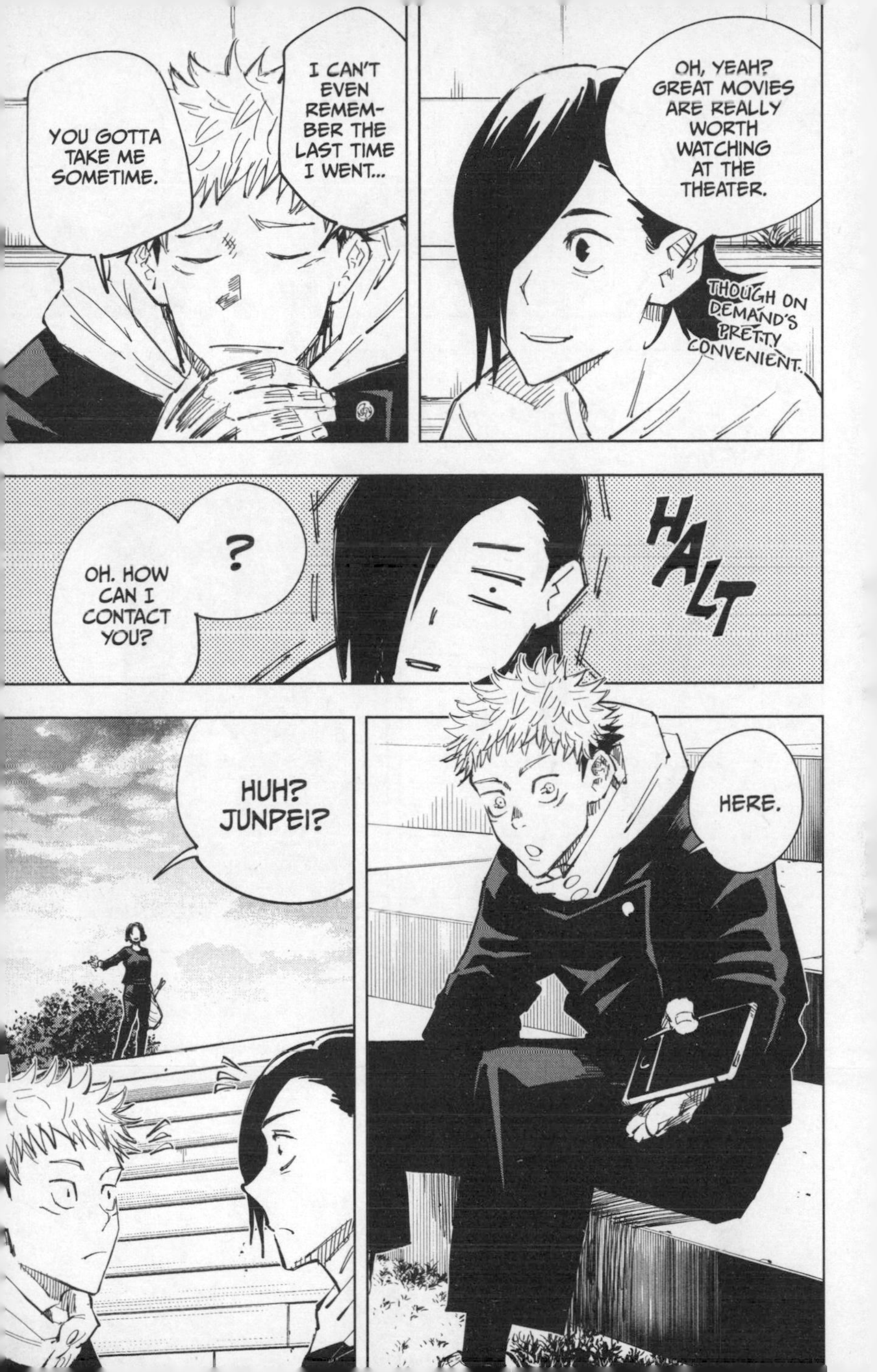
OH, YEAH? GREAT MOVIES ARE REALLY WORTH WATCHING AT THE THEATER.
THOUGH ON DEMAND'S PRETTY CONVENIENT.
I CAN'T EVEN REMEMBER THE LAST TIME I WENT...
YOU GOTTA TAKE ME SOMETIME.
HALT
?
OH. HOW CAN I CONTACT YOU?
HERE.
HUH? JUNPEI?

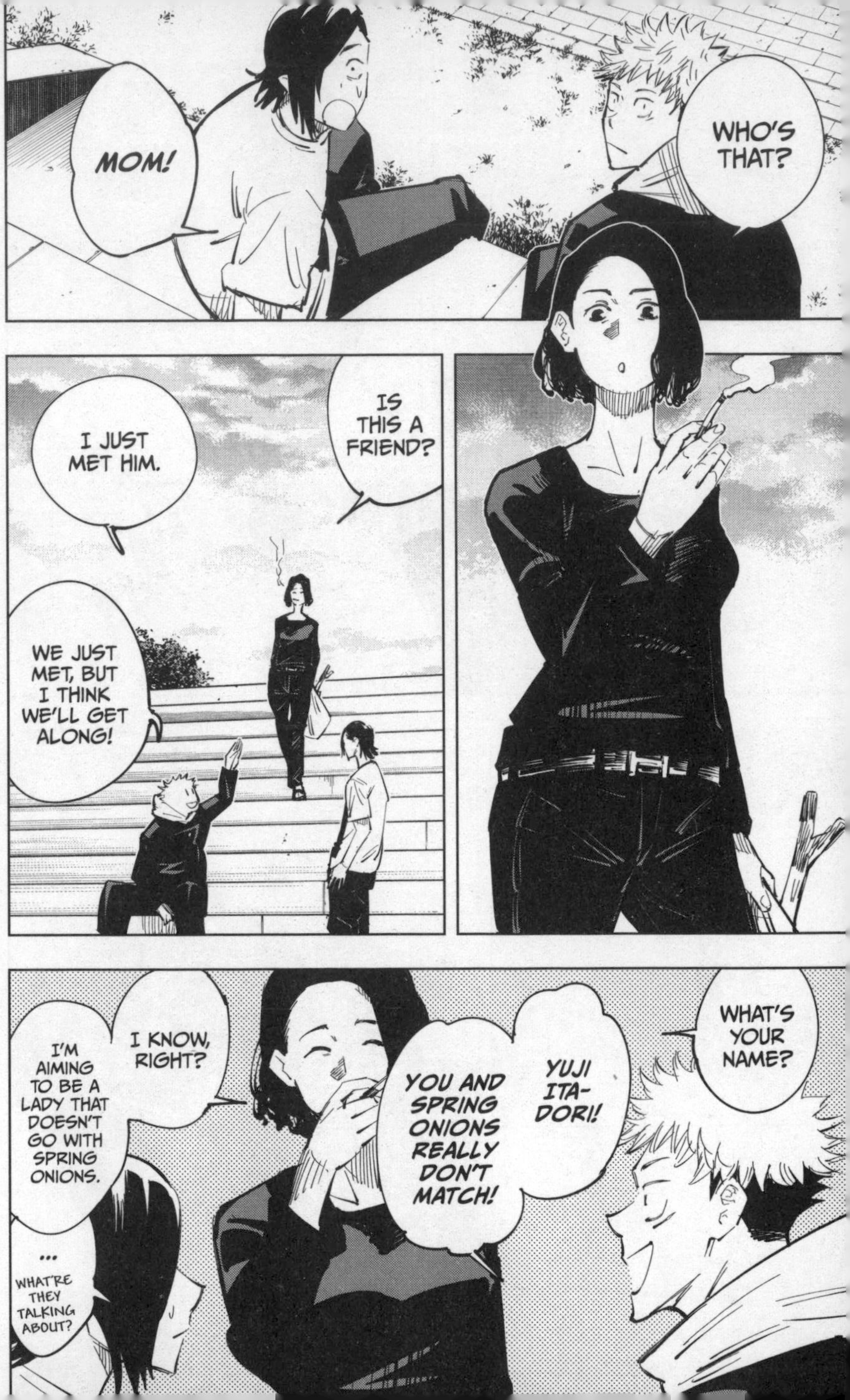
WHO'S THAT?
MOM!
IS THIS A FRIEND?
I JUST MET HIM.
WE JUST MET, BUT I THINK WE'LL GET ALONG!
WHAT'S YOUR NAME?
YUJI ITA-DORI!
YOU AND SPRING ONIONS REALLY DON'T MATCH!
I KNOW, RIGHT?
I'M AIMING TO BE A LADY THAT DOESN'T GO WITH SPRING ONIONS.
...
WHAT'RE THEY TALKING ABOUT?

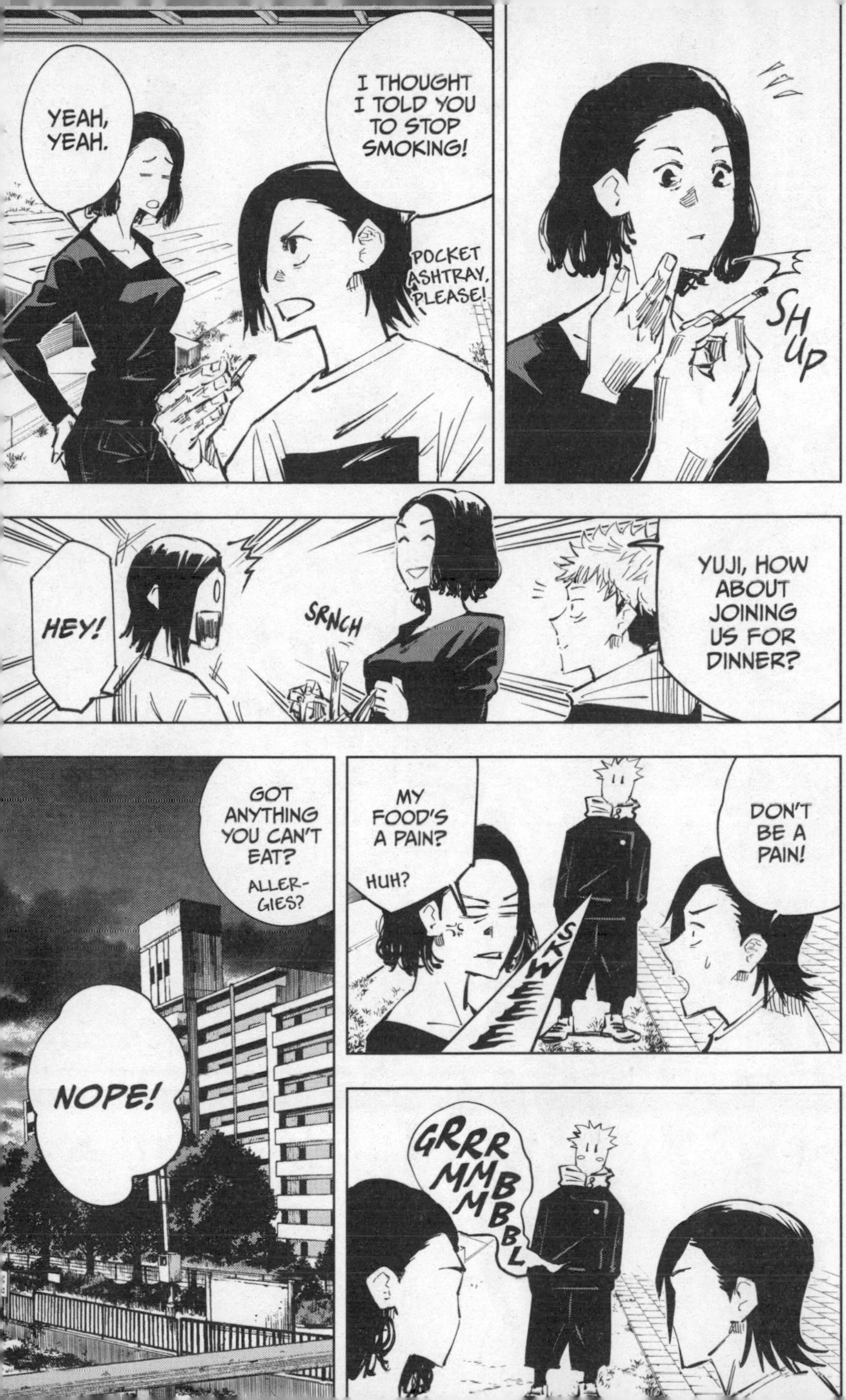
SHUP
I THOUGHT I TOLD YOU TO STOP SMOKING!
YEAH, YEAH.
POCKET ASHTRAY, PLEASE!
YUJI, HOW ABOUT JOINING US FOR DINNER?
SRNCH
HEY!
DON'T BE A PAIN!
MY FOOD'S A PAIN?
HUH?
SKWEEEE
GRRRMMMBBBL
GOT ANYTHING YOU CAN'T EAT?
ALLER-GIES?
NOPE!

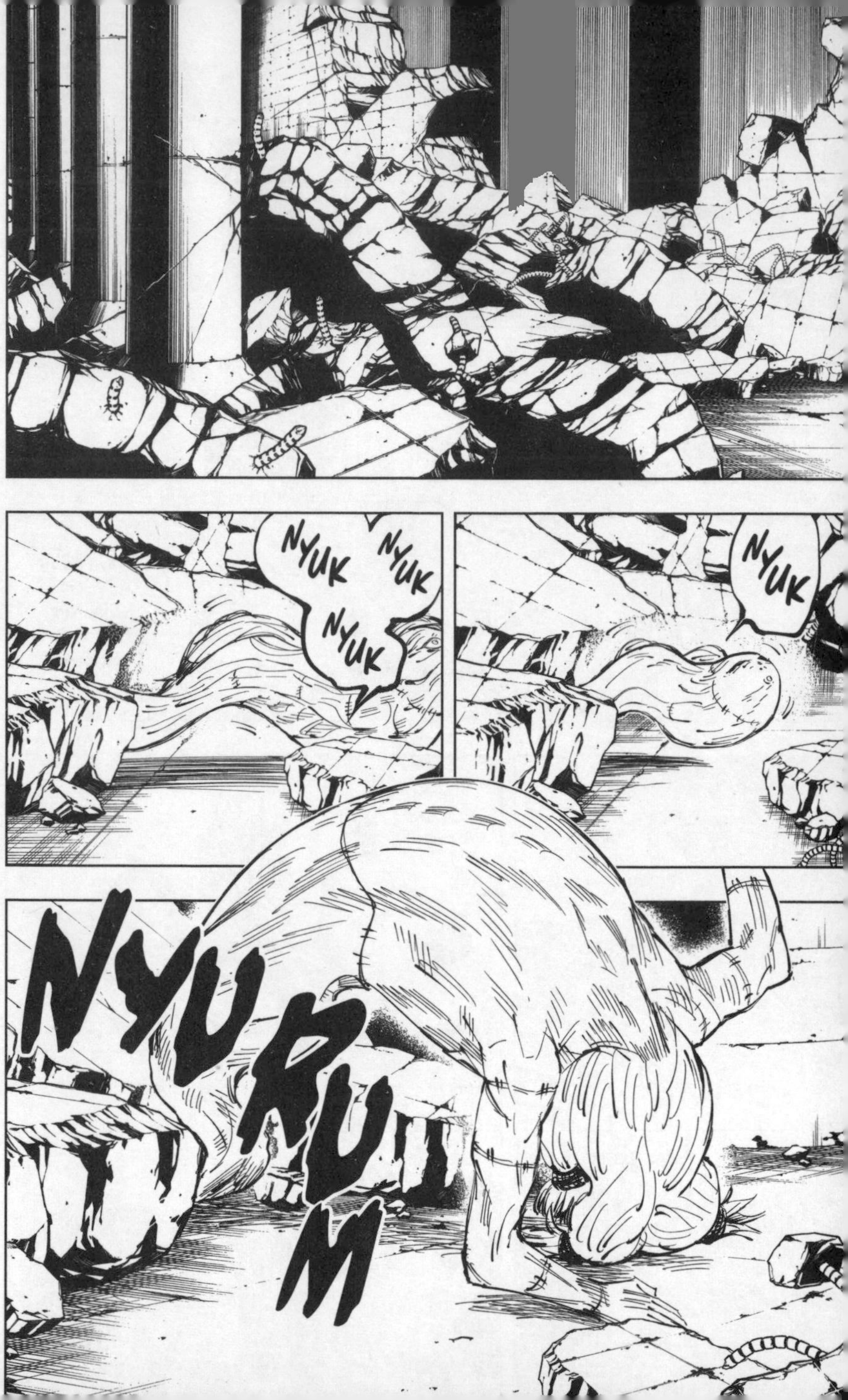
NYUK
NYUK
NYUK
NYUK
NYUK
NYURURUM

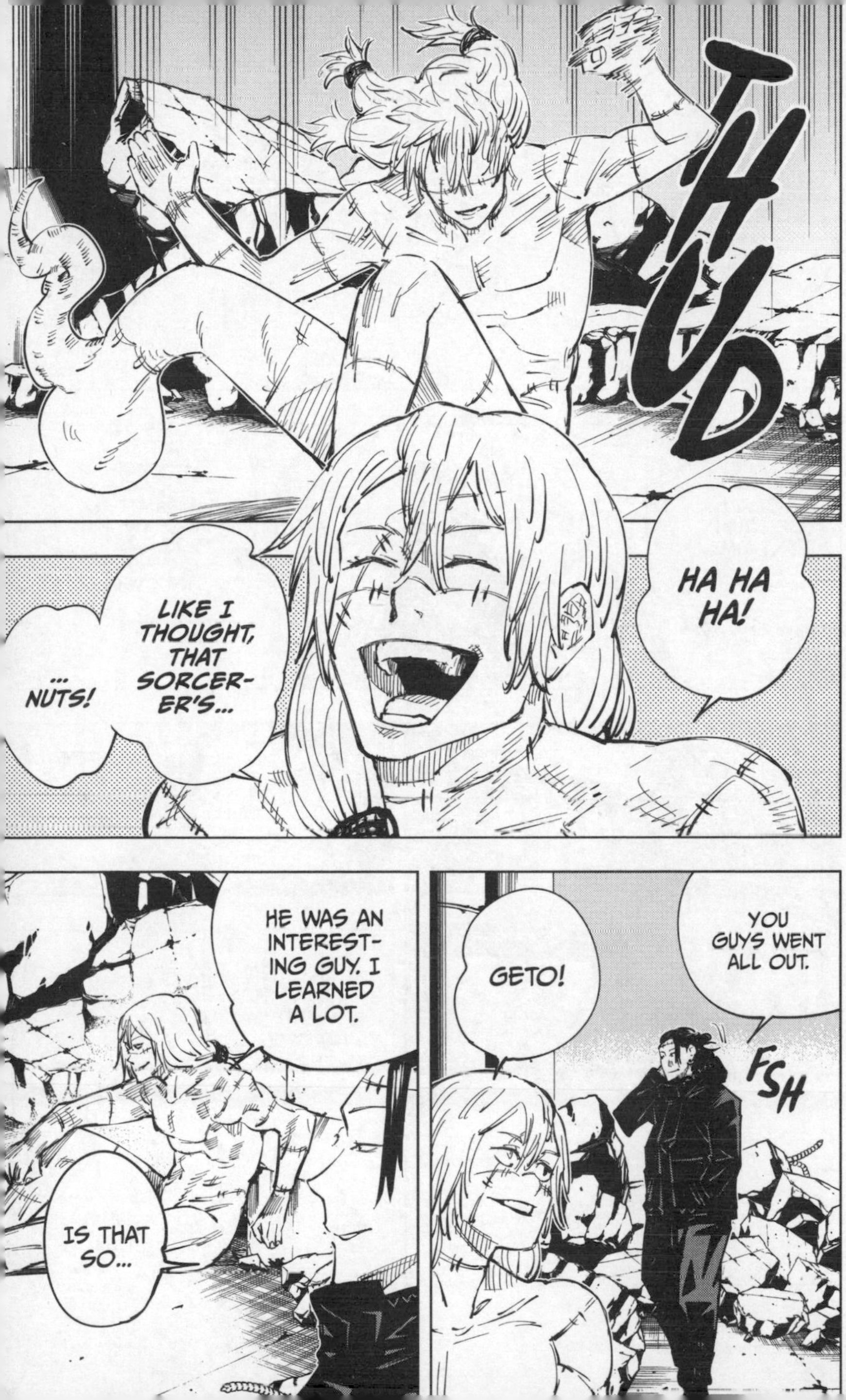
THUD
HA HA HA!
LIKE I THOUGHT, THAT SORCERER'S...
... NUTS!
YOU GUYS WENT ALL OUT.
FSH
GETO!
HE WAS AN INTERESTING GUY. I LEARNED A LOT.
IS THAT SO...

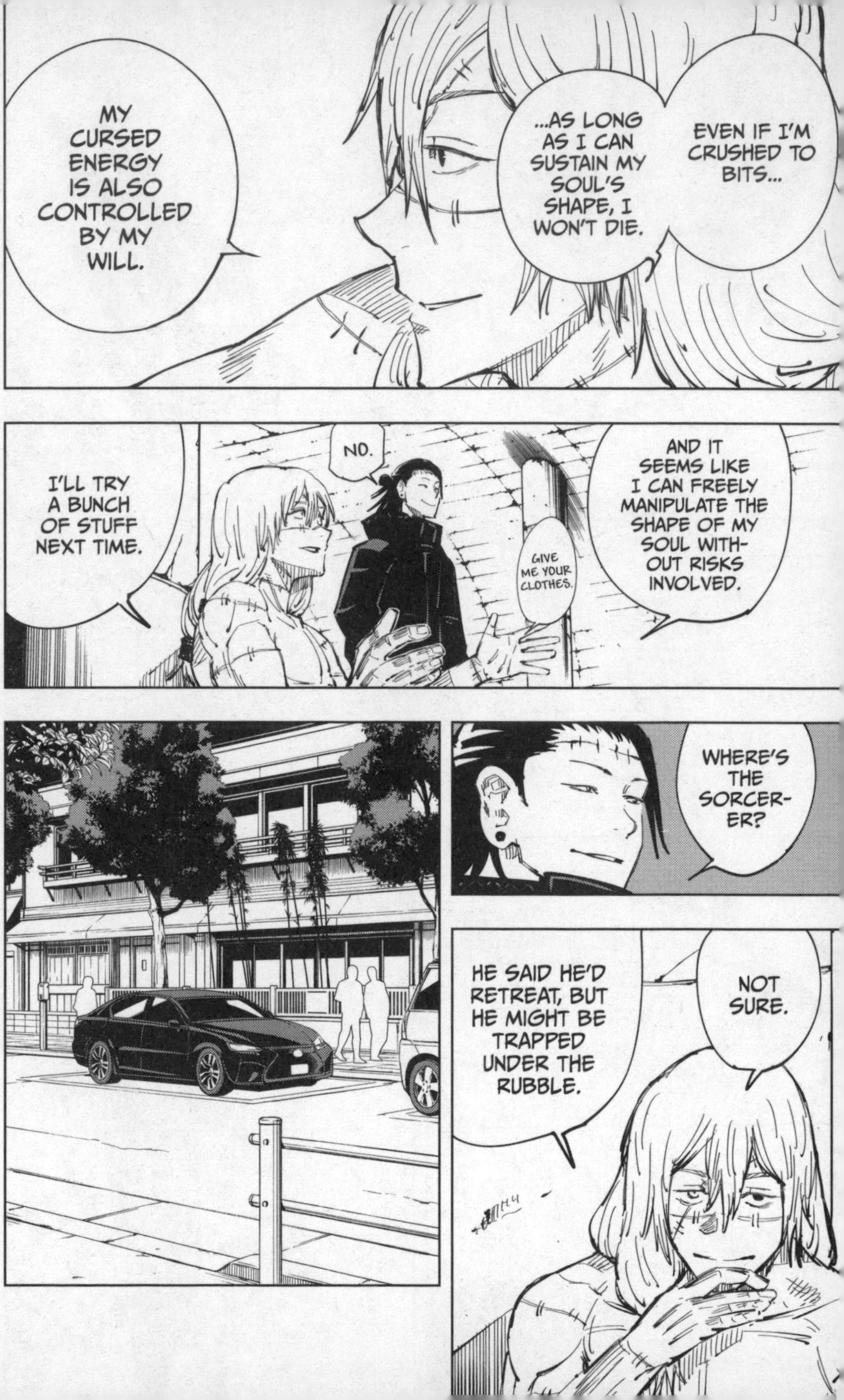
EVEN IF I'M CRUSHED TO BITS...
...AS LONG AS I CAN SUSTAIN MY SOUL'S SHAPE, I WON'T DIE.
MY CURSED ENERGY IS ALSO CONTROLLED BY MY WILL.
AND IT SEEMS LIKE I CAN FREELY MANIPULATE THE SHAPE OF MY SOUL WITH-OUT RISKS INVOLVED.
GIVE ME YOUR CLOTHES.
NO.
I'LL TRY A BUNCH OF STUFF NEXT TIME.
WHERE'S THE SORCER-ER?
NOT SURE.
HE SAID HE'D RETREAT, BUT HE MIGHT BE TRAPPED UNDER THE RUBBLE.

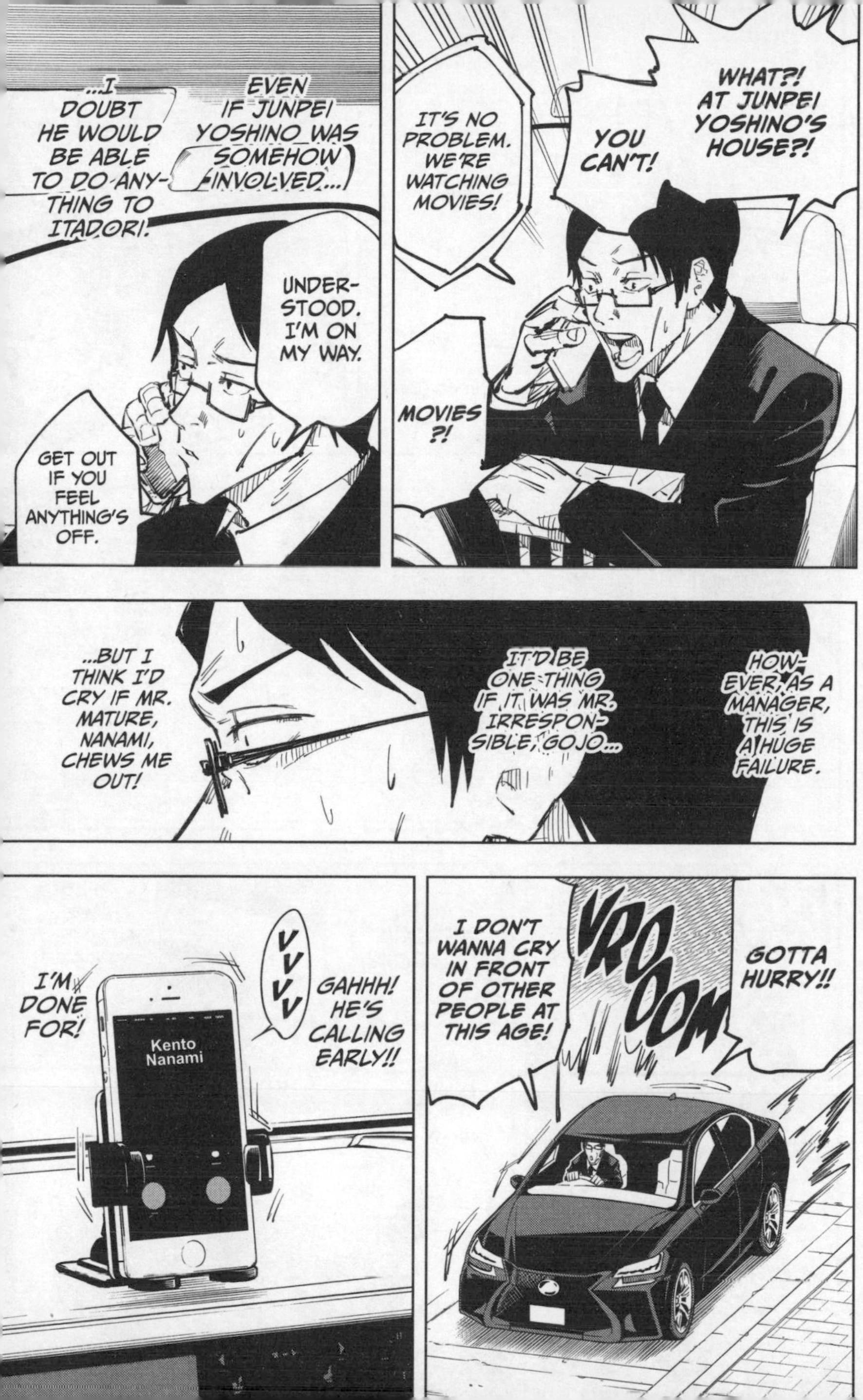
WHAT?! AT JUNPEI YOSHINO'S HOUSE?!
YOU CAN'T!
IT'S NO PROBLEM. WE'RE WATCHING MOVIES!
MOVIES?!
EVEN IF JUNPEI YOSHINO WAS SOMEHOW INVOLVED...
...I DOUBT HE WOULD BE ABLE TO DO ANY-THING TO ITADORI.
UNDER-STOOD. I'M ON MY WAY.
GET OUT IF YOU FEEL ANYTHING'S OFF.
HOW-EVER, AS A MANAGER, THIS IS A HUGE FAILURE.
IT'D BE ONE THING IF IT WAS MR. IRRESPON-SIBLE, GOJO...
...BUT I THINK I'D CRY IF MR. MATURE, NANAMI, CHEWS ME OUT!
GOTTA HURRY!!
VROOOOM
I DON'T WANNA CRY IN FRONT OF OTHER PEOPLE AT THIS AGE!
GAHHH! HE'S CALLING EARLY!!
VVVV
Kento Nanami
I'M DONE FOR!

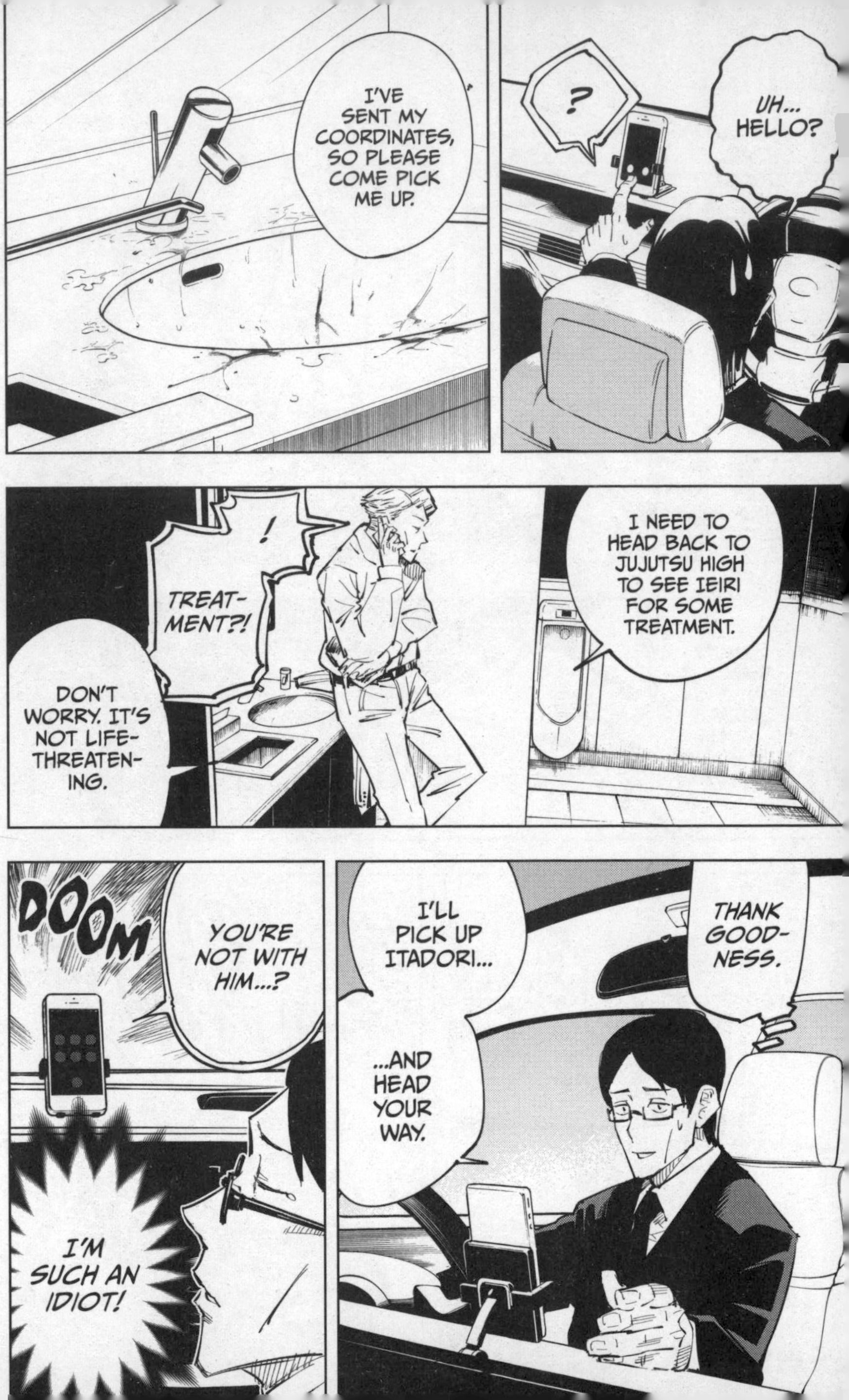
UH... HELLO?
?
I'VE SENT MY COORDINATES, SO PLEASE COME PICK ME UP.
I NEED TO HEAD BACK TO JUJUTSU HIGH TO SEE IEIRI FOR SOME TREATMENT.
!
TREATMENT?!
DON'T WORRY. IT'S NOT LIFE-THREATENING.
THANK GOODNESS.
I'LL PICK UP ITADORI...
...AND HEAD YOUR WAY.
YOU'RE NOT WITH HIM...?
DOOM
I'M SUCH AN IDIOT!

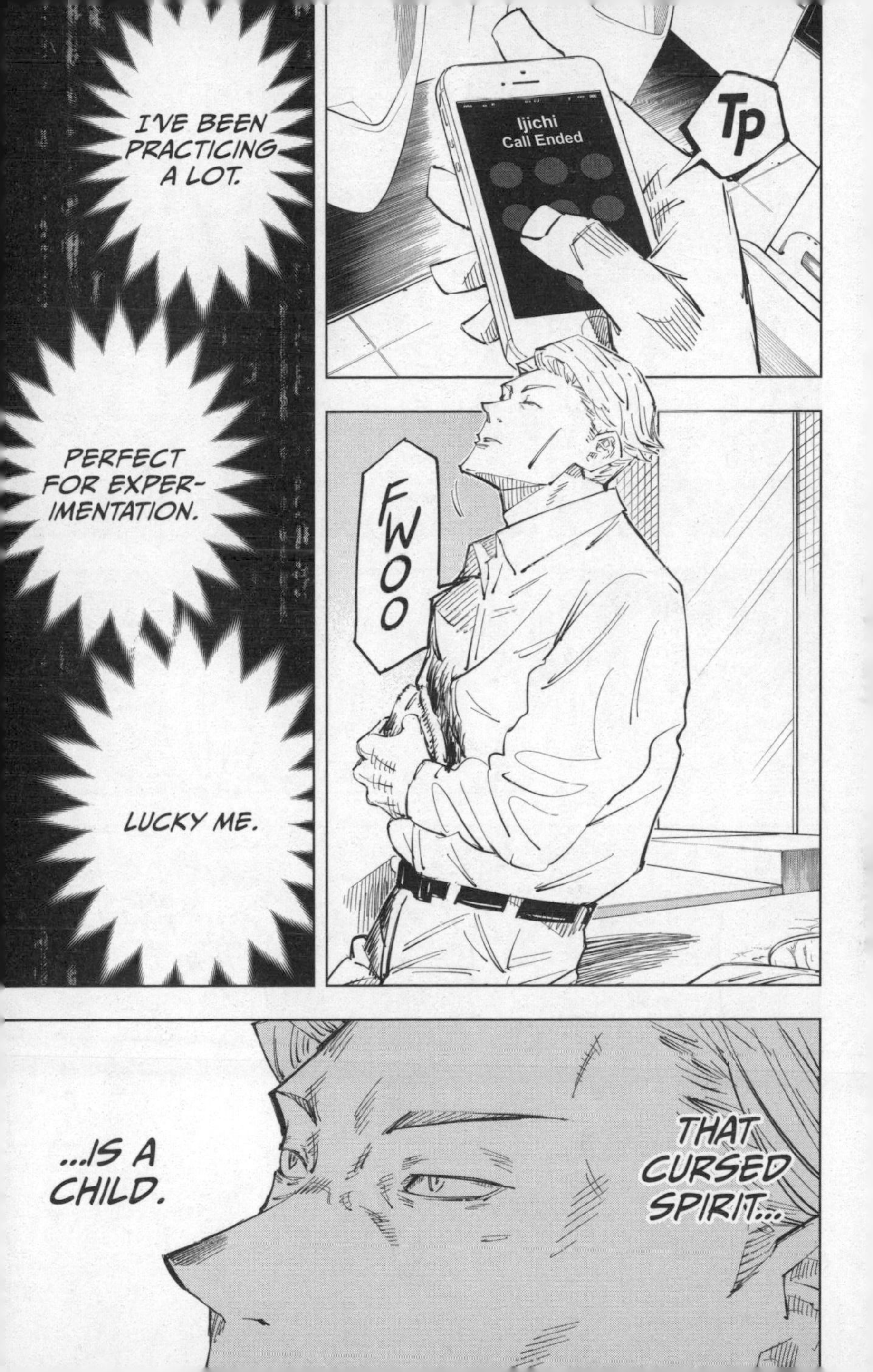
Ijichi
Call Ended
Tp
FWOO
I'VE BEEN PRACTICING A LOT.
PERFECT FOR EXPER-IMENTATION.
LUCKY ME.
THAT CURSED SPIRIT...
...IS A CHILD.

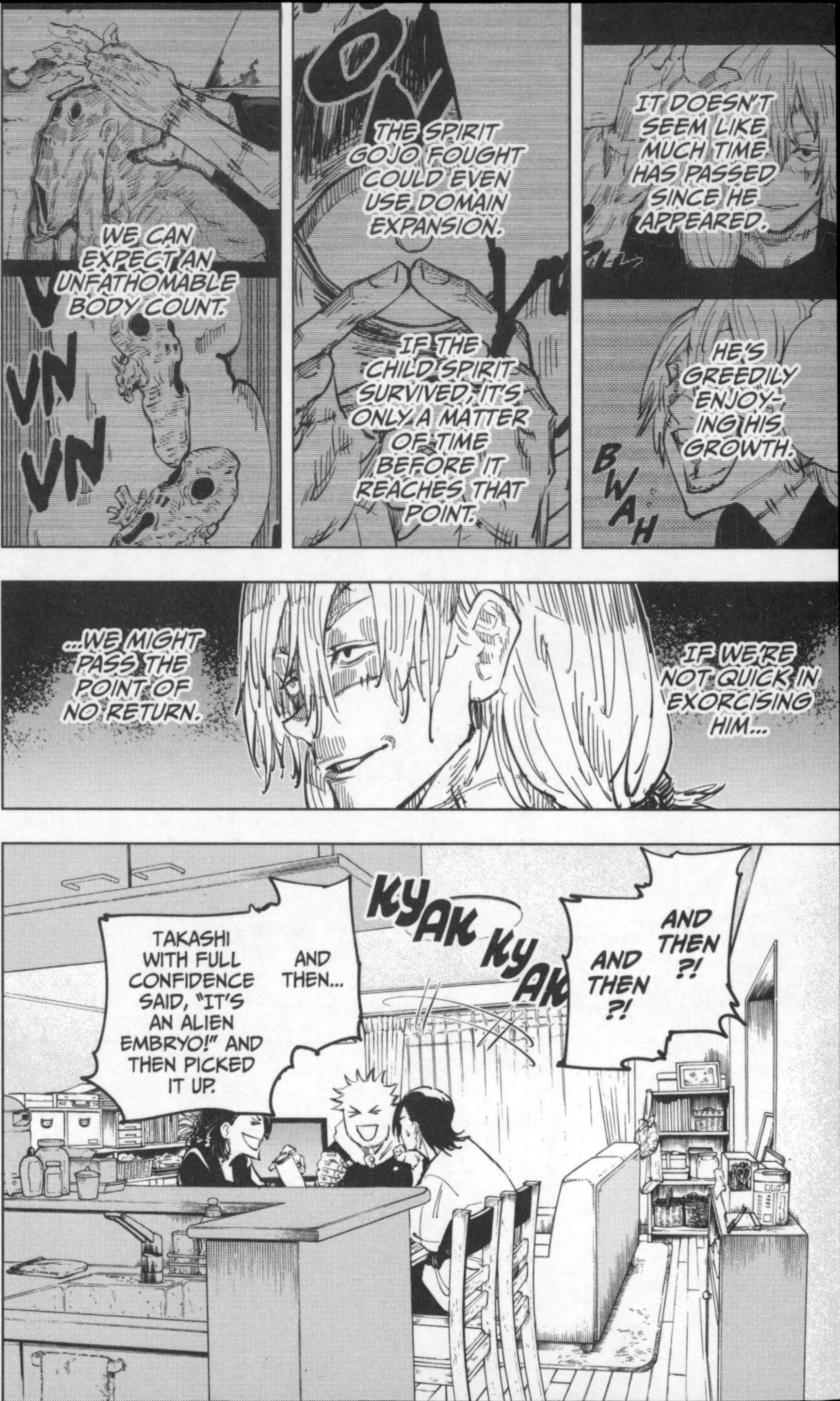
IT DOESN'T SEEM LIKE MUCH TIME HAS PASSED SINCE HE APPEARED.
HE'S GREEDILY ENJOY-ING HIS GROWTH.
BWAH
THE SPIRIT GOJO FOUGHT COULD EVEN USE DOMAIN EXPANSION.
IF THE CHILD SPIRIT SURVIVED, IT'S ONLY A MATTER OF TIME BEFORE IT REACHES THAT POINT.
WE CAN EXPECT AN UNFATHOMABLE BODY COUNT.
VN VN VN
IF WE'RE NOT QUICK IN EXORCISING HIM...
...WE MIGHT PASS THE POINT OF NO RETURN.
AND THEN ?!
AND THEN ?!
KYAK KYAK
AND THEN...
TAKASHI WITH FULL CONFIDENCE SAID, "IT'S AN ALIEN EMBRYO!" AND THEN PICKED IT UP.

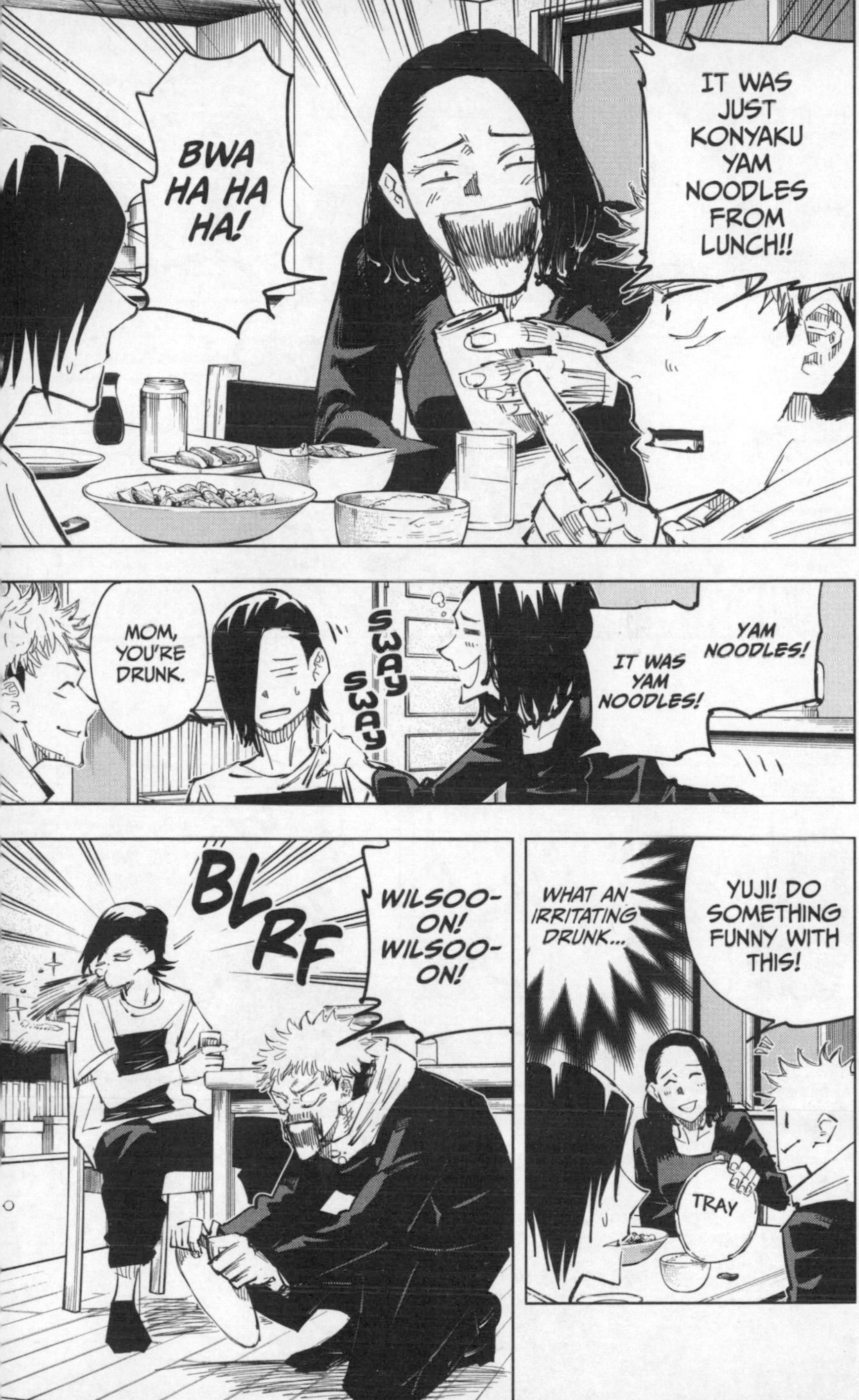
IT WAS JUST KONYAKU YAM NOODLES FROM LUNCH!!
BWA HA HA HA!
YAM NOODLES!
IT WAS YAM NOODLES!
SWAY SWAY
MOM, YOU'RE DRUNK.
YUJI! DO SOMETHING FUNNY WITH THIS!
WHAT AN IRRITATING DRUNK...
TRAY
WILSOO-ON! WILSOO-ON!
BLRF

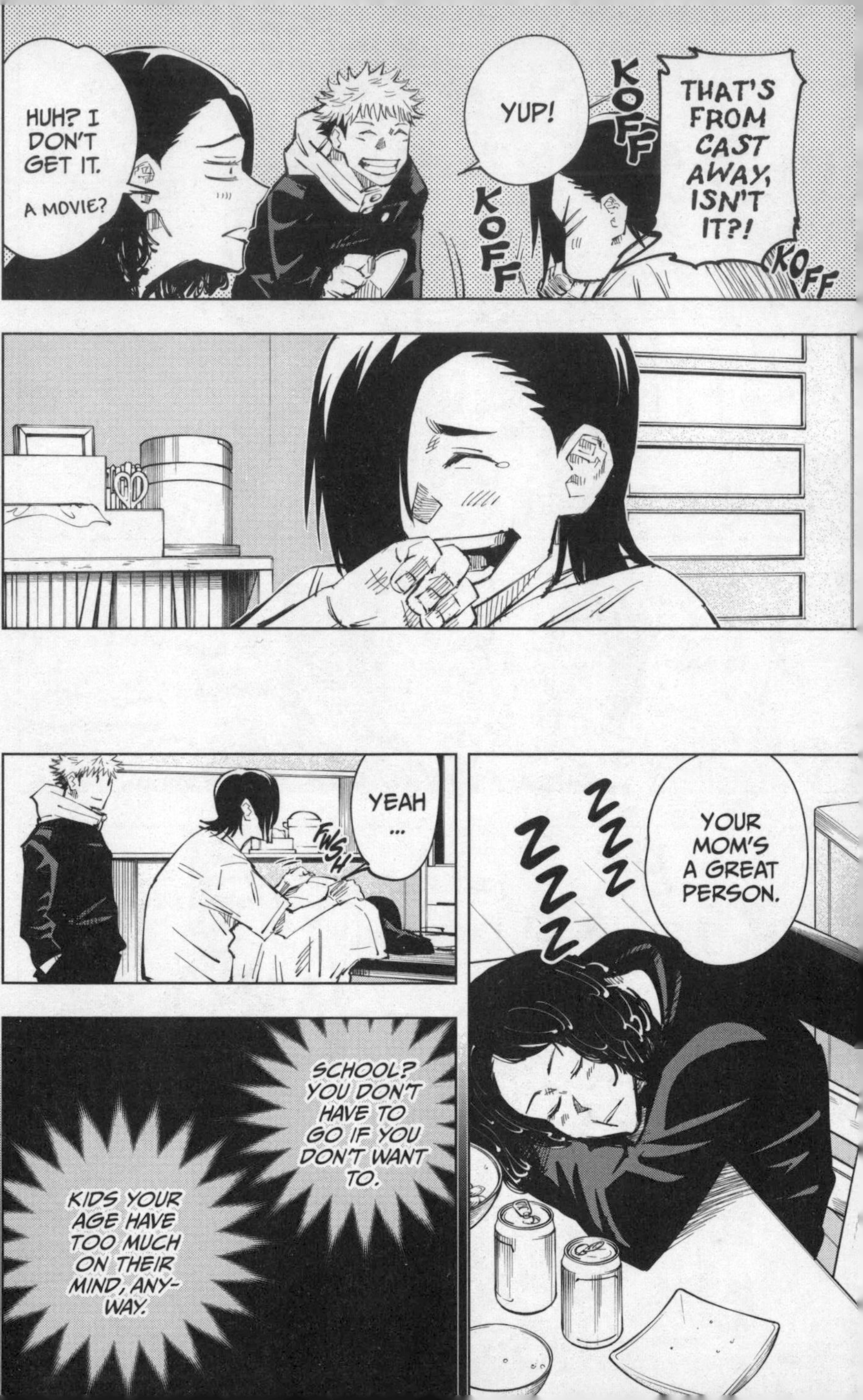
THAT'S FROM CAST AWAY, ISN'T IT?!
KOFF
KOFF
KOFF
YUP!
HUH? I DON'T GET IT.
A MOVIE?
YOUR MOM'S A GREAT PERSON.
ZZZ
ZZZ
YEAH ...
FWSH
SCHOOL? YOU DON'T HAVE TO GO IF YOU DON'T WANT TO.
KIDS YOUR AGE HAVE TOO MUCH ON THEIR MIND, ANY-WAY.

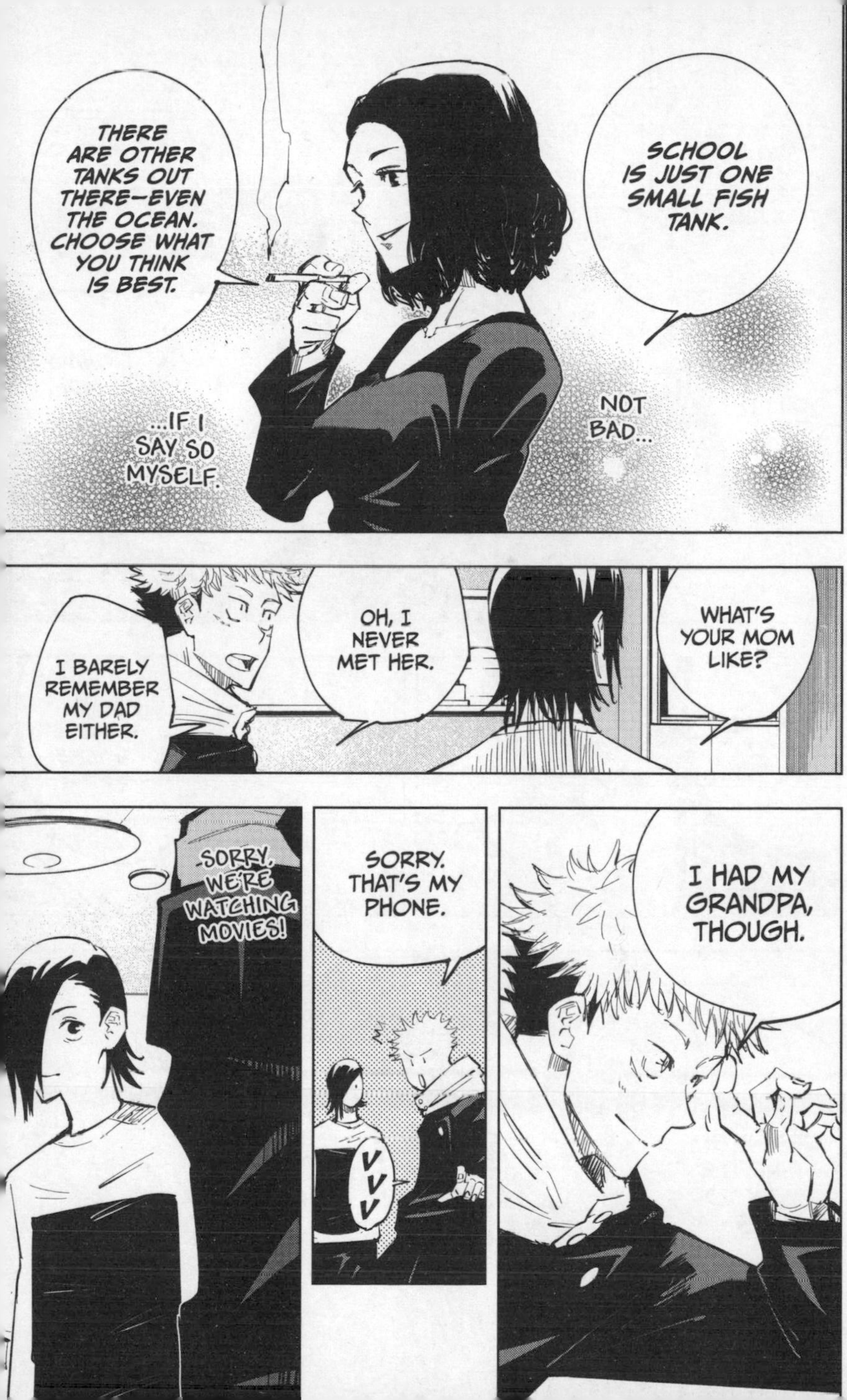
SCHOOL IS JUST ONE SMALL FISH TANK.
NOT BAD...
THERE ARE OTHER TANKS OUT THERE—EVEN THE OCEAN. CHOOSE WHAT YOU THINK IS BEST.
...IF I SAY SO MYSELF.
WHAT'S YOUR MOM LIKE?
OH, I NEVER MET HER.
I BARELY REMEMBER MY DAD EITHER.
I HAD MY GRANDPA, THOUGH.
SORRY. THAT'S MY PHONE.
VVV
SORRY. WE'RE WATCHING MOVIES!

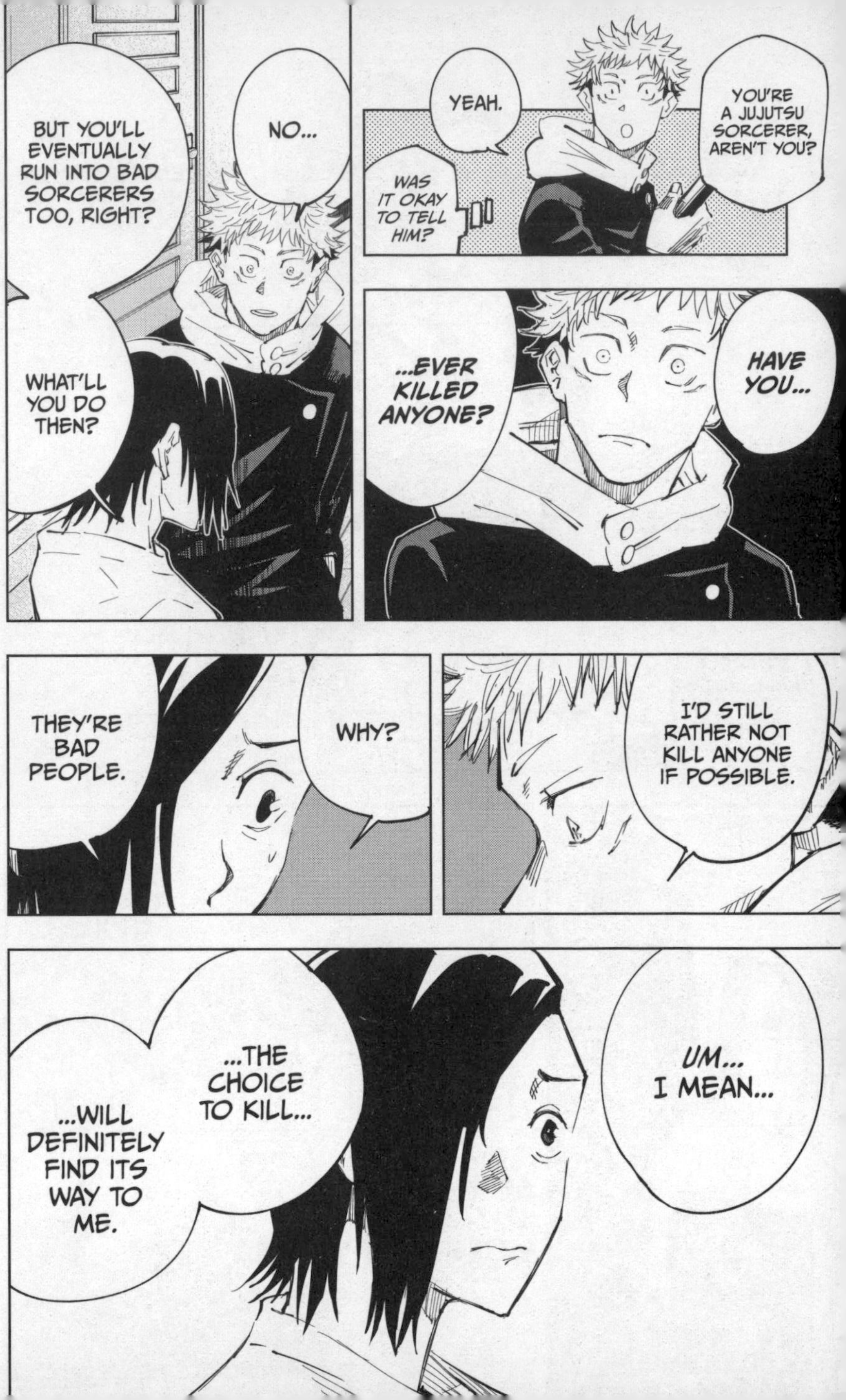
YOU'RE A JUJUTSU SORCERER, AREN'T YOU?
YEAH.
WAS IT OKAY TO TELL HIM?
HAVE YOU...
...EVER KILLED ANYONE?
NO...
BUT YOU'LL EVENTUALLY RUN INTO BAD SORCERERS TOO, RIGHT?
WHAT'LL YOU DO THEN?
I'D STILL RATHER NOT KILL ANYONE IF POSSIBLE.
WHY?
THEY'RE BAD PEOPLE.
UM... I MEAN...
...THE CHOICE TO KILL...
...WILL DEFINITELY FIND ITS WAY TO ME.

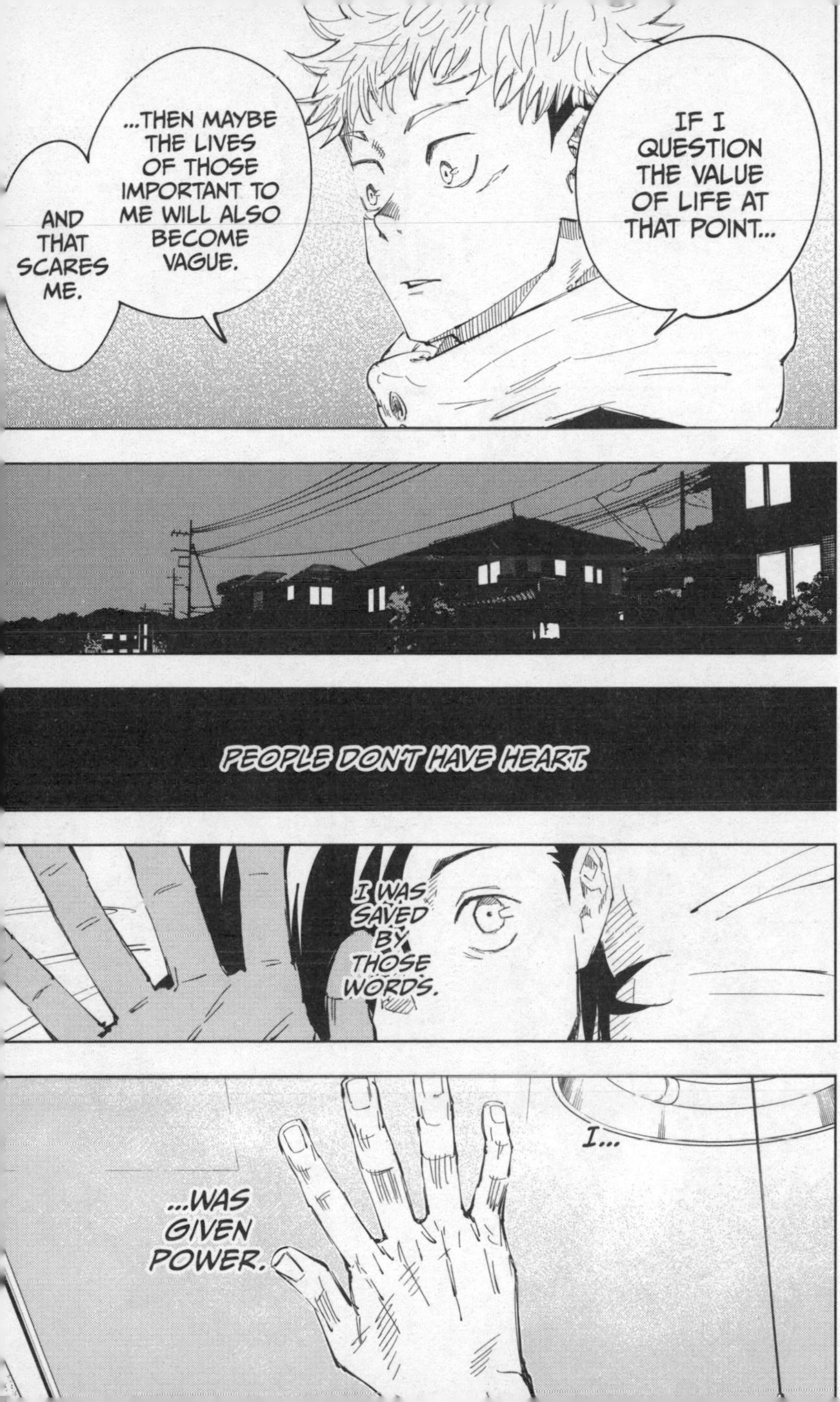
IF I QUESTION THE VALUE OF LIFE AT THAT POINT...
...THEN MAYBE THE LIVES OF THOSE IMPORTANT TO ME WILL ALSO BECOME VAGUE.
AND THAT SCARES ME.
PEOPLE DON'T HAVE HEART.
I WAS SAVED BY THOSE WORDS.
I...
...WAS GIVEN POWER.

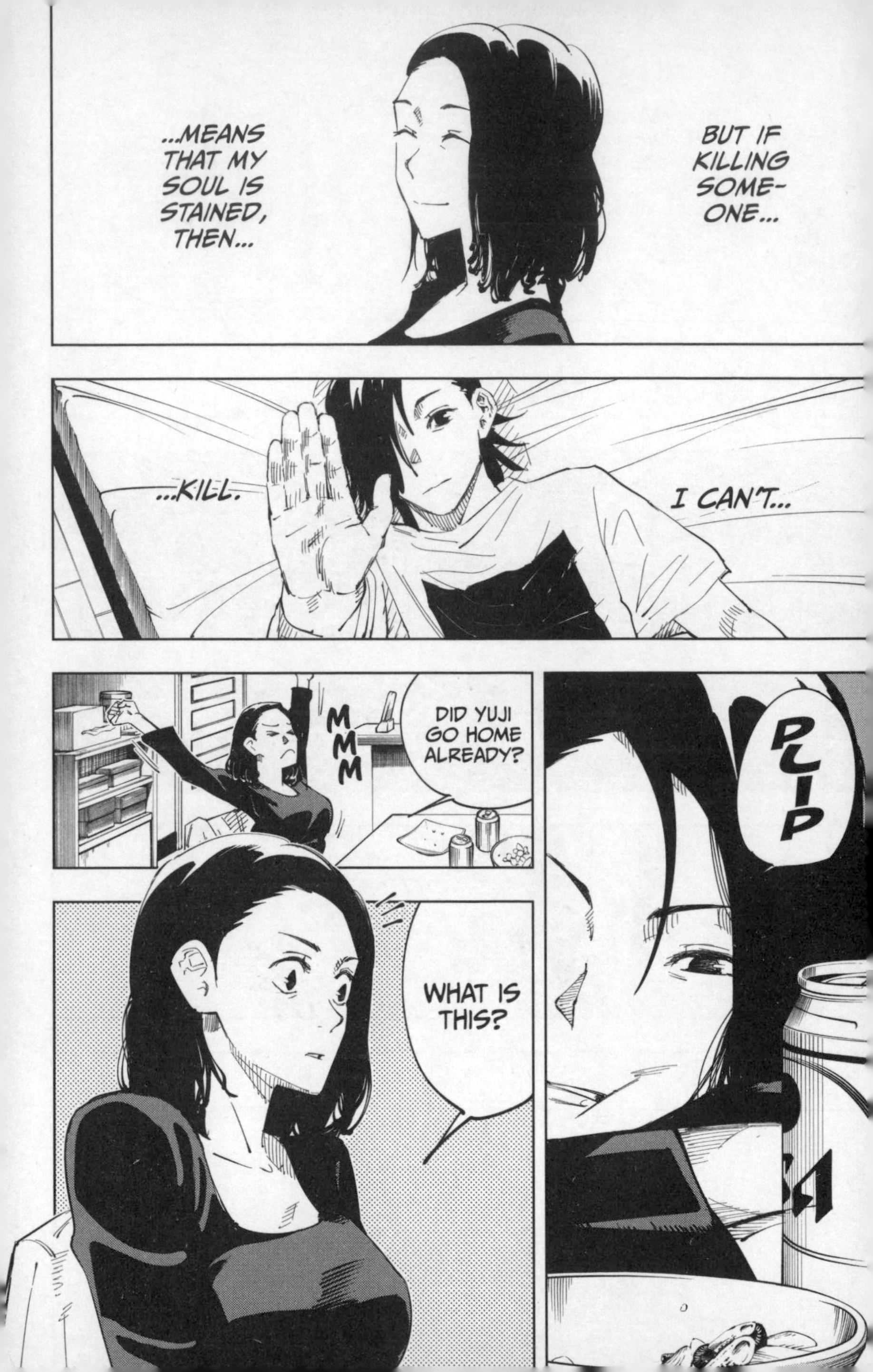
BUT IF KILLING SOME-ONE...
...MEANS THAT MY SOUL IS STAINED, THEN...
I CAN'T...
...KILL.
PLIP
DID YUJI GO HOME ALREADY?
MMM
WHAT IS THIS?

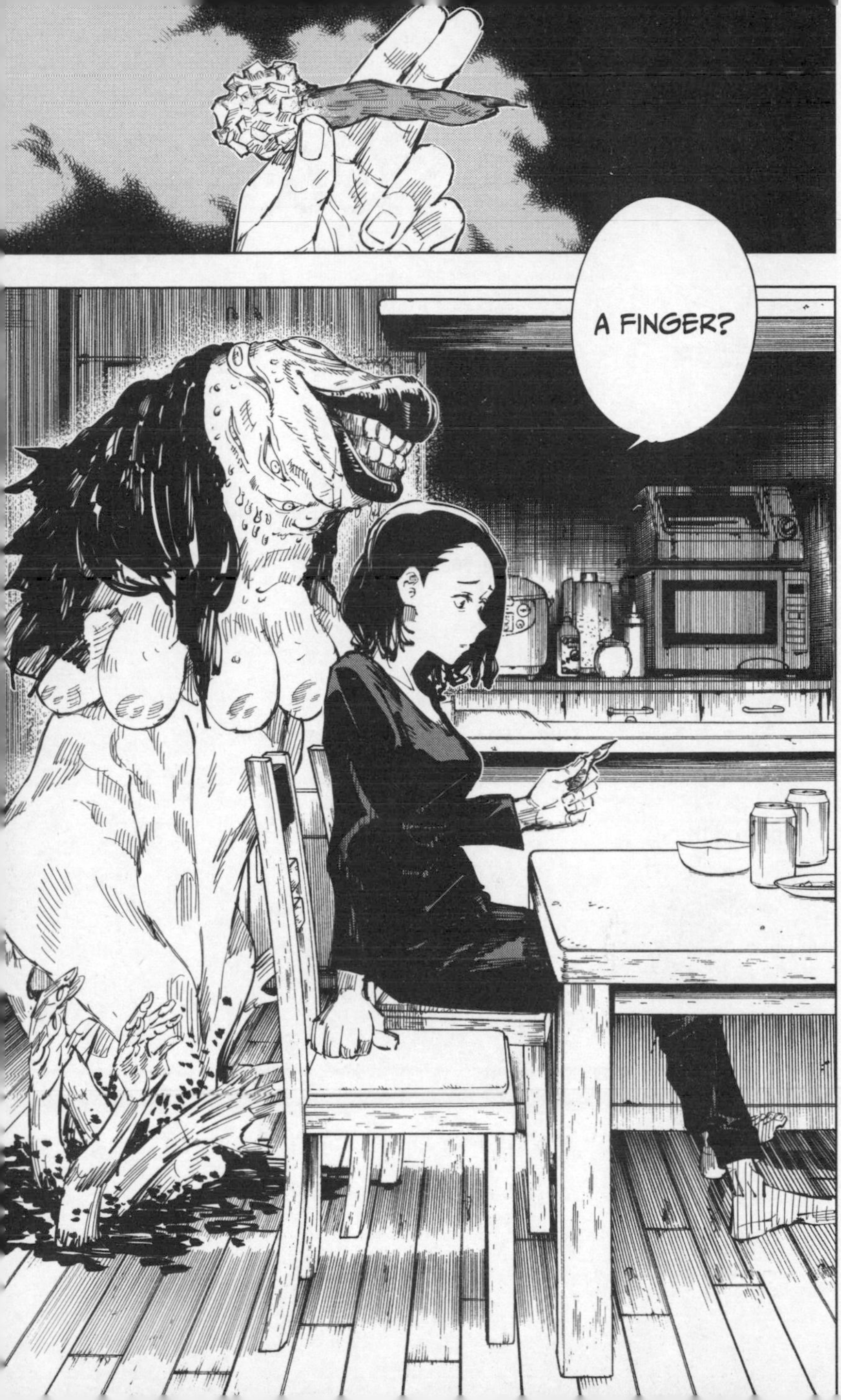
A FINGER?

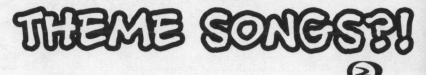

THEME SONGS?! ②

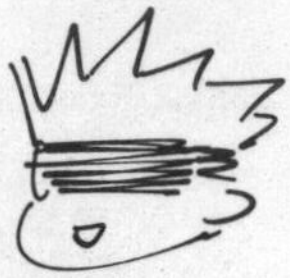

Gojo

- Asian Kung-Fu Generation - "Mada Minu Asu Ni"
- Avicii - "Shame on Me"

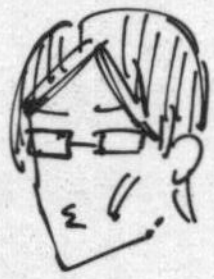

Ijichi

- Yasuyuki Okamura - "Do Nacchaten Dayo"
- Noriyuki Makihara - "SPY"

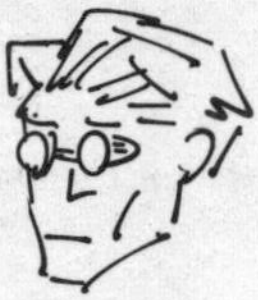

Nanami

- Yura Yura Teikoku - "Yura Yura Teikoku De Kangaechu"
- Fujifabric - "Saboten Record"

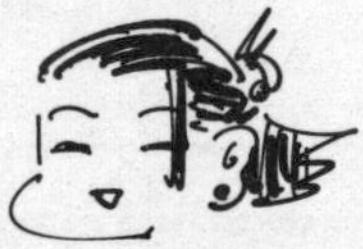

Geto

- →Pia-no-jaC← - "Paradiso"
- Two Door Cinema Club - "Come Back Home"

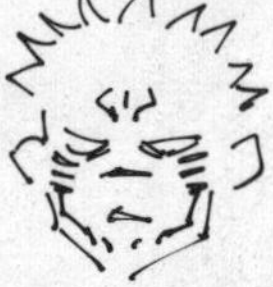

Sukuna

- Marilyn Manson - "(S)AINT"
- Susumu Hirasawa - "Day Scanner"

To be continued...

FOLLOWING THE INCIDENT AT SATOZAKURA HIGH SCHOOL, THE DEAD BODY OF JUNPEI YOSHINO'S MOTHER, NAGI YOSHINO, AND AN EXPOSED SUKUNA FINGER (LEFT EXTRA-ARM PINKY) WERE FOUND AT HIS HOME.

NAGI YOSHINO IS BELIEVED TO HAVE BEEN KILLED BY A SPIRIT DRAWN TO THE FINGER. HER BODY WAS SEVERED AND MISSING THE BOTTOM HALF.

NO VISIBLE EVIDENCE OF BLOOD WAS FOUND AT THE SCENE OF THE CRIME. NAGI YOSHINO WAS FOUND IN HER BED, STUFFED WITH AN ENORMOUS AMOUNT OF ICE PACKS.

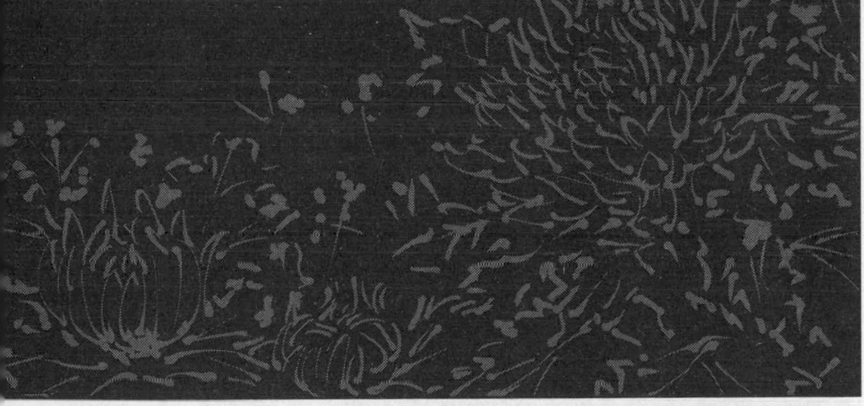

CHAPTER 25

NARROW-MINDED

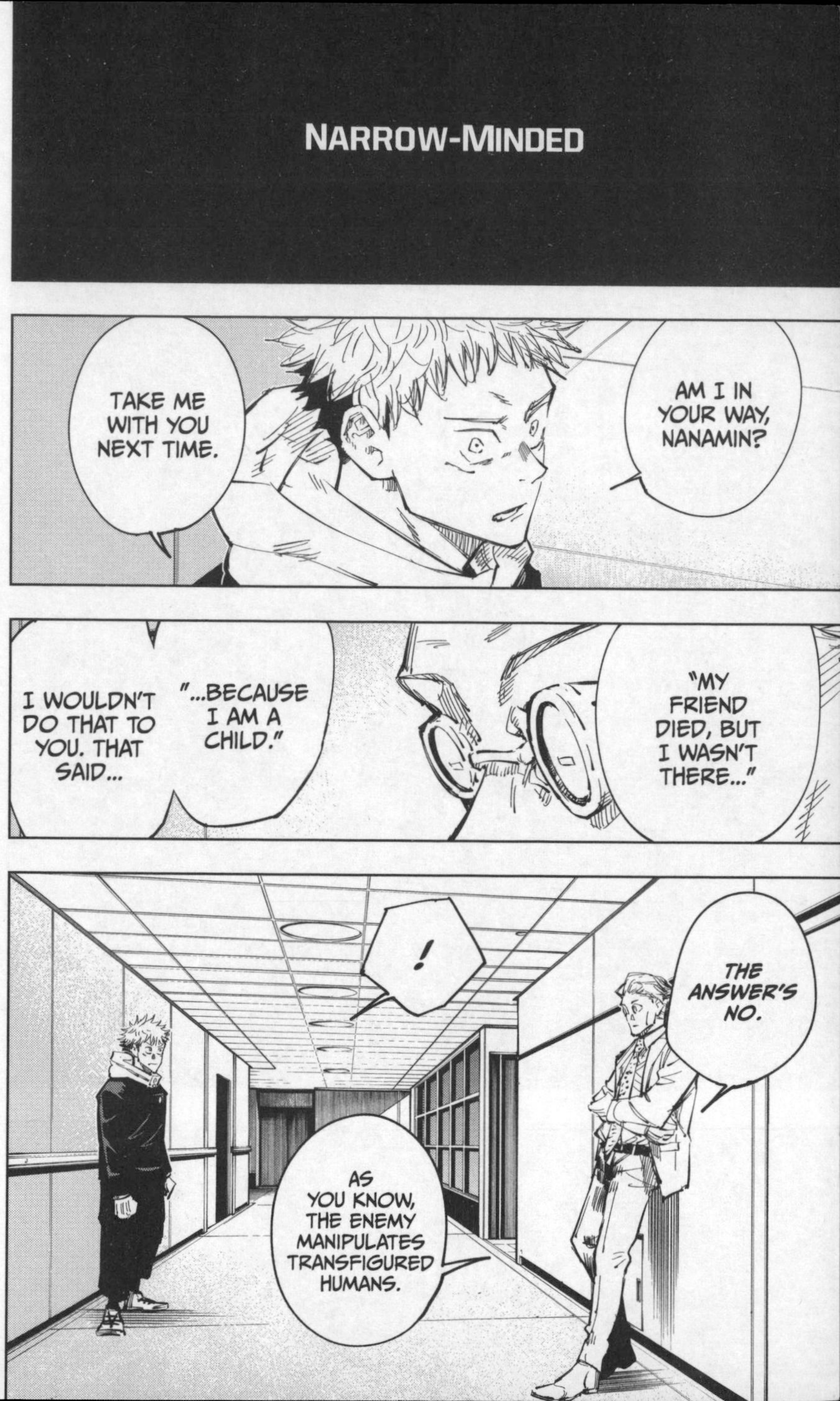
AM I IN YOUR WAY, NANAMIN?
TAKE ME WITH YOU NEXT TIME.
"MY FRIEND DIED, BUT I WASN'T THERE..."
I WOULDN'T DO THAT TO YOU. THAT SAID...
"...BECAUSE I AM A CHILD."
THE ANSWER'S NO.
!
AS YOU KNOW, THE ENEMY MANIPULATES TRANSFIGURED HUMANS.

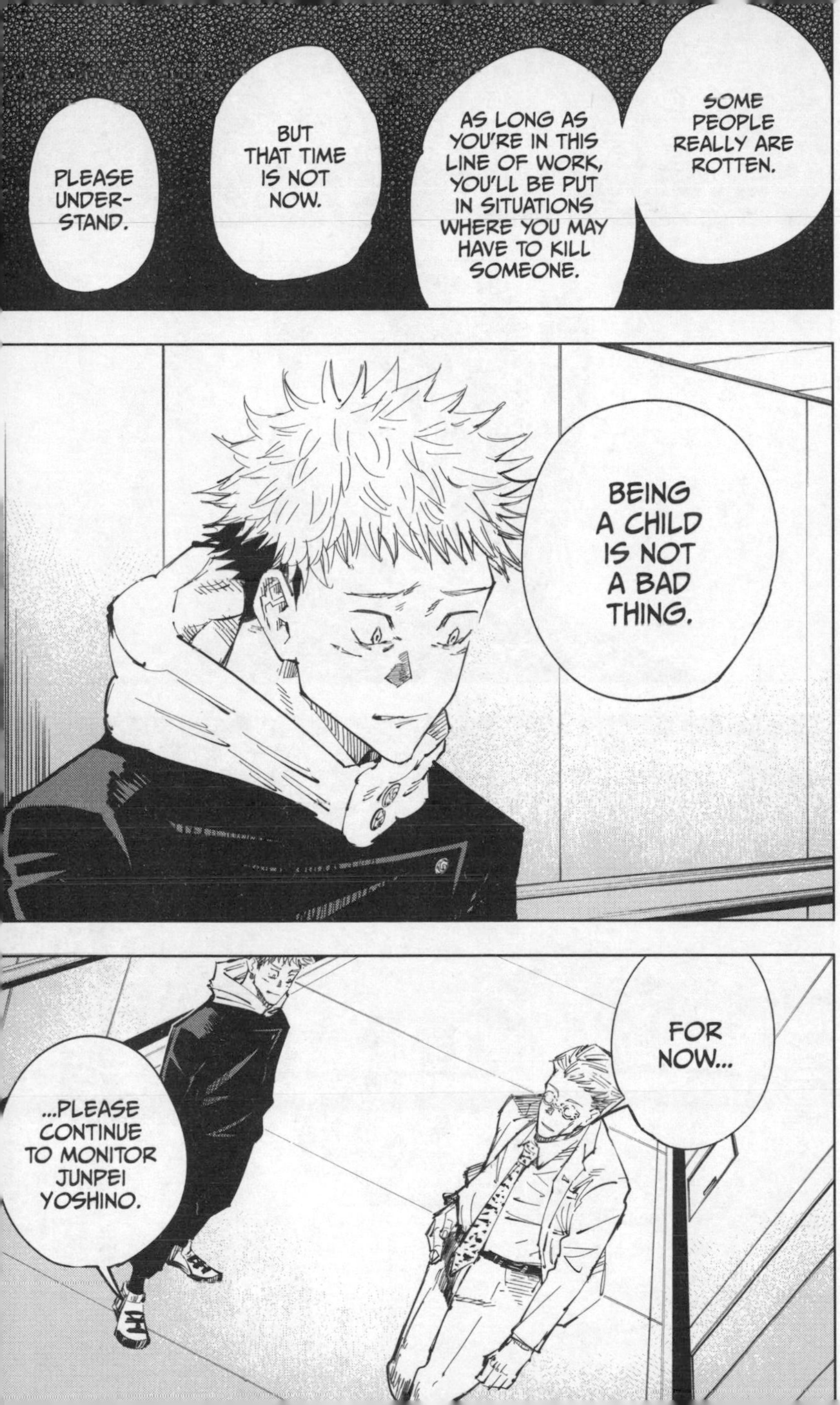
SOME PEOPLE REALLY ARE ROTTEN.
AS LONG AS YOU'RE IN THIS LINE OF WORK, YOU'LL BE PUT IN SITUATIONS WHERE YOU MAY HAVE TO KILL SOMEONE.
BUT THAT TIME IS NOT NOW.
PLEASE UNDER-STAND.
BEING A CHILD IS NOT A BAD THING.
FOR NOW...
...PLEASE CONTINUE TO MONITOR JUNPEI YOSHINO.

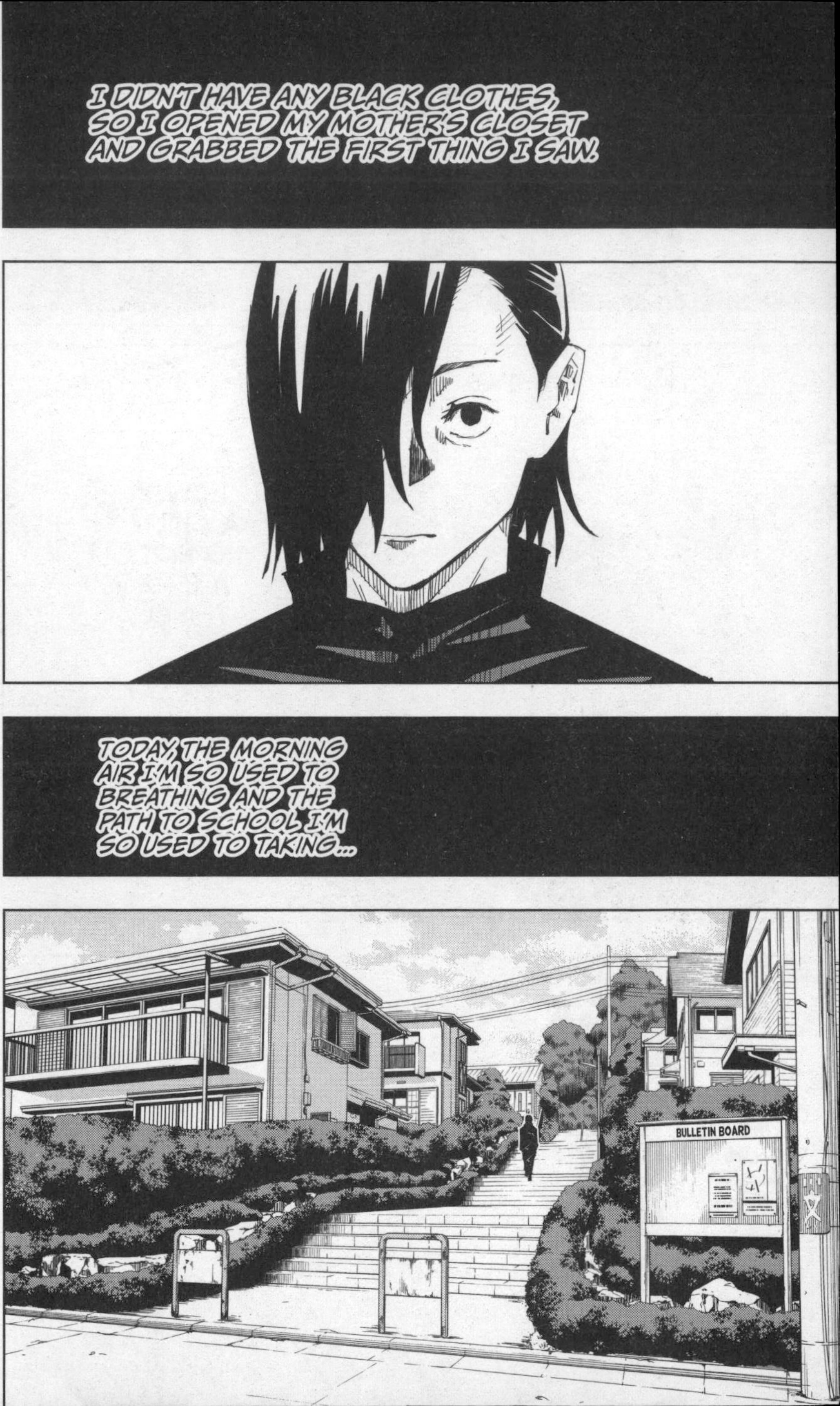
I DIDN'T HAVE ANY BLACK CLOTHES, SO I OPENED MY MOTHER'S CLOSET AND GRABBED THE FIRST THING I SAW.
TODAY, THE MORNING AIR I'M SO USED TO BREATHING AND THE PATH TO SCHOOL I'M SO USED TO TAKING...
BULLETIN BOARD

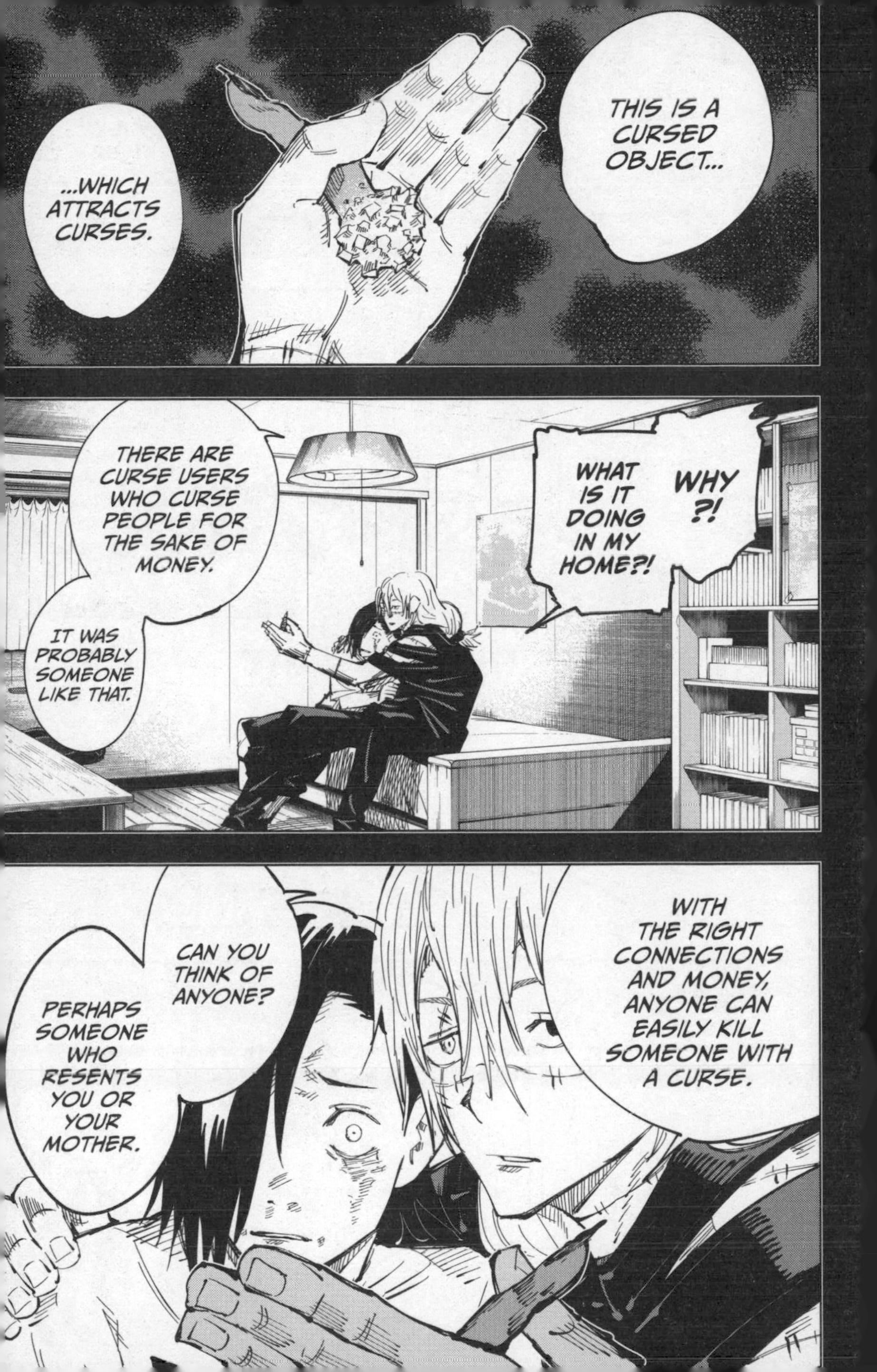
THIS IS A CURSED OBJECT...
...WHICH ATTRACTS CURSES.
WHAT IS IT DOING IN MY HOME?!
WHY?!
THERE ARE CURSE USERS WHO CURSE PEOPLE FOR THE SAKE OF MONEY.
IT WAS PROBABLY SOMEONE LIKE THAT.
WITH THE RIGHT CONNECTIONS AND MONEY, ANYONE CAN EASILY KILL SOMEONE WITH A CURSE.
CAN YOU THINK OF ANYONE?
PERHAPS SOMEONE WHO RESENTS YOU OR YOUR MOTHER.

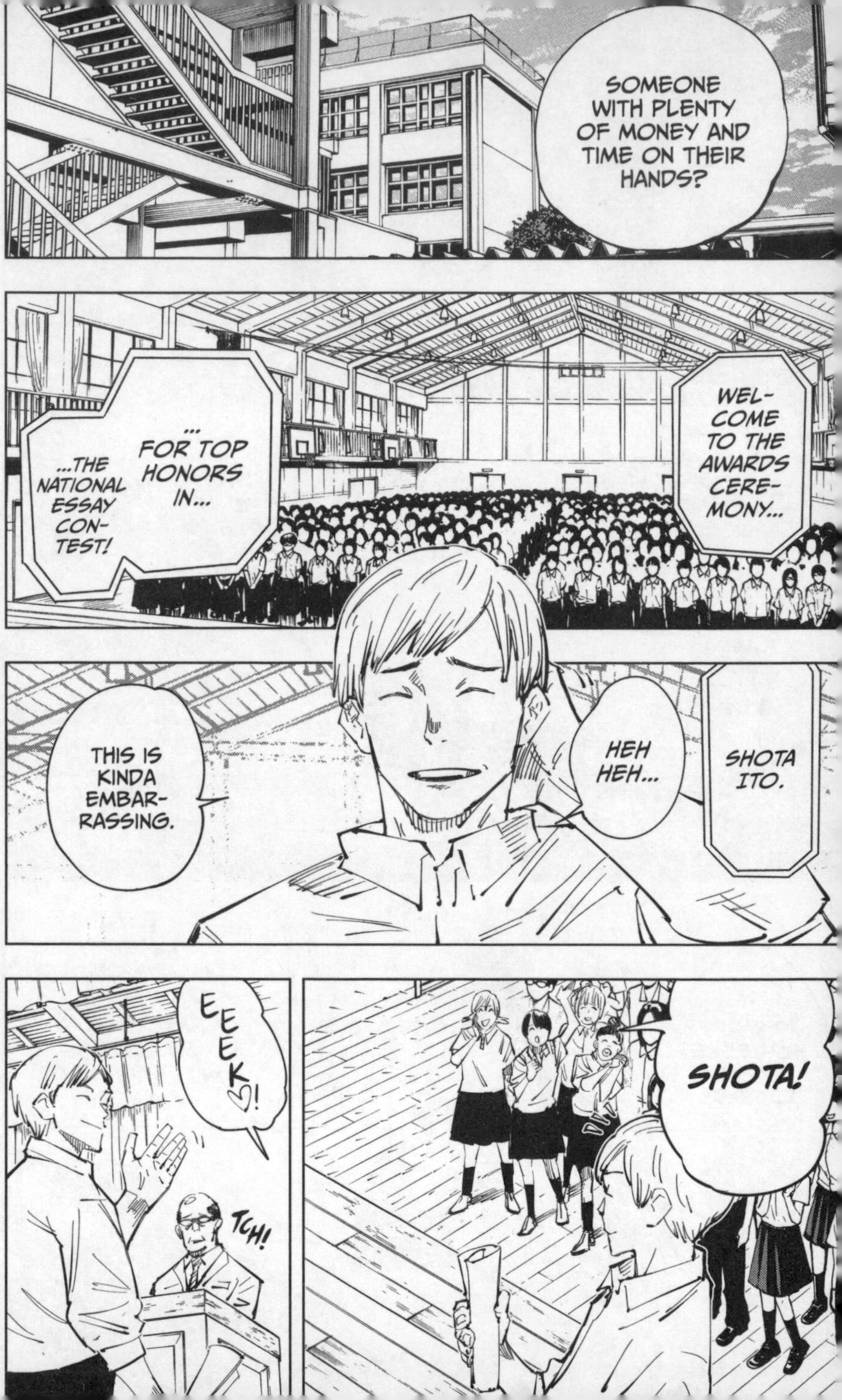
SOMEONE WITH PLENTY OF MONEY AND TIME ON THEIR HANDS?
WEL-COME TO THE AWARDS CERE-MONY...
...FOR TOP HONORS IN...
...THE NATIONAL ESSAY CON-TEST!
SHOTA ITO.
HEH HEH...
THIS IS KINDA EMBAR-RASSING.
SHOTA!
EEEK♡!
TCH!

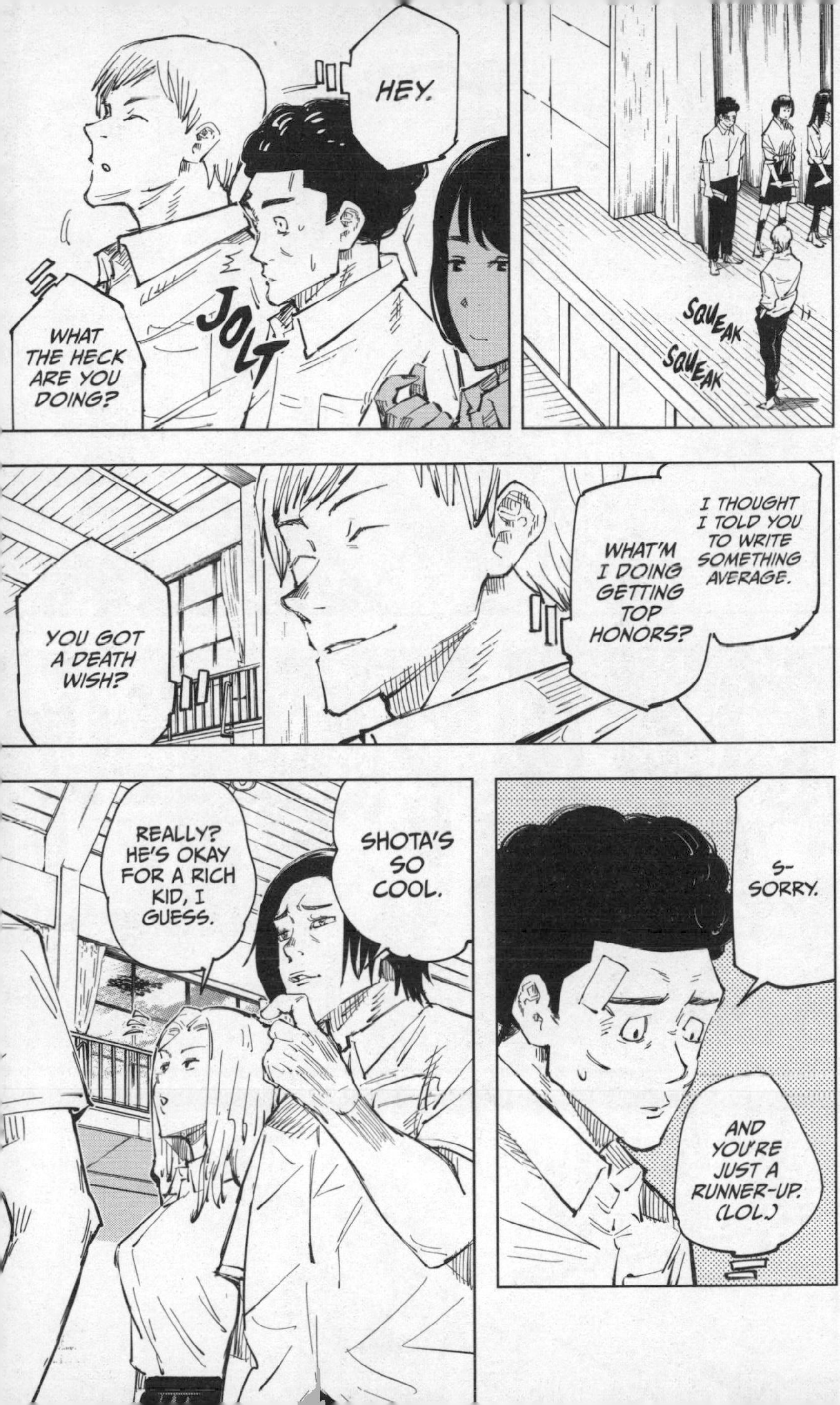
SQUEAK
SQUEAK
HEY.
JOLT
WHAT THE HECK ARE YOU DOING?
I THOUGHT I TOLD YOU TO WRITE SOMETHING AVERAGE.
WHAT'M I DOING GETTING TOP HONORS?
YOU GOT A DEATH WISH?
S-SORRY.
AND YOU'RE JUST A RUNNER-UP. (LOL.)
SHOTA'S SO COOL.
REALLY? HE'S OKAY FOR A RICH KID, I GUESS.

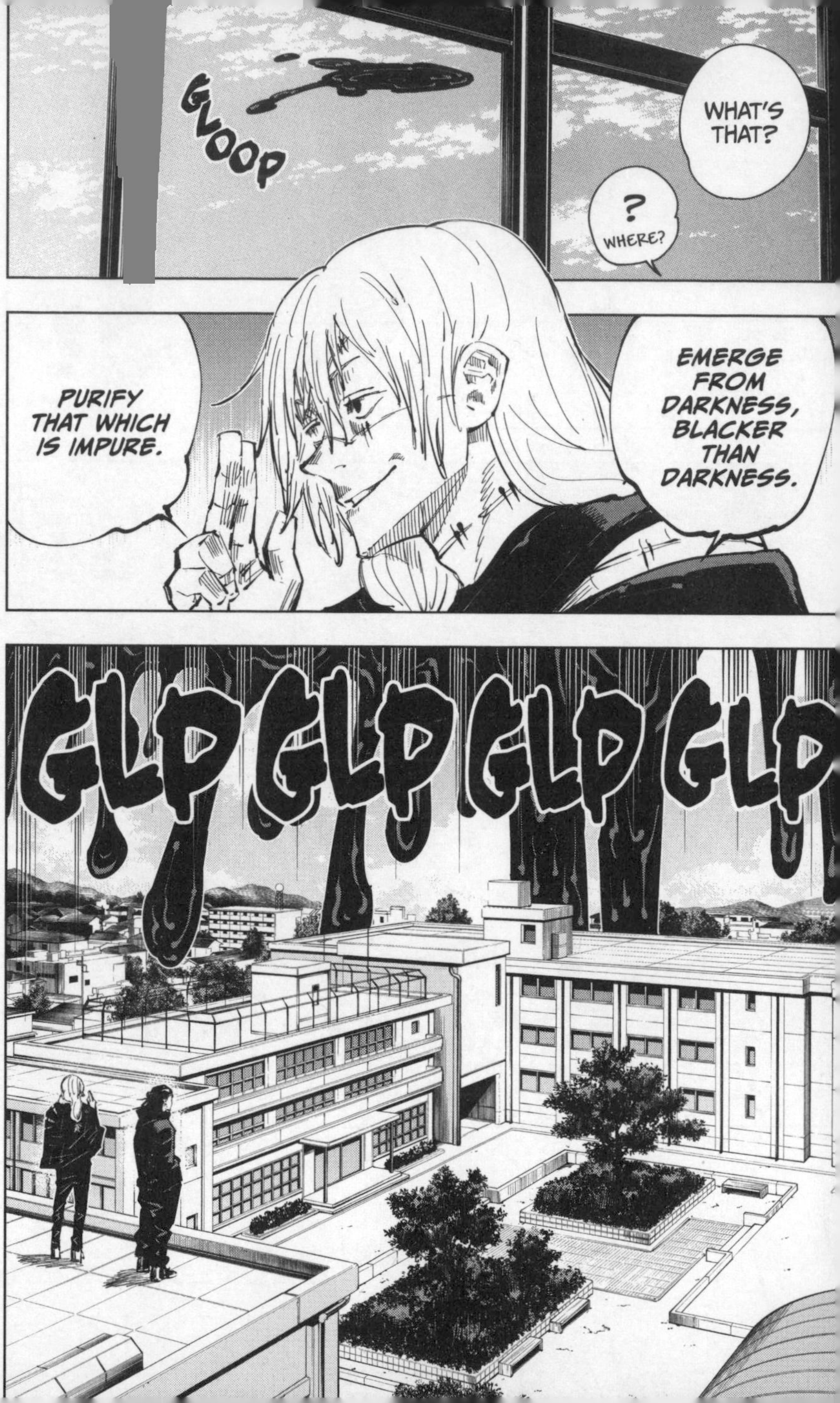
WHAT'S THAT?
?
WHERE?
GLOOP
EMERGE FROM DARKNESS, BLACKER THAN DARKNESS.
PURIFY THAT WHICH IS IMPURE.
GLP GLP GLP GLP

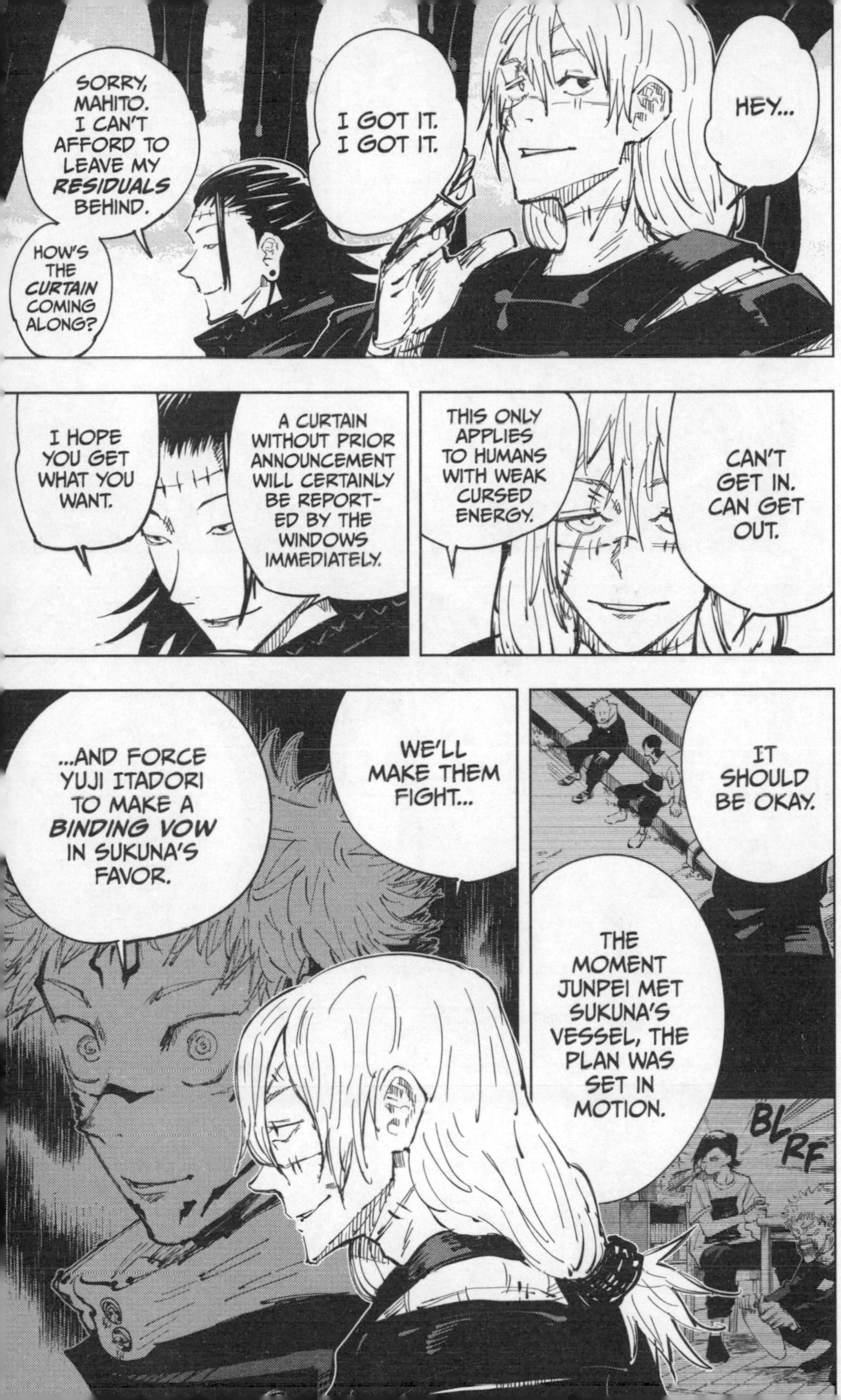
HEY...
I GOT IT. I GOT IT.
SORRY, MAHITO. I CAN'T AFFORD TO LEAVE MY RESIDUALS BEHIND.
HOW'S THE CURTAIN COMING ALONG?
CAN'T GET IN. CAN GET OUT.
THIS ONLY APPLIES TO HUMANS WITH WEAK CURSED ENERGY.
A CURTAIN WITHOUT PRIOR ANNOUNCEMENT WILL CERTAINLY BE REPORT-ED BY THE WINDOWS IMMEDIATELY.
I HOPE YOU GET WHAT YOU WANT.
IT SHOULD BE OKAY.
THE MOMENT JUNPEI MET SUKUNA'S VESSEL, THE PLAN WAS SET IN MOTION.
BLRF
WE'LL MAKE THEM FIGHT...
...AND FORCE YUJI ITADORI TO MAKE A BINDING VOW IN SUKUNA'S FAVOR.

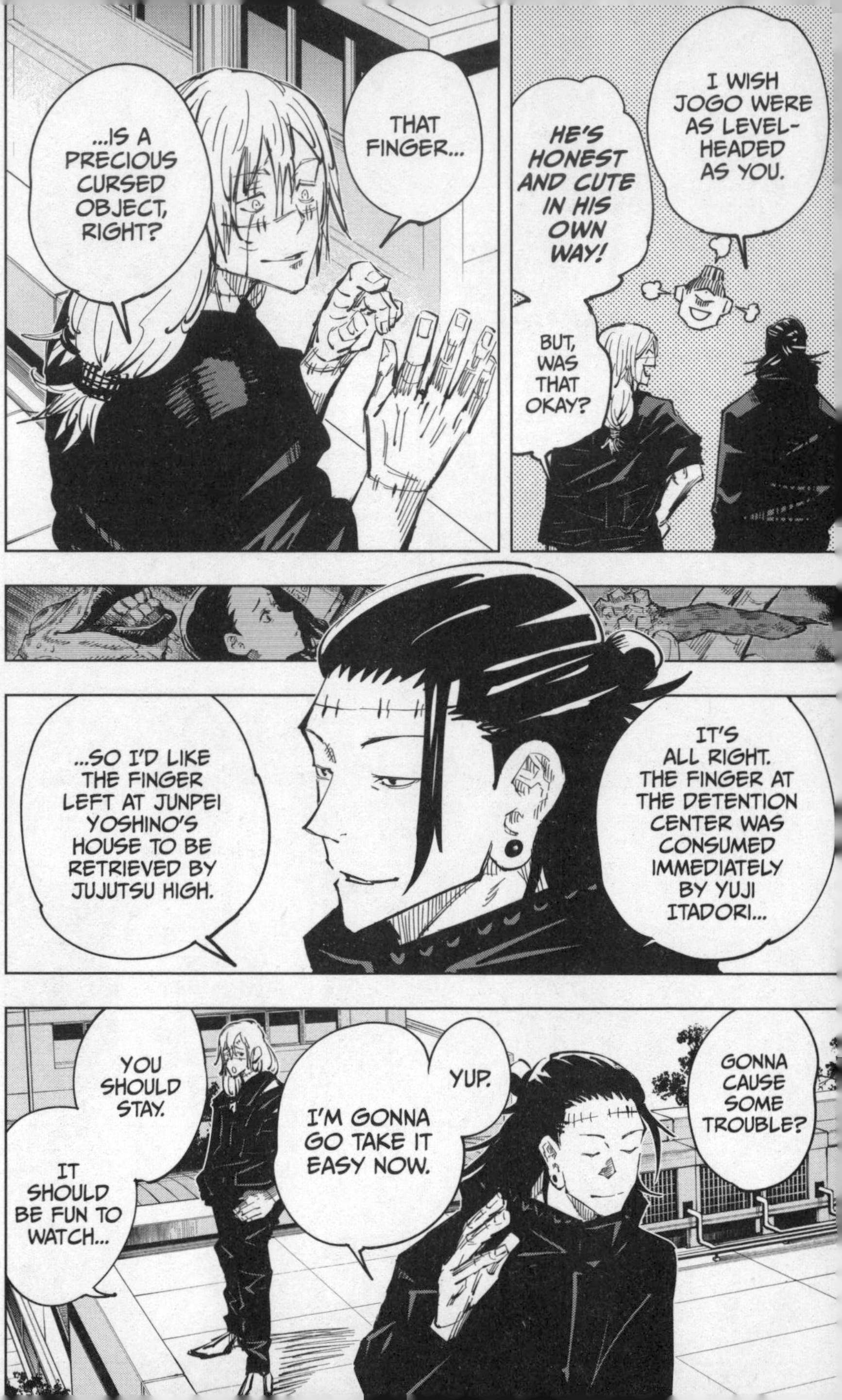
I WISH JOGO WERE AS LEVEL-HEADED AS YOU.
HE'S HONEST AND CUTE IN HIS OWN WAY!
BUT, WAS THAT OKAY?
THAT FINGER...
...IS A PRECIOUS CURSED OBJECT, RIGHT?
IT'S ALL RIGHT. THE FINGER AT THE DETENTION CENTER WAS CONSUMED IMMEDIATELY BY YUJI ITADORI...
...SO I'D LIKE THE FINGER LEFT AT JUNPEI YOSHINO'S HOUSE TO BE RETRIEVED BY JUJUTSU HIGH.
GONNA CAUSE SOME TROUBLE?
YUP.
I'M GONNA GO TAKE IT EASY NOW.
YOU SHOULD STAY.
IT SHOULD BE FUN TO WATCH...

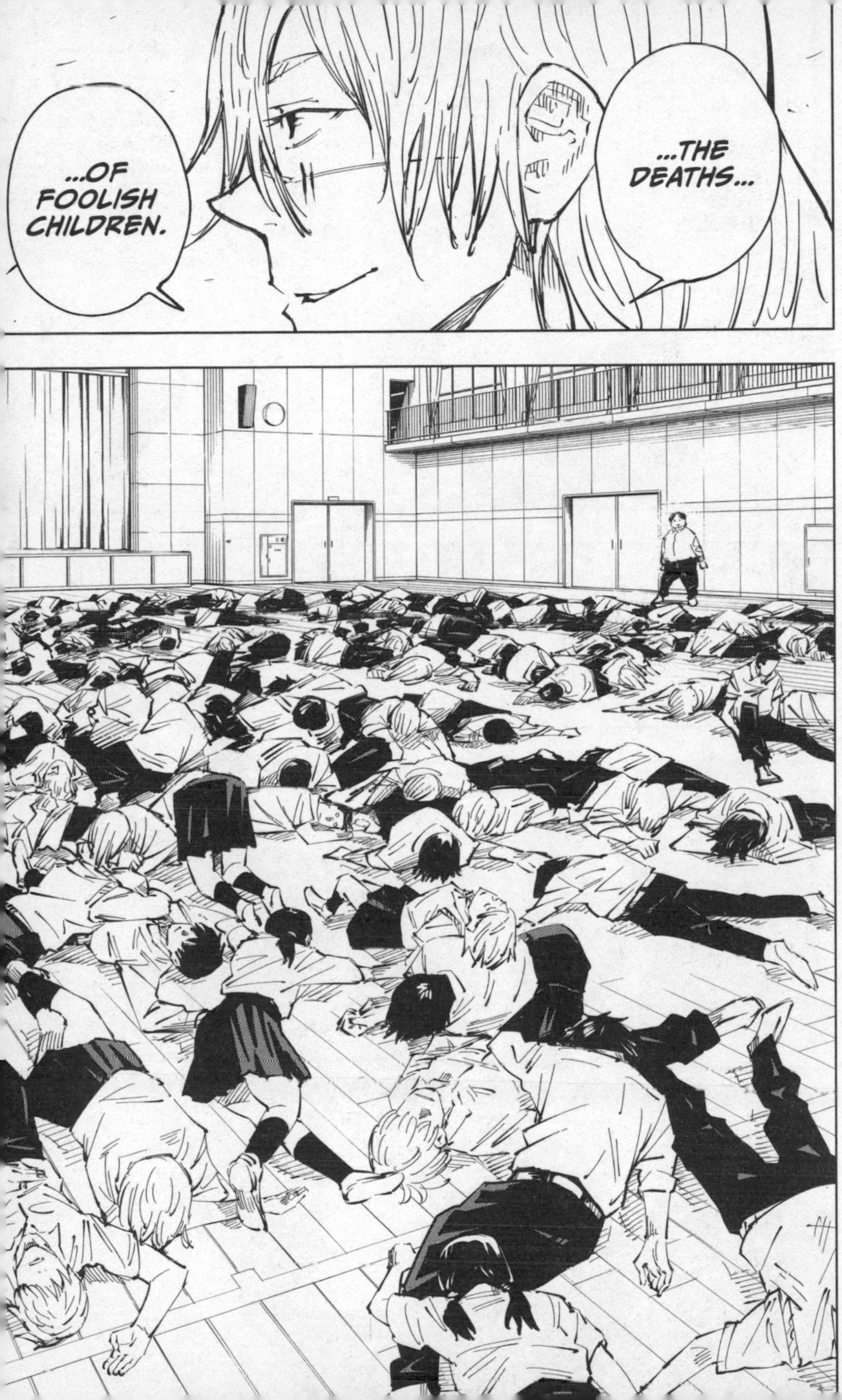
...THE DEATHS...
...OF FOOLISH CHILDREN.

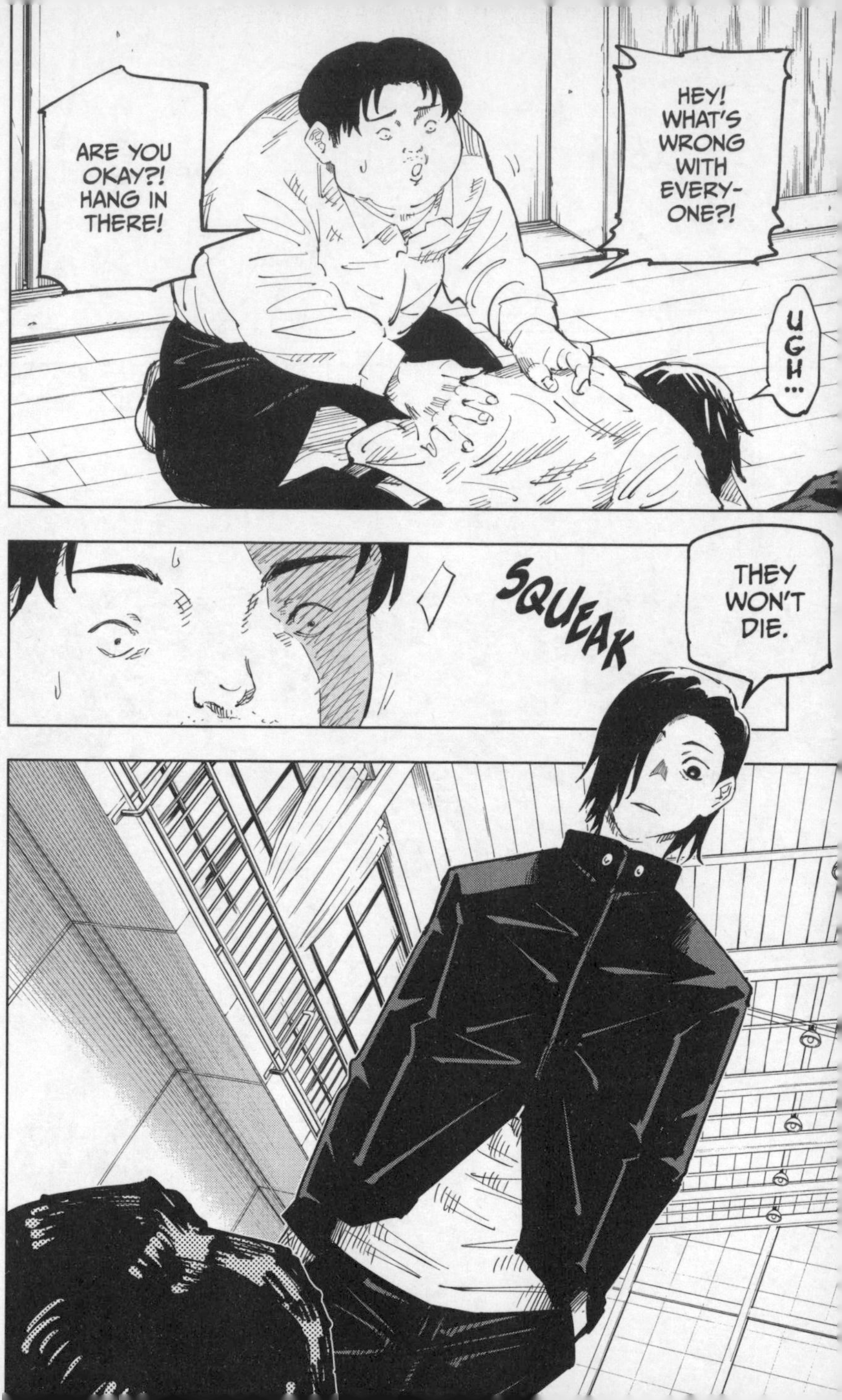
HEY! WHAT'S WRONG WITH EVERY-ONE?!
ARE YOU OKAY?! HANG IN THERE!
UGH...
SQUEAK
THEY WON'T DIE.

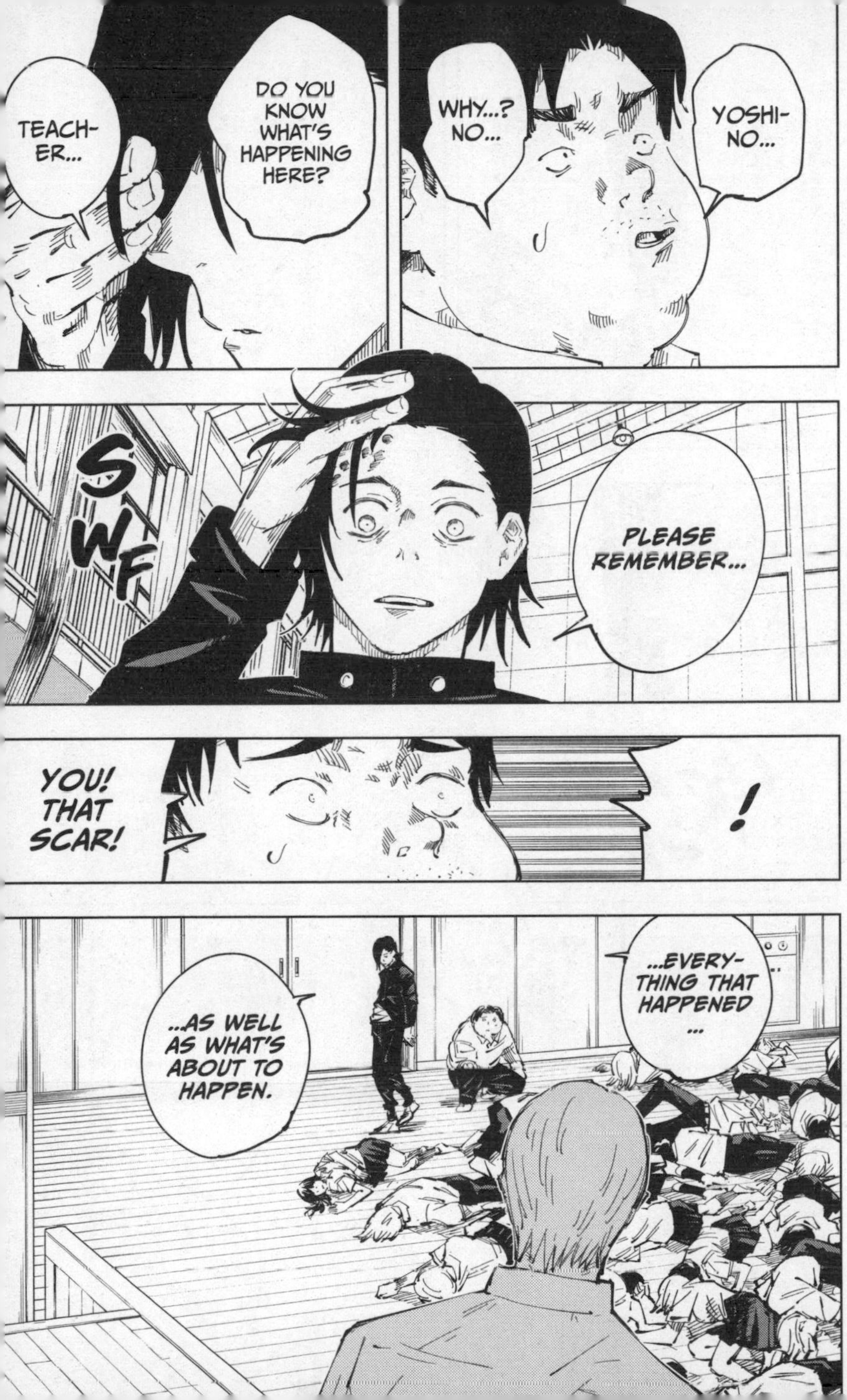
YOSHI-NO...
WHY...? NO...
DO YOU KNOW WHAT'S HAPPENING HERE?
TEACH-ER...
PLEASE REMEMBER...
SWF
!
YOU! THAT SCAR!
...EVERY-THING THAT HAPPENED ...
...AS WELL AS WHAT'S ABOUT TO HAPPEN.

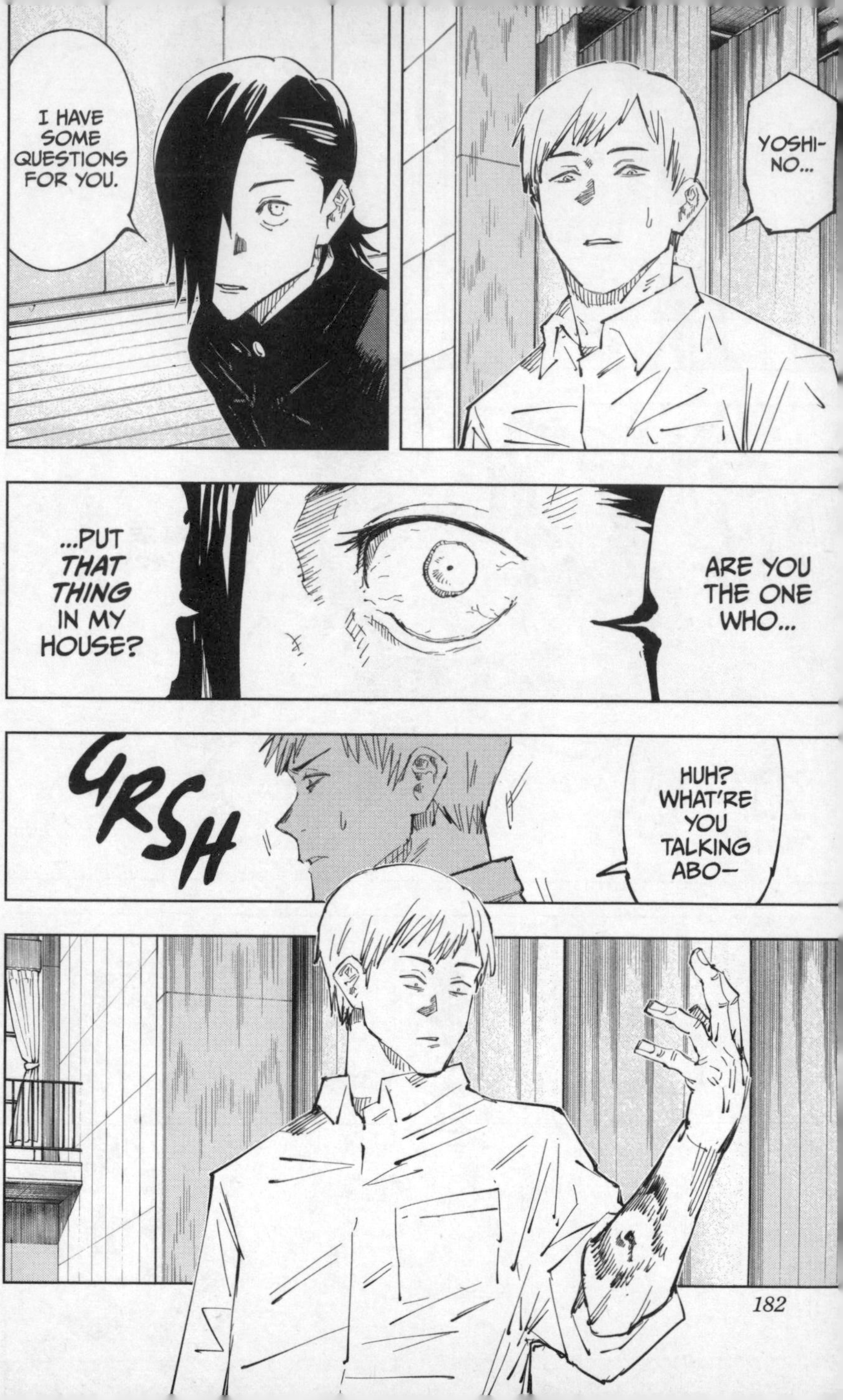
YOSHINO...
I HAVE SOME QUESTIONS FOR YOU.
ARE YOU THE ONE WHO...
...PUT *THAT THING* IN MY HOUSE?
HUH? WHAT'RE YOU TALKING ABO–
URSH

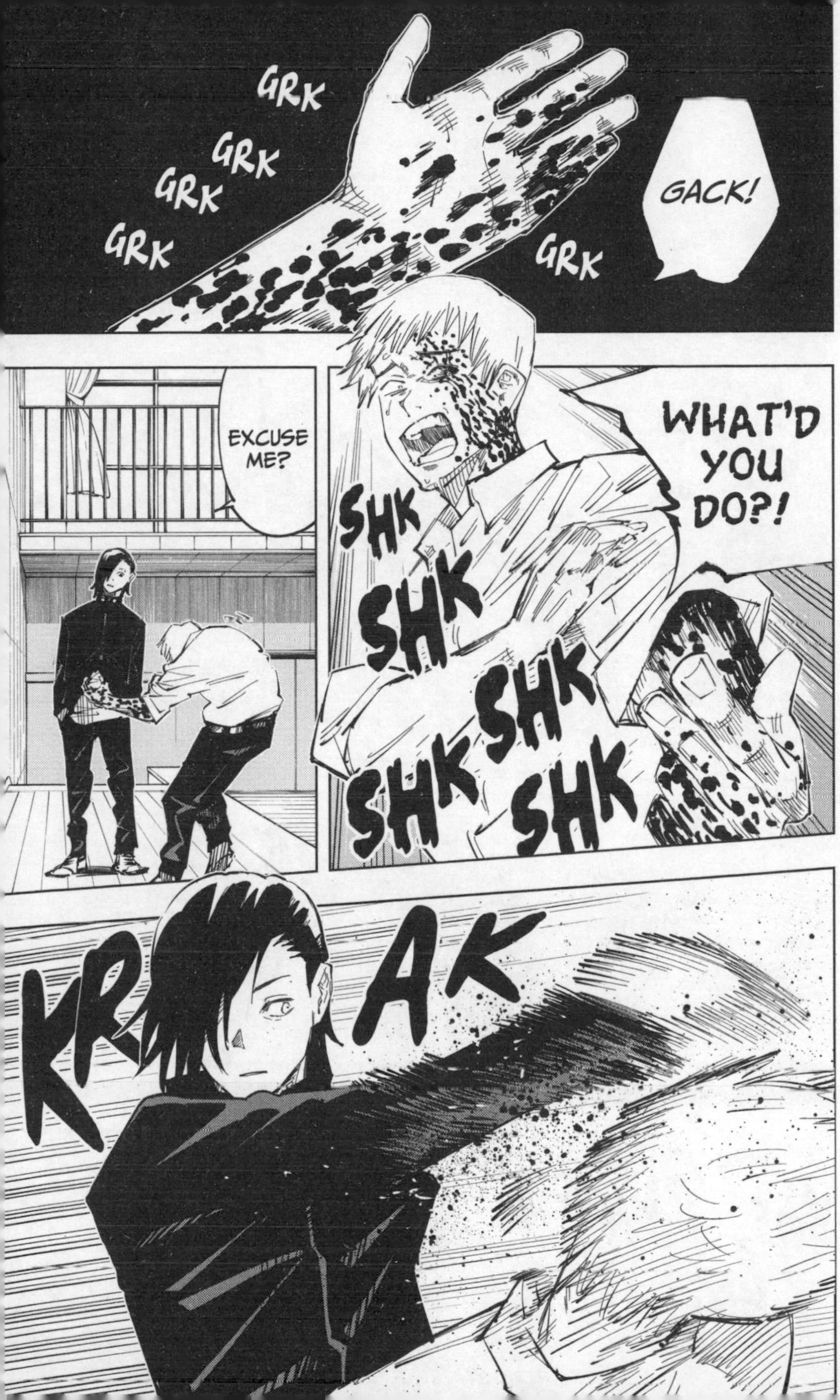
GACK!
GRK
GRK
GRK
GRK
GRK
WHAT'D YOU DO?!
SHK
SHK
SHK
SHK
SHK
SHK
EXCUSE ME?
KRAK

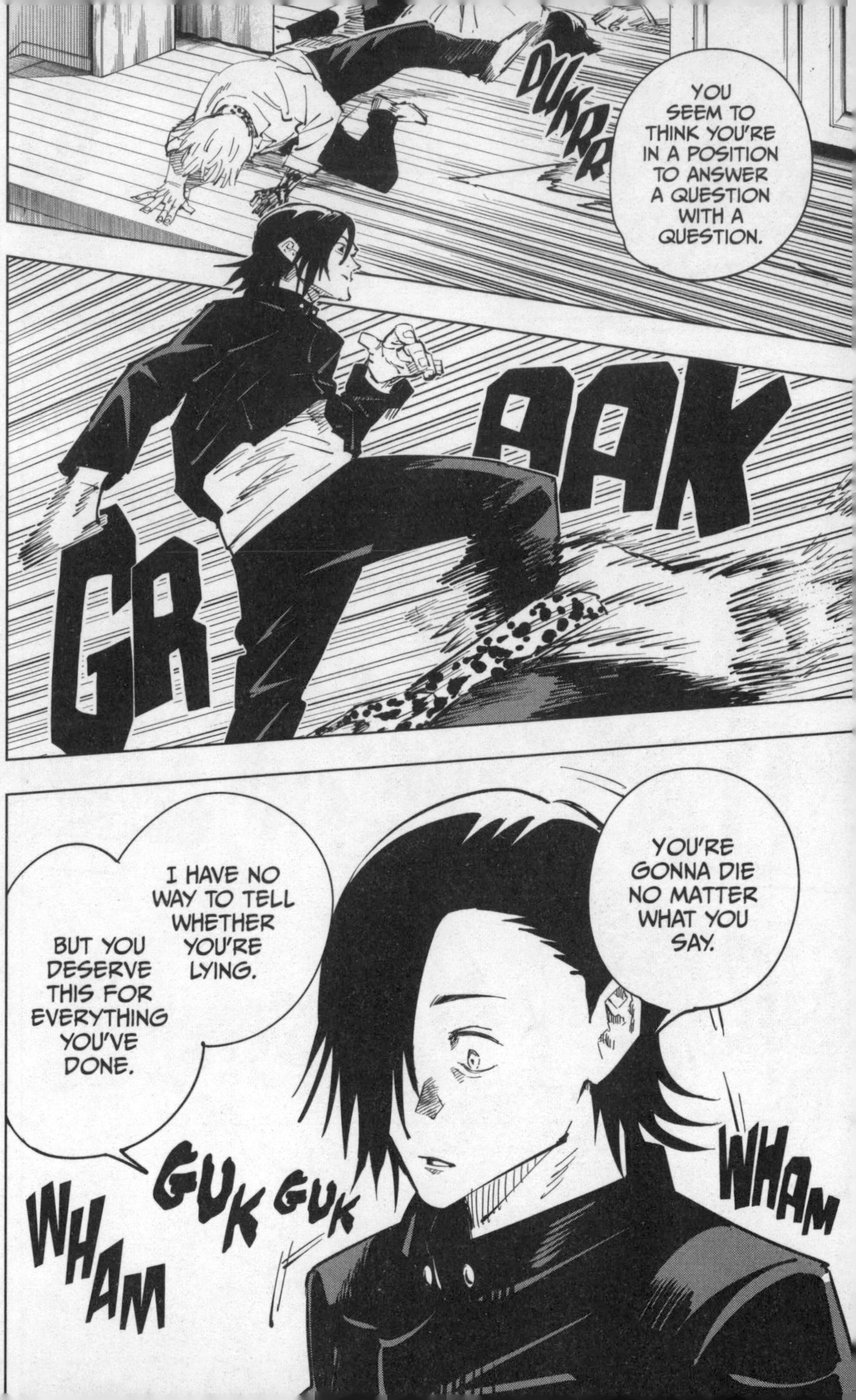
DUKRR
YOU SEEM TO THINK YOU'RE IN A POSITION TO ANSWER A QUESTION WITH A QUESTION.
GRAAK
YOU'RE GONNA DIE NO MATTER WHAT YOU SAY.
WHAM
I HAVE NO WAY TO TELL WHETHER YOU'RE LYING.
BUT YOU DESERVE THIS FOR EVERYTHING YOU'VE DONE.
GUK GUK
WHAM

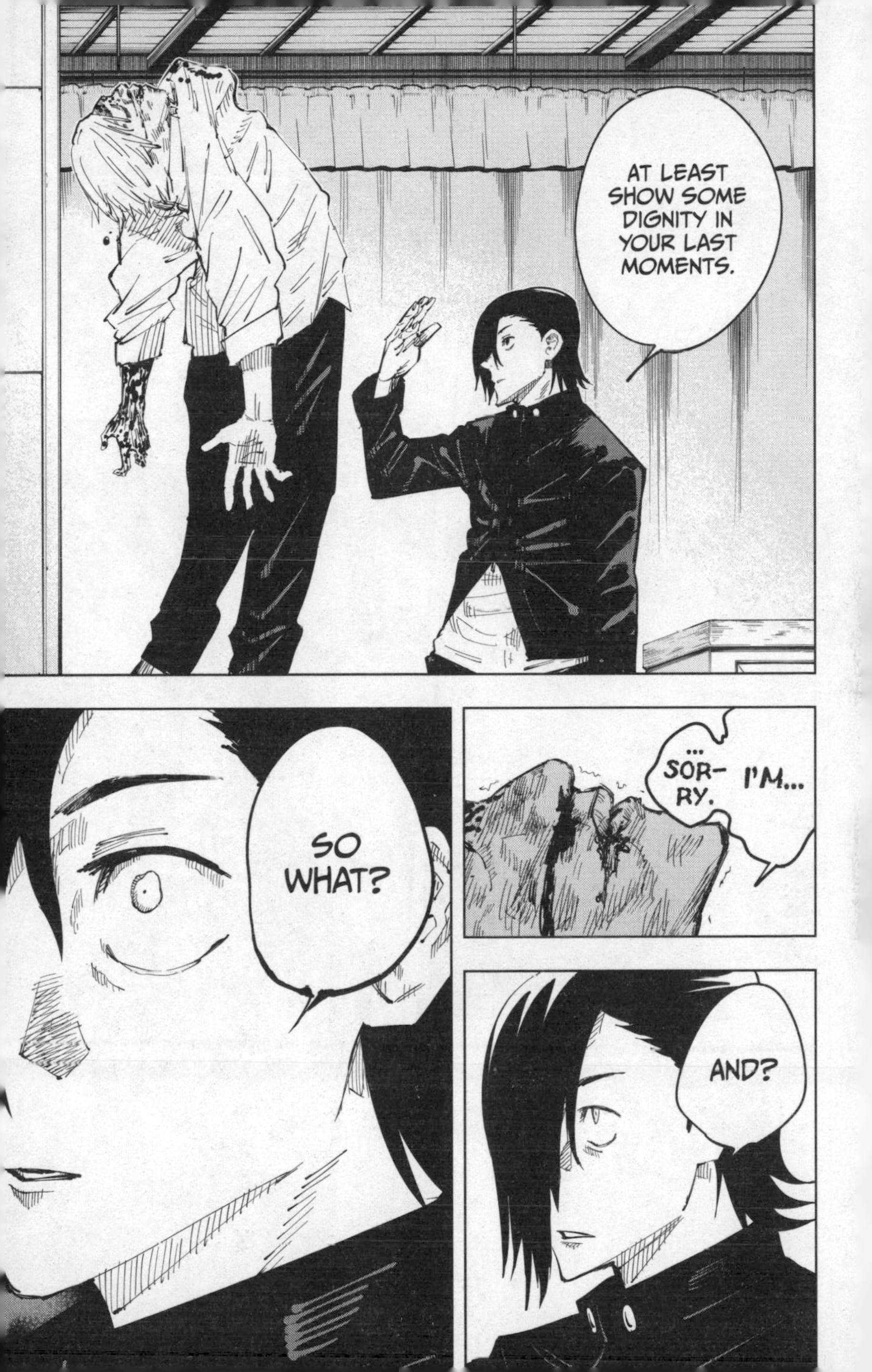
AT LEAST SHOW SOME DIGNITY IN YOUR LAST MOMENTS.
I'M...
...SOR-RY.
AND?
SO WHAT?

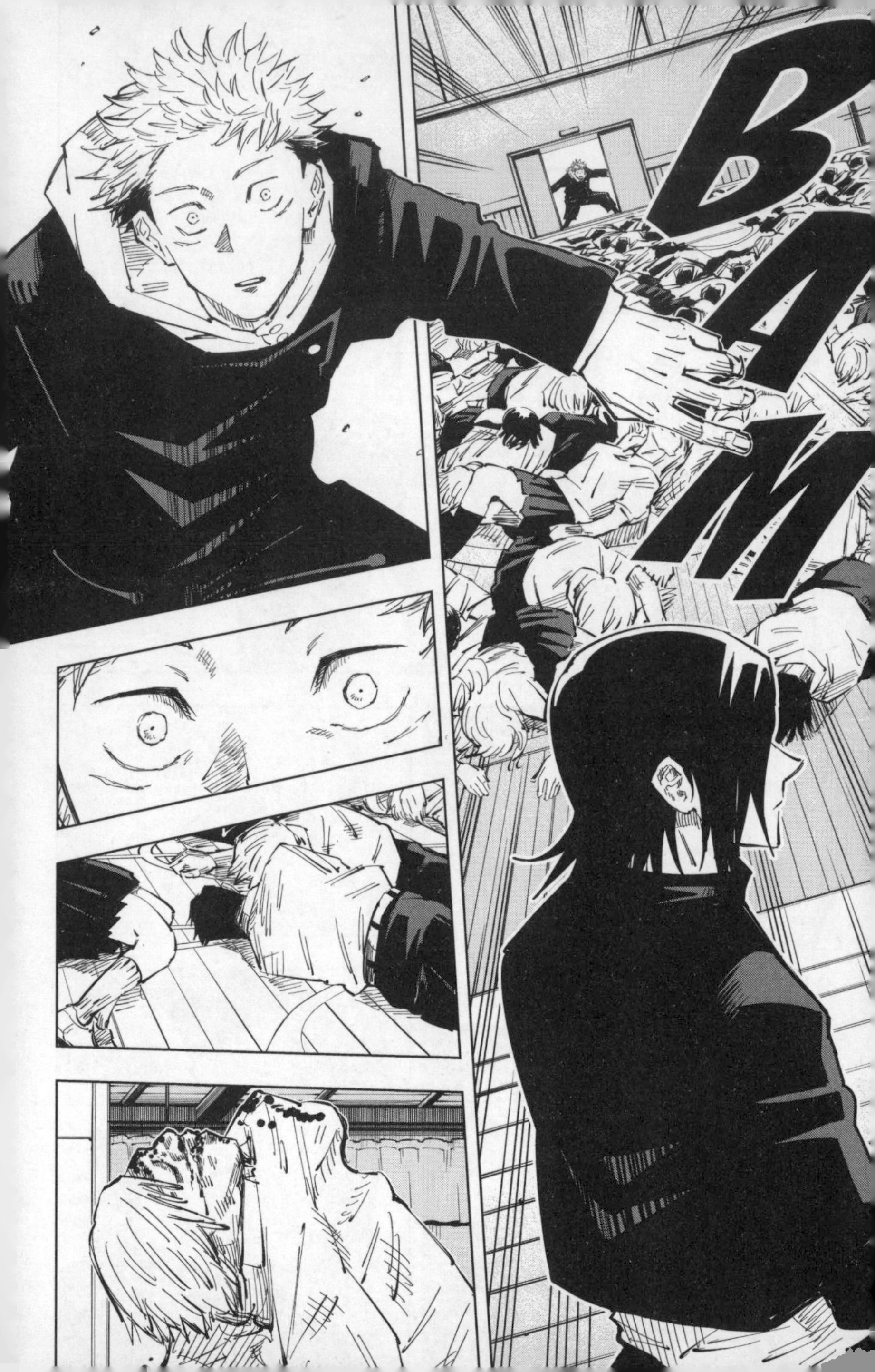
BAM

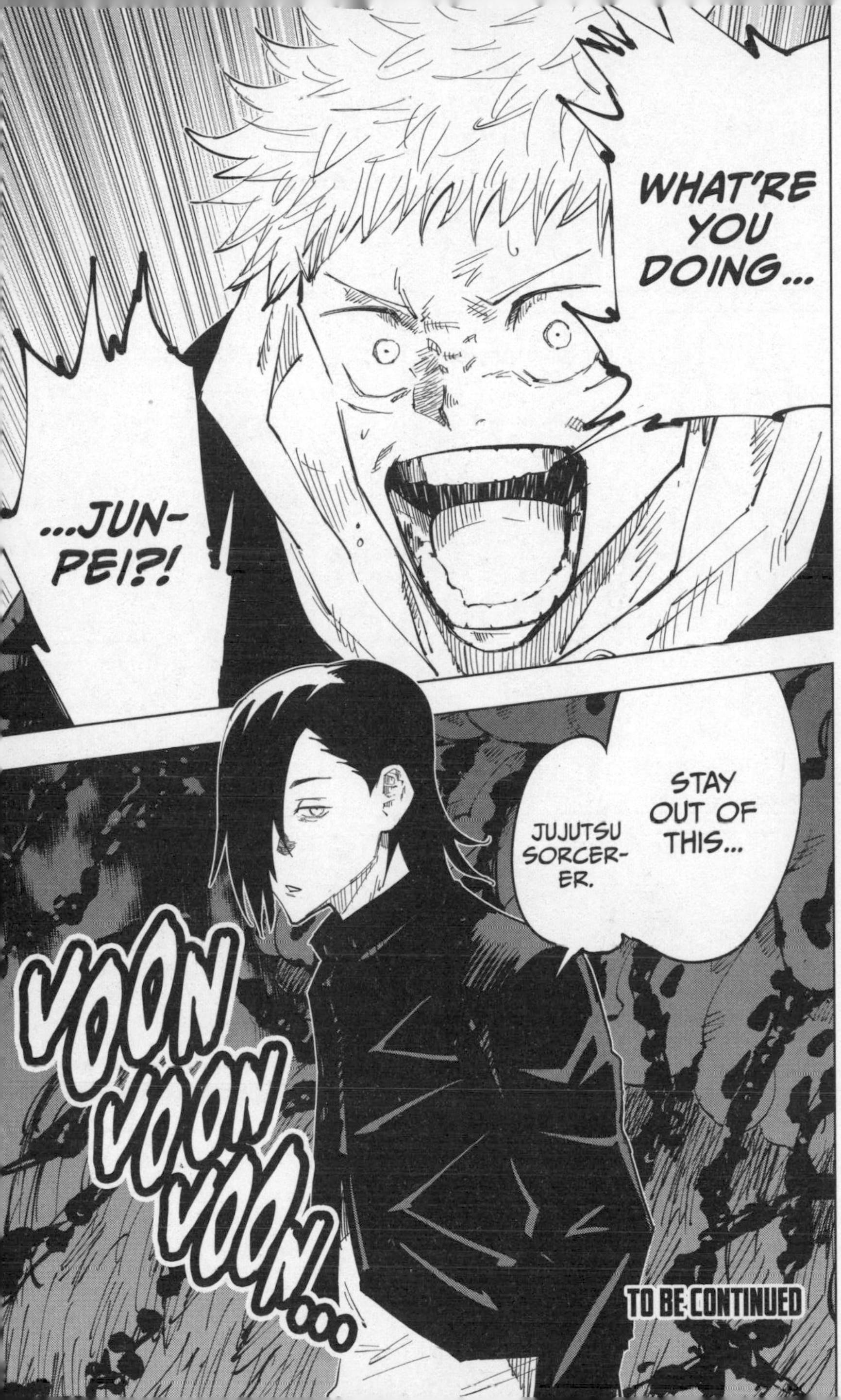
WHAT'RE YOU DOING...
...JUN-PEI?!
STAY OUT OF THIS...
JUJUTSU SORCER-ER.
VOON VOON VOON...
TO BE CONTINUED

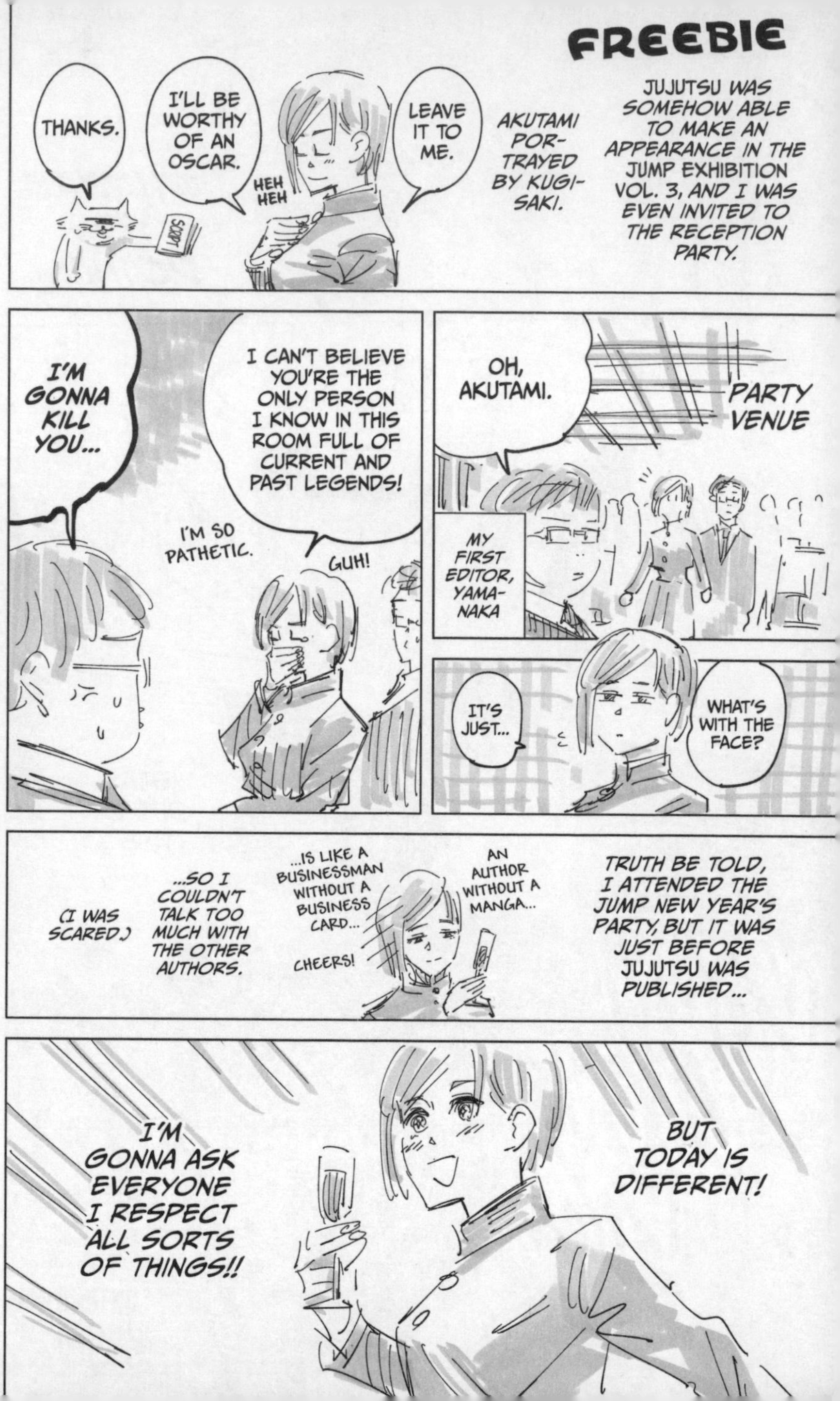
FREEBIE
JUJUTSU WAS SOMEHOW ABLE TO MAKE AN APPEARANCE IN THE JUMP EXHIBITION VOL. 3, AND I WAS EVEN INVITED TO THE RECEPTION PARTY.
AKUTAMI PORTRAYED BY KUGISAKI.
LEAVE IT TO ME.
HEH HEH
I'LL BE WORTHY OF AN OSCAR.
THANKS.
SCRIPT
PARTY VENUE
OH, AKUTAMI.
MY FIRST EDITOR, YAMANAKA
WHAT'S WITH THE FACE?
IT'S JUST...
I CAN'T BELIEVE YOU'RE THE ONLY PERSON I KNOW IN THIS ROOM FULL OF CURRENT AND PAST LEGENDS!
GUH!
I'M SO PATHETIC.
I'M GONNA KILL YOU...
TRUTH BE TOLD, I ATTENDED THE JUMP NEW YEAR'S PARTY, BUT IT WAS JUST BEFORE JUJUTSU WAS PUBLISHED...
AN AUTHOR WITHOUT A MANGA...
...IS LIKE A BUSINESSMAN WITHOUT A BUSINESS CARD...
CHEERS!
...SO I COULDN'T TALK TOO MUCH WITH THE OTHER AUTHORS.
(I WAS SCARED.)
BUT TODAY IS DIFFERENT!
I'M GONNA ASK EVERYONE I RESPECT ALL SORTS OF THINGS!!

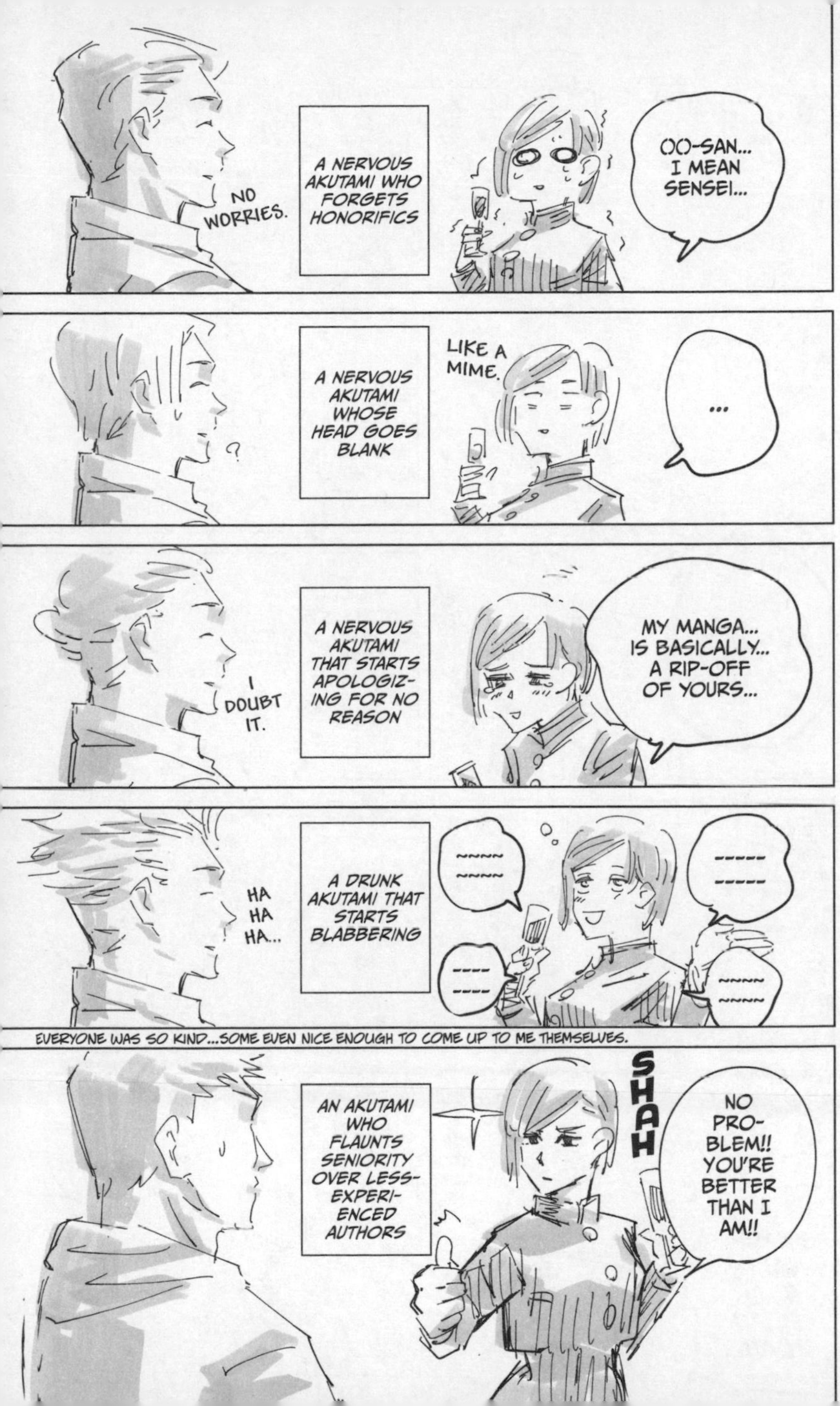
OO-SAN... I MEAN SENSEI...
A NERVOUS AKUTAMI WHO FORGETS HONORIFICS
NO WORRIES.
...
LIKE A MIME.
A NERVOUS AKUTAMI WHOSE HEAD GOES BLANK
MY MANGA... IS BASICALLY... A RIP-OFF OF YOURS...
A NERVOUS AKUTAMI THAT STARTS APOLOGIZING FOR NO REASON
I DOUBT IT.
A DRUNK AKUTAMI THAT STARTS BLABBERING
HA HA HA...
EVERYONE WAS SO KIND...SOME EVEN NICE ENOUGH TO COME UP TO ME THEMSELVES.
NO PROBLEM!! YOU'RE BETTER THAN I AM!!
SHAH
AN AKUTAMI WHO FLAUNTS SENIORITY OVER LESS-EXPERIENCED AUTHORS

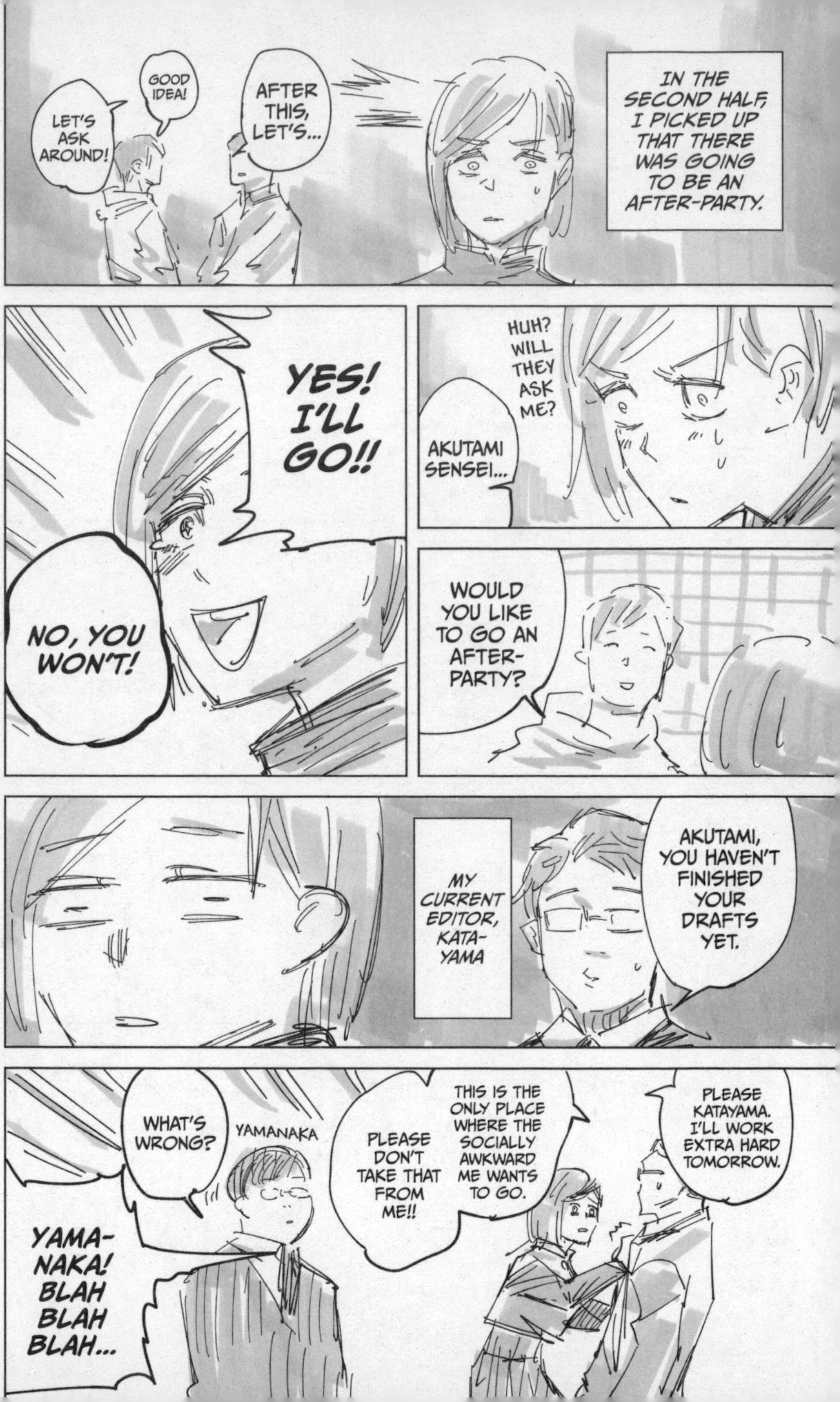
IN THE SECOND HALF, I PICKED UP THAT THERE WAS GOING TO BE AN AFTER-PARTY.
AFTER THIS, LET'S...
GOOD IDEA!
LET'S ASK AROUND!
HUH? WILL THEY ASK ME?
AKUTAMI SENSEI...
WOULD YOU LIKE TO GO AN AFTER-PARTY?
YES! I'LL GO!!
NO, YOU WON'T!
AKUTAMI, YOU HAVEN'T FINISHED YOUR DRAFTS YET.
MY CURRENT EDITOR, KATA-YAMA
PLEASE KATAYAMA. I'LL WORK EXTRA HARD TOMORROW.
THIS IS THE ONLY PLACE WHERE THE SOCIALLY AWKWARD ME WANTS TO GO.
PLEASE DON'T TAKE THAT FROM ME!!
YAMANAKA
WHAT'S WRONG?
YAMA-NAKA! BLAH BLAH BLAH...

GEGE AKUTAMI

Heart. Technique. Body.
They're all lacking.

GEGE AKUTAMI published a few short
works before starting *Jujutsu Kaisen*, which began
serialization in *Weekly Shonen Jump* in 2018.

JUJUTSU KAISEN

VOLUME 3
SHONEN JUMP MANGA EDITION

BY GEGE AKUTAMI

TRANSLATION Stefan Koza
TOUCH-UP ART & LETTERING Snir Aharon
DESIGN Shawn Carrico
EDITOR John Bae
CONSULTING EDITOR Erika Onabe

JUJUTSU KAISEN © 2018 by Gege Akutami
All rights reserved.
First published in Japan in 2018 by SHUEISHA Inc., Tokyo.
English translation rights arranged by SHUEISHA Inc.

The stories, characters and incidents mentioned
in this publication are entirely fictional.

Printed in the U.S.A.

Published by VIZ Media, LLC
P.O. Box 77010
San Francisco, CA 94107

10 9
First printing, April 2020
Ninth printing, January 2022